LANGUAGE OF THE HEART
A Sufi Interpretation of Form and Meaning
in Contemporary Society

LANGUAGE OF THE HEART

A Sufi Interpretation of Form and Meaning
in Contemporary Society

Eva Désirée van den Berg

BLUE DOME

Published by Blue Dome Press
535 Fifth Avenue, Ste.601
New York, NY 10017-8019

www.bluedomepress.com

Library of Congress Cataloging-in-Publication Data Available

ISBN: 978-1-935295-14-3

Printed by
Pasifik Ofset Ltd. Şti.
Ser No: 12027
Cihangir Mah. Güvercin Cad. Baha İş Merkezi
A Blok Haramidere Avcılar İstanbul
Tel: (0212) 412 17 77

Contents

Introduction vii

Chapter One
World of Form (*Sura*) and Meaning (*Mana*) 1
    1.1 The Multiplicity of Names 3
    1.2 Message of the Time 14
    1.3 'No god but God' (*lā ilāha illā' Llāh*) 21
    1.4 Nature as a Manuscript 32
    1.5 The Unifying Expression 35
    1.6 From the World without Sounds and Letters to the
         World of Sounds and Letters 43
    1.7 The Universe as a Dome 45

Chapter Two
World without Meaning (*Mana*) 51
    2.1 *Ayat*—Universal Expression 53
    2.2 Consumerism and the Mall 54
    2.3 Home 58
    2.4 Car 63
    2.5 Food 66
    2.6 Church 72
    2.7 Language 75
    2.8 Language that Distorts 76
    2.9 Language as Commodity 81
    2.10 Language that Corrupts Thought 83
    2.11 Language that is Blubber-Rich 85
    2.12 Language that Knows no Wonder 88

Chapter Three
Conflicting Voices 91
    3.1 The Commanding Voice of Ego 93
    3.2 Ego and the Voices of Others 102

    3.3 Ego and the Voices of Animals 109
    3.4 Ego and the Voice of the Earth...119

Chapter Four
Finding Meaning (*Mana*)...133
    4.1 Knowing with the Heart..135
    4.2 Knowing the Real...136
    4.3 Knowledge as Commodity...158
    4.4 Meaningful Expression...170
    4.5 Creativity of the Heart..179

Chapter Five
Being Meaningful...187
    5.1 Coursing through the Arteries of the World............................189
    5.2 *Ishq*—'Dying for Love' 191
    5.3 Love and Beauty...195
    5.4 Bringing forth Images 206
    5.5 Bringing forth Realities 215
    5.6 Submitting to Quietness..221
    5.7 *Baqa* and the Economy 232
    5.8 Freedom..237

Conclusion 245
Bibliography...249
Index..269

Introduction

This book seeks to examine how Sufi thought might provide critical understanding of contemporary life and a pathway towards the recovery of a more meaningful existence. Rumi's mystical teachings are, I argue, of great value at a time of rampant materialism and indiscriminate consumerism, and have the potential to illuminate the precarious state of the world, as well as revitalise contemporary social critique, ecophilosophy and biosemiotics in what is increasingly being regarded as a post-secular age.

Jalaluddin Rumi was born in Balkh in present-day Afghanistan in the year 1207, the son of an educated preacher and jurisprudent in the Islamic tradition. Rumi himself began studying the exoteric sciences including Arabic, *Shariah* law, the Qur'an, *Hadith* (the sayings of the Prophet), theology, philosophy and mathematics at an early age, becoming a doctor of law and following in his father's footsteps at the age of twenty-four (Chittick, 1983, 2). While his erudition and professional standing earned him respect and material success, it is not for these reasons that we remember Rumi today. In 1244 the wandering dervish Shams ("sun") of Tabriz stepped into the doorway of his life, illuminating its every shaded corner and awakening his slumbering heart. 'Love's fool', emptied of self, serving only as capacity for that other, the sober jurisprudent was transformed into intoxicated lover whose poetic outpourings on love's joy and pain ensured that he would never be forgotten.

Still known today as *Mevlana*, Our Master, Rumi is considered above all others perhaps, the essential voice of Sufism (Shah, 1979). Although Rumi's universe is shaped by the Qur'an, the overriding reality of his existence is the Sufi understanding of unity, which gives his message its universality. His poetry tells just one story—his soul's search for the Beloved. According to Chittick his verses are "an inexhaustible ocean" (1983, 20) and Nicholson hails him as the greatest mystical poet of any age. Goethe drew inspiration from his poetry and the celebrated poet Jami from Persia said of him: "He is not a Prophet, but he has written a Holy Book". Rembrandt drew him from a miniature painting, Gandhi frequently quoted verses such as: "To unite is why we came / to divide is not our aim", and in 1958, Pope John XXIII expressed what many felt: "In the name of the Catholic world, I bow with respect before the memory of Mevlana" (Esirgen, 2007).

Written in the Persian language (Farsi) and Arabic and emerging from the heart of the Islamic tradition, Rumi's work, while always of literary and academic interest, was not widely read in the West until little more than a decade ago. Reynold A. Nicholson's scholarly translation and explication in the 1930s of the *Mathnawi*'s 25,700 verses, published in five volumes, were instrumental in making this work more widely accessible, as were William C. Chittick's translations of selections from Rumi's and Ibn al-Arabi's work, and his insightful thematic exposition of these a half-century later. Nicholson's translations of the oldest manuscripts available and both his and Chittick's critical notes and commentaries are invaluable resources for the student of Rumi, and in this work I have relied heavily on their knowledge and insight. It was, however, the publication of Coleman Barks' 1995 volume, *The Essential Rumi*, which sparked North America's interest in the great Persian-language poet. With no knowledge of Farsi or Arabic, the Tennessee-born poet succeeded in his mission to release Rumi's poems from the cages of their academic context and to transcribe them in a simpler, freer form for a wider audience. Rumi has since become the most popular and best-selling poet in the United States, a position he has maintained for the last ten years (Holgate, 2005), despite the emergence of strong anti-Islamic sentiments during that period, triggered by the events of September 11, 2001.

The growing awareness of the relevance of Sufism's ancient wisdom teachings embodied within Rumi's poetry culminated in UNESCO's tribute to him (International Year of Rumi—2007) in celebration of the 800th anniversary of his birth on 30th September 1207 in present-day Afghanistan. This endorsement of Rumi's mystical teachings affirms their relevance within the 21st century secular, materialistic, Western world context, even though his heart-centred approach is at odds with current perspectives privileging a rational, analytical, logical approach. I will argue that such an entirely different approach is necessary if we are to resolve the current high levels of conflict and dissatisfaction evident at so many levels.

The International Year of Rumi coincided with a clash of cultures opposed by many in the West, but it was the 2008 global financial crisis which more than any other event changed the public mood and intensified the new discourse, one with distinct moral overtones. As wealth and power are threatened, ideologies shaping economies, education, societies and politics are challenged. Hegemonic discourses, once believed to reflect the truth, no longer appear reliable.

In a world characterized by division, where self-interest appears to be the prime motivator and violation of human rights widespread, the rediscovery of the Sufi message of unity is timely. And so it is that in the most scientifically enlightened, affluent society people appear to be searching for love and meaning in the passionate verses of a Sufi poet from a distant age and culture. Materially richer than ever yet impoverished by our obsession with wealth and appearances, people are dissatisfied and unfulfilled, chained to the treadmill their lives have become while they yearn for freedom and happiness. It is to these needs and wants that Rumi speaks through his poetry, a celebration of unity through love—transformation through passion. In his sacred world, form (*sura*) and meaning (*mana*) are one. Form matters because it is the locus of manifestation of meaning.

This book therefore positions itself at the intersection of religious and philosophical studies, ethics, and cultural critique, since it takes the form of a critical analysis of contemporary society, and is informed by Sufi philosophy, which, I indicate, is largely consistent with other wisdom traditions. Although I draw on sociological research, this is not a work of sociology, nor is it one of literary criticism. It is a mystical hermeneutic—a *tawil* of the heart—which seeks the mysterious One, the divine face veiled by the multitude of forms, and the divine voice that resonates in all things; the One which, like Rumi's Beloved, gives meaning to life. Since Rumi has, I argue, much to contribute to contemporary social critique and the recovery of meaning, I bring him into conversation with contemporary cultural critics and moral philosophers such as Michael Northcott, Elizabeth Farrelly and Clive Hamilton and ecological thinkers such as Freya Mathews, Wendy Wheeler and Wendell Berry, who share similar concerns but do not themselves engage with Sufism, and in so doing, I contribute not only to contemporary social critique and ecological thought, but to the study of Sufism itself.

Three strands of research inform the book, namely research on Sufism and the Sufi poet Rumi, research drawing on empirical sociological studies, as well as the area of contemporary cultural theory, ethics and ecocritique.

In support of my Sufi perspective, I draw not only on translations of original texts written in Farsi and Arabic by Rumi and Ibn al-Arabi, but also on other significant Sufi texts written in English. I make use of various translations of Rumi's and Ibn al-Arabi's poetry, such as those of Reynold A. Nicholson. His is a scholarly translation of, and detailed commentary on, *The Mathnawi of Jalalu'ddin Rumi* (3rd ed., 2003) in five volumes, first published in 1930. Rumi himself called the *Mathnawi* "the roots of the roots of the roots of the (Islamic) Faith", emanating from God; the essence of the Qur'an. Many passages indicate his belief that it is nothing less than an inspired exposition of the esoteric content of the Qur'an—the divine truth contained, not in the formalism of the orthodox religion, but in the mysticism of the Sufis, and pre-eminently, in the *Mathnawi* (Nicholson, Commentary I: 3). Nicholson's successor in the Chair of Arabic at Cambridge, Professor A. J. Arberry, also rendered valuable services to the study of Sufism, and his translation of Rumi's work *Fihi ma fih* (In It What's in It), *Discourses of Rumi*, provides further access to the poet's thought.

I owe the biggest debt of gratitude to William C. Chittick for his translation of excerpts from various works by Rumi, including the *Mathnawi, Diwan-i Shams-i Tabrizi, Fihi ma fihi*, as well as *Maktubat, Majalis-i sab'a* and *Ruba'iyyat*, thematically arranged and explicated in the form of the *Sufi Path of Love* (1983). For love poet Rumi the loving way leads to meaning, but the heart, in Sufi literature, is the locus of knowledge (*marifa*) rather than of love; knowing is therefore the rightful activity of the heart. According to Ibn al-Arabi (1165–1240), the Sufi path is a path of knowledge of which love is the consort. Chittick expands on the *Sufi Path of Love*, based on the work of Rumi, in his *Sufi Path of Knowledge* (1989), an in depth study of the doctrine of unity (*tawhid*) and the concept of mystical knowledge (*marifa*). Chittick's *Sufi Path of Love* and *Sufi Path of Knowledge* are invaluable in making these Persian and Arabic texts accessible to readers unfamiliar with those languages. Other works by Chittick, such as *Me and Rumi, the Autobiography of Shams-i Tabrizi* (2004), a portrayal of the unlikely figure who stole Rumi's heart, and *Imaginal Worlds - Ibn al-Arabi and the Problem of Religious Diversity* (1994) provide further insight into the meaning of unity as understood by the Sufi.

Another invaluable source of Sufi theory is *The Sufi Message* of Hazrat Inayat Khan (1990), a compilation of his teachings in thirteen volumes. Pir-o-Murshid Hazrat Inayat Khan, as he is respectfully known, is the great Sufi teacher who left India in 1910, aged twenty-eight, to bring his music to the West but instead gave the ancient Sufi teachings of unity, which had been largely inaccessible to the West, new relevance at a time when the world was at war. The volumes contain a wealth of information about many aspects of Sufism, and no matter how abstruse the subject, his insights, always poetically rendered, are expressed with clarity and simplicity, qualities whose value he endorses throughout. His *Message* deals not only with esoteric aspects of traditional Sufi teachings, but with the practical issues constituting everyday life and focuses on the underlying unity of all experience; he reconceptualises Islamic mysticism as the universal message of love, harmony and beauty.

In addition to the above primary texts, the work of numerous scholars has been taken into account. Annemarie Schimmel's *Mystical Dimensions of Islam* (1975), for example, provides an excellent overview of the teachings and rich literature of Sufism. In *The Persian Sufis*, author Dominican Father Cyprian Rice pays tribute to the Persian Sufis who enriched the world with their "mystical treasures", creating awareness of the respect Sufism enjoys within the Catholic world. Rice, in his concise account of Sufism's renewal in Persia in the 12th century, explains his understanding of the Islamic connection and the contribution made by the Persian Sufis (1964, 12). Rice lauds the vigour of Persian spirituality or Sufism and points out that it was not a phenomenon which suddenly came to light at the outset of Islam and that the Persian spirit was not confined to the Islamic world. "It was there all the time (…) and has pursued its course, now open, now hidden, right down the ages" (*ibid.*). Now, centuries later as new needs have arisen, Sufi vigour is once again called for to contribute to both the revitalisation of religion and the burgeoning field of ecology. As Roger Gottlieb emphasises in *The Oxford Handbook of*

Religion and Ecology, the scope of the environmental crisis facing human-kind means that world religion has entered into an 'ecological phase' in which environmental concern is leading to the recovery of an environ-mental ethic stressing the spiritual value of 'nature', our kinship with the nonhuman, and our responsibilities to the earth (2006, 5-6). Sufism, insofar as it has always recognised "the real nature of every particle of the universe" (Rumi, cited R. C. Foltz, in Gottlieb (Ed.), 207), is ideally posi-tioned to make a meaningful contribution in this regard by turning the focus to the inner world, and working on that, so as to preserve the integ-rity of the inner and outer world and restore meaning to the earth and *all* its forms.

Werbner's *Pilgrims of Love* (1975) is an anthropological account of what she terms a Sufi "cult", and Lings's *What is Sufism* (1975) is useful for the range of definitions it provides. Besides Martin Lings, other 'perennial philosophers' on whose interpretation of knowledge as *scientia sacra* I draw, are Seyyed Hossein Nasr's *Knowledge and the Sacred* (1981), Frithjof Schuon's *Language of the Self* (1959) and *Eye of the Heart* and A. K. Coomaraswamy's *Indian Art* (1969).

Idries Shah's *World of the Sufi* (1979) is a collection of essays by schol-ars from divergent fields, addressing the impact of Sufism in the modern world. Shah's claim that "Sufism is, in operation, pragmatic" (p 2) led me to an exploration of Dewey's pragmatism theory, and accounts for affinities with Richard Sennett's interpretation of craftsmanship in *The Craftsman* (2008), and Peirce's perspective as elaborated by Wendy Wheeler (2006).

Psychologist Llewellyn Vaughan-Lee, author of *Sufism: The transfor-mation of the Heart* (1997), and *Love is a Fire: The Sufi's Mystical Journey Home* (2000) belongs to an order known as the 'silent Sufis', named after the 14th-Century Sufi, Baha-ud-Din Naqshband (1318–1389), who taught that the Beloved is silent and is most easily reached in silence. Naqshband was renowned as an interpreter of dreams, and dream work and symbology are considered extremely important, as Karl Jung explained many centuries later. Vaughan-Lee's interpretation of concepts such as *qalb* (heart) and *ishq* (love) reflect the fire and intoxication of 'Love's Idiots', whose purpose is not to escape from pain and suffering, but, driven by the soul's homesickness, to find meaning by losing them-selves in union with their divine Beloved.

In addition to the above, extensive reference to journals such as those of the *Muhyiddin Ibn 'Arabi Society* and *The Fountain Magazine*, and to the publications of Carl W. Ernst, a specialist in Islamic studies, provides further insight into contemporary Sufi scholarship. Some of the dominant themes identified are as follows: Sufism's role in conflict resolution, Sufis as 'bridge builders', Sufism's "daring and prescient universalism" (el-Khazari, 2006), its role in interfaith dialogue and the revitalisation of religion, Sufism's explicit environmental ethic, and inevitably, Sufism's commoditization in a process which Ernst refers to as "the publication of the secret" (2009, 10)—"Sufism for Westerners" (Hammer, in Westerland (Ed.), 2004) which downplays the Islamic connection and mystical aspects while emphasising more popular ones.

At the heart of these diverse themes is the central issue of 'going beyond' the surface, of plumbing the depths to find meaning within the multiplicity of forms, and being enriched by it—the essence of all Sufi teachings and so too of Rumi's poetry. Insofar as three modern-day philosophies share this perennial, mystical concern with meaning, my contribution to this field of inquiry is to bring ecophilosopher Freya Mathews' panpsychism, Clive Hamilton's metaphysical-psychology and Wendy Wheeler's biosemiotics into the conversation, because their thought, essentially mystical as I will argue, resonates clearly with Sufi teachings and therefore has the potential to further extend the scope of Sufi thought within the western context (or: demonstrate its universalism?).

Most citations of Rumi and other Sufi poets in this book are translations from Persian or Arabic by either Nicholson or Chittick. In order to avoid frequent, unwieldy references to translations by Nicholson or Chittick, I have chosen to follow Chittick's example and use the abbreviation *SPL* when referring to Chittick's *Sufi Path of Love* (1983); *SPK* when referring to Chittick's *Sufi Path of Knowledge* (1989), and Nicholson followed by the volume when referring to translations by Nicholson. When citing from any of Pir-o-Murshid Hazrat Inayat Khan's thirteen volumes, I refer simply to the volume and page number without the author's name in order to avoid using the surname without the honorific, (meaning master or wise spiritual father (Rice, 13) or saint, spiritual guide or Sufi mystic (Werbner, 327)). In a further attempt to avoid clumsy circumscription, I refer to the Beloved as He. Of course, Truth is neither masculine nor feminine but all-inclusive and limited only by our language and thought. Fur-thermore, I make use of the masculine pronoun when referring to 'the Sufi' since such references generally relate to Rumi, although occasionally they are non-specific in which case I retain the masculine for reasons of consistency. I acknowledge that this approach is exclusive of the sacred feminine aspect and is therefore not entirely satisfactory, but trust that the heart with its unifying potential has the capacity to transcend the divisive-ness of language's form.

I draw on empirical sociological studies in order to disclose various aspects of contemporary society. Guided by architect and social critic Eliz-abeth Farrelly (*Blubberland: The Dangers of Happiness*, 2007) through our culture's constructed forms, as well as by Mathews (*Reinhabiting Reality*, 2005), who attributes to "block-logic" the "wholesale terminations" (p. 8) of our suburbs, I note that the "fat form", is ubiquitous; blubber threatens the health of the world. I find support for this perspective in *Affluenza* (2005), by Clive Hamilton, formerly Executive Director of The Australia Institute, and Richard Denniss, Deputy Director of the same institute—Australia's "foremost public interest think tank" (p. i). Although theirs is a critique of Australian society in particular, it would be fair to say that the condition they describe is not limited to Australian society but is common to all affluent societies today. According to the authors, afflu-enza is the condition from which contemporary society suffers, and is defined as follows: The bloated, sluggish and unfulfilled feeling that results from efforts to keep up with the Joneses; an epidemic of stress, overwork, waste and indebtedness caused by dogged pursuit of the Aus-tralian dream, and an unsustainable addiction to economic growth (p. 3). People infected by affluenza are plagued by psychological disorders, dis-connectedness and distress. What they want above all is for their lives to have a purpose, but "finding meaning is not easy" (p. 182), according to the authors, who conclude that we need "a new political philosophy". Rumi's mystical philosophy, I argue, has the potential to address these needs as acquisitiveness no longer appears to be the Zeitgeist—it is being superseded by the deeper need for meaning.

In my critique of linguistic forms I draw on Wendell Berry's *Stand-ing by Words* (1983) and George Orwell's *Politics and the English Language* (1945), *Collected Essays, Journalism & Letters of George Orwell* (Electronic version). "If thought corrupts language, language can also corrupt thought", wrote George Orwell with reference to the decline, as he perceived it, of the English language and culture. Authenticity and sufficiency are all too often replaced by phoniness, deceit and surfeit, resulting in a 'cacophony of voices'; often shrill and strident, competing to be heard. In order to hear the "moral voice" (2008) of which Hamilton also speaks, the shrill voices must be stilled.

My critique of our approach to eating draws on a substantial body of evidence that suggests that human, animal and environmental interests are not being served by the international meat industry as we know it today. The full range of horrors to which animals are regularly subjected is documented by the following authors on whose work I draw: Clive Hamilton (*Affluenza*, 2005); animal ethicist Peter Singer (*Animal Liberation*, 1975); Wendell Berry (*The Unsettling of America*, 1996; *Life is a Miracle*, 2000); Eric Schlosser (*Fast Food Nation: The Dark Side of the All American Meal*, 2001); Karen Davis (*Prisoned Chickens, Poisoned Eggs*, 1996); Gail Eisnitz (*Slaughterhouse: The Shocking Story of Greed, Neglect and Inhumane Treatment Inside the U.S. Meat Industry*, 2006). These accounts document the suffering, first and foremost by animals, but theirs becomes a collective suffering for which animals, humans and the environment ultimately pay the price.

In my critique of the commodification of the natural world, I draw on Scottish ethicist Michael Northcott (*A Moral Climate: The Ethics of Global Warming*, 2007) and American poet, essayist, novelist and farmer, Wendell Berry. Though grounded in the Christian tradition, Berry's perspective is that of the mystic or ecophilosopher with a heightened awareness of the mystery of life. At the heart of our engagement with forms, he argues, is the *logos* embodied in our word; and our obligation to stand by it and uphold its integrity (1983). Acknowledging Berry's influence on his own thought, Northcott argues that our materialistic worldview, having reduced all things to commodities, denies their moral or spiritual significance.

The third aspect of the study relates to contemporary eco-cultural thought, in particular ecophilosopher Freya Mathews' panpsychism as developed in *For Love of Matter* (2003) and *Reinhabiting Reality* (2005); Wendy Wheeler's work in the emerging field of biosemiotics, *The Whole*

Creature: Complexity, Biosemiotics and the Evolution of Culture (2006), as well as the metaphysical psychology of Clive Hamilton's *Freedom Paradox: Towards a Post-Secular Ethics* (2008).

The ecophilosophical worldview is based on the principle of interconnectedness, where everything is seen as implicating and being implicated in the identities of other things; a worldview which is by no means new. Indeed, Aristotle and his student Theophrastus were early forerunners of ecological thought and are considered the Greek fathers of animal and plant ecology respectively (Macauley, D., *Greening Philosophy and Democratizing Ecology*, 1996, 1). In their search for a hidden *arche*, an underlying *logos*, or a guiding *telos*, the first Greek philosophers reflected not simply upon the human psyche but "directed themselves foremost toward the yawning heavens, the turnings and reversals of fire, the rhythm and play of water, and the outcroppings of rock and earth" (*ibid.*). The earth's symbolic expression was for a long time considered revelatory; its communications invited scientists and philosophers to participate dialogically in its mysterious nature.

What is distinctive about the new environmental or ecophilosophy, is its more emphatically ethical and political orientation. Responding to ecological crisis, it seeks to rethink our assumptions about 'nature' and 'humanity' with a view to advancing environmental sustainability and interspecies justice. Mathews outlines the assumptions underpinning its perspective as follows: ". . . an *ecocentric* perspective situates humanity *in* nature rather than apart from and above it, and thereby removes the traditional justification for anthropocentric attitudes. The idea of interconnectedness can function as an organizing principle not only within metaphysics and ethics, but in many different theoretical and practical contexts (. . .). In the theological context, spirit is seen as immanent in matter, body, Nature. Spirituality thus involves celebration of and reverence for our corporeal existence, and affirmation of the natural world and our enmeshment in it. In the sociopolitical context, society is seen not as an aggregate of social atoms—essentially mutually independent individuals—but as a collective, in which individuals are constituted through their relations with one another" (Mathews, 1998).

The term 'ecophilosophy' was coined fairly recently; probably in 1973 by the Norwegian philosopher Arne Naess, who was influenced, amongst others, by Spinoza, Gandhi, logical positivism and the nature-centredness of the Norwegian folk tradition (*ibid.*). Naess's 'deep ecology' started as "a doctrine of biospheric egalitarianism" and is, according to Brennan, the best-known "radical (environmental) ethic" (Brennan, 1998). It involved "challenging prevailing philosophical and ideological assumptions about our relation to the natural world", unlike 'shallow environmentalism' which "sought environmental reform within existing philosophical and ideological parameters" (Mathews, 1998). It is a "philosophy of 'self-realization', according to which individuals can overcome their culturally acquired alienation from the natural world by recognizing the ultimate ontological seamlessness of reality", and gradually developing an "extended sense of self", an "ecological consciousness" which is a notion of selfhood beyond individual identity (*ibid.*). However, Naess's deep ecology is just one strand of a much wider field which includes social ecology, founded by Murray Bookchin, and ecofeminism. Bookchin's work constitutes just one variant of social ecology, alongside socialist, liberation and feminist ecologisms (Cudworth, 2005, 24). There are also a number of individual ecophilosophers, who, according to Mathews, remain unaffiliated with any of these.

In a field characterised by transdisciplinarity and "extreme" diversity (Cudworth, 2), the various ecophilosophical forms nevertheless share a common concern with socio-political systems of domination and environmental exploitation. Social ecologists are most concerned with issues relating to "intra-human domination", regarding it as the immediate cause of environmental abuse and exploitation, while eco-socialists identify the specific use which capitalism makes of industry as the cause of environmental degradation. Liberation ecologists argue that 'de-development' of the first world is critical to ensuring environmental justice, "wealth being a greater threat to the environment than poverty" (Guha and Juan Martinez-Alier, 1997, 59, in Cudworth, 37). Ecofeminists, such as Val Plumwood and Carolyn Merchant, draw on deep ecological theory to the extent that they interpret human relations with 'nature' as a form of domination. They have a particular interest in the link between the domination of women and of nature, and argue for the positive revaluation of the connection between women and nature (*op. cit.*, 101). There is a distinct spiritual dimension to some ecofeminism and deep ecologism, and some ecofeminists attribute to women particular knowledge or iden-tification with 'nature', claims which are occasionally dismissed as 'essen-tialist'. Cudworth, however, argues that such critiques are reductionist in their almost exclusive focus on human agency in social relations and their failure to take biological considerations into account. Charges of essential-ism, she says, are more often than not based on insufficient knowledge and de-contextualization (*op. cit.*, 102).

Predominant in Mathews' work is the ecofeminist understanding that nature is real (Soper, 1995, in Cudworth, 119), and deep ecology's notion of ecological selfhood, but her 'panpsychist' ecophilosophy distin-guishes itself from other ecophilosophies insofar as it offers a *modus viven-di* in the form of "a conscious, devotional pursuit of the Way" (2003, 9) to counteract modernity's assault on the world. It not only restores to reality its psychic dimension but offers a "world-inclusive spirituality" (*op. cit.*, 1) which seeks to "resacralize the taken-for-granted ground beneath our feet" (*op. cit.*, 5) by "liberat(ing) reason into a larger field of meta-physics" (*op. cit.*, 6), and in doing so, can be seen to have much in com-mon with Sufism. Prefiguring aspects of ecophilosophy, Sufism teaches a holistic worldview based on unity of form. Like panpsychism, Sufism teaches that matter should be approached mindfully. The alternative, Mathews argues, is modernity's materialistic culture which regards the entire world as "raw resource, inert and uncommunicative", in which we assume an attitude of "bruteness and blindness", and increasingly repre-sent "little more than highly sophisticated instruments of human assault on world" (2005, 15).

Andrew Dobson (1990, 13-18) suggests that ecologism is, by defini-tion, radical (in Cudworth, 2005, 16), and as Roger Gottlieb notes in the preface to Merchant's *Radical Ecology* (1992, xii), many have claimed that such visions are really "unrealistic fantasies". And indeed, ecofeminism has been dismissed by some as a "mishmash of mysticism (and) morality" (Moore 1990, endorsed by Pepper 1993, cited in Cudworth, 2005, 33). It is this commonly held misconception of mysticism and its association with fantasy, evident in both Mathews' and Wheeler's work, which I will address in this book, illuminating their interpretation from a Sufi perspec-tive, thus enriching this particular field of inquiry with Sufism's unbound-ed vision.

Wendy Wheeler's *Whole Creature* (2006), her work on complexity, biosemiotics and the evolution of culture, contributes to the field of bio-semiotics—the study of signs and significance in all living systems—stemming from the semiotics of Charles Sanders Peirce (1867–1893), the biology of Jakob von Uexküll (1940), and Sebeok's study of zoosemiotics (1984), the study of animals' use of semiosis (Wheeler, 2006). Wheeler details the paradigm shift, the 'complexity revolution' occurring in the sciences during the past sixty to seventy years, which physicist Robert Laughlin in 2005 describes as the move from the Age of Reductionism to the Age of Emergence in which the reality of mind-body-environment holism (such as the Sufis described) once again becomes conceivable.

During the twentieth century, explains Wheeler, the idea that social change is an evolving process became unfashionable. In the Romantic philosophy of the late eighteenth and early nineteenth century, as with the work of Marx and Engels, for example, there was a stronger awareness of nature and society as a complex and evolutionary process, and this was linked to an ideal of progress. But in the late nineteenth century and in the twentieth, the idea arose that society should be conceived of as essentially static, seeking always to return to a state of equilibrium which could be reductively analysed into component parts. Under the banner of post-modernism, says Wheeler, the idea of processual change was equally rejected. It was elided with an idea of progress felt to be scientistic, possibly ethnocentric, and tainted by Enlightenment rationalism (Wheeler, 38). A complexity view of nature and culture is obviously in contrast with neoliberal ideologies which have resulted in an economic and utilitarian focus on markets and job-skills and consequent degrading of "non-instrumental" life in all its forms (*op. cit.*, 21). Wheeler explains that complexity theory represents a new scientific paradigm shift across the disciplines, allowing us to think about all life forms in different ways, and she does this by setting the methodological power of reductionism in science within a larger frame of understanding.

Against the individualism asserted by liberal doctrine, Wheeler affirms the crucial importance to physical and mental well-being of human solidarity. "Monadic individualism is a fiction", she argues, and individual parts are "close to meaningless" (p. 99) when taking systemic complexity into account. Our interconnectedness naturally affects our flourishing, and for humans, says Wheeler, maximal flourishing consists in the richness of our semiosis: our contacts, our ability to be heard and responded to, our sense of being supported and effective in a rich number of ways (p. 109).

Insights of this nature were arrived at intuitively by mystics and poets, particularly of the Romantic era, who sensed the essential unity of all things despite their differences, and indeed Wheeler refers to poets such as Coleridge and Wordsworth in this regard. Yet, like Mathews, she appears anxious to distance herself from mysticism, and turns instead to Buddhist philosophy which, as she explains, is not based on belief but is a system of mental culture, a philosophy of lived experience. Wheeler speaks of "mindful practice" (p. 98), and of furthering "the path, the process of self-understanding of the world" (*ibid.*), yet hastens to explain that "this is not a matter of some mystical fantasy of being 'good'" (*ibid.*). I address this obvious misconstrual of mysticism as a belief system, an escape from harsh realities (which has arguably contributed to its popular appeal), and the notion of 'being good', which is not the mystic's primary objective but rather a consequence of *Suluk*—the journey of the heart, which, like the mindfulness of Buddhist practice leads to right action, which, after all, is necessary for maximal flourishing. Hamilton explains this fundamental difference between the 'good' life, whose objective is the attainment of virtue, and the 'meaningful' life which is the mystic's goal (2008).

Mindfulness underpins morality, which leads me to the work of Clive Hamilton, Professor of Public Ethics at the Centre for Applied Philosophy and Public Ethics, a joint centre of the Australian National University, Charles Sturt University and the University of Melbourne. Hamilton's *Freedom Paradox: Towards a Post-Secular Ethics* (2008) counters the rationalist ethics of Immanuel Kant (1724–1804), the emblematic philosopher of the European Enlightenment, and of Arthur Schopenhauer (1788–1860), who took the transcendental aspect of Kant's idealism one step further. Reason, according to Kant, is the essence of our humanity—the basis of self, of order and of morality. Yet, he concedes, reason is unable to apprehend existence "in itself" (2008, 73). In a world of appearances, argues Kant in *Critique of Pure Reason*, there must be something that appears—"an object independent of sensibility", the "thing considered as it is in itself" (*ibid.*). Kant adopts the terms 'phenomenon' and 'noumenon' to distinguish between the thing as it appears to us and the thing as it is in itself. Against Kant's "epistemological modesty" (*op. cit.*, 97), Schopenhauer in *The World as Will and Representation* was willing to argue for the existence of a form of "heart-centred" (*op. cit.*, 167), "non-sensible intuition" (*op. cit.*, 76) that would allow us to understand the noumenon. Although he believed that the essence of humans lay in their "life in the noumenon" rather than in their rational capacity, he denied that life in the noumenon had any purpose, a position Hamilton believes "imbued his philosophy with relentless pessimism" (*op. cit.*, 244).

Departing from Schopenhauer, drawing instead on Eastern philosophies, Hamilton recognises and expands on the purpose of "life in the noumenon", the fixed point from which emerges the "moral self", "the most immediate expression of the noumenon in the phenomenal world" and the source of "fellow feeling" (*op. cit.*, 190) or "metaphysical empathy" (*op. cit.*, 146). "The moral self is our better nature" (*ibid.*). Finding the path to the noumenon, Hamilton suggests, entails following a "metaphysical-psychological" path, a path of humility, the objective of which is to overcome our subjectivity by transcending identification with the ego-self in the phenomenon (*op. cit.,* 227). Such a path, he believes, might reveal the stream of meaning running beneath the surface of life. Unlike the pleasant and the good life whose respective goals are pleasure and virtue, the meaningful life, according to Hamilton, has few advocates (*op. cit.*, 243). The Sufis, however, advocated the kind of path Hamilton proposes, and his "metaphysical psychology", I maintain, is analogous to the Sufi path, although its name, abstract and passionless, conjures up none of the "purity of passion" (*op. cit.*, 226) required on such a path.

Sufi poets, advocates of the meaningful life, are, I believe, ideally positioned to stir in the hearts of those who come to know them the passion that might lead them to "transcend the phenomenal preoccupations of lives pleasant and good" (*op. cit.*, 231). Indeed, Hamilton affirms the artist's role in giving form to the noumenon: "The true value of great art lies in its ability to remind us of our existence in the noumenon and to do so in spite of all the distractions that keep us confined to the world of everyday appearances" (*ibid.*). I therefore contend that the way revealed to us by Sufi poets such as Rumi exemplifies the path that Hamilton envisages.

Hamilton, Mathews and Wheeler would, I claim, find support for their respective philosophies in Sufism's ancient wisdom teachings, with which they are largely compatible in view of their shared concern with connectivity. In Chapter One, I provide an overview of Sufi cosmology and introduce the defining principle of unity, *tawhid*, which affirms the One's all-encompassing reality and unequivocally counters Cartesian dualism's conception of deanimated, meaningless matter. I signal affinities between Sufism and other wisdom traditions, ranging from the writings of Plato and the mystic Plotinus, to Buddhism and Taoism, as well as the work of modern-day scientists such as Fritjof Capra and David Bohm which reflects a perception of reality that goes beyond the post-Enlightenment scientific framework to an intuitive awareness of the oneness of all life. I argue that Sufism's animating impulse has re-emerged in the form of three modern-day philosophies focusing on ethical engagement with an intrinsically meaningful world, and propose that Mathews and Wheeler, rather than eschewing mysticism, might acknowledge the mystical inspiration at the heart of their thought, as Hamilton is more ready to do.

In light of the Sufi understanding that the universe is a collection of signs that carries a message, a concept which finds new life in new forms in the work of Mathews and Wheeler, I observe, in Chapter Two, some of the signs of our constructed world, to see what they reveal about the nature of our existence. 'Going beyond form', which Rumi urges us to do, necessitates prior traversal; in this chapter, therefore, I engage extensively with forms, attending to the cultural landscape, noting its bloated appearance, its superficial enhancements, endeavouring to understand the message in the context of the whole, the theme of the sacred script being *tawhid*.

Contrasting sociobiology's and objectivism's reductive interpretation of the fundamentally competitive nature of human interaction with Wheeler' more optimistic argument from biosemiotics which presupposes a complex non-reductive and non-positivistic semiotic biology and culture as co-determining how genetic traits and communication-systems develop, I argue in Chapter Three that refinement of *nafs* (ego) is essential, since its strident voice breaks the stillness in which other voices might be heard—the voices of others, of animals and of the earth. Finding at the heart of our obesogenic environment the obese ego, a disorder which appears to have no name, I coin the term 'egobesity' to affirm its reality.

In Chapter Four, I contrast the Sufi concept of *marifa* with the modern understanding of knowledge, the neoliberal association of knowledge with the economy, and the commoditisation of knowledge, making reference to Nasr's thought on the modern desacralisation of the *scientia sacra* and signaling affinities with Polanyi's account of the passionate structure of tacit knowledge on which Wheeler draws. I compare the Sufi concept of *amal*, knowledge in practice, as exemplified by Rumi's analogy of 'the Worker, hidden in His Workshop', with pragmatist Sennett's interpretation of craftsmanship. I argue that the modes of knowing as elaborated by three contemporary philosophers, namely Mathews' understanding of 'encounter' as opposed to "epistemological probe" (2003, 76), Wheeler's of 'semiotic knowledge' and Hamilton's of 'moral certainty' are 'new' forms of a perennial, mystical concern with knowledge and meaning.

In Chapter Five, I introduce the concept of mystical love, *ishq*, the creative energy generating all forms, and elaborate its centrality to *fana* (annihilation of ego) and *baqa* (subsistence), Sufi concepts which, I argue, also resonate with concepts central to Mathews' panpsychism and Hamilton's metaphysical-psychology.

At a time when meaning tends to be forgotten and submission to ego's commanding voice the norm, I argue in this book that the language of the heart should be heard—pure language, as spoken by Sufi poets like Rumi, who urges us to go beyond form, to seek meaning, and in heeding his words, as we journey from superficial complexity to the simplicity at the centre, we might, I suggest, hear the heart's own silent expression, and be transformed by it. And while mystics and poets have always offered us meaning, their ancient wisdom teachings have, until recently, been consigned to oblivion as postmodernism problematized their "metanarrative" (Lyotard, 33). Capturing the new mood, however, are three modern-day philosophies—panpsychism, biosemiotics and metaphysical psychology, and it is within this framework that I incorporate Rumi's mystical insights with which, I claim, they resonate so clearly. This book is an exploration of Sufi principles within this context and as such I believe it represents a recovery of knowledge, in the traditional sense, and a new contribution to knowledge, as currently understood.

CHAPTER ONE

World of Form (*Sura*) and Meaning (*Mana*)

World of Form (*Sura*)
and Meaning (*Mana*)

I n this chapter, I will provide an overview of Sufi cosmology and introduce Sufism's defining principle of unity, *tawhid*, which, in affirming the One's all-encompassing reality, unequivocally counters Cartesian dualism's conception of a deanimated, meaningless world. I will bring the new biosemiotic understanding of communication as all-pervasive in the living world into conversation with Rumi's depiction of a world in which form and meaning are inextricably linked. I will signal affinities between Sufism and other non-dualist traditions, ranging from the writings of Plato (though some would classify him as a dualist) and the mystic Plotinus, to Buddhism and Taoism, including the work of modern-day scientists such as Fritjof Capra and David Bohm which reflects a perception of reality that goes beyond the post-Enlightenment scientific framework to an intuitive awareness of the oneness of all life. I will argue that Sufism's animating impulse has re-emerged in the form of three modern-day philosophies focusing on ethical engagement with an intrinsically meaningful world, namely Mathews' panpsychism, Wheeler's biosemiotics and Hamilton's metaphysical-psychology, and will propose that Mathews and Wheeler, rather than eschewing mysticism on account of its unscientific appearance, might acknowledge the mystical inspiration that could be seen to underpin, and certainly to lend support to, their thought.

1.1 The Multiplicity of Names

From the initial encounter the Western student of Rumi is faced with a bewildering array of names whose strangeness and inconsistency make them impenetrable symbols that reveal far less than they conceal. In their multiplicity these names are analogous to all forms (*sura*) whose appearance is many and varied but whose meaning (*mana*), according to Sufi thought, is One.

Discerning meaning is, for Rumi, a matter of finding the Beloved, who, though present in all things, is manifest in an infinite range of modalities. All names are His names, the Sufis tell us, and every name reveals something of the divine presence while concealing an infinite range of aspects. In answer to the question "Where can I find Him?" we are told "Wherever He is present, which is everywhere, since all things are His acts. But no act is identical with Him, who encompasses all things and all acts, all worlds and all presences. Though He can be found everywhere, He is also nowhere to be found" (*SPK*, 6). To find the Beloved is to fall into bewilderment (*hayra*), the bewilderment of affirmation and negation, finding and losing, knowing and not knowing, since "None knows God thoroughly but God" (*SPK*, 4).

Similarly, grasping the meaning of Rumi's name is problematised by the ambiguity of its many forms which vary from one text to another and even within the same text. In Nicholson's translation of the *Mathnawi*, for instance, we find throughout the text the form Jalálu'ddín Rúmí, but on the cover we find a less elaborate Jalalu'ddin Rumi as well as an even simpler Jalaluddin Rumi inside it. Chittick uses the form Jalāl al-Dīn Rūmī; Vaughan-Lee favours Jalaluddin Rûmî; UNESCO policy document 175 EX/11 (3 October 2006) refers to him as Mawlana Jalal-Ud-Din Balkhi-Rumi but also as Mevlana Celaleddin Belhi-Rumi. Both Nicholson's and Chittick's credentials as translators and interpreters of ancient Sufi texts are impeccable yet their representations of Rumi's name differ in the detail. Hazrat Inayat Khan tells us that Persians and Afghans refer to him as Jalāluddīn Muhammad Balkhī (IX, 53). The name Balkhi (Belhi) tells us that he is originally from Balkh in present-day Afghanistan and we cannot be sure when this name was conferred on him. Since he spent most of his life in Anatolia, the land colonised by the Romans whose capital was at Konya where he settled (in present-day Turkey), he also came to be known as Rumi. Şefik Can tells us that his name is Muhammad and his title is Jalal al-Din, and that he is also called Hudavendigar (Can, 2005, 12). In some poems he uses nicknames such as *khamoosh* (silent) or *khamoosh kon* (be silent) (*op. cit.,* 40). In all likelihood the names by which we know him today are quite different from his real name. How then to resolve the dilemma of the name? Rumi offers the following advice:

Pass beyond form, escape from names! Flee titles and names toward meaning! (Rumi, *SPL*, 20)

Mindful of Rumi's instruction, I recognise that the form of the name in no way captures his boundless spirit, and refer to him simply as 'Rumi'. Unaware of the meaning concealed within the various adornments that some translators have retained in the anglicized form of the name, I heed Rumi's words and in my own usage opt for the simplest form of his name. We are not to be deceived by the appearance of the myriad forms, he tells us repeatedly, and though each form displays its own limited meaning, its real meaning goes beyond the limitations of its form.

Of course Rumi's instruction does not give us license to disregard particularity; particulars after all reflect the rich diversity of the Beloved's acts and as such must be encountered mindfully. Explaining the importance, in respect of discerning meaning, of attending to particulars, Mathews affirms the One subjectivity: "communicative cues reside *deep within* the particularity of things", and initiating communication with the world at large "requires awareness of intricate *patterns of unfolding*, attunement to the minutest details in the *order* and *sequence* of things. . ." (2005, 16) (my italics). Rather than focus exclusively on particulars and risk overlooking commonality and connection, the Sufi always seeks the unifying essence concealed by veils of infinite variety—the eternal patterns of unfolding that tell of order and sequence, deep within. In the ensuing chapters, therefore, I will look closely at the particulars of various forms, but always with a view to their animating impulse. Our embrace of the infinite is mediated by the finite, says Mathews (2003, 106), to which the Sufi might add, recognising the infinite leads to an embrace of the finite. "He can be experienced as immanent only after he has been experienced as transcendent", says Nasr (1981, 137). Over-attention to the constantly changing finite might prevent recognition of the infinite. As long as we remain bound to the particulars, or the letters—as Sufi Niffarī (d. 965) put it—we are in some sense fettered by appearances instead of reaching the place in which there are no more letters (Schimmel, 1975).

It is appropriate that Rumi's name should not be the subject of speculation since the Sufi *sheikh* (master) is traditionally "without a face and without a name" (Vaughan-Lee, 1997, 144), the relationship with the teacher being an impersonal one despite its spiritual intimacy. Empty of self, the ego having annihilated (*fana*), the master embodies a space in which the lover can meet the Beloved—a mirror reflecting the student's own inner light. Rumi in fact writes much of his poetry not under his own name at all but under the name of his beloved spiritual master, Shams (1185–1248), the one he has chosen to serve; the *Diwan* for instance, is entitled *Diwan-i Shams-i Tabriz*, 'Poems of Shams, the sun of Tabriz', while the *Mathnawi* is the *Husamuddin*, 'the book of Husam, the latter filling the void left by Shams' disappearance (Nicholson, I, 5). In Shams and Husam Rumi recognises the perfection of his Beloved, and in a state of spiritual union, having shed his ego (*nafs*), participates in their attributes. This is not a self-conscious act of appropriation or colonisation, but rather a selfless act of devotion. Devoid of ego, there is only the eternal and infinite presence of the Beloved. In his pursuit of selflessness and meaning, he eschews the "narrow abode" of his own name, for "self-consciousness is names, names!" (Rumi, *SPL*, 174).

The Sufis themselves have never referred to themselves by this or any other name. In *The Necessity for the Rise of the Term Sufi*, Victor Danner tells us that the name 'Sufi' is used to translate both *sūfī* and *mutasawwif*, which denote respectively one who is at the end of the spiritual path and one who is on the path (Cited in Lings, 45). The term *mutasawwif* would therefore more accurately name the self-purification of spiritual wayfarers who have not yet realised the state of perfect selflessness designated by the name 'Sufi', while those who had would not be concerned about what name was given to them. The name 'Sufi' was always given to mystics by others and various explanations of the term have been offered (Shah, 1968, 14), the most common being that the name was derived from the Arabic *sáf* meaning 'pure' (VIII, 23) or *sūf* meaning 'woollen', (Lings, 46) and by extension 'wearers of wool' since woollen dress was associated with spirituality in pre-Islamic times. Other possibilities include a reference to the *Sáfa,* the Brotherhood of Purity whose doctrine was: "Know thyself and thou wilt know God" (Lings, 15), or possibly their enthusiasm for the wisdom of the Greek *Sophia* (Shah, 1979, 123). Perhaps the word needs no derivation, suggests Brent, "being simply itself". The sound *soof* of the Arabic letters S, U, F (*Soad, Wao, Fa*) in this same order of use has its own power, "a value based on the universe's hidden currents of meaning" (Cited in Shah, 1968, 16). Those who were, like Rumi, lovers of

God, did not want to draw attention to themselves and were determined to be free from labels and distinctions.

The essence of life cannot be fixed or limited, and in the process of naming a thing we delimit the boundlessness that makes it sacred. "The Tao that can be described is not the eternal Tao; the name that can be defined is not the unchanging name. . ." (Lao-Tzu, Cited in D'Adamo, 162). Naming implies that we have grasped a thing's meaning and that it is knowable in its entirety. Martin Heidegger, whose later work has been seen as consistent with Sufi thought (Leckey, 2009), draws attention to the problematic nature of naming when he says: "How is one to give a name to what he is still searching for? To assign the naming word is, after all, what constitutes finding" (Heidegger, 1959, 20). Names effectively conceal the all-encompassing, unknowable nothing—"the Nothing that is Everything" (XI, 9)—that gives them being and sustains them.

It is inevitable that Sufism has been called an "imprecise tradition" (Brent, Cited in Shah, 1979, 7), in which a vaguely defined method for achieving an incommunicable experience was handed down from master to disciple through the generations, and as such, both the derivation of its name and its origins are shrouded in obscurity. According to Witteveen (1997), Sufism is a confluence of mystical currents, some of which have been reliably traced back to the Hermetic tradition of about 3000 BCE and given an essentially universal character at the beginning of the twentieth century. Rice likens Sufism to a great oak tree, standing in the middle of the meadow; "no one witnessed its planting, no one beheld its beginning, but now the flourishing tree speaks for itself, is true to its origins which it has forgotten, has taken for granted. . ." (Cited in Shah, 1979, 9)

Ibn al-Arabi envisages the universe as the manifestations of *wujud*, a reality that is one in every respect, variously translated as 'sheer Being', 'utter Plenitude', 'pure Consciousness', or 'Light'. He explains the dependence of all beings on this reality: "the Necessary Being is that reality which cannot not be (. . .) and the possible things come into relative existence within the cosmos through their partaking of it" (*SPK*, 7). Various terms are used in an attempt to identify this reality which Chittick translates as 'Necessary Being', 'the One Entity' and 'Essence of God' (*SPK*, 82). To Rumi, the lover, God is the Beloved but is not limited to Love, since 'all names are God's names'. His names, attributes and acts are unlimited and provide knowledge of his mysterious essence. The scientist might not conceive of energy as God, though it too might be described as absolute, eternal and aquiver with potential—sheer existence, independent of any other entity (Siahpush, 2009). Names given to it cannot confine it since all names are its names, all things belong to it and all things are its radiance, its properties and attributes, representing its visible, knowable aspects. The cosmos is thus conceived of as a living, pulsating manifestation of spirit in which the many arise from the one whose reality they continuously express.

"Being is Oneness" is Sufism's primary teaching, just as Islam taught from the first that Allah is One (*SPK*, 6). The name Allah is the "all-comprehensive name" (*SPK*, 66), designating every other name referring to relatively specific attributes of Being. Chittick explains that within the loci of their manifestation the names are multiple but in themselves the names remain one, in respect of Allah's oneness. Everything is from Allah. The all-comprehensive nature of the name Allah as it is so powerfully conveyed in Arabic is not adequately rendered by the nearest English equivalent 'God'. My recourse, in this book, to the translation is therefore not entirely accurate.

What is Sufism? It is neither a religion nor a cult, sect, secret society or theory. It is not a recent phenomenon nor is it a modern-day fad born of a makeover culture desirous of instant results. It has no dogma, does not proselytize or promise fulfilment. It neither acknowledges allegiance to any other form, nor does it demand it of anyone. It does however offer seekers of truth an alternative to religion in the form of a mystical, philosophical vision which is in some respects in harmony with contemporary scientific thought. Of the many definitions available, Martin Lings's "movement of return, ebb," is probably most apt. From time to time, he says, a Revelation 'flows' like a great tidal wave to the shores of our finite world, and Sufism is "the vocation, the discipline and the science of plunging into the ebb of one of these waves and being drawn back with it to its eternal and infinite Source". Each wave emanating from the ocean of unity has its own characteristics according to its destination, that is, the particular needs of time and place towards which and in response to which it flows, but Sufis do not concern themselves with their varying shapes. The Source is within as well as without, and the path of the Sufis is "a gradual awakening in the direction of the root of one's being, a remembrance of the Supreme Self which infinitely transcends the human ego and which is none other than the Deep towards which the wave ebbs" (Lings, 1975, 13).

Like a speck of foam seeking reabsorption by the ocean, the Sufi holds on to his memory of intimacy and longs to return to the One from whom the earthly journey takes him. Experiencing a merging with the One, losing himself in the Beloved's embrace, the Sufi has been called a mystic. According to Robinson (1998), Sufism and Sufi metaphysics or gnosis (*al-marifa*, *'irfan*) are paradigmatic of mystical philosophy since 'knowledge' to the Sufi means 'knowledge of mysteries' (*'ulum al-asrar*). "Sufism is nothing short of divine knowledge for, in the words of the sacred *Hadith*, when God loves his servant he becomes 'the hearing with which he hears, the sight with which he sees'" (Ibn al-Arabi, *SPK*, 331).

The term 'mysticism' is commonly misunderstood and not infrequently mistaken for a display of paranormal phenomena. Like 'mystery' (Greek *mysterion*), the adjective 'mystical' (Greek *mystikos*) is derived from the Greek verb *myein* ('to close', especially the eyes and lips), suggesting something secret, concealed and too precious to be spoken about inappropriately. The term was used by Christian authors of the patristic era to refer to the 'mystical sense' of Scripture, the hidden presence of Christ in the Biblical text and, by extension, in the sacraments, especially the Eucharist (Payne, 1998). The existence of 'concealed' or veiled divinity is a fundamental principle in Sufism, and mystical consciousness is of 'pure undifferentiated unity', which Stace and Pike (Cited in Payne, 1998) describe as (apparent) union with God if it comes as the culmination of a sequence of states in which the subject–object distinction seems gradually to disappear as God and the soul draw closer. This definition corresponds with the Sufi's goal of returning to the Source (*'irfan*).

Philosopher and scientist William James provides the following insight into the mystical experience:

> The fountain head of all religion lies in the mystical experiences of the individual. All our theology, all our ecclesiasticism, are only secondary growths that are superimposed. These experiences belong in the region deeper and more vital and practical than that which our intellect inhabits. They convince us there is a sphere of life larger and more powerful than our usual

consciousness. They help us to live; they melt our hearts, and communicate significance and value to everything. (From a letter to Henry William Rankin, dated June 16, 1901, cited in Wright, 2000)

The terms Sufism, mysticism and spirituality are used interchangeably in the literature. They are not contradictory or mutually exclusive, since all three derive from the mysterious impulse that inspired religious doctrines. The Hebrew and Greek words for 'spirit', *ruah* and *pneuma* respectively, are rooted in the notion of the intangible movement of the air (*Glossary for the Message of H. I. Khan*); the Spirit, like the wind, "blows where it pleases; you can hear its sound but you cannot tell where it comes from or where it is going" (*John* 3: 8). Like the Spirit, spirituality is elusive, mysterious and dynamic (Wright, 7), and refers to the primary and universal religious experience as opposed to the secondary and culturally diverse expressions that constitute religion.

Spirituality, according to Mircea Eliade (1987, 46), is the capacity to encounter the sacred in the midst of the profane. It is a celebration of the inherent mystery of life. Spiritual experience "suggests a mystery, an unseen reality, beyond the life of the individual, pervading the entire world order, with which human persons are invited to enter into relationship and communion".

For David Tacey, the key word is 'interconnectedness', spirituality being the art of gaining access to "the greater mystery to which we are connected and in which we are profoundly situated". "Spiritual experience replaces the isolation of the individual ego with the unitary awareness of the larger or cosmic self", he believes (2006, 19-20). It is not 'otherworldly'; spirituality does not disdain the world, nor is it escapist and delusional (*op. cit.,* 23).

Chittick avoids the word 'mysticism', partly, he says, because of its overwhelmingly negative connotations (2003). Most people nowadays, he explains, especially in the academic community, seem to understand the word in terms of Webster's (3rd ed.) third definition, namely "vague speculation, belief without foundation". Mysticism commonly signifies "mystification, madness, or mindless mush", he says, adding that many would agree with Bertrand Russell's argument in *Mysticism and Logic* that mysticism and rationality are irreconcilable (though Aahlia Khan (2009) claims that "no responsible student now identifies mysticism with confusion of thought"). Chittick does, however, agree that Webster's second definition of mysticism as "the doctrine or belief that direct knowledge of God, of spiritual truth, or ultimate reality . . . is attainable through immediate intuition, insight, or illumination and in a way differing from ordinary sense perception or ratiocination" reflects the Sufi approach to understanding God and the world.

Like other exponents who say that Sufism is essentially a mysticism derived from the Islamic religion, Chittick emphasises Sufism's direct link to Islam, saying that Sufis hold that this direct knowledge (unveiling/*kashf*) must be rooted in the Qur'an and the *Sunnah* (the practices and sayings of the Prophet Muhammad). Among the various approaches that Muslims took to their religion, Chittick explains, the Sufi approach was most concerned with imitating the Prophet by ascending to God in this life, whereas other Muslims maintained that the meeting with God promised in the Qur'an was reserved for the afterworld. In general, he says, the Sufis criticised the juridical approach because of a common perception that correct bodily activity is sufficient to make someone a good Muslim. They were also critical of the theological and philosophical approaches whenever these implied that one can understand God and the world adequately by the mere exercise of the rational mind. They held that the best way to understand God, the world, and oneself was to search for God in one's own heart. Chittick explains that Sufis were differentiated from ordinary Muslims by their single-minded dedication to actualizing their spirit ('polishing the mirror of the heart') and living in the presence of God. Keeping God constantly in mind (*dhikr Allâh*), forgetting self, they longed for access to spiritual reality and real being, just as the Prophet was given access to them.

On the nature of mysticism, Nicholson, on the other hand, says: "All manifestations of the mystical spirit are fundamentally the same, and we shall not be astonished to encounter in remote lands and different ages of the world one set of principles variously combined" (Cited in Star, 1992, xviii). In Sufism, this one unifying principle appears through a kaleidoscope of religious practices and philosophies which can be traced back from Antiquity, through Arabia and into Persia, where it came under the influence of Plato and Socrates, of Christianity, of Hinduism and Buddhism due to Persia's proximity to Greece, Egypt and India. Since Sufis were often ostracized by the established religions for their non-conformity, Sufism found its outlet in poetry and music, spreading through the works of poets such as Omar Khayyam (1048–1122), Nizami (circa 1141–1209), Sa'di (circa 1213–1292), Hafiz (circa 1320–1388), Jami (1414–1492) and Rumi (1207–1273).

Other scholars who claim that Sufism is the essence of the Islamic religion include Martin Lings who claims that "Sufism is nothing other than Islamic mysticism, which means that it is the central and most powerful current of that tidal wave which constitutes the Revelation of Islam" (1975, 15), though he acknowledges that "it can if time and place concur, pluck flowers from gardens other than its own.

Other exponents insist that Sufism precedes Islam. Arberry (1942) tells us that according to Nicholson it was Dhul-Nun al-Misri (d. 830) who was inspired by the Hermetic wisdom which had the same vision of unity with God who above all others gave Sufism its permanent shape. According to Khaleb el-Khazari "the first Sufi is generally held to be Hasan al-Basri (d. 728)" (el-Khazari, 2006). Hazrat Inayat Khan describes Sufism as the essence of all religions, antedating Islam and others. It was always without limiting principles, according to Witteveen (1997), respecting all religions without espousing any of their dogma, its central theme being the freedom of the soul.

Rice, in his concise account of Sufism's renewal in Persia in the 12th century, shares his understanding of the Islamic connection and the contribution of the Persian Sufis (1964, 12). It was the humiliating defeat the Persians suffered at the hands of the Arabs and the consequent imposition of the Arabic language and the Qur'an that gave rise to a vast body of mystical poetry written in the Persian language. The Persian Sufis challenged all forms of rigidity and formalism. Rice emphasizes the vigour of Persian spirituality or Sufism and points out that it was not a phenomenon which suddenly came to light at the outset of Islam and that the Persian spirit was not confined to the Islamic world. "It was there all the time . . . and has pursued its course, now open, now hidden, right down the ages" (*ibid.*). "Sufism existed from the beginning, because man has always possessed the light which is his second nature; and light in its higher aspect may be called the knowledge of God, the divine wisdom—in fact, Sufism" (VIII, 14).

In attempting a definition, Brent concludes that Sufism is unlike other schools of thought. It is "in short, something on its own. It is a different kind of entity . . . Sufism is a study" (Cited in Shah, 1979, 225). Sufis, however, emphasise that it is not a study but a way of life, a discipline—a practice. "It is more than a school: it is life itself . . ." (VIII, 20) Oneness of Being or Unity of Existence (*wahdat al-wujud*) cannot be realised theoretically; it must be experienced. Sufism is about *transforming the self* in order to serve society to the fullest extent. Interaction with the world is the test of the Sufi's desire to travel the path towards truth (*haqq*); retiring from society and adopting solitude in order to further one's spiritual development does not lead to finding.

Whilst there is clearly a degree of uncertainty regarding the origin and extent of influence of the various religions and philosophies on Sufism, "the essence of all religions" (VIII, 13), this neither alters nor diminishes its worth. What is clear however, and more important, is that we are dealing with a significant body of values regarded by many as timeless. Kinney sums up as follows: "The Sufi steps beyond Sufism, or any other -ism... But until we reach that point (whatever we may call it) the Sufi conundrum continues" (1994).

We have looked at the ambiguous nature of names as they reveal and conceal their various meanings, and noted that mysticism's meaning may have been embraced but its name has been widely rejected. As science confirms concepts that Sufis have long intuited (Ch. 1.5), mystical truths are espoused, but mysticism's name is spurned. There is some evidence of this in the work of Mathews and Wheeler, and to a lesser degree, Hamilton in whose modern-day philosophies Sufism's ancient teachings appear to have re-emerged—Mathews' panpsychism, Wheeler's biosemiotics and Hamilton's metaphysical-psychology—focusing on ethical engagement with a world pulsating with meaning, as Sufis claimed centuries ago. Yet both Mathews and Wheeler appear anxious to distance themselves from mysticism, and Hamilton provides few clues that his is essentially a mystical path. Mathews and Wheeler provide reasons why theirs is not a mystical approach, and I will examine them; Hamilton's reluctance can be surmised. Thus Mathews turns to Taoism and Aboriginal thought, and Wheeler to "the sophistication of Buddhist philosophy" (2006, 97) while the ideas put forward, particularly in the case of panpsychism, are also consistent with Sufism. We must go beyond the name of mysticism and reveal its meaning.

1.2 Message of the Time

As Sufi poetry is described as one of the most reliable sources of Sufi wisdom (Rice, 1964, 29), and Rumi's *Mathnawi* an inspired exposition of the esoteric content of the Qur'an (Nicholson, 2003), UNESCO's tribute to Rumi and his work can be interpreted as an endorsement of Sufism itself, and its unifying potential is indeed being recognised more widely. According to Seyyed Hossein Nasr, Professor of Islamic studies at George Washington University, for example, Sufism is the most powerful antidote to religious radicalism as well as the most important source for responding to the challenges posed by modernism as reflected in globalisation and materialism, since it rejects the search for power and wealth in favour of a more spiritual path (Cited in Lampman, 2007). "Its influence is immense," says Nasr. "Sufism has kept alive the inner quality of ethics and spiritual virtues, rather than a rigid morality . . . and it provides access to knowledge of the divine reality, which affects all other aspects of one's life" (*ibid.*).

Sufi Sheikh Abdoulaye Dieye of Senegal, for example, evokes this 'inner quality' in his 2002 address in California, in which he touches on issues such as ecology, poverty and the effects of globalization, before his concluding remarks calling for peace:

> "Many wars have been waged in the name of religions but the real reason for these armed conflicts and other acts of violence are only greed and the desire for power. This is true for Muslims and Islam, for the Jews and Judaism as well as for Christians and Christianity. . . . Let the Jewish and Muslim scholars meet in a part of the globe to ask for peace and reconciliation between these two nations. At the dawn of this millennium when it has been proved that violence merely aggravates the conflict and politicians can only acknowledge their inadequacy, I appeal to Muslim Sufis and Jewish Rabbis to find common grounds for better relations. Let them pray together, so that God Who is Merciful and Gracious, extinguishes with the flow of His Mercy all the areas seething with conflicts in the Middle East and the fire of despair that is consuming the heart of so many women, children and men" (cited in Ernst, 2009, 29).

And while Sufis have been persecuted in some countries such as Saudi Arabia and Egypt, Sufism is thriving in Iran, Pakistan, and India outside the modernist cities, according to Washington-based anthropologist, Akbar Ahmed (Cited in Gioia, 2008). A 2006 survey conducted by Ahmed indicates that young Turks' top choice of role model is Sufi intellectual, Fethullah Gülen, who has built a large system of schools and is known for his promotion of interfaith dialogue. "The Gülen Movement is similar to a well-conducted symphony as its basic aim is to unite people and bring about solutions to their problems," said Pakinam El Sharkawy from Cairo University. It is a movement which "tries to respond to strong winds by creating a soft and soothing atmosphere" (Yeşilova, 2009). Of interest to note is Turkey's emergence as the main mediator in the troubled Middle East, a position formerly held by "diminishing giant" US (ABC news, 13 January 2009).

Sufism, in the first instance, applies itself to 'heart', less so to periphery; its practices of 'refinement' counter a 'heartless' approach to life, and seek to reduce the inner turbulence of which the outer crisis is simply the externalisation. As Jane Clark explains, with reference to Ibn al-Arabi's teachings, "the important thing about our knowledge of the external world—the only important thing—is that it is an indicator of something in ourselves" (Clark, 2001). For Fethullah Gülen, speaking metaphorically of "perpetual breezes", "terrifying blizzards, typhoons, and thunder storms" (2010), external crises clearly have their origins not in the 'environment' but deep within the heart of humankind. Already in the 1960s Nasr was addressing the issue of humankind's disharmony within itself and therefore also with the environment (Nasr, 1968). Gülen's achievements indicate that Sufi thought can play a pivotal role in reducing conflict by conducting interfaith dialogue, for instance, which might in turn facilitate the revitalisation of religion in general, so that common ground can be established and a clear environmental ethic emerge, an urgent requirement at this time of unprecedented exploitation. Like other religious traditions, the Islamic tradition, with its affirmation of divine unity, already makes ample provision for a caring, nonexploitative environmental ethic. Three central concepts of Islam—*tawhid* (unity), *khilafa* (stewardship), and *akhirah* (accountability in the Hereafter) suffice to support such an ethic. Islamic scholar Mustafa Abu-Sway, for example, argues convincingly that *khilafa* is a test. Basing his argument on passages from the Qur'an, such as "Then We have made you heirs in the land after them, to see how you would behave" (10:14), and *Hadith* such as "Verily, this world is sweet and appealing, and Allah placed you as vicegerents therein; He will see what you will do. . .", Abu-Sway says: "It is rather clear, now, that the Islamic world-view indicates that vicegerency on earth forms a test which includes how human beings relate to the environment. . . Life on earth entails great responsibilities. It is a test with accountability" (Abu-Sway, 1998).

However, as Richard Foltz points out in his essay "Islam", "Whether the true essence of Islam is proenvironment or not, in practice throughout most of its history Muslim theologians, philosophers and laypersons have focused almost exclusively on the relationship between Allah and humanity. Iqtidar Zaidi (1981, 36) implicitly confirms this when he states that "we are seeking a religious matrix which maintains man's position as an ecologically dominant being" (Foltz, in Gottlieb (Ed.), 213). What is undeniable, however, is the explicit environmental ethic to be found in Sufism, exemplified by lines from Rumi's poetry because, for the Sufi, lover and Beloved, or creation and Creator, are one in accordance with *wahdat al-wujud* (unity of Being) as expounded by Ibn al-Arabi. Thus Rumi says:

> Since God hath made man from dust, it behooves thee to recognize the real nature of every particle of the universe, That while from this aspect they are dead, from that aspect they are living; silent here, but speaking yonder. . . They all cry, "We are hearing and seeing and responsive, though to you, the uninitiated, we are mute" (Cited Foltz, in Gottlieb (Ed.), 207)

Foltz reminds us (as does Bülent Rauf in his article *Concerning the Universality of Ibn 'Arabi*, 1987, and Souad Hakim who provides an extensive list of al-Arabi's many opponents in *Unity of Being*, 2004) that Ibn al-Arabi has always been a controversial figure. Foltz says ". . . many have accused him of holding pantheist or monist views. . . Likewise, the notions of certain Sufi mystics are felt by many Muslims to blur dangerously the distinction between the Creator and creation. This discomfort appears most often in accusations of *shirk* ('associating partners with God') which is considered by many Muslims to be 'the one sin that Allah cannot forgive'" (Foltz, in Gottlieb (Ed.), 210). As Cecilia Twinch explains in a paper entitled *The Circle of Inclusion* (2006), Ibn al-Arabi "constantly refers back to the source of the revealed words of the Qur'an rather than relying on subsequent interpretations of Islam. In this way he brings out the true meaning of the religion ... which shows the uniqueness of the single reality of Being and its infinite possibilities expressed in endlessly changing forms and images". Frequently quoting the Qur'anic verse, "We shall show them Our signs on the horizons and in themselves until it is clear to them that it is the Real", al-Arabi's writings illuminate the indivisibility of the inner and outer reality, of the invisible and visible worlds, and of the all-inclusive One whose attributes and names appear in all things yet remains unconfined by the limitations of anything (*ibid.*).

According to Foltz, some Muslim environmentalists argue that the *Shariah* (Islamic legal tradition), "if applied to the letter, contains adequate restrictions to ensure a use of natural resources that is both sustainable and just" (*op. cit.*, 211). Such an approach might be problematic in view of the changed cultural, political and economic conditions facing Muslims today. Sufi thinkers, on the other hand, were "more inclined than their exoteric counterparts to view Islam from a wider perspective and deal meaningfully with religious difference", argues Vincent Cornell in a paper on the relevance of Sufism in the modern era. In part, he explains, this was because "they understood theology in its original sense as the 'study of the nature of God', and followed their inquiries wherever this definition took them" (Cornell, 2004). Indian scholar and statesman Rafiq Zakaria calls Sufis "bridge builders" who risked persecution and dared to oppose orthodoxy in their tireless pursuit of unity (el-Khazari, 2006). By 'returning to the source', Sufism has, I believe, an important contribution to make in this regard; its heart-centred approach could provide that much-needed "hermeneutical space in which critical thinking can take place" and counteract the "radical superficiality" (*ibid.*) as well as "doctrinal rigidity" (el-Khazari, 2006) which has for too long limited religious thought.

"A more comprehensive cosmological worldview of the interdependence of life is being articulated", says Mary Evelyn Tucker, noting that the emerging field of religion and ecology is playing a role in this (Gottlieb (Ed.), 2006). Religions, in this role, says Tucker, should be understood "in their largest sense as a means whereby humans recogniz(e) the limitations of phenomenal reality", "connect humans with a divine presence" and "link humans to the larger matrix of indeterminacy and mystery from which life arises, unfolds, and flourishes" (*ibid.*). Clearly, Sufism's recognition of the sacred value of the earth, its "daring and prescient universalism", and the "peace, goodwill and mutual understanding" (el-Khazari, 2006) that Sufis strive to generate, attest to Sufism's particular relevance within this burgeoning field at this time.

Sufism put into action also bridges the gap between spirituality and economics and could lead to improved material conditions of large masses of people in impoverished countries, according to Dr Johannes Witteveen, ex-minister of Finance in Holland and former Managing Director of the International Monetary Fund. Spirituality and economic science are not mutually exclusive but are by necessity complementary, he says, adding that globalisation, technological and economic progress demand that we find ways of balancing the sacred and the profane and so overcome this apparent polarisation (Witteveen, 2003), an urgent requirement at this time of financial and ecological crisis. Of interest to note is the shift in sentiment that has taken place since TIME Magazine's reference to Witteveen as "an austere mystic and strict adherent of the obscure Sufi religious cult" in the 15 August 1977 edition. Three decades later Sufism is no longer obscure, nor is it regarded as a cult.

The Sufi message might well be, as Hazrat Inayat Khan claimed and UNESCO implied, the message of the time; "the answer to the call of every soul" (VIII, 21). The need for such a message is evidence of particular problems whose origins lie deep within—problems which indicate that we regard only the outer while ignoring the inner, like the drunkards of the *Mathnawi* in the tavern of ruin, thirsting for dregs (*durd*) rather than pure wine (*saki*). The Sufi message is one of love, harmony and beauty, and as such is in direct contrast with postmodern culture, which has reduced these fundamental concepts to their most superficial level (Farrelly, 2007). Alexander Nehamas, for example, argues that "the twentieth century forgot the essence of beauty, namely love, and in rejecting love it rejected beauty also, replacing it with frigid abstractions" (Cited in Farrelly, 2007, 38). Conflict, confusion and loneliness affect all aspects of life.

Within the secular system it appears that mystical knowledge is not valued and awareness of the sacred is not cultivated. According to Bennett, people are left to flounder when darkness descends. "We find ourselves pitted against powerful external forces or those we ourselves have unleashed. We know loss, defeat, and humiliation—unbidden and unwanted catastrophes that seem to leave to our choice only how to deal with them. Facing these sad and barren times, some of us lash out in anger and resentment, while others give up in bitterness—satisfied to be less than their gifts call them to be" (2006, 4). "Sad and barren times" manifest at all levels: personal, societal, national, international and environmental.

According to Alexander W. Astin (2006), the contrasting values—the material and the spiritual—have literally traded places since the early 1970s, a time when developing a meaningful philosophy of life was the number one value for American students. Today "being very well off financially" is the top value, while developing a meaningful philosophy of life has dropped right down on the list. A focus on the spiritual interior has been replaced by a focus on the material exterior. By promoting acquisitiveness, materialism and commercialism have contributed to a major shift in values and a near-total absence of critical reflectiveness, Astin concludes.

The Archbishop of Canterbury, Rowan Williams, sees modern society as "trivial, obsessed by celebrity, damaging to children and marked by a moral vacuum". He talks of a "broken society" where lonely, dysfunctional people lead segregated lives, have no aspirations and suffer from feelings of "imprisonment" while yearning for love (Cited in Sylvester, 2007). We are living in the age of anxiety according to psychologist Jean Twenge (2009), who lists factors such as crime, divorce, living alone, isolation, lack of trust and a general increase in social problems that contribute to increased anxiety in all age groups. Twenge argues that until people feel connected to others, malfunctioning is likely to continue.

The interconnectedness of all things is the cornerstone of Sufism. Awareness of this underlying unity provides a different perspective of self in relation to world. An understanding of the nature of our need sheds light on our dissatisfaction and desire for gratification and distraction, which has led to accusations of "commoditization" and "cretinization" of parts of Western culture (Kinney, 1994, 11), and "hedonistic" lifestyles in an "atheistic world" (Wright, 2000, 54). Misguided attempts to satisfy individual demands are often indiscriminate and always unfulfilling. Sufi teachings elucidate our notion of individual ego (*nafs*) by revealing the unity of all things.

Separation and division as features of a rational reality are limiting, and limited beliefs, ideals, and points of view invite conflict. The twentieth century will be remembered for its large-scale wars between nations, causing immense suffering and damage to humans, animals and environments. As *khalifa* (stewards) we often fail, yet we cling tenaciously to our limited points of view. When unity is sacrificed for group or personal gain, and esoteric aspirations are replaced by exoteric ones, conflict is inevitable. Atrocities have been perpetrated in the name of religion and political ideas; we have known anti-Semitism, anti-Catholicism, anti-Protestantism and current anti-Islamic sentiment as we struggle to arrest the wave of extremism engulfing those same countries where the Sufi message of love and unity bloomed centuries ago. Anti-Islamic sentiment and Islamic fanaticism are fast becoming the cancer of the century.

In "this hour of cultural need" (Mathews, 2003, 7), how are we to find meaning in life's bewildering array of forms? Dominican Father Cyprian Rice, his allegiance to Catholicism notwithstanding, suggests that the Sufi way might inspire us with humility, "when we realize what mystical treasures we ourselves may have let slip through carelessness or dissipation" (Rice, 1964, 15). Sufism's mystical treasures enable us to move beyond the apparent duality of the world of forms to encounter the formlessness of the one true Beloved. The concept of unity and harmony seems inconceivable in a world characterised at all levels by conflict, separation, segregation and division. We see ourselves as separate and aspire to become independent, autonomous individuals, identifying only with particular social groups or organisations whose point of view we share, shaped by the national culture or social subculture in which we are immersed. We lose sight of the much greater whole when we focus exclusively on our limited being, our body in the here and now, our mind with its thoughts and emotions, our fragile egos, our religious organisations, educational institutions, social groups, our nation, our culture, our language, all with their own peculiarities and limitations. When division is so entrenched, conflict is inevitable since a particular perspective must be defended or risk being replaced by a foreign one (Jones, 2006).

Sufism lifts the veils mindfully, respectfully and above all, lovingly, since it seeks, through a transformation of the heart in love, to win a higher form of knowledge, a direct vision of that divine reality that transcends the sphere of the senses. It is a philosophy to which Mathews could turn for a defense of the ideas she calls panpsychist, and in which Hamilton would find support for his metaphysical-psychology, as both these are, I argue, essentially mystical paths. Sufism can, I claim, sort "genuine metaphysical nourishment" from "the chaff that is proliferating in this time of ideological instability" (Mathews, *op. cit.*, 7).

1.3 'No god but God' (*lā ilāha illā' Llāh*)

'No god but God' proclaims God's *wahdat al-wujud*—Only God is self-existent: He is like a sun and everything else like shadows. There is nothing in independent, necessary, and eternal existence save the Divine Presence, Its Essence, Its Attributes, and Its Acts (Hakim, 2004). Ontologically, there is only One Being (*SPK*, 356). Nothing is without Being—the cosmos is God's self-disclosure (*tajalli*) (*SPK*, 16). Rumi's Beloved is the One whose reality is the only certainty (*ibid.*); a reality which is experienced at every moment. The Sufi poet Shibli (d. 946) describes Sufism as the guarding of the heart from the vision of 'other', since God is the only reality and 'other' does not independently exist (Schimmel, 1975). 'Panentheism' is perhaps a near equivalent to Sufism's *wahdat al-wujud*, but John Chryssavgis makes the point that "the term panentheism is neither always clear in meaning nor always consistent in usage, inasmuch as it is adopted by thinkers and theologians of all persuasions" (in Gottlieb, 2006, 103). *Wahdat al-wujud* denies the self-existence of creation for the sake of God, whereas pantheism denies God's self-existence for the sake of creation.

> At the level of their existence, all things are equal, manifesting the Essence inasmuch as they exist (*SPK*, 346). In this respect all paths of belief are considered equal, since each exists. Therefore whether we seek truth through religion, philosophy, mysticism or science, Sufism teaches that truth, which is one, will ultimately be found. This all-inclusive perspective, perhaps best reflected in the Sufi saying "The paths to God are as numerous as the breaths of the creatures" (*SPK*, 439), does not reflect "fundamentalist proclivities" (Mathews, 2003, 7), since Sufis do not claim to have grasped the one and only truth and have no interest in proselytising; it simply reflects Sufism's principle of oneness of being, or *wahdat al-wujud* as expounded by Ibn al-Arabi, whose metaphysical outlook has been described as follows: "(I)t is extremely important—it is a kind of tolerance, openness and metaphysically-inspired generosity . . . It is the kind of outlook which will have nothing to

do with the petty and the mean-spirited or the dogmatic and the intolerant
. . . There is a vastness about Ibn 'Arabi's metaphysics which makes it anti-
thetical to any narrow religious fundamentalism or closedness and inflexibil-
ity of mind. (It) reflect(s) the strength, generosity and grandeur inherent in
the vision of the original unity alluded to in the description *Wahdat al-
Wujud*" (Coates, 1999). As Cecilia Twinch (2006) explains, the Islamic
instruction to seek knowledge is "an invitation to discriminate between a
lesser vision of reality and a greater one, to abandon a partial view for a more
comprehensive and complete one, to progress through our own personal
Lord to the Lord of Lords, the all-inclusive God who encompasses all names
and qualities and where all opposites are united".

Sufism's vision of unity is one of harmony realised through transformation of one's own heart, not through conversion of others. "We need
today the religion of tolerance", says Hazrat Inayat Khan (X, 54) as prejudice and distrust cause discord within and between nations, each
absorbed in its own interest. Religion might have helped bring about harmony, but with discord and strife evident at all levels, it is clear that religion has brought about neither a spirit of tolerance nor unity. Attempting
to define and delimit by rational means what can only be known by the
heart, formal religion has long reinforced the distinction between sacred
and secular. Hanging on to religious and ethnic differences has led to conflict throughout the ages. In July 2007 the American Center for Reduction of Religious-Based Conflict (CRRBC) lists eighteen hotspots of religious conflict in the world where differences in form are considered sufficient grounds for inflicting harm. Religious intolerance shows no sign of
abating; on the contrary, in his analysis of religious-based conflict, *Beyond
Tolerance (2004)*, Terry Trowbridge argues that it is destined to increase
in this century.

Although all the major world religions seem to be involved to a greater or lesser extent in this conflict, the religion of Islam appears to be over-
represented in its aggressive involvement, with Muslims featuring in conflict in the Balkans, the Caucasus, Egypt, Ethiopia, Pakistan, Indonesia,
Iraq, Malaysia, the Middle East, Nigeria, Philippines, Sudan and USA
(*ibid.*). Consequently we are seeing a growing vilification of Islam by non-
Muslims which Rabbi Professor Jonathan Magonet refers to as the
"demonisation of Islam" by Western society (2007). However, as Karen
Armstrong writes, Western culture has "a long history of Islamophobia

that dates back to the Crusades, and Christian monks of the twelfth century in Europe already insistently defamed (the Prophet Muhammad)" (cited in Altay, 2008). Some fundamentalists have insisted on a literal interpretation and application of the Qur'an and Islamic law, the *Shariah*, and in doing so have set out to wage a 'holy war', *jihad*, on all 'unbelievers'. But similar battlefield metaphors are used in other religious texts, such as in the *Bhagavad-Gita* when Krishna describes the battle of contrary desires. A literal interpretation of metaphors deviates from Islamic tradition, which emphasises individual responsibility towards God and a spirit of tolerance reflected in Qur'anic verses such as "We do not make a distinction between any of His prophets" (2:285, as Cited in Can, 2005, 6). Apart from obvious political and economic factors leading to the spread of fundamentalism, the violence of the reaction intensifies when perpetrators identify their religion—which is so sacred to them—with its form: its dogmas, rituals and laws, forgetting its meaning, the impulse which gave rise to it. The Prophet's dream was one of reconciliation (Muhaiyaddeen, *Islam and World Peace*, 2002), of healing the schism between minds, as he looked out upon the disputes of the numerous Christian sects and rites on Arabian and near-Arabian soil (Rice, 1964). His proclamation of Allah's all-encompassing reality, "There is no god but God", is understood by the Sufis as a declaration of unity, not of exclusivity (*ibid.*).

In classical Islam, the divine attributes were enumerated but divine essence was deemed to lie beyond human knowledge. It was nevertheless the study of these attributes in all their wondrous glory that was to guide and benefit humanity. Islamic fundamentalism, however, shifted the focus of the study to Islam's essence and attributes, rather than God's, thereby losing sight of the essential inner aspect of the religion (Choueiri, 1998; Ernst, 2009). The outer forms of religion are veils concealing inner meaning, making them vulnerable. We need both of course, but as Tacey points out, form and meaning, or religion and spirituality, find themselves in an uneasy alliance, and religion, standing accused of "mere institutional authority", has come under attack (Tacey, 2000, 28).The Sufi emphasis on the validity of all beliefs is of particular relevance to us today. As Cecilia Twinch explains, when Ibn al-Arabi exhorts us to be the "substance of all beliefs", he is appealing for vision, entreating us to see that the One who appears in everything and takes on the forms of all beliefs, is the

Essence of everything. Anissian, drawing on Corbin, explains that the inner meaning of the Qur'an, its *haqiqat* (reality), is symbolized (*mathal*) in the exoteric (*zahir*) text of the Qur'an. The *tawil* (returning to source) leads back to the hidden reality. The soul (heart) cannot return text to the truth until it itself returns to its *haqiqat*. "The *tawil* of texts supposes the *tawil* of the soul" (Corbin, cited in Anissian, 2006, 47). For this reason it has been said that the Qur'an, rich with metaphor is "above all, the book of a minority," although "it is the book of the whole community" (Lings, 27).

In many verses the outer and inner meanings apply to quite different domains. For example, on one occasion, when returning from a battle against the infidels, the Prophet said: "We have come back from the lesser *jihad* to the greater *jihad*". His companions asked: "What is the greater *jihad*?" The Prophet answered: "The war against the soul." According to Lings, here lies the key to the inner meaning of all those verses in the Qur'an which refer to *jihad* and 'infidels'. Hazrat Inayat Khan refers to this war as "the annihilation of the false ego in the real, which raises the mortal to immortality and in which resides all perfection" (I, 21). Shahid Athar also explains that in Sufi tradition, the ego is the enemy and conquering it is the best form of *jihad*, allowing the Sufi to be at peace with himself and thus closest to his Creator. The word *jihad*, he explains, comes from the Arabic root JHD, meaning striving or struggle (2010). From this perspective the verses "Wage war on the idolaters totally" (9:36) and "Fight them until there is no longer any sedition, and religion is all for God" (8:39) are not calls to take up arms against an external enemy at all. Rumi makes this clear in innumerable verses replete with warring metaphor, for example in the following lines he talks about the conflicting aspects of human nature— ego with its sensual passions and desires versus 'heart' with its propensity for knowledge. When there is tension between these two aspects it becomes necessary to engage in one's own spiritual 'warfare':

> One of you is an unbeliever and one of you a believer: In your existence two persons are warring. (*SPL*, 87)
> The first spiritual combat the prophets and saints undertake in their quest is the killing of the ego and the abandonment of personal wishes and sensual desires. This is the Greater Holy War. (*SPL*, 154)

The Islamic testification *lā ilāha illā'Llāh*, there is no god but God, forms the basis of Sufism. The word Sufi, most widely believed to be derived from *sáf*, (pure), could be taken to mean that Sufism is purified of ignorance, superstition, dogma, egotism and fanaticism, as well as free from religious, ethnic and racial limitations. "There is no god but God" means that the Essence is one in every respect. Rumi's description of his own transcendence of duality illustrates the Sufi understanding of unity:

I am no Christian, no Jew, no Magian, no Musulman.
Not of the East, not of the West. Not of the land, not of the sea.
Not of the mine of nature, not of the circling heavens,
Not of earth, not of water, not of air, not of fire;
Not of the throne, not of the ground, of existence, of being;
Not of India, China, Bulgaria, Saqseen;
Not of the kingdom of the Iraqis, or of Khorasan;
Not of this world or the next: of heaven or hell; Not of Adam, Eve, the gardens of Paradise or Eden;
My place placeless, my trace traceless.
Neither body nor soul: all is the life of my Beloved . . .

The enlightened being of Rumi's poem is, like the Beloved Himself, free; free from the limitations of form and nondelimited by any attribute whatsoever. The universe is His manifestation and it tells of unity. Throughout history there have been countless accounts of it. Thus, in the prayer *Salat*, Sufis ask:

Let us know Thee as Abraham, as Solomon, as Zarathustra, as Moses, as Jesus, as Muhammad, and in many other names and forms, known and unknown to the world.

The same principle of unity is expressed by many religions, for example in the Christian religion we are told:

I am Alpha and Omega, the beginning and the end (Revelation 21:6)

In the Bhagavad-Gita we read that everything is a manifestation of the Absolute. Lord Krishna tells Arjuna:

I am the ritual, I am the sacrifice, I am the offering, I am the herb, I am the clarified butter, and I am the oblation. I am the supporter of the universe, the father, the mother, and the grandfather. I am the object of knowledge, I am the goal, the supporter, the Lord, the witness, the abode, the refuge, the friend, the origin, the dissolution, the foundation, the immutable seed ... There is no truth superior to Me. Everything rests upon Me, as pearls are strung on a thread. I am the taste of water, the light of the sun and the moon, the syllable 'om' in Vedic mantras; I am the sound in ether and the ability in man. I am the original fragrance of the earth, and I am the light in fire; I am the light of all that lives. I am immortality as well as death; I am both the eternal Absolute and the temporal, O Arjuna. I am everything and inexhaustible (p. 130).

"If God alone is real, God alone is, and there is no being but His Being" (Lings, 65). According to the Islamic doctrine of unity, the Divine Infinitude is without parts; the "Indivisible One-and-Only" (*ibid.*). What the eye sees and the mind records is an illusion, since every apparently separate and finite thing is the presence of the One Infinite. "Wheresoever you turn, there is the Face of God" (II: 115). Many religions conveyed the same message of unity, love and service in a way that was most appropriate to the culture of the time, therefore the exoteric forms of the message differed but Sufis believe that in their essence they are the same. In a materialistic world, however, this mystical essence has been replaced with explanations and elaborations that rationally thinking followers have given to them. This might have helped satisfy their longing for certainty, but the dogma was often rigid and limited the inspiration as truth became veiled.

When the Prophet Muhammad delivered his message of peace to the people at the time, he said: "There is no god but God, the living, the self-subsistent who revealed the law" (III: 1). He described a living, eternal God, unlimited by his people's image of Him, and a pre-existing, eternal law which was being revealed again. Jesus also said he came to "fulfill the law", not to create a new one; in the Bhagavad-Gita Shri Krishna says: "When Dharma (duty) decays, then I am born". In other words, when there is a need for it, the law is revealed. Sufism recognises this one divine law, veiled by the many forms of religion. Rumi's poetry is an almost inexhaustible description of his vision of unity, his Beloved inseparable from any part of the whole. He says "My religion is to live through Love. . . The intellect is bewildered by the Religion of Love—even if it should be aware of all religions" (*SPL*, 213). Hazrat Inayat Khan says:

> How thickly veiled man's eyes must be by the religion, the faith, the belief he holds, for him to accept only one messenger and to reject the message given by other prophets, not knowing that the message is one and the same! (IX, 241)

Likewise in *God and the Universe of Faiths*, John Hick observes that differences of form . . .

> must express, surely, diverse encounters with the same divine reality. These encounters have taken place within different human cultures by people of different ways of thought and feeling, with different histories and different frameworks of philosophical thought, and have developed into different systems of theology embodied in different religious structures and organizations. These resulting large-scale religio-cultural phenomena are what we call the religions of the world. But must there not lie behind them the same infinite divine reality? (Wright, 33)

Sufism sees the same infinite divine reality behind all things. In His manifestation the One has become many; unity manifests as diversity. Conflict arises when we see only diversity and ignore the underlying unity, when we confuse unity with uniformity and when we attempt to delimit the One as the outcome will be as limited as our language and our thoughts. The Persian language, used by Rumi and other Sufi poets, makes no distinction between genders in nouns and pronouns and as such allows a portrayal that is more appropriate than the English translations since it is not limited by the duality emphasised by the pronouns 'he' and 'she'. Because the neutral 'it' is distant and abstract, English translations depict a predominantly masculine God, although liberal use of names such as 'Beloved' could suggest a feminine aspect. Some religions have attempted to overcome the limitations of gender by offering male as well as female God ideals; the Hindu god Shiva for example combines both male and female qualities.

In our attempts to make the Only Being comprehensible, we have intellectualised and thereby reduced the incomprehensible to a comprehensible, anthropomorphic derivative. "Attributing to God deficiencies by which we are constrained . . . is a great mistake", says mathematician Nuh Aydın, who believes that the mathematical concept of infinity is intimately connected to the concept of divinity and the Attributes of God. "An incorrect understanding of infinity in mathematics leads to seemingly irresolvable paradoxes; likewise, an incorrect understanding of the Attributes of God leads to an incomplete or incorrect understanding of creation", says Aydın (2009). By reducing the One to a comprehensible level, we disregard the fundamental unity of being on which hinges the mystery and sanctity of life.

We diminish the power that not only transcends but permeates all things, that One from whose superabundance all things flow.

The doctrine of unity (*tawhid*), fully expounded by Ibn al-Arabi, builds on the classical Greek tradition and was first postulated by Pythagoras, whose teachings influenced successors such as Heraclitus, Parmenides, Plato, Aristotle and Plotinus (Sedley, 1998). Rumi and Ibn al-Arabi were steeped in the Platonic and Neo-Platonic tradition and regarded Plato as a sage and lover of Truth, so it is inevitable that their work draws on his thought. In fact al-Arabi and Shams-i Tabrizi refer to him as "the divine Plato", "rare among scholars", because they believed he attained knowledge of the Truth by way of 'tasting' (i.e. experientially, like the Sufis themselves) rather than merely intellectually, and in recognition of a kindred spirit, al-Arabi came to be surnamed 'the Platonist, the son of Plato', Ibn Aflatun (*SPK*, 203).

While Platonic thought may be interpreted as dualistic by some, for example by ecophilosopher Val Plumwood (*Feminism and the Mastery of Nature*, 1993), others, such as Gabriela R. Carone (*Plato and the Environment*, in *Environmental Ethics* (1998) 20 (3):115-133), refute this interpretation. Hamilton also recognises in Sufi and Platonic writings and in the works of Spinoza and Christian mystics the same concept of one essence, the undifferentiated noumenon, manifest in all phenomena. There is no doubt that Rumi and Ibn al-Arabi would have read Plato with an eye toward unity; the heart, seat of mystical knowledge, would effect this union with its infinite unifying capacity, in accordance with *tawhid*— "all things must be taken back to the One" (*SPK*, 147). Platonic terms such as 'this world' and 'other world', and 'Forms' (*eidos*) and 'sensible things' closely resemble the pairs of opposites Rumi himself uses metaphorically to describe different aspects of the one reality and the illusory form-meaning dichotomy. To name meaning (mana) or essence in the Sufi sense, Plato uses the term '*eidos*', (Brennan, 2002) which could be translated as 'idea' but is most commonly translated as 'Form' by Platonists. Platonic 'Form' is therefore synonymous with Rumi's 'meaning', rather than with Rumi's 'form', which corresponds with Plato's 'sensible things'. While Sufi terminology may therefore also appear to reflect a dualistic perspective, the metaphor's inner meaning (*batin*) always pertains to Oneness of Being, and this conviction would have influenced their reading of Plato. Indeed, Mathews' 'One "and" the Many' might also be interpreted as dualistic on the grounds of terminology, as though somehow the Many were additional to, and therefore separate from, the One.

Plotinus is particularly explicit about the unified nature of the One from which all derives and which is unique and involves no variation or limitation. It is as a result of his vision of union with the One, a union which transcends conceptualisation, that Plotinus has been called a mystic. His understanding of the One is similar to that of the Sufis:

> The One, perfect in seeking nothing, possessing nothing and needing nothing, overflows and creates a new reality by its superabundance. The One is all things and yet no one of them. It is the source of all things, yet not itself all things, but their transcendent Principle . . . (*Selected Passages from the Enneads*, Cited in Emilsson, 1998).

That moment when the ego is effaced and perceptions of duality are overcome is the moment of perfect bliss the Sufi strives for:

> My eyes see only the face of the Beloved.
> What a glorious sight
> For that sight is beloved
> Why speak of two?—
> The Beloved is in the sight
> And the sight is in the Beloved.
> (Rumi, in Star, 1992, 6)

This mystical vision of the One from whose superabundance all things flow takes form again in Mathews' panpsychist vision of 'the One and the Many', according to which "all things are included in one all-embracing consciousness" (2003, 28). The world-inclusive spirituality Mathews describes as 'panpsychism' emerged from what she perceives as a "metaphysical void at the core of society" (*op. cit.*, 5) resulting from widely held philosophical presuppositions of physical reality as mindless and therefore devoid of intrinsic meaning. According to Mathews, such an impoverished world view invites exploitation on a grand scale, devalues all life and underpins the current ecological crisis. In this regard Mathews (1998) cites Plumwood who argues that the reason/nature dichotomy is used to elevate humanity above nature, and in so doing rank one group above another within society, making of it an ideological instrument of domination and oppression. Mathews characterises *"any* view that reunites mentality with materiality, and thereby dismantles the foundational dualism of Western thought, as panpsychist" (2003, 4). Panpsychism offers a pathway to the reanimation of reality within a Western frame of reference, an attempt to "resacralize the taken-for-granted ground beneath our feet" by "liberating reason from old epistemological certainties into the larger field of metaphysics" (*op. cit.*, 5) and in so doing to address the yearnings of society in this time of ideological instability.

Deeply influenced by Spinoza and non-Western perspectives such as those of indigenous Australia and specifically Taoism as expounded by Lao-Tzu in about 500 BCE, Mathews refers to the panpsychic way as "the Way of the One and the Many", after the Chinese notion of the Tao, which, she acknowledges, "the present Way closely resembles" (*op. cit.*, 9). Whilst modelling panpsychism on this particular form of Eastern thought, Mathews warns of "exotic imports" (*op. cit.*, 7) when she asks where those are who might in this hour of cultural need render insights derived from inspirational traditions to provide genuine spiritual nourishment. "Where indeed?" she asks, revealing a certain inconsistency that should not pass without comment, nor the entreaty ignored, particularly since inspirational Sufi poetry, dedicated to the One within the Many, has the potential to address the very yearnings Mathews describes. Imports are rendered 'exotic' by their appearance; their differing forms conceal the one meaning-giving core which Rumi urges us to seek, as Mathews has done with regard to Taoism and might wish to do with regard to other 'exotic' teachings embodying similar truths. The legacy of Rumi and other Sufi poets is effectively to restore meaning to the world's many and varied forms.

Although sharply different in some respects, various traditions share these core insights, and it is to their unifying vision that Hamilton turns for support for his "post-secular ethics"—the writings of the Platonists and the Sufis, Spinoza (on whom Mathews also draws), and Hindu and Buddhist teachings. Hamilton's numerous references to Sufism include Ibn al-Arabi's description from *Kernel of the Kernel* of the one all-encompassing reality: ". . . whether it be in the interior or whether it be in outside existence, whatever is manifested is the Absolute Being; that existence is One Existence, One Soul, One Body; it is neither separated nor individuated" (Cited in Hamilton, 2008, 102). It is appreciation of this unity of all things and the understanding that grows from that, says Hamilton, that is the path to the noumenon (*op. cit.*, 227). Such a path, he suggests, might reveal "the stream of meaning that runs beneath the surface of daily life" (*ibid.*).

Hamilton reminds us that Kant's and Schopenhauer's attempts to define the noumenon and discern modes of approaching it were preceded by earlier and in particular by Eastern philosophies, and it is on these he draws in constructing his argument. In Eastern traditions it has long been understood that the noumenon, the 'universal' or 'subtle essence' (2008, xiii), can be known only by transcending rational forms of understanding. Departing from Schopenhauer, Hamilton recognises and expands on the purpose of "life in the noumenon". The noumenon, he argues, is that fixed point the ancient Greek mathematician Archimedes was seeking when he wrote, "Give me one fixed point and I will move the earth" (*ibid.*); a point, Hamilton argues, we are able to intuit if we are sufficiently attentive. From this fixed point emerges the "moral self" (*op. cit.*, 146); universal but also personal, in accordance with the unity of all things. "The moral self", he says, "is the most immediate expression of the noumenon in the phenomenal world, implicating each individual by virtue of the universal Self in one all-encompassing reality". It is the aspect of our selves in the phenomenal world that most directly reminds us of our origins. The failure of humanism and all Kantian ethics, says Hamilton, demands that we "allow the noumenon back into ethics" (*op. cit.*, 220).

Sufism teaches that the whole material world—life in its entirety—is sacred because "everything is the manifastations of His Beautiful Names". The Vedanta philosophy teaches it in its *advaita* (*a-dvaita*, or non-dual): there is no such thing as 'two'; the whole is one and the same being. Jesus says, "I and the Father are one" (John 10: 14); in the state of Nirvana Buddha finds a condition "wherein there is neither consciousness, nor space nor a void . . . not a coming, not a going, nor a standing still, nor a falling, nor a rising" (Mascaro, 1973, 19). Krishna says: "I am the same to all beings, and my love is ever one" (*ibid.*). Sixteenth century Spanish mystic, Saint John of the Cross, asks: "What more do you want, o soul! And what else do you search for outside, when within yourself you possess your riches, delights, satisfaction and kingdom—your beloved whom

you desire and seek?" (*ibid.*). Similarly, Emperor Marcus Aurelius expresses the Stoic perspective as follows:

> All things are interwoven with one another; a sacred bond unites them.
> Everything is coordinated; everything works together in giving form to the
> one universe. The world order is a unity made up of multiplicity: God is
> one, pervading all things; all being is one, all law is one and all truth is one
> . . . (Aurelius, 1964, 106)

Revelation has come in different forms to different people in different periods of the world's history and so there are many sacred texts, natural and cultural, and different religions and philosophies, but when we
look beyond the veils of form, we recognise the same divine impulse giving rise to them.

1.4 Nature as a Manuscript

Nature, as cultural theorist Raymond Williams points out (*The Long Revolution*, 1961), is a word of great complexity, and as Wheeler reminds us
with reference to Kate Soper's exposition in *What is Nature?* (1995), it
has been the subject of much dispute between postmodernists who claim
it is only a discursive construction, and those of a materialist and ecological persuasion who insist it is real and has intrinsic value. Wheeler's own
usage is influenced by Michael Polanyi's account of nature as something
about which "more can be known" (2006, 86).

Mathews' endorsement of Timothy Sprigge's definition in the *Routledge Encyclopedia of Philosophy* of panpsychism, which allows any theory
according to which "all things are included in one all-embracing consciousness in a manner which displays itself as their containment within a
single spatiotemporal system" (2003, 28), would suggest an equally inclusive understanding of the term 'nature', corresponding with Sufism's nondualistic understanding of a seamless reality. Mostly, however, the term is
not used either by Mathews, presumably on account of the dualism it
implies, or in Sufi literature, where the term "Supreme *Barzakh*" appears
to be synonymous with 'Nature', i.e. the cosmos as a whole, or 'every real
thing' in respect of the Universal Reality's all-inclusiveness. "All *haqqs*
have a single reality", according to the *hadith* to which al-Arabi alludes in
his explication of the Supreme *Barzakh*, and here Chittick understands

haqq to mean "real thing" (*SPK*, 138). Therefore Wheeler's reference to "mystical fantasy" (2006, 98) is unfortunate as it misconstrues the nature of mysticism, which does not concern itself with fantasy (*wahm*) but with the Real (*al-haqq*). Mathews also refers to all-inclusive nature as "the real". In order to arrive at a nondualistic form of "knowing the real", says Mathews, reason should be "guided by the heart" (2003, 174).

Mathews signals "a certain affinity" between panpsychism and Romanticism, in particular the Romantic tradition of nature philosophy, which, she says, "prefigured the current ecological view of nature in its general organicism" and its "emphasis on relationality and the interconnectedness of all things" (*op. cit.*, 172). In their imputation of spirit to matter, Mathews explains, German philosophers such as Schlegel, Schleiermacher, Schelling, and to some extent Hegel, and poets in England, such as Coleridge, Shelley and Wordsworth, rejected Cartesian dualism and the mechanistic view of matter to which it led (*ibid.*). However, the Romantic tradition falls short of the panpsychist ideal, Mathews believes, in that it remained "in the grip of anthropocentrism" with its emphasis on "humanity as the telos of the World Soul" (*ibid.*). Nevertheless, despite the tradition's perceived shortcomings, in accordance with *tawil*, I will call upon poet and cultural critic John Ruskin's occasional witness since a philosophically-informed critique of modernity and its reductive materialism that is cognate with aspects of Sufism emerges within Western society during the Romantic period and continues through to the present in the work of cultural critics and moral philosophers such as Northcott, Farrelly, and Hamilton and ecological thinkers such as Mathews, Wheeler and Berry.

Mathews' argument for the reality of matter challenges the traditional understanding of materialism as the deanimation of the world—a world incapable of communicating and signifying. In this endeavour she is by no means alone. Bio- and ecosemioticians are concerned with producing an integrated account of the biosphere as a highly articulated semiosphere, where the whole world is a signifying milieu and semiosis is common to all life—where, in fact, "the definition of life may coincide with the definition of semiosis", as Thomas Sebeok writes in *Biosemiotics: the semiotic web* (1991) (Cited in Wheeler, 28). Similarly countering the reductive, mechanistic metaphor introduced by seventeenth-century science, Wheeler's argument from biosemiotics follows in the tradition of Raymond Williams, whose "ecological" understanding of a communicative order at the heart of the complex web of life's many forms also rejects "positivism's sharp distinction between subject and object, and also its reduction of either to a simple machinery" (2006, 13). Biosemiotics is consistent with the Sufi (and panpsychist) understanding that all of life communicates (as Hamza Aydın also emphasises in his most recent article, *Connection, Always and Everywhere*, 2009), that semiosis is not peculiar to humans, but "goes all the way down" through interrelated, complex systems characterised by "the ongoing throbbing of all life" (Wheeler, 108). The entire universe is "perfused with signs" (Peirce, C. S., cited in Wheeler, 103).

According to this perspective, communication is indeed the unifier, the mechanism that allows the organism to be one. Sufism in fact insists that there is nothing on earth that does not communicate. In recognition of the divine impulse animating all things, the Prophet reminds us not to disturb objects unnecessarily "because they are in a state of praise" (Can, 2005, 140). Hazrat Inayat Khan explains as follows:

> Every aspect of life communicates . . . Life is communicative, the soul is communicative . . . Life is intelligence, everywhere, and the more one communicates with life, the more one feels that even the rock is not without life, that through it pulses the blood of the universe. And when we look at life from this point of view, we see that there is no place, no object which is not sacred; that even in a rock one may find the source and goal of all things in that particular form (VIII, 29).

The signs and symbols of the manuscript of nature form a living text for us to read and interpret at every moment without mediation if we are able. "Such revelation gushes forth as from the source and is not painfully conveyed over man-made aqueducts . . . It comes from the sphere of 'My Lord has educated me' and not from the sphere of 'My father told me' . . ." (Attār, Cited in Shah, 1979, 13). To understand symbology means to understand divine consciousness, the language of nature (IX, 25) and to perceive in all forms not only their superficial differences but the underlying shape of the cross, most ancient symbol of totality, and understand its meaning. Its perpendicular line speaks to the mystic of ascending and descending paths and the inevitable conflict between them, the horizontal depicts the embrace of the Real; the intersection tells of the destruction of *nafs* (ego), and the return to source (Mambrino, Cited in Bosco, 1976). The intersection conceals the heart, the centre and seat of mystical knowledge.

'Divine vibration' (*Nada*) results in the mystic sounds of the Eternal, the cosmic sound from which all other sound derives and which can be heard during deep meditation. It is from this vibration, mystics say, that all life emanates. "God most High created the world from a Word, for He said, 'Be!' and it is" (Rumi, SPL, 269). At the heart of Islam is God's Word, the Qur'an, and Rumi has a great deal to say about the Word (*kalam*). Likewise, the Bible tells us that "In the beginning was the Word, and the Word was with God, and the Word was God" (John 1:1). The 'word' or *logos* as it was originally used by Heraclitus suggests the everlasting cosmic order whose contrasting aspects or phases disclose an underlying unity; Plato associates the term with truth and stability; in Aristotle's metaphysics *logos* equates with the essence of things (*eidos*), and to the Stoics *logos* embodies the universe's supreme directive principle (Stead, 1998). Sound, audible vibration, is creative; Sufis 'know' that all things have their origin in it. It is the natural and only name of the Nameless, proclaimed, audibly and inaudibly, throughout manifestation. There is nothing on earth or in the heavens that does not declare His glory (Can, 2005). "This (the cosmic sound) is the spirit of all sounds and of all words, and is hidden within them all, as the spirit is hidden in the body" (II, 64). It does not belong to any language, but the root of all languages reaches into its depths.

1.5 The Unifying Expression

The nature of life is, above all, a mystery, unfathomable by reason or logic. Sufism teaches not the certainty of science but the conviction of mystics whose hearts have, throughout the ages, responded to the universe's own communication. Both scientist and Sufi, however, tell of a similar vision of ultimate unity, which the former observes with detachment and the latter turns towards, as a wave seeking renewal, turns to the ocean.

Wheeler, in particular, argues that religion, art and science are not fundamentally different sorts of human endeavour, but must be understood as related activities and emergent features in the complex evolution of what

Robert Laughlin refers to as "towers of truth" (2006, 81). Human creativity, whether of a scientific or non-scientific nature, involves 'surrender' (Ch. 5), which Wheeler explains as follows: "The experience of surrender as immersion in, as a form of giving one's self over to experience . . . is, of course, a process of active semiosis in which I do not simply receive signs, but actively embrace them" (*op. cit.*, 87). Although in agreement with the general trend of Wheeler's argument, I believe that acknowledgement of mysticism, as the intuition of truth, would have been appropriate, given the numerous references to aspects of mystical experience, such as "the sacred", "the experience of surrender", "sacred knowledge", "surrender to the mystery", "passionate drive towards more knowledge of an ordered universe. . . an unfolding towards an unthinkable consummation" and "passionate and pleasurable, warm surrender . . . to the mysterious actions of . . . 'the becoming of tacit knowledge'" (*op. cit.*, 86-91). But in an attempt to formalise the quest for truth in the "official modern world of modern science", Wheeler admits, "this is heresy" (*op. cit.*, 91). Consequently mysticism remains unnamed and unacknowledged.

With the development of complexity science and the emergence of "substantial research" backing up "strongly felt", (but 'unscientific') "hunches and intimations", Wheeler explains, we understand better our connectedness and co-arising being (*op. cit.,* 82). It is to overcome a false idea of objectivity, Wheeler believes, which has led increasing numbers of scientists to turn to non-western ways of conceiving the world and living skilfully in it (*op. cit.,*87). As Mathews turns to Taoism and Aboriginal thought, and Hamilton to the ancient Greeks and Eastern philosophy generally, it is on Buddhist philosophy that Wheeler draws, its insights being compatible with "General Systems Theory's idea of subjectivity as located and processual" (2006, 81), which Wheeler advances.

In support of this move, Wheeler notes that Western philosophers have long made explicit use of its ancient wisdom teachings (2006, 94). Others, I would add, have been influenced by the unifying vision of Sufism—one thinks, for example, of Johann Wolfgang von Goethe, whose *West-östlicher Divan* and his poetic tribute to the Prophet, *Mahomets Gesang*, exemplify his "grand response" (Nasr, 1981, 96) to Sufism.

The silent life 'appears as death' in comparison with the life of activity on the surface (II, 16). According to Sufi teachings, life begins with the activity of consciousness, sometimes referred to as vibration, and every vibration starting from the same original source, differing only in its tone and rhythm. "Rhythm is a law of creation and it is in accordance with this law that every form is determined and every condition manifests to view" (XI, 45). Mineral, vegetable, animal and human life results from a gradual change of vibration, and the vibrations of each plane differ from one another in their weight, breadth, length, colour, effect, sound and rhythm (*ibid.*). Plotinus, whose perception of the creative principle is similar to that of the Sufis, refers to this activity of consciousness as 'Soul' or 'Sympathy':

> A Sympathy pervades this single universe, like a single living creature; every interval, both large and small, is filled with Soul . . . Like parts lie not in contact but separated, with other parts between, yet by their likeness they feel sympathy . . . and in a living and unified being there is no part so distant as not to be near (Selected Passages from the *Enneads*, Cited in Emilsson, 1998).

Similarly, the Sufi says:

> Vibrations work through the chord of sympathy existing between man and his surroundings . . . and are perceived not only by man but by animals and plants . . . (II, 19)

It is the gradually increasing activity which causes vibrations to materialise, and it is the gradual decrease of the same which transmutes them again into spirit. Incessant flux characterises all matter: "all that is of the body is as coursing waters", interrupted by the "simple dissolving of the elements whereof each living thing is composed", says Aurelius; a ceaseless forming and re-forming. (Aurelius, 1964, 64).

The inward and essential part of every entity is composed of fine vibrations; the external part is formed of gross ones. The finer part we call spirit and the grosser part matter, the former being less subject to change and destruction and the latter more so (II, 17). Intrinsically matter and spirit or form and meaning have the same composition, the difference being one of degree of fineness of vibration. Sufism is a path of 'refinement', the focus of which is to rekindle the spiritual aspect by refining the instrument. In this regard Sufi thought is in line with the earliest mystical writings of the Hermetics, according to which "nothing rests; everything moves; everything vibrates". According to the Hermetic principle of rhythm, "everything flows, out and in; everything has its tides; all things rise and fall; the pendulum-swing manifests in everything; the measure of the swing to the right is the measure of the swing to the left; rhythm compensates" (Ramacharaka, 1904). The goal of Rumi and other Sufi mystics is the 'annihilation' of the ego—Inayat Khan prefers the more moderate 'refinement' of the ego. In a materialistic age characterised by coarseness, or what Mathews refers to as the "block" mentality of "bruteness and blindness" (2005, 15), the pendulum-swing towards refinement might restore the sensitivity which Australian philosopher Raimond Gaita argues is lacking in much human activity today. He too draws our attention to the "coarsening of public morality", recommending a more spiritual outlook (Gaita, 2008).

Until the advent of rationalism in the seventeenth century, the pursuit of science had a spiritual foundation. Its objective was to come to know the Creator and His creation more fully. As the pendulum-swing to materialism led to forgetfulness of the spiritual aspect the methodologies of science and religion became more and more divergent. However, it appears that the pendulum is swinging back once again and it may no longer be heresy to include mysticism in the conversation. Witteveen makes the following observation: "Western science has developed a materialistic causal-deterministic theory quite opposite to religious and mystical visions. But these lines again converge and begin to touch each other in certain fields. Accordingly some scientists have found parallels between the vision of earlier mystics and some aspects of modern science, which is more organic, more holistic and sees creation as an indivisible dynamic whole" (Witteveen, 1997, 54). According to Witteveen, Hazrat Inayat Khan's mystical philosophy is, in many respects, in harmony with insights which modern scientific thought has reached in an analytical way. He explores this convergence with particular reference to Fritjof Capra's *The Turning Point* and *The Tao of Physics* and the theories of physicist David Bohm, on which Wheeler also draws.

Capra's understanding of the "living Void" is no different from that of Hazrat Inayat Khan's descriptions of vacuum. In his book *The Tao of Physics* (p 223) Capra writes:

> The relation between the virtual particles and the vacuum is an essentially dynamic relation; the vacuum is in reality a 'living Void', pulsating in end-

less rhythms of creation and destruction. The discovery of the dynamic quality of the vacuum is seen by many physicists as one of the most important findings of modern physics. From its role as an empty container of the physical phenomenon, the void has emerged as a dynamic quantity of utmost importance. The results of modern physics thus seem to confirm the words of the Chinese sage Chang Tsai: 'When one knows that the Great Void is full of Ch'i (vital energy) one realizes that there is no such thing as nothingness.' (Cited in Witteveen, 1997, 55)

In *The Essential David Bohm* physicist Bohm explains how vacuum (plenum) is capable of unfolding the forms we experience in the sensual world. His ontological explanation and philosophy of consciousness are in complete harmony with Hazrat Inayat Khan's mystical perspective. Bohm's account tells of an "enfolding-unfolding universe", the reality of consciousness and the activity of a "super-implicate order" that accounts for the universe's ordered manifestation. It is the super-implicate order, Bohm explains, which infuses the universe with active information, and this in turn generates various levels of organization, structure and meaning. He introduces the concept of "soma-significance"; here 'soma' refers to the body, and by extension to all matter, while 'significance' refers to mind or meaning. With this model he suggests that "active meaning is enfolded and unfolded throughout the whole of existence". Wholeness is understood to be more than a theoretical construct, "it is a meaning-field, a living totality that includes us" (2002, 158). He describes the universe as being "woven together in a dynamic, tapestry-like configuration" in which "all the interactions constitute a single structure of indivisible links, so that the entire universe has to be thought of as an unbroken whole".

Capra expresses this interconnectedness in similar terms: the universe, he says, is "one indivisible, dynamic whole, whose parts are essentially inter-related and can be understood only as patterns of a cosmic process . . . As we penetrate into matter, [creation] does not show us any isolated building blocks, but rather appears as a complicated web of relations between the various parts of a unified whole" (Cited in Witteveen, 62). These various parts, Witteveen explains, are now viewed as packets of energy (quanta) that behave like particles or waves, depending on the approach being taken.

Quantum theory thus reveals a basic oneness of the universe. All parts of this 'complicated web of relations' can therefore only be fully understood through their interrelations and cannot be defined as isolated entities. Similarly, and supported by the science of epidemiologist Michael Marmot and psychoneuroimmunologist Paul Martin, Wheeler's 'whole creature' swims in a semiotic world or *Umwelt* (2006, 107-108). This principle of interrelatedness is at the heart of what Inayat Khan calls the "threefold aspect of nature" which characterises all things (XI, 50-51). They might be referred to as past, present and future; source, journey and goal. Sufis of all ages, and Rumi more than any other, have expressed these three aspects which they have identified in all things as love, lover and beloved while Ibn al-Arabi interprets them as knowing, the knower and the known.

The work of scientists Erwin Schrödinger, Michio Kaku and Jennifer Trainer on vibration also seems to be in harmony with Khan's views. "It seems we may reduce the entire manifestation to vibrations, to 'superstrings', minuscule vibrating strings. . ." (Kaku & Trainer, *The Cosmic Quest for the Theory of the Universe,* 1995, Cited in Witteveen, 1997, 59). When asked whether 'every atom of the manifestation can be said to have a soul', Inayat Khan replied in the affirmative:

> . . . every atom of this universe, mental or material, is an outcome of that eternal source and cannot exist without having part of that heavenly radiance within it. Even a mote of dust has radiance behind it and if it were not for this radiance it would not have manifested to our view. We see it because it has light in it; it is its own light that shows it to us. That is its soul. (I, 41)

According to Arthur D'Adamo (2004, 62-87) scientists today accept a monist description of the physical universe, since they believe that every physical phenomenon is a manifestation of one entity, energy. Energy is the ultimate ground of existence, depending on nothing for its existence; independent, self-sufficient. He examines terms that have been used both by science to describe energy, and by religion with reference to God, such as the one, the pure, the unmixed, the unadulterated and the eternal and supports not only their religious and philosophical but also their scientific relevance. When viewed through the lens of biosemiotics, energy is information (2006, 155), which can, according to Wheeler, under the right conditions, become life in a universe perfused with signs. On the ultimate level nothing exists but energy. On that level, energy is 'the one'. Because energy alone exists on the ultimate level, it is the single, unique root and source of all that exists. It is pure, unmixed and unadulterated. As the ultimate substance, energy pervades every corner of the cosmos. It is omnipresent, infinite and unlimited with respect to time and space.

What was observed by science in the late twentieth century has been known for millennia in the hearts of mystics, who perceive the One in all things. In a paper entitled *Levels of the Soul and the Levels of Time* (2007), Caner K. Dağlı elaborates how the metaphysics and cosmology of Ibn al-Arabi, in particular, prefigured the recent findings of physics. Sufis, lovers, are not only filled with wonder and awe, but a longing to transcend the divisions of form and merge with the eternal and infinitely divine substance of their Beloved (Athar, 2009). Science, on the other hand, had for centuries ignored connections to the larger whole, focusing on observable details rather than speculating about our place in the universe, our relation to the eternal totality and our ultimate meaning (D'Adamo, 79).

To the Sufi, matter, as manifestation of the One, is sacred. According to Mathews' panpsychism, mentality, rather than life or divinity, is a property of all matter (2003, 188), hence the distinction between panpsychism and hylozoism and pantheism, and also Sufism. Sufism is neither hylozoism nor pantheism, but nor does it subscribe to the exclusion of the properties of life and divinity from any existent. What, after all, can be the mentality of a grain of sand or mote of dust if not its participation in the one life-force, the universal mind? And although Mathews' various definitions exclude the attribute of divinity from matter, the sacred dimension is palpable throughout her work, and indeed, she says "To adopt a panpsychist outlook is to enter the terrain of 'spirituality'" (*op. cit.*, 10). Mathews not only describes her own strong sense of the sacred and experiences usually associated with it—wonder, exultation, beauty and awe, and feelings of being, on occasion, "at the heart of the Mystery—at the heart of Creation" (2003, 2), but also appeals to that of her readers. The attribute of mentality alone does not inspire this depth of emotion; even when mentality is recognised, as it surely must be with regard to humans and animals, our interaction with these is seldom characterised by wonder and awe, and is often, in fact, unethical, as I will illustrate in Chapter 3. As an attribute, I believe, mentality is insufficient to change the modus operandi of society, which Mathews clearly seeks to do. It appears incongruous therefore that these other important aspects have by definition been excluded.

Recognising mentality alone does not enable us to "imagin(e) the innerness of things" (*op. cit.*, 25) or to "imagin(e) them as imbued with an interiority analogous to ours . . . a subjective form of self-presence . . ." (*ibid.*). Such imagining, like Sufi *marifa*, I argue, invites us into the *mundus imaginalis* (Corbin, 1969) where this particular outlook might be "intuitively clinched" (Mathews, 2003, 25) and meaning found—meaning which quantum physics cannot bestow. The Sufi understanding that all things are sacred precisely because they are imbued with meaning does, I claim, refine the nature of our engagement with them. (In Chapter 4 I will look more closely at the need to find meaning in things by imagining their innerness.)

The findings of Henry Margenau and Ray Abraham Varghese would indicate, if not a universal shift in thinking, certainly a real interest among the scientists interviewed in cosmological questions with metaphysical implications. *Cosmos, Bios, Theos* (1992) details the perspectives of sixty eminent, contemporary scientists, twenty-four of whom are Nobel Laureates, on the relationship between their scientific enterprise and their view of reality. Most of the participating scientists see no conflict between science and spirituality, which they view as complementary, recognising from the outset that science is limited in its methodology and domain of inquiry. Thus, while they regard questions of origin as legitimate for science, the general consensus is that ultimate answers cannot be provided by science alone. Physicist Henry Margenau, rejecting the view widely held half a century ago that regarded science and spirituality as incompatible, calls for a new metaphor to describe the prevailing relationship between them, since science has been introduced "to a world of awe and mystery that is not far removed from the ultimate mystery that drives the religious impulse" (1992, 58). Similarly, "(p)assion is, secretly, what animates scientific research", says Wheeler, drawing on Polanyi's argument (2006, 86).

A solid faith has propelled many a scientific quest, such as that of Isaac Newton which culminated in the Law of Gravity. Charles Birch, one of the great Australian scientists and theologians, expresses the relationship between belief in God and science thus: "The key ideas of modern science were wrought in the imagination of men who battled in thought with what at first they only dimly saw, though firmly felt". Of his own faith, Birch says: "It is . . . a sense of being grasped by something of tremendous importance that calls forth from a man all his powers of imaginative thought and of feeling and of action" (Birch, Cited in Kohn, 2007). Hence the openness of Birch's faith to the unfolding history of the natural world, with its ever more complex discoveries from genetics to the outer galaxies.

Marcus Aurelius posed the question at the heart of religion and in the mind of science: "How do we discover the truth of all this?" and obliges us with the following answer: "By distinguishing between the matter and the cause" (1964, 68). Similarly Rumi writes that the "science of bodies", without a direct and living vision of meaning, is incomplete since it is limited to the outer, observable features of form:

> The sciences are all paintings. When they gain spirits, their lifeless bodies receive a spirit.
> The root of all these sciences is from Yonder, but they have been transported from the world without sounds and letters to the world of sounds and letters (Rumi, *SPL*, 26)

The 'root' of all things, the Sufis teach, extends deep into the totality, and the leaves and branches springing from it carry their own special image of that same totality which religions attempt to reveal and scientists endeavour to discover. Its visible parts reflect the attributes of that mysterious world without sounds and letters in whose silence all things are born and come to rest.

1.6 From the World without Sounds and Letters to the World of Sounds and Letters

> The body did not exist and I was a spirit with Thee in heaven;
> Without composition and one in substance, we were all on yonder side, headless and footless.
> Like the sun we were one substance, like water we were pure and without ripples.
> When that pure light entered into form,
> Multiplicity appeared like the shadow of a battlement. (Rumi, *SPL*, 70)

The 'one substance' of which Rumi speaks is 'pure' and 'without ripples'. From this one substance form takes shape and multiplicity appears. As spirit materialises, it conceals itself from the eyes of those who look at life from the outside. Rumi develops this mystical concept of concealment in numerous verses, referring to the veils covering the Beloved's face as 'intermediaries', since their purpose is to shield the eyes from the "Heart-ravishing Beauty of the Face unveiled" (Rumi, *SPL*, 267)—beauty of such magnitude that mortals cannot bear to look at it until they are ready, or until they no longer look at life from the outside. Likewise, in Plato's *Phaedo*, Socrates refers to his attempts at contemplating 'true existence' and his fears that his soul might be blinded if he gazed at the sun directly (*The Works of Plato*, 1956, 165). Senses and intellect, like a bird with one wing, need heart to affirm wholeness and lift the veils of form. Without love, or in Rumi's words, when love is 'in separation', forms only are perceived.

In this materialistic world the focus is almost exclusively on form (*sura*). Though lacking the attributes of meaning (*mana*), form is not insignificant since it provides capacity (*akasha*) for meaning. The form-meaning dichotomy is an illusion since they are the outward and inward aspects of a single reality—"He is the Outward (*al-zahir*) and the Inward (*al-batin*)" (*SPK*, 89)—each important in its own way:

> Form also has tremendous importance. No, much more than importance, for it participates in the kernel.
> Just as nothing can be done without the kernel, so also nothing can be done without the shell . . . (Rumi, *SPL*, 24)
> The spirit cannot function without the body, and the body without the spirit is withered and cold,
> God made the body the locus of manifestation for the spirit (Rumi, *SPL*, 29)

Forms (*sura*) are loci of manifestation for meaning. Ibn al-Arabi explains: "God (Being) says 'Be!' and the thing receives coming to be. Its reception of coming to be is the fact that it becomes a locus of manifestation for the Real. This is the meaning of His words, 'Be! And it is'" (*SPK*, 90). The Real therefore stands beyond the realm of appearances, but all things are signs (*ayat*) of its reality which they in turn, by virtue of their being, express and communicate. This, the language of the birds of the spirit which fly in God's presence (Attar, 1984) can be heard when stillness prevails. Sufis tell us that the universe of Being, the Supreme *Barzakh*, speaks it. It is this subtle communication, I suggest, that Mathews intuit-ed, from which her panpsychist outlook emerged, and indeed, she affirms that a communicative order is, from the panpsychist point of view, funda-mental to the nature of reality. The world in its entirety can thus be seen as a "potentially active co-respondent, ready to respond to our overtures" (2003, 40). Thus she describes how she becomes aware that there is "an innerness to the reality (of things) as well as an outerness", and "the dif-ferences between (the most disparate things) no longer registered" (2003, 25). As the Sufis have long told us and science is discovering, every exis-tent has properties that spread beyond itself, communicating silently and mysteriously by way of ceaseless vibratory activity. It follows that nothing is devoid of potential and significance. The prerequisite to becoming active co-respondents, capable of responding to the world's subtle over-tures, not merely it to ours, however, is the awakening of the heart.

1.7 The Universe as a Dome

"The pulse of space beats ceaselessly because life is continuity. This life is a capacity in which Being manifests, and in it everything, once given birth, is taken care of and is raised and brought to fruitfulness" (II, 220). Noth-ing is lost though forms will change in time. The One's Hindu name, Brahman, reveals this mystical truth particularly clearly. Derived from the Sanskrit verb root *brh*, meaning 'to grow', the name means 'that which grows' (*brhati*) and 'which causes to grow' (*brhmayati*) (*Bhagavad-Gita*, *Glossary*, 287). The One, whatever its name—Brahman, spirit, light or life, manifests in all things, which from the densest to the finest pursue their course. Every word, deed, thought or feeling is like a seed thrown to the ground by a passer-by, who has forgotten it by the time it takes root, while the elements have preserved it and brought it to fruition.

"The universe is like a dome: it vibrates to that which you say in it, and echoes the same back to you" (V, 30). Vibrations can be understood as both cause and effect, enabling every word or action to live on. The strength of the vibration determines the intensity of the echo. Since all things are connected, visibly or invisibly, any disturbance of the slightest part of life disturbs the greater; similarly, peace achieved in a small way comforts many. According to Sufi teachings, all occurrences take place in accordance with this law and it is from this law that the religious doctrines of reward and punishment, the notion of heaven and hell, and Judgment Day originated. According to the Sufi principle of unity, heaven and hell are part of the here and now (Tatari, 2008), as are all other states, and people create their own state of harmony (when ego has been refined) or discord (when ego predominates) and consequently experience the effects of that particular state.

The Sufi understanding is that each person is his or her own judge and that in the conscience of each individual resides the faculty of judging. "Not one moment of time, not the blinking of the eye passes without a judgment" (V, 48). The 'Day' of Judgment refers to that moment when the heart is awakened and the darkness of ignorance is dispelled. Then we see the results of our actions, clearly, not 'through a glass darkly'; when the seeing faculty is not dimmed and we differentiate between illusion and reality. Similar metaphors illustrate the same truth in Plato's *Phaedo* (p 166) when Socrates refers to the limitations of sight, and in the Bible in 1 Corinthians 13:12: "For now we see through a glass, darkly; but then face to face: now I know in part; but then shall I know even as also I am known." Hazrat Inayat Khan refers to "a record in the memory of every action, thought, and word"; the consequences of our deeds, the reality of which must be confronted. Similarly, the focus of Plato's *Apology* is precisely on this theme of self-reflection. So committed is Socrates to his mission of examining all things that he would rather lose his life than abandon the practice. Examining himself and others, he says, is "the greatest good of man", since "the unexamined life is not worth living" (1956, 84). The Sufi approach differs from the Socratic approach, however, in that the Sufi examines only the state of his own heart, not that of others.

Fate, in Sanskrit, is called Karma, meaning the rhythm of past actions (V, 30). Sufi teachings do support the general concept that the present is the echo of the past and the future is the reflection of the present, and although in its broadest application the concept of Karma is in harmony with Sufi thinking, the law of karma as it is understood in Buddhism, for example, appears too restrictive in its application since it is highly individualised and therefore ignores the interconnectedness of all things. According to the Buddhist understanding, an individual's karma determines the nature of that individual's rebirth (Mascaro, 1973), whereas according to Sufism's principle of unity, the burden of negative action is borne by all, not only by the perpetrator, and positive action does not only reward the doer. Sufism's main objective is to diminish the thought of self as a separate entity and to promote a holistic perspective. In this regard, I believe Wheeler would find greater support for her vision of "inter-related and co-dependent co-arising of all life" (2006, 97) in Sufism than in Buddhism, since Sufism seeks a constructive, synthetic view that focuses on unity of the whole.

Heaven and hell are both part of our reality here and now, and this, the present moment, is where the focus lies for the Sufi, who knows that in the course of time the elements of which all things are composed will return to the earth and the individual being will gradually dissolve in the ocean of eternal Being. And so the Sufi poet Hafiz writes:

Sing oh Singer, the new song of the new life every moment (IV, 27)

Life is potential and spirit is creative therefore every moment offers the possibility of revision, reconstruction and renewal. Like form and meaning, harmony and discord lie side by side; when one is revealed, the other is simply concealed. In Sufism, all is one; every thing and every being needs the two opposite qualities to exist, to act, and to fulfill the purpose of life, each aspect being incomplete without the other.

Pain and pleasure follow in each other's footsteps, Plato explains, with recourse to imagery similar to that of Rumi: "Their bodies are two, but they are joined by a single head" (1956, 112). When the one is hidden, the other is manifest. What outwardly has every appearance of hell might hold concealed below the surface a thing of beauty, as Fethullah Gülen explains in *Our World and Its Inherently Exquisite Mystery* (2009). "This world has always smiled gently on its children . . . softening the painful and harsh storms of reality with its magical hope-inspiring essence, and even in the most hellish conditions, cooled down the heat of those who took shelter in it with a peaceful '*bard al-salam*'" (Gülen, 2009). By allowing the world to speak to us, we might observe heavenly aspects in the most unlikely places. In the midst of hell, life still has meaning and happiness is possible, as psychiatrist and concentration camp survivor Viktor Frankl recalls in *Man's Search for Meaning,* his account of the indomitable human spirit confronted by the horrors of Auschwitz. When it seemed conditions could become no worse, he describes what he calls "some of the most idyllic

hours I have ever spent" (1984, 84). On another occasion, robbed of all
but the spirit within, he recalls "how content we were; happy in spite of
everything" (*op. cit.*, 68). Despite all the tragic aspects of human existence,
life holds potential meaning under any circumstances (*op. cit.*, 17). Even
when the sounds of hell are deafening, celestial music can be heard and its
powerful message brings comfort and joy.

What is manifest we recognise; what is hidden we are wont to
ignore. The illusory form-meaning dichotomy is the dominant theme in
Rumi's poetry, and the terms most often used to express it are: secondary causes (*asbab*) and First Cause (*musabbib*), outward (*zahir*) and
inward (*batin*), dust and wind, foam and ocean, picture and painter, and
shadow and light:

> People look at secondary causes and think that they are the origin of every-
> thing that happens. But it has been revealed to the saints that secondary
> causes are no more than a veil . . . One must have an eye which cuts through
> secondary causes and tears aside all veils. Whoever looks upon secondary
> causes is for certain a form-worshipper. Whoever looks upon the First
> Cause has become a light which discerns Meaning (Rumi, *SPL*, 21)

Spirit and matter are inextricably intertwined to form one—the form-
meaning dichotomy is an illusion. Life appears as a puzzle of duality—
harmony and discord, joy and sorrow, reward and retribution seem to
have little in common with each other. Knowledge is acquired by learning about pairs of opposites; the characteristics of one shed light on the
opposing other. Only after having distinguished between them does it
become apparent that they represent two aspects of one thing and when
their oneness is evident, it becomes possible to rise above their apparent
duality. What is most important to the Sufi is to recognise their unity so
as to overcome distinction and division, seeking neither joy nor avoiding
sorrow. The Sufi, like the follower of Hamilton's metaphysical-psychological path, seeks neither the "pleasant life" nor the "good life" (Hamilton,
2008, 241) but rather the meaningful life in which opposites coincide.
"Life is peace among opposites" (Rumi, *SPL*, 51). The "coincidence of
opposites" where opposition is effaced can be experienced in union with
the one Being, who cannot be known, having no opposite to 'make Him
clear' (*ibid.*). Viktor Frankl speaks of having experienced contentment in
a death camp. This is the peace that passes all understanding, the silence

that comforts more than any language, the 'colourless' world that holds the key to all colours, which the Sufi aspires to reflect in his own being and whose rhythm he seeks to make his own:

> Each opposite inflicts reciprocal annihilation upon its opposite; when opposition disappears, subsistence alone remains . . . Colourlessness is the root of all colours, peace the root of all wars (Rumi, *SPL*, p 52)

In the intersecting lines of the cross symbolising all forms we see that conflict is a natural aspect of existence. We experience it at every level and all life is exposed to it. The continuous process of construction and destruction of forms is, according to Sufis, at the heart of all conflict (XI, 63). The process of refining the ego, a prerequisite if conflict is to be reduced, demands constant self-reflection, but the task of judging and appraising one's actions with honesty and detachment calls for an awakened heart. A constant guide on our way is available in the form of the manuscript of nature with its wealth of sounds and letters, silently addressing the hearts of travellers. What are its sounds and letters telling us at this time? Do they reveal the fineness of the heart or the coarseness of its shadow—the ego? This is the question that we will proceed to address in the following chapter.

CHAPTER TWO

World without Meaning (*Mana*)

World without Meaning (*Mana*)

In light of the Sufi understanding that the universe is a collection of signs that carries a message, and Wheeler's argument from biosemiotics that semiosis is not peculiar to humans, but "goes all the way down" (2006, 28) in a universe "perfused with signs" (Peirce, C. S., cited in Wheeler, 103), I will look closely at some of the signs exemplifying contemporary western culture. 'Going beyond form', which Rumi urges us to do, necessitates prior traversal—the beyond can be reached only via thoroughfare; in this chapter, therefore, I will engage extensively with forms, attending to the cultural landscape, its appearance, its superficial enhancements, endeavouring to understand the message in the context of the whole, the theme of the sacred script being *tawhid*.

2.1 *Ayat*—Universal Expression

> These words are for the person who needs words in order to perceive. As for him who perceives without words, what need has he for words? After all, the heavens and the earth are all words for him who perceives. They are born from words, for 'Be!' and it is. (Rumi, *SPL*, 269)

Words, says Rumi, are snares, and Beauty, like exotic birds, will not be caged. He advises us to listen to the universe's own silent expression if we wish to hear the Beloved's voice. Despite being extremely powerful, words, says Wheeler, are only one aspect of semiotic communication; central to the non-reductionist realist ontology underpinning biosemiotics is a mind-body-environment holism whose reality is expressed non-verbally (2006, 17). Nasr explains that the universe's own expression might be said to take the form of *ayat*—the verses which not only make up the Qur'an, but the divine words and letters (signs) which comprise at once the elements of the macrocosmic world and the inner being of man. To the extent that the *ayat* of the sacred book reveal their inner meaning, and the human heart has been awakened, the message can be read, written as it is in the most subtle manner on "the cliffs of high mountains, the leaves of the trees, the faces of animals and the stars of the sky" (Nasr, 1981, 192). Similarly, Mathews believes that life assumes a poetic structure for those who are awake to the world's "endless communicativeness" and that everything is "an expression of the unfolding of world" (2005, 20).

2.2 Consumerism and the Mall

The materialist view of matter is, according to Mathews and Hamilton, characterised by an ethos of consumerism and an ideology of progress. More, bigger and bolder appears to be the prevailing mindset. While the environment groans under the weight of the useless stuff that fills our endless malls, factories produce it faster than ever as consumers in increasing numbers shop around the clock in the hope that the objects they pursue hold the key to their happiness. In no time however, the shine wears off and the stuff is discarded, to be replaced by more items—bigger and costlier. But as the subtitle of Hamilton's *Affluenza* suggests, *too much is never enough*. Furthermore, the maximally extractive profit-driven economics which drives such mindless consumerism represents an unsustainable assault on the world.

The things we think will make us happy don't, yet the wanting continues. "Nineteenth century economists predicted that the abundance made possible by technological advance and the modern organisation of work would result in the emergence of 'post-materialist' humans—people existing on a higher plane, where their cultural, intellectual and spiritual powers are refined" (Hamilton, 2005, 4-5). Instead of our growing wealth freeing us of our materialist preoccupations, however, it seems to have had the opposite effect, says Hamilton. It appears that no matter how much we have, we feel we need more. The threshold of desire is raised as goals are reached, creating an "endless cycle of self-deception" in which our desires always seem to stay ahead of where we are. Richard Easterlin describes this phenomenon as a "hedonic treadmill" (cited in Hamilton, 2005, 6), a cycle of hope and disappointment which, Hamilton believes, lies at the heart of neoliberal economic policies that have set out to promote higher consumption as the road to a better society (*ibid.*).

As our own achievements never appear to be enough we find ourselves "in the grip of a collective psychological disorder", where our view of reality becomes distorted (*op. cit.*, 6). Surrounded by affluence, we indulge in the illusion that we are deprived, says Hamilton. Brink Lindsey's *Age of Abundance* (2007) and Robert Frank's *Richistan: A Journey through the 21st Century Wealth Boom and the Lives of the New Rich* (2007) paint a disturbing picture of emptiness and meaninglessness to which many in western society can relate. Sydney-based author and critic Elizabeth Farrelly cites American psychologists Daniel Gilbert and Timothy Wilson with reference to 'miswanting': we tend to "want all the wrong things, things that are wrong not just morally or environmentally but even in their capacity to deliver the satisfaction they promise" (Farrelly, 2007, 30). And so the cycle of desiring, acquiring and discarding continues relentlessly, and little thought is given to destructive habits and huge eco-footprints.

Conspicuous consumption, stimulated by the transformation of ubiquitous malls and supermalls into entertainment destinations, has become a defining feature of western life. Retail has become the most popular therapy, with people shopping voraciously, for fun rather than of necessity. In vast malls the glittering wares are displayed, seducing shoppers with their promise that happiness lies merely a purchase away. America now has more shopping malls than high schools and shopping centre space has increased by a factor of 12 in the last 40 years (Farrelly, 145). Shopping, not baseball, has emerged as the preferred national pastime in the USA according to Dr Irwin Kellner, chief economist for Market Watch, and a 2006 ACNielson survey indicates that shopping is a 'hot pastime' in seven Asian countries. About 93 percent of respondents in Hong Kong and Singapore said they would go shopping even if they did not plan to buy anything, and 34 percent said they would go shopping just for entertainment about once a week (*China Daily*, 2006-07-21). The survey of 22,000 Internet users in 42 markets found that 74 percent of the world's consumers admit to shopping as entertainment when they do not need anything (*ibid.*). According to Hamilton, similar trends have emerged in Australian cities.

"It's where we go to be together with our loved ones: Chaddy," writes Helen Razer of Melbourne's favourite shopping mall, Chadstone, where "a community now plays its intimacy out in a new kind of church" (*The Age*, 2007-12-26, *Opinion*, p 15). "For many," she says, "shopping is an opiate far more potent than religion and Boxing Day is a compelling

Haj", with the Myer stores alone enticing more than 528000 shoppers through its doors in Victoria on that one day. Contemporary western society has become so dominated by consumerism that consumption activities play a major role in the construction of the self as people define themselves through the products they buy in a mall-based culture. Psychologists such as Helga Dittmar argue that all buying is to some degree an attempt to bring our actual self into accord with our ideal self, a theory to which Hamilton subscribes (2005, 13). We complete ourselves symbolically by acquiring things that compensate for our perceived shortcomings, only to be confronted by a different set of problems: impossible-to-obtain ideal images presented by advertising, the lack of adequate resources for appropriate self-construction, the quandary of being rich in things and poor in time, and the risk of losing the self when shopping becomes not merely the acquisition of things but the buying of identity. Then the mall becomes a cage in which the material 'good life' appears to be purchasable (Dittmar, 2007).

The impact on our wellbeing of the consumerist culture with its 'toxic ideals' is extremely detrimental (*ibid.*). While desiring and acquiring are both necessary for survival, the insatiability of much of our consumption has ominous implications. Compulsive shopping disorder, a condition marked by binge shopping and subsequent depression and financial hardship, is now recognized as a disease which Stanford University Medical Centre researchers have begun treating with a drug commonly prescribed as an antidepressant. The drug is reputed to be able to curb uncontrollable shopping urges. According to Lorrin Koran, professor of psychiatry and behavioural sciences at Stanford, this 'very real disorder' is estimated to affect between 2 and 8 percent of the U.S. population. Symptoms include preoccupation with shopping for unneeded items and the inability to resist purchasing such items (Koran, 2003). According to Hamilton, compulsive shopping, also known as 'oniomania', has been called the 'smiled upon' addiction because it is socially sanctioned (2005, 15). He suggests another name for this and similar conditions—'akrasia', from the Greek *a-kratos*, meaning 'without power', otherwise interpreted as 'lack of self-control' (*op. cit.*, 39).

We seek, through our acquisitiveness, to own the world, and "comport ourselves as invaders, conquerors, buying up the matter that means nothing to us, and trashing it when tired of it", says Mathews (2005, 36). When "the entire world is treated as raw resource, inert and unspeaking", the fundamental modus operandi of society becomes one of "callous insensitivity" and "we ourselves assume an attitude of bruteness and blindness", Mathews believes. "We must march through the world unseeing and unfeeling, turning away from the poetic order that unfurls about us, closing our ears to the inexhaustible eloquence of things . . ." (2005, 15). This attitude finds its expression in the image and language of the 'block', according to Mathews. "The block sees, hears, feels nothing"; it "stolidly refuses to acknowledge all that is fluid, living, expressive, responsive, subtle, multivalent, multilayered, interleaved, elusive *and* present, capable of self-veiling and self-revelation" (*ibid.*).

Mindful of the importance of longing and its power to awaken and purify the heart, Rumi stresses that not every hunger should be satisfied, nor should every desire be fulfilled. "Don't look for water, be thirsty", he says, welcoming longing as the heart's remembrance, its consciousness of separation. Longing is the primal pain of the soul separated from its source, says psychologist Vaughan-Lee, and leads into the arena of love, a love that transforms as it burns, emptying us of ourself until all that remains is our Beloved (2000). The love affair begins when by an act of grace the heart is 'turned' (*tawba*) and experiences a deep longing that seeks to be fulfilled. The heart's cry is heard by the Beloved who then begins to guide the lover home. Rumi tells us that the heart will not be satisfied by material offerings:

> Pleasure derives from hunger, not from new sweetmeats; hunger makes bread better than sugar. Why is it you are not bored with shopping, haggling and gossip? How is it that in sixty years you have not become sated? (*SPL*, 274)

Not only have people not become sated since the time of Rumi's writing, their insatiability has become cause for alarm. As Hannah Arendt says: "No object of the world will be safe from consumption and annihilation through consumption" (Arendt, 133). "The unhappier people profess to be, the more they head out to the malls," says Kellner (2007). We remember that when Viktor Frankl experienced deep contentment, he had lost all material possessions. And William James told us more than a century ago that "lives based on having are less free than lives based on either doing or being" (Wright, 79).

> One must have an eye which cuts through secondary causes and tears aside all veils; earnings and shops are but phantoms materialized upon the highway, so that the period of heedlessness may endure sometime longer (*SPL*, 21)

Rather than indulge the ego's petty passions, Rumi advises we should engage our intellect by discriminating between first and secondary causes. 'Intellect' and 'heart' are often used synonymously, heart being the domain of mystical knowledge (*marifa*), our shield against the follies of ego. Eight hundred years before the advent of the supermall and the diagnosis of compulsive shopping disorder, Rumi urged people not to act indiscriminately but to look within, warning them of the dangers of ignorance, greed and the chains of desire:

> Your properties are determined by that which predominates, oh self-worshipper! Close the ass's eye and open intellect's eye for the ego is like an ass, and avarice is its bridle. Sensuality is a chain: it drags people towards shops and fields (*SPL*, 88)

2.3 Home

To accommodate the mountains of stuff we buy we want bigger houses than previous generations dreamed of, and nowhere is there greater evidence of this than in burgeoning McMansion Land. The McMansion trend began in the late 1980s in the United States where the term was coined and has since spread to most parts of the western world (Farrelly, 2007). The McMansion or McPalace describes the biggest house on the smallest block for the lowest price. Mass-produced, it comes complete with triple garages, faux facades, spiral staircase, four or five bedrooms, multiple bathrooms, office, games room, home theatre, spa, imposing front door with vaulted entry, feature portico with columns, stencilled concrete driveway, small manicured lawn, rows of small matching plants, and feature letterbox. In affluent nations average household sizes are shrinking; in Australia they have decreased from 3.7 people in 1981 to 2.7 in 2001, yet average house sizes have increased 60 per cent since 1990, from 169 square metres to 270 square metres (*ibid.*). In Baulkham Hills

Shire in Sydney's north-west, the average new home size in 2002 was 418.5 square metres (*ibid.*).

The primary target of excessive consumption spending in western societies is generally the home, according to Hamilton (2005, 20), but this form's allure lies in its surface rather than in its obviously lacking depth. Architect Andrew Andersons points out that these oversized houses are totally environmentally unsustainable. They have no shady trees, and their clipped eaves and exposure to the afternoon's western sun means air-conditioners are a necessity. Washing-lines are regarded as unaesthetic so dryers churn away. Since there is usually inadequate public transport in these newer areas, there is heavy reliance on motor vehicles and roads become choked (Cited in Hawley, 2003). Large tracts of land are bulldozed and life-giving trees sacrificed to make room for developments whose little gardens—tamed, fenced, sometimes entirely paved, offer none of the benefits of natural spaces.

Mathews remembers how taking the route through Melbourne's Braeside always made her cry, its eponymous "brae" (creek) concreted into an open drain, older houses and paddocks obliterated, and in their place immense, featureless, concrete "blocks". It is a familiar scene, she says, which tells of the negation of architecture and the denial of beauty— "a final *reductio ad absurdum* of modern civilization" (Mathews, 2005, 6). Concrete, "brutal like an overwhelming destruction", a "base and quantitative sort of counterfeit stone", has invaded the whole world, says Schuon (1959, 124), and in it the spirit of life has been replaced by an anonymous and brutal heaviness.

Andersons refers to the anomalous situation of creating suburbia without the benefits of suburbia. "Houses are so close that you must keep windows shut, have tinted glass, or blinds and curtains drawn . . . to get visual and acoustic privacy" (Hawley, 2003). The traditional backyard has gone, along with its trees, vegetable patch, shed and space where children could let their bodies and imaginations run free and build tree houses, dig in the dirt and invent games. Instead, the McMansion boasts ornamental exteriors and children are entertained indoors by television and computer games, and driven to organised sport or trips to the mall as the superficially enhanced form ill accommodates meaning.

"Image has become more important than quality," says Graham Jahn, past president of the Royal Australian Institute of Architects (*ibid.*). McMansion Land has been referred to as the 'slums of the future', and Professor Jim McKnight, head of the school of psychology at the University of Western Sydney, and a licensed builder says, "we've seen built-in obsolescence in everything else, so why not in project houses?" Cracking walls, shoddy brickwork, short cuts in materials, design and finish, rattling hollow-core doors, second-rate carpentry, plasterwork and plumbing highlight this form's impermanence. McKnight indicates visual tricks that interior designers use to make the low ceilings look higher and interiors look bigger, such as dining room tables and chairs with shortened legs, short beds and tall, skinny vases and candles on long, thin pedestals (*ibid.*). 'The look' is all-important while functionality is compromised and artifice becomes a substitute for authenticity.

It is the old abandoned farm house of Barramunga, stripped of all adornment, on the brink of no longer being habitable as it gradually returns to the earth, whose authenticity provides Mathews with entry into "the inner presence, the nurturing, beautiful, poetic presence—of reality" (2005, 197). Its peaceful rhythm as things follow their natural course allows her to recover her "ground state, which is simply a steady state of cheerful tranquillity" (171). It is a contemplative state in which subsistence activities become daily rituals and create a sense of perfect order and structure in place of the disintegrating physical one. The stillness of the house and the simplicity of the life it offers invite attentiveness to reality's "inexhaustible text"—the profusion of flowers and trees, the legions of birds, animals wild and tame, hilltop vistas, forest depths, weather patterns and "celestial light" (173). Spiritual nourishment derived from her "sympathetic attention" produces, at times, "a kind of wand-struck astonished plenitude" (198). At Barramunga, Mathews finds herself "transported into a noumenal realm" and "called to direct encounter with (reality's) veiled presence" (*ibid*).

Similarly, poet John Ruskin, alive to the smallest features of the visual world and a firm believer that human construction should be in harmony with the natural environment, describes the sacred nature of home:

> It is the place of Peace; the shelter, not only from all injury, but from all terror, doubt and division. In so far as it is not this, it is not home; so far

as the anxieties of the outer life penetrate into it, and the inconsistently-minded, unknown, unloved or hostile society of the outer world is allowed by either husband or wife to cross the threshold, it ceases to be home . . . But so far as it is a sacred place, a vestal temple, a temple of the hearth . . . and roof and fire are types only of a nobler shade and light,—shade as of the rock in a weary land, light as of the Pharos in the stormy sea;—so far it vindicates the name, and fulfils the praise of Home (158-159)

The contrast between this mystical 'vestal temple' with its palpable divine presence and the modern home, infused with 'terror, doubt and division', emanating mainly from the centrepiece, the ubiquitous entertainment centre, could not be more stark. 'Anxieties of the outer life' have been welcomed into the modern home, where computer and ever larger television screens give life to images as they replace reality. The heart of the home is no sacred place and family time not one of meaningful sharing (Hamilton, 2005; Olfman, 2005), but rather an individualistic experience in which participants are outwardly engaged but oblivious of those nearest to them. Home is less of a sanctuary where the spirit dwells than an obligatory pit stop before we hit the road again.

Whereas lights in the modern home, mall and city often burn wastefully, the light radiating from Ruskin's house is a guiding light that leads to a place of safety. It burns purposefully and is, Ruskin implies, a divine light. Similarly, in the shimmering light of the hearth fire, to whose living presence Mathews is drawn after outings, "as to the warm and comforting lap of a mother", she glimpses the very "core of creation" (2005, 176). In the black of night, she says, "it feels right" in her "little lighted ship, becalmed though derelict, in space" (*ibid.*) From a mystical perspective, light has always had a divine aspect; the word divine has its origin in the Sanskrit word *deva*, the root of which means light. In the *Allegory of the Cave* as told in Plato's *Republic* the prisoners ascend from the darkness of the cave, the limited world of sight, towards the universal Light, the world of knowledge, and in the *Dhammapada* Buddha speaks of the lamp that dispels deep darkness (Mascaro, 146). In the Christian Bible we read in the Gospel according to St. John: "In Him was life; and the life was the light of men. And the light shineth in darkness; and the darkness comprehended it not (I, 4-5). Mystics throughout the ages have understood the divine to be the Eternal Light. Hesychasm, a mystical tradition of the

Eastern Orthodox Christian Church, is particularly explicit in this regard. Symeon, a Hesychast saint who lived a thousand years ago, writes:

> God is light, a light infinite and incomprehensible . . . one single light . . . simple, non-composite, timeless, eternal . . . The light is life. The light is immortality. The light is the source of life . . . the door of the kingdom of heaven. The light is the very kingdom itself. But, Oh, what intoxication of light, Oh, what movements of fire! Oh, what swirlings of the flame in me . . . coming from You and Your glory! . . . You granted me to see the light of Your countenance, that is unbearable to all. . . . You appeared as light, illuminating me completely from Your total light (Cited in D'Adamo, 2004)

Light burning brightly in areas where there is no activity and the continuous flickering light of idle appliances is a powerful symbol of irreverence. At a more fundamental level it represents a rejection of the natural ordering of time—the refusal to be restricted by the limiting rhythm of creation (Northcott, 2007). Our perceived right to freedom from such natural restrictions is indicative of the imperial nature of our engagement with the world. The form of light has been reduced to nothing more than a commodity, vital yet disposable and replaceable, devoid of intrinsic meaning. At a time of rampant materialism, light is perhaps the most recognisable sign of a point of sale rather than the mysterious symbol of Being.

Though bathed in light the mall is designed to make visitors feel "needy, inadequate and dreamily disoriented" since the worse they feel, the more they buy (Farrelly, 150). "The place is designed as a disconnect," says Farrelly, "separating you from your reality and from your higher, warmer self" (151). Standish refers to deliberate decentering of spaces in an attempt to direct attention towards the periphery as a typical feature of the postmodern age. The disorientation it causes, he says, compels people who use these spaces to seek authoritative information telling them where to go (Standish, 1995). Postmodern architecture embraces principles of complexity and contradiction rather than of unity, harmony and purity of form; it is at times rigid, monotonous and sterile, and its effect has been described as vertiginous (Jameson, 1991).

Similarly, Hawley comments on the feeling of disconnectedness experienced on entering a McMansion: "Cosiness is out and a lot of it feels like dead space", she says. Farrelly refers to architecture as "the art of cladding the human spirit" (2007, 97). What then do our homes and public spaces reveal about the human spirit that they house? Disconnectedness, or separation, the destruction of traditional ties, is the antithesis of Sufi aims—restoring unity; re-investing form with meaning. Our buildings are bodies without hearts and the human spirit within them like birds with one wing, never knowing the freedom of flight. Cosiness in a home is the warmth and heartbeat of the body—form alive with meaning, *Batin* within *Zahir*. Cosiness is an attribute of interior rather than exterior, of heart rather than of appearance. Rumi reminds us that interior is all-important and that exterior exists only to serve it. He praises the 'People of the Heart' and admonishes the form worshippers who are forgetful of meaning—the 'people of clay':

> Shame on the world's inhabitants, shame! Look at these ignorant fools in their fine exterior, but inwardly—God does not inhabit the house! (*SPL*, 147)
> "Blubber-rich but meaning-poor" is Farrelly's summation of the excess apparent at so many levels, where the meaning we crave is lacking. With reference to the central intuition of "most mystical traditions, from Sufism to Jung to the Aboriginal Dreaming", she urges her readers to "grasp the essential connectedness of everything, and re-invest in (their) source of meaning, or die" (2007, 11).

Unlike the People of the Heart, the 'people of clay' are ignorant, says Rumi:

> The ass does not smooth out his place in order to stay: he knows this is no place to pass his life. Your sense perception is less than that of an ass, for your heart has not jumped up out of this mud. You interpret this mud as a special dispensation since you do not want to detach your heart from it (*SPL*, 121)

2.4 Car

Regarded alternately as necessity or luxury, the car has almost become an alter ego we invest in because it makes a statement about how we would like to be and how we would like others to see us. The sense of identity thus derived, however, is completely lacking in authenticity. People who buy large 4WDs, for example, have been found, by some researchers, to be "insecure and vain . . . nervous about their marriages and uncomfortable about parenthood . . . self-centered and self-absorbed, with little interest in their neighbors and communities". They "tend to like fine restaurants a lot more than off-road driving . . ." according to Hamilton

(2005, 45), citing Keith Bradsher (*High and Mighty SUVs*, 2002), yet the vehicles they select might symbolise quality family time, confidence and a spirit of adventure, or like the McMansion, the more-is-better approach to consumerism.

Promising freedom and providing convenience, comfort and status to millions, motor vehicles are responsible for 20–22 per cent of greenhouse gas emissions in the United States and the United Kingdom (Northcott, 2007), but this figure does not take into account the energy involved or resources consumed in manufacturing, maintaining, selling and scrapping vehicles or in constructing roads, garages and parking facilities to accommodate them. Encapsulated within our own personalised space, we move through the landscape at the speed of our choice, in temperatures that we control, to the sounds and scents we select to make our experience more pleasurable, and experience an illusion of freedom and control over our increasingly polluted, congested physical environment. Alienated from natural rhythms, removed from the landscape through which we move effortlessly and swiftly, we become oblivious of the world as it flashes past, and oblivious of the fact that we are causing harm.

On the other hand, walking through the landscape establishes a bond between people and earth that rapid mechanical journeys cannot replicate. The artificial sense of autonomy and control that boosts the driver is in stark contrast with the wanderer's spirit of encounter and openness to the gifts and trials that each step brings. Exposure to the regular rhythm of nature, the harmonious rhythm of *sattva*, is beneficial to health by regularising the rhythm of stress, *rajas*, and by enhancing awareness. Already in the nineteenth century Ruskin was distressed by the speed at which we viewed the world, overlooking simplicity, subtlety and detail: ". . .the really precious things are thought and sight, not pace", he says. "It does a bullet no good to go fast; and a man, if he be truly a man, no harm to go slow; for his glory is not at all in going, but in being" (*The Moral of Landscape*, in *Modern Painters*, from *The Works of John Ruskin*, Cook & Wedderburn (Eds.), V, 381). Noticing the "bumps and curves of actual things, the particularity of the actual ground on which we stand", we might begin to view the world less as mere scenery to be transformed than as "a 'spirit thing' with ends and meanings of its own which it can in principle communicate to us and in which we can participate" (Mathews, 2005, 199-200).

Walking, alone, at Barramunga, Mathews is acutely aware of life all around, of poetics blossoming in her footsteps (2005, 170). "It's all to do with attentiveness", she says, "with the way everything awakens under the gentle beam of one's sympathetic attention" (*op. cit.*, 169). The English Romantics, and in particular William and Dorothy Wordsworth, had already popularised the idea of walking in the western literary imagination, taking it from a mode of transport to a way of being in the world (Wallace, 1993), but in other cultures the tradition goes much further back. Fundamental to them all, however, are the concepts of attentiveness and humility, and harmony derived from regularising one's rhythm, transforming the act of walking into spiritual practice or meditative activity, which is perhaps why walking has always been an important part of pilgrimage.

Satish Kumar, for example, explains how Tibetan Buddhists, when going on pilgrimage, prostrate themselves every inch of the way. "They start by standing, their hands held in prayer, then they kneel and, bowing down, lie facing the earth and touching her with their forehead in humility. Then they make a mark on the ground with their nose, stand up and walk to the spot marked by the nose (to ensure that they do not miss a fraction of the path). Then they stand and repeat the process, and this they do all the way to the temple, which might be one hundred miles away" (*No Destination*, 1992, 176, cited in Mathews, 2005, 220). In similar vein, on his peace walk from India, his own sense of awareness heightened, Kumar awakens to the world: "In wandering I felt a sense of union with the whole sky, the infinite earth and sea. I felt myself a part of the cosmic existence. It was as if by walking I was making love to the earth itself. Wandering was my path, my true self, my true being. It released my soul-force; it brought me in relation with everything else" (*op. cit.*, 221).

For thirteen hundred years the vast majority of Muslims made the *hajj*, the pilgrimage to Mecca, on foot (Murata & Chittick, 1994). It was not a matter of taking a hurried trip or even an extended vacation; it was a life-changing encounter with reality to which years of thought needed to be given. The difficulty of the journey meant that they had to assume they might never return, and make all the necessary preparations for that eventuality. The *hajj* was a move from preoccupation with externality and trivia to occupation with God; return, if it occurred, was a rebirth (*ibid.*). Today the *hajj* is accomplished much more easily, and perhaps its benefits are diminished accordingly, but the heart of the holy site, the Ka'ba, is still circumambulated in contemplative manner, symbolising the traveller's journey from the periphery to the centre of his being.

For the Sufi, this journey to the centre is the most important 'walk'— from *sura* to *mana*, a walk which requires no displacement, therefore Rumi advises "Keep walking though there's no place to get to; don't try to see through the distances . . . move within" (tr. Barks, 1995, 27). This does not, of course, imply that Rumi considered the *hajj* of little importance, having himself accomplished it under the most difficult circumstances (Arberry, 1961), but simply that meaning must always prevail. The search for meaning takes us on a journey inwards, says Hamilton, from the frenetic striving of the world on the surface to the centre, the noumenal world, which is a place of peace (2008, 242).

2.5 Food

Blubber most aptly describes the quantity and quality of food consumed throughout the western world. Some blubber protects and ensures survival in times of need, but in a culture characterised by excess rather than scarcity, blubber is more likely to compromise health than to preserve life. We know that the incidence of obesity has increased to epidemic proportions. "Without remorse", writes Berry, "with less and less interest in the disciplines of thrift and conservation . . . we are eating thoughtlessly, as no other entire society ever has been able to do" (1977, 81). Excessive consumption and abundant supply have seen obesity rates among American adults double and the number of overweight adolescents triple. Currently, two-thirds of American adults are overweight or obese and recent population surveys suggest that these trends are set to continue despite numerous public health efforts to reverse them (Morris, M *et al*, 2008). According to Hamilton, Australia also has an 'obesogenic' environment, that is, a social environment that promotes and facilitates obesity (2005, 118). "The insidious, creeping pandemic of obesity is now engulfing the entire world, led by affluent Western nations," claimed Professor Paul Zimmet, director of Monash University's International Diabetes Institute in September 2006 (Cited in Farrelly, 103).

Shut your lips to food and drink, hurry to the table of heaven!

urges Rumi (*SPL*, 211), reminding us of the importance of spiritual sustenance. Stripping the form of its meaning carries a hefty price. Obesity is associated with an increased risk of coronary heart disease, stroke, hypertension, type 2 diabetes and certain cancers (Kuchler and Bellenger 2002; Pi-Sunyer 1993, Cited in Morris *et al*, 2008). In the US, direct medical and lost productivity costs attributable to obesity were estimated at $117 billion in 2000 (*ibid.*). Obesity related chronic disease is no longer an adult-only public health concern. Twenty years ago, 5% of American children were overweight. Today, 31% are overweight or are at risk of becoming overweight and their rates of developing type 2 diabetes continue to rise, thereby placing them at risk of becoming the first generation to have a shorter life expectancy than their parents (Ebbeling, Pawlack, and Ludwig 2002; Lemonick 2004, Cited in Morris *et al*, 2008). This trend is reflected throughout the western world. According to a regionally representative cross-sectional survey of 4 to 12 year olds from regional Victoria, Australia, 2003 to 2004, 19.3% were overweight and 7.6% obese (Sanigorski, *et al*, 2007). According to Sanigorski *et al*, the prevalence of obesity is increasing in Australian children by about one percentage point per year, which equates to approximately 40,000 more overweight children each year as long as the current trend persists.

Morris *et al*, citing Drewnowski and Darmon, 2005, note that American consumer food choices are driven primarily by taste, cost and convenience. Data from the National Health and Nutrition Examination Survey indicate that nutrient poor food choices high in added fat and sugars are prevalent in the American diet. On average sweets, desserts, soft drinks and alcoholic beverages account for 25% of all calories consumed (Morris, M *et al*, 2008). Food related decisions were found to be based on the following options: convenience, what makes the children happy and cost-effectiveness. Food quality, nutritional value and production methods were given less, and in many cases, no consideration. The authors suggest that to counter this emotional preference, some alternative emotional satisfaction should be provided.

Junk food, as the name implies, contains not only ingredients whose nutritional value is questionable, but also a raft of additives that have no nutritional value whatsoever as well as several that are quite harmful. Imitating nature to recreate an artificial strawberry flavour of the kind that might be found in strawberry milkshake, for example, involves the scientific blending of the following substances that are not in any way related to real strawberries: amyl acetate, amyl butyrate, amyl valerate, anethol, anisyl formate, benzyl acetate, benzyl isobutyrate, butyric acid, cinnamyl isobutyrate, cinnamyl valerate, cognac essential oil, diacetyl, dipropyl ketone, ethyl butyrate, ethyl cinnamate, ethyl heptanoate, ethyl heptylate, ethyl lactate, ethyl methylphenylglycidate, ethyl nitrate, ethyl propionate, ethyl valerate, heliotropin, hydroxyphrenyl- 2-butanone (10% solution in alcohol), ionone, isobutyl anthranilate, isobutyl butyrate, lemon essential oil, maltol, 4-methylacetophenone, methyl anthranilate, methyl benzoate, methyl cinnamate, methyl heptine carbonate, methyl naphthyl ketone, methyl salicylate, mint essential oil, neroli essential oil, nerolin, neryl isobutyrate, orris butter, phenethyl alcohol, rose, rum ether, undecalactone, vanillin and solvent (Rice, 2007). Ruth Winter lists 12,000 artificial ingredients in the sixth edition of her *Consumer's Dictionary of Additives* (2006); they impact negatively on health but still find their way into products readily available on supermarket shelves.

The industrial food supply chain that gives rise to processed foods has drastically changed our culture's eating habits, as prevailing nutritional orthodoxies are challenged and replaced with the latest scientifically-researched dietary wisdoms. In the process, a simple, nourishment-based culture of eating fresh, locally grown, preservative-free food has been superseded by a fad-culture of immediate gratification based on convenience and preference. Charting the absurdity of ancient and venerable staples such as bread, milk, flour, butter, cheese, cream and red meat abruptly disappearing from the American dinner table, only to be replaced by complex processed ones, Michael Pollan argues that as a culture we seem to have arrived at a place where whatever native wisdom we may once have possessed about eating has been replaced by confusion and anxiety (Pollan, 2005). He claims we seem to have lost the most elemental awareness of knowing what to eat and require experts to direct us in this regard. Eating industrially, says Pollen, requires an almost heroic act of not-knowing. Never before have there been so many diet books, magazine features and scientific studies telling us what to eat. We rely on food pyramids, lists of ingredients and dictionaries of additives to explain the mysterious numbers and letters, and the Heart Foundation's Tick of Approval to guide us through what has become the complexity of eating. Processed foods of questionable merit are able to make bold health claims simply because the companies manufacturing them can afford the high cost of achieving accreditation (*ibid.*), while the 'silent foods' that have come direct from the grower sit quietly on the shelf making no claims as to their benefits.

Yet the most unassuming of these tell fascinating stories to those who pay heed, as Selim Mutlu discovered. The humble carrot, for instance, is not naturally uniform in shape and colour, but as diverse as green, red, white and even purple, each differing in shape, and while its benefits to eyesight are well known, its scientifically established role in treating cancerous tumours, pneumonia and emphysema is generally unknown. As Mutlu points out, its latent benefits, too numerous to enumerate, make it an indispensable "close friend", to which there is much more than meets the eye. "The earth is a mighty pharmacy which is orderly fashioned (sic.) with numerous therapeutic qualities in the form of vegetables and herbs spread out in abundance", says Mutlu with reference to the Qur'anic verse: "Who is it that provides for you from heaven and earth?" (Mutlu, 2010).

In industrial food production processes Mathews sees another form of 'block logic', materially imposed, assuring the absence of dialogue (2005, 18). "Land partitioned into blocks loses the conversation of its parts" (*ibid.*), just as food produced by industrial methods establishes no communicative bond between grower, consumer and the earth, monocultural mass production brusquely terminating reciprocal intimacies. Production of food, like other forms of mass production, is now "strictly functional and contractual in form, rendered by anyone for anyone in exchange for cash" (*op. cit.*, 19).

Even the form of processed food we deem suitable for our pets is 'enhanced' by the addition of colourants, artificial flavours and stabilisers. Manufactured "'needs' yet to be satisfied in the pet product industry may be as limitless as humans' 'needs'", says Hamilton (2005, 30). Giant pet food manufacturers with the resources to ensure the best possible fare for our canine and feline dependents assure us of their products' goodness, but product labels tell a different story, as does veterinarian Dr Tom Lonsdale, who refers to the so-called wet and dry 'quality' pet foods as "junk food . . . laden with synthetic colourants, preservatives and a raft of other chemical additives, none with any nutritive value and all toxic to varying degrees" (Lonsdale, 2007). These chemicals depress animal immune systems and support toxin-producing bacteria in their bowels, he says.

It is not just the questionable form of what many people are eating, but the quantity consumed that is cause for concern. Since the 1970s portion sizes have continued to increase, particularly at fast food and sit-down restaurants where over half of all meals are consumed today (Rolls 2003, Neilsen and Popkin 2003, Cited in Morris *et al*, 2008). Expansive portions eaten out and at home have also contributed to the fact that between 1985–2000, average daily caloric intakes have increased by 300 kcal (Putnam, Allshouse and Kantor 2002, *ibid.*), and since the 1960s they have increased by 600 kcal (*ibid.*).

'Overeating', according to Morris *et al*, is used for comfort in the face of a poor self-image. At the other end of the consumption spectrum are equally severe eating disorders also associated with low self-esteem such as bulimia and anorexia which further exemplify our increasingly unnatural relationship with food. Dieting, bingeing and purging represent a deliberate rejection of food's gift of life in an attempt to gain a sense of control of one's life (Nash, 1999). Cultural pressures that glorify the 'perfect body' and norms that attribute value on the basis of physical appearance are just some of the social factors contributing to the increasing number of girls in particular who succumb to these disorders (*ibid.*).

Food, in other words, becomes a substitute for meaning. Meaningless form feeds the ego's sensual desires and contributes to separation from the Beloved. The practice of fasting (*sawm*) is intended to reduce absolute dependence on these desires and impulses by developing the self-control that is needed to maintain a state of harmony (Özalp, 2008). As Yüksel Aslandoğan explains, fasting, the third 'pillar' (religious duty in Islam), has many dimensions—behavioral, religious, social and spiritual (2008).

> Display the herbs and the bones! Display the food of the spirit and the food of the ego. If he seeks the food of the ego, he is defective, but if he seeks the food of the spirit, he is a chief. If he serves the body, he is an ass, but if he enters the ocean of the spirit, he will find a pearl. (Rumi, *SPL*, 101)

'Material man' is material in his outlook and pursues earthly gains (I, 98). Having mundane desires, he enjoys his food and drink, bodily comfort, momentary pleasures and passing joys, but is the slave of his passions. He is susceptible to depression and despair, though he may not be aware of their cause. "One might say that he lives to eat" (*ibid.*).

Form must become meaningful if we are to have a healthy relationship with it, but before that can happen, Rumi tells us, hunger for food must be transformed into hunger for the Beloved:

> Separation from Thee destroys me! Thy image has become my food: For my heart has gained a stomach, full of insatiable hunger for Thee . . . Whether asleep or awake, I am thirsty for that Friend . . . (*SPL*, 260)

He advises us to nourish ourselves with 'heavenly foods' and cautions against satisfying the senses alone in order to experience greater joy than form devoid of meaning can provide:

> Pollute not your lips by kissing every mouth and eating every food! Then the Beloved's lips will make them drunk and feed them sugar . . . Take heed! Keep your stomach empty, for He has set for you a table. If a dog has eaten its fill, it will not catch any game, for the running and racing of aspiration derive from hunger's fire. (*SPL*, 336-337)

Form provides capacity for meaning. Harmony cannot ensue unless their unity is restored; disconnectedness and anguish derive from separation. Through our food we are most directly connected to the earth and its inhabitants—to soil, sun, rain, grower, harvester, vendor and cook, and as connections are established, truths are revealed. Practices like Buddhist meal ceremonies (*Orioki*) that focus on living simply and sustainably are consistent with the Sufi ethos of mindfulness and the principle of unity (*tawhid*), and serve to renew connections. Maggie Gluek of the Zen Buddhist / Eco-ascetic retreat centre, Kodoji, west of Sydney, describes the Orioki meal: "Absolutely every morsel is important and nothing must be wasted . . . the meal ceremony is a particularly beautiful and somewhat intricate ritual, which encourages us to be mindful of our bowls; we unwrap the bowls which are wrapped in cloth, and we arrange them in a certain way, we put our spoon in a particular place, the meal is served in a certain order, and then at the end, we're given tea and we clean our bowls one by one, using the tea, drinking it as we go along, and it is actually quite tasty. It's not washing-up water that's been contaminated by detergent, and then we leave a little bit of this water in the bowl and that's put into a communal bowl which is taken outside and offered to hungry ghosts: suffering beings in other worlds, and in fact up here it's eaten by wombats and kangaroos and birds. So none of it is wasted" (Gluek, *Eco Asceticism*, 2009).

Similarly, in the stillness and simplicity of Barramunga mundane activities, such as meal preparation, are transformed into panpsychist praxes, since food, in the panpsychist and Sufi sense, is, in the first instance, for the heart—nourishment with calm and peace, feeding not only physical but more subtle needs. Eating is a ritual conducted with care and consideration for how the food came to be, how it came to us and how the life contained within it continues through us. When we eat we participate in the flow of creation, with the dynamic of life as it comes from the source into the outer world of forms, and then returns to its origins. When our life ceases to be cut off from its origin, it is nourished from within and then, as Vaughan-Lee says, we feel the primal joy of life lived from the source (2000).

2.6 Church

The association of the bread and wine shared during Holy Communion with the flesh and blood of Christ does not extend beyond church walls. It was the differentiation between sacred and secular itself that was the first phase in the decay of religion, concludes Charles Taylor in *A Secular Age* (2007).

Despite its shortcomings however, the church was traditionally the spiritual centre and dwelling-place of the Mystery, but like other forms, the form of the modern church has undergone a transformation in the name of populism (Farrelly, 71). The modern church, now bigger than ever before, has replaced the mysterious with the mundane and the symbolic with ordinariness. Form has been stripped of meaning as sacred music, liturgy and altar make way for stage, big band, concert lighting and dry ice (Hillsong Church). The screen is the new stained-glass window and the in-nave coffee table has replaced the communion table (Sydney's St Andrew's Anglican Cathedral) as the temple-of-God has become the house-of-the-people (Farrelly, 2007). Architecture, according to A. K. Coomaraswamy, is derived from the primordial altar, but little sign remains of its sacred foundations and rich symbolism; architecture's celestial origins as described in the ancient Vedas are no longer apparent, not even in modern church design (Coomaraswamy, 1969).

Farrelly comments as follows on the changes to the traditional cruciform church plan:

> (The plan) can be read as a symbolic Corpus Christi, making the altar rail, at the crossing or shoulders, a threshold not only between body and head but also between this world and the next; between humanity and God. But the implied distancing and subordination (of humans to God) is no popularity cinch. So the new church exchanges vertical for horizontal, gloaming for daylight, otherworld for world; relationship with God, perhaps, for a 'community of relationships, where people feel at home and welcomed'. Church, it seems, may these days be awesome, but not awe-full (72).

Like its natural equivalent the tree, the steeple was designed to conduct the eye and the soul to God, but is conspicuously absent from the flatter structures of the new church. In Hillsong Church's 3500-seat auditorium at Baulkham Hills, a phenomenal 12000 people attend the charismatic 'prosperity preaching' services each weekend (*op. cit.*, 70). The wants and needs of the body, if not the soul, are well catered for as materialism thrives in the church.

Biblical literalism has become increasingly important, but in the process of de-mystification, meaning is diminished as the text is repeatedly revised, modernised and literalised. Many events described in the Bible, when taken literally, invite incredulity. John 6: 16-21 for example, describes Jesus walking on water. When symbolism is restored to the text, it becomes meaningful. Water is the essence of life, and if we interpret the text as Jesus rising above the troubled waters of life, we understand that he mastered life by transcending it rather than becoming engulfed by it. Yet taken literally, such descriptions defy logic and subject a text rich with symbolism to scientific scrutiny, as was the case with this particular passage. On 5 April 2006 the BBC News reported the 'findings' of Professor Doron Nof, an oceanographer from Florida State University, who insisted his research pointed to a scientific rather than miraculous explanation. His study found that "Jesus may not have walked on water as the Bible claims but rather skated on ice formed through a freak cold spell" that may have occurred in what is now northern Israel from 1 500 to 2 600 years ago. (*Did Jesus walk on water - or ice?*)

The Christian church year itself is reduced to form without meaning when Easter is no more than a chocolate-feast and Christmas the biggest commercial opportunity of the year. The four weeks of Advent that traditionally represented a time of preparation to celebrate the birth of Christ serve as little more than a prelude to the greatest shopping weekend of the year. Christmas itself is nothing more than a religion-sanctioned occasion for extravagant spending when divested of meaning. We have invested Santa with omniscience, omnipotence and omnipresence as he alone knows what children want, is able to make their wishes come true and deliver their gifts on time. Christmas has become a time often marred by loneliness and disappointment when it does not deliver the happiness popular hype promises. Stripped of its mystery, Christmas becomes mundane and meaningless, as reflected by the politically correct season's greeting—Happy Holidays! and a plethora of popular Christmas songs without a hint of mystery trumpeted throughout shopping malls in order to generate greater profits, according to advertising's behaviour modification specialists, who claim that the strains of *Joy to the World* and *Silent Night, Holy Night* produce the best results of all (author unknown, *Alternatives for Simple Living*, 2007).

Depleted of what Nasr terms *scientia sacra* or sacred knowledge (see Chapter 4), contemporary religious forms are essentially meaningless (Nasr, 1981). To support this perspective, he draws on Sufi René Guénon's criticism of the modern world, particularly as it is expressed in his *Crisis of the Modern World* (1927), as well as the thought of perennialists A. K. Coomaraswamy (1877–1947), and Frithjof Schuon (1907–1998) which seeks to revive the sacred character in a world intent on its denial. Similarly, Tacey believes that the fundamental problem from which the church suffers at this time is an essential lack of faith in the reality of spirit, and that the overwhelming imperative is to "return religion to mystery and restore its claims to the mysterious depths in our own lives". Here, the need for proof fades away and the truth status of religion is restored to its rightful place (2000, 32).

Within the "stripped back" version of Christianity, Mathews recalls, like so many of her generation, she "found emptiness at the core" (2003, 2); the Mystery, of which she was so acutely aware, had been banished from the centre of her church.

2.7 Language

> The root of all things is speech and words. . . . The wise man sees speech
> as grand—speech came from heaven, it is not something paltry. (Rumi,
> *SPL*, 270)

Language as expression of thought and feeling refers to the outward
(*Zahir*) as opposed to the universe's own expression (*Batin*). As Wheeler
explains, articulate language is a form, more recently evolved, "in which
the semiosis that is apparent in all life achieves a new, and more complex,
level of articulation" (2006, 19). Language provides capacity and gives
sanctuary, like a shell safeguarding a precious kernel hidden below its surface. Therefore Rumi says: "The nutshell makes a sound when it is cracked,
but where is the voice of the kernel and the oil? It has a voice, but not in
the ear's perception; its voice is hidden in the ear of intoxication" (cited in
Ernst, 2009). If language is 'the voice of the kernel', or in the words of
Heidegger, "spoken purely" as is the case in inspired poetry, which is the
"work of the heart" (Heidegger, 1971, 138), its purpose is to reveal what
is concealed; more often than not, it acts as a veil, further obscuring the
already-concealed meaning. Of its diverse and contradictory functions,
Aahlia Khan writes: "... language has an ambivalent character; it can equally disclose and hide, construct and destroy, inspire and demoralize, liberate
and imprison, clarify and distort, heal and hurt". Sufi literature, she
believes, illustrates the paradox of the inadequacy of words to convey the
experience of the heart, and on the other hand the power of words and our
need for them. Sufi poets insist that their experience is ineffable, yet make
abundant use of them to give form to it (Khan, 2009).

When one does not "have an eye which cuts through secondary
causes and tears aside all veils", forms conceal meaning. Rumi urges us
not to be form-worshippers but to look for meaning instead:

> Whoever looks upon the First Cause has become a light which discerns
> Meaning. (. . .) the profit of every outward thing lies hidden in the inward,
> like the benefits within medicine. (*SPL*, 21)

Understanding the illusion of the form-meaning dichotomy of language has never been as relevant as at this time when sounds and letters
have become the principal feature of life and not a waking moment passes
that we are not subjected to the messages they relentlessly convey. Almost

four decades ago Heidegger wrote of "an unbridled talking, writing and broadcasting of spoken words raging round the earth" (1971, 215) and since the time of his writing, technology has spawned an unprecedented explosion of sounds and letters, of the kind he had not envisaged.

In 1970 Alvin Toffler coined the term 'information overload' in his book *Future Shock*, in which he describes its deleterious effect on people in general and on the mind in particular, since a seemingly infinite stream of information, much of it conflicting, demands attention. People struggle to keep up with the never-ending flow of language they feel compelled to access, filtering out unsolicited content only after having taken note of it. The sheer volume of information and misinformation in the form of language to which people are exposed causes confusion, stress and anxiety. The World Wide Web, the media, the entertainment industry, the world of commerce, education and inter-personal relationships all depend on language. More than ever we are bombarded with words, messages and images.

Attaching too much importance to them compromises the quality of life. Martin Wainwright (2005) argues that exposing individuals to information overload results in severely impaired IQ scores. The relentless influx of messages received by modern workers 'is a greater threat to IQ and concentration than taking cannabis', he claims. The constant interruptions faced by people in the workplace reduce productivity and leave people feeling stressed, tired and lethargic, says Wainwright. Even at leisure we remain 'on call'. Psychologist Glenn Wilson claims that the compulsion to keep 'switched on' has become an obsession and that people are in danger of being caught up in a 24-hour 'always on' mindset (cited in Wainwright, 2005). Words multiply since "the nature of creation is the doubling of one" (II, 51). "Substance has been composed in vacuum and has developed in it . . ." (XI, 60).

2.8 Language that Distorts

In the interpretation of the divine tongue, the universe's own authentic language, as perceived by prophets, mystics and sages, subtle ideas materialised into the gross terms of articulate language. "Nothing but duality enters speech's playing-field", warns Rumi (*SPL*, 275). Words remain but "meanings fly away" (276). We know that the chameleon-like form of language invites manipulation and see examples of it everywhere—the media present a particular perspective to serve their purpose and silver-tongued politicians promise peace and prosperity in exchange for a mandate. George Orwell claims that "all political language is designed to make lies sound truthful and murder respectable and to give an appearance of solidity to pure wind" (Orwell, 1945). Self-styled advisors capitalise on ignorance to sell their counsel and marketers persuade consumers to buy products they do not need. Kelley describes the language of the 'nu-marketing' paradigm as predicated on controversy, changeability, customer disorientation, intransigence, belligerence and restlessness (Kelley, 2007). Such language is, according to Kelley, the future of marketing.

According to Hamilton, the entire marketing industry is devoted to developing ways of "increasing consumers' insecurity, vulnerability and obsessiveness" (2005, 36). "Sometimes advertisers try to make us laugh or make us think, but mostly they make us feel deprived, inadequate or anxious. It is axiomatic that they make us feel bad in a way that can be cured by possession of the product they advertise" (2005, 37). Advertising does more than attempt to persuade us of the benefits of any given product, offering narrow and specific messages. Instead, says Hamilton, advertising sells a worldview, that happiness can be bought (*op. cit.*, 40). Because truth is eclipsed when meaning is overlooked, Rumi asks to be saved "from words that do not come from the heart but are just uttered by mouths" (Cited in Can, 2005, 202).

The urge to persuade is powerful and every interaction presents an opportunity to advance the speaker's cause. Persuasive language therefore takes many forms. The language of advertising is the most common of these and its distinctive features such as succinctness, largely the result of spatial constraints and the need for impact, make it easier to recognise than other forms. Words are used to manipulate the audience into perceiving a need, creating awareness of a deficiency, shaping self-esteem, exploiting anxiety and awakening desire. Thus Rumi says:

> The only profit of speech is that it may cause you to seek and incite your desire. The goal is not realized through speech (*SPL*, 272)

Terminology is often ambiguous, information pertaining to origin, content, production conditions, quality and health usually deficient and labelling practices misleading, leaving consumers confused and, in many instances, deceived. The wording on the 'Odwalla Juice' label, for example, states proudly: "Three men and a juicer" but fails to include that the company is owned by international giant—Coca-Cola (Cliath, 2007). The appearance of traditional values is used to sell a thoroughly modern product. The wording conjures up bucolic scenes of three men—brothers or mates maybe, united by their commitment to an honest product, lovingly extracting honey-sweet juice, uncontaminated by additives, from sun-ripened oranges in bounteous orchards. The image bears little resemblance to the truth.

Scientific and technical jargon is often used in advertising to impress and confound consumers who mostly have little understanding of its meaning and consequently believe the products possess superior qualities than they really do. The cosmetic industry is particularly partial to this ploy, and many of its claims are hyperbolic and lack scientific evidence to back them up, according to Lesley Regan, Professor of reproductive biology at St Mary's, London (2007). Estée Lauder, for example, invites the over-forties to "enter the age-defying world of Re-Nutriv", promising "a transcending experience" where "leading-edge technology" will bring about "a flawless, simply exquisite look". "Hydrating lotions, luxuriously silky, toning and flecked with elemental gold" rejuvenate and beautify, while "Advanced Night Repair, based on solid, scientific findings, builds a rich reserve of anti-oxidants and lipids to help replenish skin's natural protectants and protects the future by neutralizing up to 90% of environmentally generated free radicals". In addition, 'serums' (blood plasma?) "deliver high levels of long-proven hyaluronic acid" (Mayo Clinic report, 2006), which explains their effectiveness. Or does it? Words are imposters, giving dreams the form of reality. Such language does not take responsibility or stand by its words.

Bruthiaux refers to this lack of clarity created by the language of advertising as a "communicative fog" and describes it as "vacuous", "artificial" and "competitive" (2000, 305). An advertisement for salad dressing, for example, is spiced up by a heavy dose of 'feel-good' language ('superb', 'unique', 'fabulous'). "These claims border on the absurd", he says. A common product is made to appear uncommonly desirable and consumers are manipulated into believing that some of its uniqueness might rub off on them. According to Bruthiaux, "the need for writers to manipulate readers' self-image overrides the need to present content explicitly" (*ibid*.).

If content is not presented explicitly, it is implicit or concealed. Such language conceals truth. The consumer is duped by form; both by the form of the product and by the form of the words used to sell it. Rumi says:

> Man is hidden beneath his tongue. The tongue is a curtain before the spirit's courtyard. When a wind lifts up the veil, we observe the secret of the house's courtyard—whether there are pearls within or wheat, or a treasure of gold, or all is snakes and scorpions . . .
> Although in one respect speech removes veils, in ten respects it covers and conceals (*SPL*, 269)

As long as we are mindful of the axiom, *caveat emptor*, we should not be deceived by the language of advertising since we might expect a person trying to sell something to use all his or her persuasive powers to present it in as favourable a light as possible, even if this means distorting the truth or withholding information. However, the inclination to persuade is not limited to formal advertising. Bruthiaux, citing Dessalles (1998), makes the point that from an evolutionary perspective language as a whole may be considered as an "advertising device", since the successful manipulation of complex linguistic structures is bound up with the successful manipulation of complex social relationships, hence with status. Individual language users can thus be seen as advertisers, competing with one another in eloquence and persuasive skill in order to draw attention to themselves, to obtain status from their audience, and to reflect some of that status on to those who choose to associate with them.

This understanding, from sociobiology, of the fundamentally competitive nature of human interaction suggests limited potential for change and represents just one strand of evolutionary theory, albeit one for which there is overwhelming evidence in our materialistic society. Consumerism itself thrives on competition, not only at an individual level, but globally as Hamilton explains, insofar as First World countries have enriched themselves materially at the expense of the Third World (2005, 39), an approach which appears unethical and unsustainable as I illustrate in the following chapter. Sufism's principle of unity (*tawhid*), on the other hand, represents a much more sustainable mode of being with its ethos of cooperation and harmony. This view, that all life is inter-related and co-dependent, also informs complexity science and biosemiotics, and Wheeler insists that the "western emphasis on individualism needs to be understood within this wider context" which confirms that "human societies are not mere aggregates of selfish and competing individuals but living totalities in which the life of the whole exceeds the sum of the parts". This line of thought, Wheeler believes, has "tended to be occluded in direct proportion to the secularisation of western society" (2006, 41-42). I shall expand on it in subsequent chapters.

Citing Studdert-Kennedy *et al* (1998), Bruthiaux continues as follows:

> The capacity to speak . . . might afford an individual, male or female, and its close kin a selective advantage over rivals in forming coalitions, discussing plans of action, and otherwise negotiating a path to higher social status, and so to more successful feeding and mating (Cited in Bruthiaux, 4)

From a sociobiological perspective therefore language can be seen as a device for forming and maintaining alliances and outperforming rivals and thus achieving more successful reproduction through a complex social network. Individuals' inclinations to enhance personal status or advance a particular bias vary in intensity and as social relationships vary in complexity, the efficacy and power of the 'advertising' aspect of language varies. Since the more complex types of interaction require a greater degree of linguistic sophistication and more subtle persuasive techniques than simpler ones, they are less evident or may not be discernible at all, so that form becomes divested of meaning. When meaning is lost, flourishing is comprised.

Wheeler's argument from biosemiotics on the other hand is far more optimistic since it would have a complex non-reductive and non-positivistic semiotic biology and culture together determine how genetic traits and communication-systems develop, whereas sociobiology posits that traits such as competitiveness are hardwired. With reference to Eva Jablonka and Marion Lamb (*Evolution in Four Dimensions: Genetic, Epigenetic, Behavioral, and Symbolic Variation in the History of Life*, 2005) Wheeler states that it has become clear that "the gene-centred view of evolution via which neo-Darwinists have attempted to reduce the complexity of human life to a genetic determinism is seriously incomplete" (2006, 14). An incomplete understanding of a semiotically complex reality manifests as language that distorts.

Language that distorts uses words that "are not just the innocent tools that allow us to describe reality. They select. They emphasize. They embody a bias . . . If words or their meaning can be changed, the quest to change hearts and minds will be achieved" (Cited in Marker & Smith, 2004). Engineered more subtly, words misinform less overtly. Words are not neutral, says Dutch euthanasia practitioner and ethicist Dr. M.A.M. Wachter, and the range of definitions of voluntary euthanasia to which he refers illustrates his point. Euphemistic forms such as 'gentle-landing', 'deliverance' and 'dignity in dying' dispel the spectre, which might have haunted some, of a lethal syringe-wielding physician intent on killing a loved one—words effectively first blurred, then completely obliterated, the line between what might either be considered desirable or repugnant. The clear light of truth becomes penumbral; meaning is blurred as words, like veils, conceal. "In one respect speech removes veils, in ten respects it covers and conceals", Rumi reminds us, which is perhaps why Marker and Smith conclude "It's as if 'up' were now 'down' and 'hot' were now 'cold'. Words only mean what the speaker intends them to mean . . ." (*ibid.*); but do they, in reality?

2.9 Language as Commodity

In an age of materialism characterised by rampant consumerism and an obsession with wealth, we witness the explosion of language usage as well as the commoditisation of language in general and of the English language in particular. Language as outer form has become a highly prized consumer good, valued for its status-enhancing potential. In *The Value of Language* (2005), Krishna S. Dhir assesses the economic value of language as a commodity, and given such conception of language, Dhir concludes, corporations should begin to think in terms of "a portfolio of language assets much in the same way as they think of portfolios of financial currency assets". In *Hypercapitalism* (2006), Phil Graham explores the problems of understanding the emergent form of a global political and economic organisation in which every possible aspect of human existence, and most notably language, has become a commodity.

Having achieved global domination, the English language has become an intensely desirable commodity and selling it is highly profitable. It is now used more by second language users (over one billion) than first (about 380 million) (Clyne, 2007). According to Wheeler, "the long

hegemony of liberal individualism, supported by the economic and imperial power of the West, can be understood as the hegemony of a certain
language" (2006, 33). Clearly that language is English, a "predatory" language according to Catalan author and translator Teresa Solana (Solana,
2009). The price of proficiency, both financial and emotional, is high, and
often entails compromise of students' heritage culture and language mastery (Zhou & Kim, 2006), sometimes even total loss of the heritage language. According to sociologist Ruben Rumbaut, North America has
proven for centuries to be a language graveyard where immigrant families'
native language is almost always lost by the third generation (Cited in
Mcgee, 2007).

But temptingly arranged together with all the other products on display, the new language appears to be the key to a better education, a more
lucrative career and an enviable lifestyle. The allure of the product gives
no hint of the sense of dislocation, the anxiety and loneliness that accom-
pany foreign students in their quest to achieve this form of success (Sallis,
2009). Bob Beaver and Bryan Tuck monitored the adjustment of Asian
students at a tertiary institution in New Zealand and noted considerably
higher levels of anxiety, deficient study skills and difficulties interacting
socially compared with local students. Sallis describes the process of *learning a foreign language as an "unravelling" of the self (ibid.) as preconceptions
and certainties are traded for the allure of the unknown.*

Mastery of a foreign language often proves elusive and superficial
knowledge of a language does not automatically lead to inclusion within
the group of native speakers. When pursuit of the new commodity leads
to alienation from the heritage language and culture, the acquired language ceases to be an attribute (Griego, 2002) and becomes instead an
obstacle, creating a vacuum of history, culture, tradition and customs that
will never be known (Brewer, 2002).

Rumi reminds us of the impermanence of form and the inevitability
of conflict, and forms of language are no exception: "Like a fish, it flops
a moment on dry ground. A while later you see it lifeless" (*SPL*, 271). Of
the estimated 7000 languages spoken today, linguists estimate that at least
75% are likely to disappear this century. On average, one falls out of use
every two weeks. Australia remains one of the global hot-spots for language extinction, with about 110 of 145 remaining indigenous languages

critically endangered (Clyne, 2007). No form is immune, Rumi reminds us; the hegemony of language is not enduring as other cultures become resurgent (see Chapter 5) and today's commodity becomes tomorrow's waste. "Foam thrown up from the ocean", says Rumi of form; sooner or later it returns to its source. Conflicting forms of language fall silent, as foam returns to the ocean, revealing in the stillness of the heart the meaning that is one.

2.10 Language that Corrupts Thought

"If thought corrupts language, language can also corrupt thought", wrote George Orwell in 1945 with reference to the decline, as he perceived it, of the English language and culture (*Politics and the English Language*). The English language, he says, "becomes ugly and inaccurate because our thoughts are foolish, but the slovenliness of our language makes it easier for us to have foolish thoughts". In other words, cause becomes effect and vice versa. As Wheeler says, language is causally efficacious; "it can change the way we think and feel about things dramatically" (2006, 23). What would Orwell have made of the changes that have taken place in the forms of language, culture and thought since the time of his writing more than sixty years ago? The horrors of war have not ceased, nations and individuals still seek to dominate, peace and goodwill to all have not materialised and language and thought reveal no more beauty or truth now than they did in Orwell's time. Nor is there any evidence to suggest that Nietzsche's words that years of painstaking effort were required to produce fine writing were ever heeded. He recommends "some ten years of practice", writing tirelessly, describing, relating, listening, reflecting, "disdaining no signpost for instruction, so that what is then created in the workshop would be fit to go out into the world" (Nietzsche, 1996, 163), since mastering the language of 'truth' is an infinite process of remaking and overcoming.

Like Orwell, Nasr is fiercely critical of the degradation of language, brought about by its secularisation and the attempt to substitute quantity for symbolic significance in the reading of the cosmic text. The link between divine and human language broke down, he says, leaving the latter to undergo successive "falls" or stages of secularisation which have resulted in various forms of "bastardization" of languages which exist merely to express experiences of triviality (Nasr, 1981, 47). As Nasr points out, language has been unleashed in an unprecedented manner; relentlessly, excessively and indiscriminately. The same conspicuous consumption that is the hallmark of our time bedevils current language usage. Quality is sacrificed for quantity as mass-communication is a prerequisite to making money. More language equals greater profits. As a result much of it is superfluous—superficial, trivial and uninspired. Its exterior is, perhaps, enhanced, augmented, nipped or tucked, but what lurks below the surface is often of little concern. Irredeemable features are liposuctioned away, while redeemable ones are repositioned, reshaped, enlarged or reduced to enhance and streamline the body. It's all about form, surface and adornment, while meaning is often forgotten.

Farrelly notes that "ugliness is pretty much a constant" (2007, 100) and despairs at "the heartbreakingly, wrist-slittingly obvious fact that this—this—is what people like" (*op. cit.*, 98). It's about kitsch, she concludes, the opposite of authenticity. "The materials themselves (. . .) all selected for cheapness, lightness and convenience—reinforce this dissociative effect" (*op. cit.*, 115). Ugliness is apparent in all constructed forms and our language is no exception. Many words in popular usage are euphemistically described as 'strong language', in spite of their obvious lack of strength, and warnings such as 'coarse language may offend sensitive viewers' have become commonplace in a culture characterised by addictive consumption. Coarse language has become the community standard (Burris, 2007) with nearly three-quarters of Americans saying they frequently use or experience the use of profanity in public. Children are particularly adept at acquiring language, especially 'strong' language used by adults all around them (Perry, 2008). Years of watching television and film leave children's speech peppered with the meaningless trademark phrases of American youth, as well as forthright and explicit, vulgar, offensive or disparaging references to sexual or excretory functions and words which denigrate certain racial, ethnic or social groups.

Language corrupts thought not only by giving a voice to the trite, vulgar and offensive, but by reinforcing separateness and division. Language by its very nature is divisive and entrenches separatism, loosely uniting some while excluding others, reinforcing distinctions and differences. Misunderstanding is common when speakers of different languages attempt to bridge the linguistic gap that keeps them apart, and interpretation is hazardous as meaning stubbornly conceals itself. Furthermore, in translation meaning is often lost; modern transcriptions of Rumi's poetry attest to this. Aahlia Khan notes the common misunderstanding by some western readers that Sufi poetry is strongly tinged with sensuality and replete with bacchanalian symbolism when in fact it clads divine love in secular words. Interpretations yoked to political or national agendas may manipulate language to construct meaning not originally intended, she says (2009). Nor does sharing a language ensure unity as linguistic idiosyncrasies determine who will be included within the linguistic community. Like all 'stuff', language has an exclusionary role. Its form polarises its consumers in the same way that other goods do, hindering unity by promoting exclusion. Like the supermall and McMansion that close themselves off from the life-giving flow—"sealed and air-conditioned, cul-de-saced and pest-proofed, security-equipped and . . . gated" (Farrelly, 117)—language has become a closed temple to worldliness, rather than the unifying expression of life.

The "symbolist spirit" (Nasr, 1981, 155) of the Sufi poets who lived in a world where everything was sacred, on the other hand, was directly reflected in their language, within the structure of which was embedded "the treasury of metaphysics" (*ibid.*), which, as Nasr reminds us, is still taught in Sufi schools. As the Sufi poets well understood, the significance of the root meaning of words, reflecting the symbolic possibilities hidden within words, is in itself symbolic of that mysterious presence whose sacred reality animates all things. However, as Aahlia Khan reminds us, our western orientation being based on a set of presuppositions that deny mysticism and sacredness a central role in the constitution of reality, translating and interpreting correctly the densely metaphoric, intertextual language used to extend meaning and reality in Sufi poetry can be extremely difficult (2009).

2.11 Language that is Blubber-Rich

Language, like all forms, has its adornments that make it blubber-rich but meaning-poor. In his *Essais,* the sixteenth century French philosopher Montaigne wondered whether scholars would have appreciated Socrates, a man they claimed to respect above all others, if he had approached them in his old cloak, speaking in plain language, devoid of the prestige of Plato's dialogues, since "we can appreciate no graces which are not pointed, inflated and magnified by artifice. Such graces as flow on under the name of naivety and simplicity readily go unseen by so coarse an insight as ours" (Montaigne, 1991, III, 1173). "Writing with simplicity requires courage", says Alain De Botton, "for there is a danger of being overlooked, dismissed as simpleminded by those with a tenacious belief that complexity is always preferable to simplicity and that impassable prose is a hallmark of intelligence. Simple language appears base and commonplace", he says, "since we are never aware of riches except when conspicuously paraded" (2000, 158).

The tendency for obscure communication or what human rights and refugee advocate Julian Burnside AO QC calls "nonspeak", most commonly found in complex and jargon-ridden language used by governments and business, leads to the "wilful misuse" of language in public utterances (Burnside, 2009, 342). Instead of conveying accurately what they mean, users of nonspeak betray the central purpose of language by "carelessness, foolishness or malevolence", Burnside argues, citing examples such as *illegals* (innocent victims of oppression), *collateral damage* (killing innocent civilians), *energetic disassembly* (nuclear explosion), *incontinent ordnance* (bombs which hit schools and hospitals by mistake) and *active defence* (invasion) (*op. cit.*, 76). As a result, he says, "the world is awash with . . . empty rhetoric dressed up in the finery of rococo elegance, vacuous new-age gush, or the yawning post-modern fashion of abstraction piled on abstraction—all devoid of real content. These are the empty calories, the fast food of modern discourse" (*op. cit., 74*).

Like the unnaturally elongated, uniform and almost eyeless Russet Burbank, or the most recent Monsanto invention, the New Leaf, which McDonald's demands of its potato growers, public language, according to Don Watson, has not only been bleached of all meaning, but actually stifles the capacity for thought and, in doing so, saps the will to live. In *Death Sentence: the Decay of Public Language (2003) and Bendable Learnings (2009)* he describes the seepage of managerial jargon into all areas of public language: education, commerce, the bureaucracy and politics. Empty code words which are "learned, practised, expected (and) demanded" throughout the networks of management in Australian society (2003, 15) have transformed clear, everyday communication into "depleted and impenetrable sludge" (2003, 24). Abstract nouns abound—*synergy* and *strategy, uptake, outcomes, outputs* and *inputs, key performance indicators, drivers* and *customer experience,* even if 'customers' are in fact hospital patients. Vacant expressions (*culture of productivity, initiatives going forwards, goal alignments, groupthink, effortings* and *learnings*) and sterility (*historically dry circumstance* instead of 'drought', or *synergy-related headcount reduction* instead of 'sacking people') render language "incapable of carrying mood or emotion" (2003, 48). The new language is deliberately obscure and falsely scientific, Watson believes, but what concerns him most is that those who use it seem to have lost the ability to think clearly. Words like *commitment, flexibility, innovation, integrity* and *diversity,* have become "icons the true meaning of which has long been forgotten or never understood" (2003, 97).

Stripped of meaning language serves no purpose. Abstract language, however, has concrete effects, and Watson illustrates this most poignantly with reference to the Country Fire Authority's failure to alert residents appropriately in the face of Black Saturday's bushfires in Victoria. They lacked the language to describe fires whose terrifying speed and stature were unprecedented. "Incredible as it seems, they didn't have the words—simple, concrete words", says Watson, "to say, in advance, 'look out; deadly fire'". When asked why warnings that would have got people out of their homes were not issued, the leaders of the Country Fire Authority are reported to have said that they'd spent the day in management training, where they had participated in "value adding, populating the document and watching Google Earth" (Watson on ABC PM, 2009-10-09).

Grammar is not the problem, says Burnside. "This language is systemically ill", he believes, "and does not respond to any form of massage or manipulation". The obese form is in need of radical reshaping. "Surgery may help, but then there'd be more on the floor than on the table and you'd realise that it has been a corpse all along, composed entirely of dead matter" (Burnside, 2009). Concrete words and fresh metaphor can revive the simple heart of language so that expression does not stifle meaning or the capacity for thought.

Sufism teaches that our love of complexity leads us away from truth. Linguistic embellishments, like wood veneers, marble look-alikes and fake chandeliers enhance the form's appearance while masking meaning or absence thereof. Difficult or incomprehensible language might just not be truthful. Mystics, according to Hazrat Inayat Khan, very often appear to be simple because sincerity makes them feel inclined to express truth, which is essentially simple, in simple language. "But because people value complexity, they think these simple things are meaningless" (X 71). "Truth is simple and plain", he says (VIII 53).

Forms—those secondary causes which Rumi urges us not to mistake for primary cause—are reduced to trappings, hype, spin and gloss with powerful seductive, deceptive or demeaning powers when devoid of meaning. Instead of being enriched by the beauty of their depth, we find ourselves impoverished and disenchanted by the deficiency of surface. Authenticity and sufficiency are replaced by phoniness, deceit and surfeit, resulting in a 'cacophony of voices'; often shrill and strident, competing to be heard (von Heyking, 2004). Rumi reminds us, as we find ourselves in the midst of superfluity, that forms are veils; when language becomes deafening, he calls for stillness and when people seek adornment, he reminds us that beauty is in the heart.

2.12 Language that Knows no Wonder

The way in which we organise language reveals our attitude towards the world. Our fondness of the passive voice, for example, might betray a reluctance to assume responsibility for our words (Berry, 1983), since it keeps them at a safe distance while the speaker remains conveniently anonymous. Furthermore, the passive sentence conveys information that has the appearance of not being limited or biased by a particular perspective or vested interest. It has the all-important 'look' of knowledge though it might be mere opinion; descriptions of economic processes, for example, are often in the passive voice, creating a sense of inevitability that deflects people from imagining alternatives (Salleh, 2009).

Questions and exclamations betray a sense of inquisitiveness and wonder that appears to have become distinctly unfashionable (Robinson, 2002). The questioning mind seeks a response which may or may not, in time, be forthcoming. But this means first acknowledging a not-knowing, opening oneself up to uncertainty and entering a state of receptivity, waiting patiently and hopefully, trusting that the answer will come. Asking suggests ignorance and need, and implies dependence. It entails listening.

This, in turn, entails stilling one's own voice. Then there remains the chance that the answer might not be to one's liking and that one would be required to suppress one's own preconceptions. One would have to accommodate the answer and this might be inconvenient. Thus, in a sense, questions draw people into relationships, and relationships entail commitment. "Whatever" is the generational watchword, Hamilton reminds us (2008, 126), a word which expresses a generation's aversion to commitment. Little wonder then that questions are not in vogue.

Exclamations of surprise and wonder are also in short supply as people focus almost exclusively on material things. Robinson argues that the exclamation mark is too emphatic, too childish for our sophisticated ways, unlike semicolons which imply a capacity for complex, dialectical formulations appropriate to our predilection for complexity. Punctuation may be sparse as in email or lacking entirely as in most text messaging, trading clarity and care for ambiguity and haste.

The organisation of language hints at the meaning concealed within form. The signposts of language indicate that the reader should anticipate, listen, exclaim, wonder, slow down; their omission gives permission to accelerate at whim instead of attending and observing closely. Without their direction the continuous flow of words might be devoid of meaning, like beads without a string to bind them. Punctuation unites words in a logical way, making the whole intelligible, unified and rhythmic. Frequent pointers instruct us to pause for breath or stop, reflect, and then, refreshed, to proceed anew. Punctuation controls pace and creates harmony by ordering stillness in which a listening can occur. Rumi created a similar effect by appending his nickname *khamoosh kon* (be silent) to his verses, allowing meaning to come to the fore in stillness, and reminding us that language proceeds from silence and returns again to it.

All forms corporealise meaning and as such are dynamic symbols communicating not only their own existence, but the impulse that inspired it. Yet, subjugated by materialism, we are deprived by our crowded, noisy lifestyles of the stillness from which truths might emerge; relentless consumers of form, we become forgetful of meaning concealed below the surface. Reflecting divine qualities, forms have the power to be "occasions for recollection" as in the Platonic sense, assuming a "metaphysical transparency" (Nasr, 1981, 191), inviting us to see the Beloved everywhere.

Such recollection involves considering the implications of one's choices and promotes connectivity and therefore individual flourishing. Only the discordant voice of ego, most shrill and strident, breaks the stillness in which other voices might be heard.

CHAPTER THREE

Conflicting Voices

Conflicting Voices

In light of modern humans' defacement of the manuscript of creation, I will argue that refinement of *nafs* is essential, since its strident voice breaks the stillness in which other voices might be heard—the voices of others, of animals and of the earth.

3.1 The Commanding Voice of Ego

Ayn Rand, founder of Objectivism, the philosophy of rational individualism which holds that there is no greater moral goal than achieving happiness, is the author of *The Virtue of Selfishness* (1961), in which she defines selfishness as "serious, rational, principled concern with one's own wellbeing". Underpinning her philosophy is "the concept of man as a heroic being, with his own happiness as the moral purpose of his life" (Rand, 1957, vii). Rejecting altruism and the concept of self-sacrifice as the moral ideal, she argues that the ultimate moral value for each human individual is his or her own wellbeing. Since selfishness is a prerequisite for the attainment of wellbeing, it is, according to Rand, a virtue. She defines virtue as an action by which individuals secure and protect their rational values—ultimately, their life and happiness (Atlas Society, 2007).

Rand's philosophy found fertile ground in the United States where the pursuit of happiness was written into the Constitution as a basic human right. Despite its 1075 pages making it one of the longest novels ever written in any European language, *Atlas Shrugged* met such wide appeal that, according to a 1991 United States survey by the Library of Congress and the *Times* Book of the Month Club, it was the book that made the greatest difference in readers' lives after the Bible (Shermer, 2008). It was in this book that Rand introduced the theme of selfishness as a virtue that she would subsequently develop into the philosophy of Objectivism.

This perspective clearly counters Sufism's *tawhid*, mystical and eco-philosophical intuitions of unity, as well as complexity science's more recent understanding of systemic interrelatedness and codependence. It also counters the social philosophy of Jean-Jacques Rousseau and, later, socialist economics premised upon cooperation and shared wealth. But, as Hamilton explains (2008, 190) with reference to the 'socialist' motive for moral behaviour identified already by Plato and Schopenhauer, societies have shown they can construct for a time a social basis for 'fellow feeling'; this after all was the goal of socialism, "but to the extent that such plans can succeed they must be constantly recreated as society changes in response to technological, demographic and economic forces" (*ibid.*). Only the noumenon, the essential source of fellow feeling, says Hamilton, is constant. With the rise of secularism and materialism, however, the focus shifted from neighbour to self, and there has been considerable support for the view that selfishness, self-centredness and self-interest not only are, but ought to be, powerful determinants of behaviour (Miller, 1999). Classical economists, in particular, assume that individuals are motivated by self-interest above all else. Economist and forerunner of this line of thought, Adam Smith (1723–1790), claims that in commercial society individuals in pursuit of 'vain and insatiable desires' through an invisible hand 'advance the interest of society' (Oneill, 2001). While Adam Smith and Thomas Hobbes (1588–1679) denied that self-love should be identified with avarice or the love of gain, both argued that commercial society and the rules of property allowed self-interested agents moved by gain to act to the mutual benefit of all. This thought has been expanded in recent economic theory, which argues that in certain ideal conditions market exchange between rational self-interested agents can realise optimal outcomes.

Outcomes are seldom optimal however as the failure of the 'free-market' economy illustrates, and instead of advancing the interest of society, individuals are bound by what Northcott refers to as a 'coercive social and economic contract' governed not by law or virtue but by economics and statistics (2007, 63) since all activity is reduced to a calculation of costs and benefits. Self-interest invariably disregards the common good and exchange values override all other goods. Instead of being liberated by the modern economy and its technological and scientific advances, every individual is increasingly dependent at every moment on the necessity of their connection with the labour market and with an economy in which natural wealth is transformed into stored money values (*ibid.*). In accordance with *tawhid*, however, economics is effectively integrated into ethics, the law of creation (*shariah al-fitriyya*) being all-encompassing, and adherence to it ensures that self-interest is held within bounds and the wellbeing of all is safeguarded (Rice, 1999, 348).

The economy and technology may have freed many in the west from physical toil, but we are arguably less free and self-sufficient than before, since we are now subservient to a global economy over which we have no control and whose tentacles reach into every corner of our lives. Northcott continues: 'Just as all forms of goodness, truth and beauty are . . . rendered exchangeable by the economy . . . all forms of human making, including the family and human natality, along with all forms of species being, are drawn into the process of the accumulation of monetary values, and increasingly subjected to the governance of the mechanistic procedures of market economics' (p 65). The moral climate fostered by the global economy is far from ideal for fostering 'fellow feeling' or responding to the clearly visible signs of stress presented by an increasingly ailing earth.

Richard Dawkins, author of *The Selfish Gene,* claims that 'we are born selfish' (1989, 3). He bases his argument largely on Charles Darwin's theory of struggle for existence, commonly referred to by the more controversial catch-phrase of evolutionary theory, 'survival of the fittest'.

Wheeler details the essential continuity of internal world (*Innenwelt*) and external world (*Umwelt*), of organism and environment, arguing that while individualism identifies an ontological difference between individuals and societies, there is, in fact, no such difference (2006, 124). Citing Raymond Williams (*Long Revolution*), she says "the consciousness is part of the reality, and the reality is part of the consciousness" (*ibid.*). Altruistic forms of behaviour appear to be ubiquitous in nature, occurring in creatures "from bacteria to mammals" (Sayoran, 2009). Therefore for the sake of our collective flourishing we need to broaden our egocentric perspective or, in the words of Rumi, look beyond form and seek meaning.

Mathews believes it is "the habit of inattentiveness that is the legacy of materialism (which) locks us into an effective, if inadvertent, solipsism"; "when (. . .) *nothing* other than our own selves can really matter to us" (2005, 17). We fail really to register others except as "discursive ciphers" in our own story, as "the consciousness of individual human beings itself becomes increasingly blocklike" (*ibid.*).

Our self—its security and happiness—appears to determine our behaviour. We noted the ubiquity of the 'fat form', blubber-rich but meaning poor, as evidenced by the bigger-is-better-is-beautiful mentality. We saw that obesity has become a western world epidemic, resulting from over-indulgence in food that is often harmful and devoid of nutritional content, and we also saw the bombardment by advertising and the media, the "plethora of messages to assault our eyes and ears" (Hamilton, 2005, 38), which has diminished people's well-being. But excess does not pertain only to stuff in supermalls, suburban sprawl and the clamour of signs and sounds that constitute our reality. The obese form is everywhere, but none is more hazardous than the obese ego that casts its shadow over the heart and compromises flourishing. One might coin the term 'egobesity' to affirm the reality of the ego's unhealthy, bloated condition which jeopardises the health of the world yet has no name.

But, asks Rumi, "who has ever seen a part greater than the whole?" (Nicholson, I, 159). By aggressively pursuing the ego's demands, happiness remains elusive. Mathews elaborates the insidious and pervasive environmental and social effects resulting from the autoic (self-regarding) rather than alteric (other-regarding) orientation privileged in the western tradition (2003, 59). Seeking purely its own increase, the autoic self is construed as essentially "hedonic"—instrumentalising and subordinating the world to itself (Mathews, 2003, 59). For this reason, Mathews believes, this predominantly autoic orientation must be redressed. Self-knowledge, the secret of happiness (I, 5), is crucial for this purpose. "Man seeks happiness, not because happiness is his sustenance, but because happiness is his own being. Therefore, in seeking happiness, man is seeking himself" (*ibid.*). In other words the pursuit of happiness is the natural response to a feeling of having lost something which was previously an intrinsic part of one's being. But we forget the true nature of our own being and conclude that the key to happiness lies in acquisition, so we set out in pursuit of it. Franz Kafka (1883–1924), described by French writer and philosopher Hélène Cixous as a mystic, "a religious writer without religion" (Cixous, 1999), also recognises happiness as the natural state of the world. It should not be pursued but must be unmasked, he says, and that can only occur when the observer is in a state of receptive stillness:

You do not need to leave your room. Remain sitting at your table and listen. Do not even listen, simply wait; do not even wait, be quite still and
solitary. The world will freely offer itself to you, to be unmasked, it has no
choice, it will roll in ecstasy at your feet (Brod, M. (Ed.), *The Diaries of
Franz Kafka*, 1964)

Our strident voice, however, drowns out all others and stops us from
listening. The 'unmasking of the world', freely offering of its joyous
nature, is overlooked as we readily succumb to the dictates of what political philosopher Hannah Arendt calls "the catastrophic interiority of the
selfish I", whose tyranny threatens not only all our actions but the very
survival of humanity (Arendt, 39), though it is merely an "ontological
bubble" (Schuon, 1959, 233).

Thomas Jefferson's injunction to the people of America to pursue
happiness is deplored by American essayist John Perry Barlow (b. 1947)
as "a toxic stupidity (. . .) a poison that sickens our culture (. . .) and produces a monstrous, insatiable hunger inside our national psyche that
encourages us ever more ravenously to devour all the resources of this
small planet, crushing liberties, snuffing lives, feeling ourselves ordained
by God and Jefferson to do whatever is necessary to make us happy" (Barlow, 2001). In a desperate attempt to fulfil what has practically become a
national imperative, says Barlow, contemporary Americans turn to phar-
maceuticals for the desired effect: "What am I to think of my people who,
during the year 2000, while feeding at the greatest economic pig-trough
the world has slopped forth, ate $13.4 billion of Prozac and other antide-
pressants?" (*ibid.*). In Australia this largely silent epidemic was thrust into
the spotlight by the death of actor Heath Ledger, a regular like countless
others, at some of the most exclusive New York nightclubs, in January
2008. "Acute intoxication by the combined effects of oxycodone, hydro-
codone, diazepam, temazepam, alprazolam and doxylamine" was given as
the official cause of the actor's death (CNN.com, February 6, 2008).

Howard Markel, professor of paediatrics and psychiatry at the University of Michigan, maintains that the misuse of legal drugs has become
one of the major health problems of our time. In the US, where pharma-
ceuticals are advertised on prime-time television, pill-popping has become
a normalised, socially acceptable means of alleviating stress, sleeplessness
or anxiety, he maintains, and the practice of prescribing drugs has meta-

morphosed from a medical treatment of last resort to a way of life (Markel, Cited in Day, 2008). According to the 2006 National Survey on Drug Use and Health, 49.8 million Americans over the age of 12 have reported non-medical use of illicit drugs in their lifetime. Among teenagers aged 12–17, prescription drugs are second only to marijuana in popularity, and in the past 15 years there has been a 140 per cent increase in painkiller abuse. It is the fastest-growing type of drug abuse in the US, as prescription drugs appear to be a legal, seemingly safe, way to recreate a high. As a result, mishandled drugs now kill 20,000 a year, nearly twice as many as 10 years ago (*ibid.*).

Spiralling antidepressant use is not limited to the US. Pointing to an explosion in the use of antidepressants, with 31 million prescriptions issued in 2006, including 631,000 for children, Liberal Democrat leader Nick Clegg says "Britain has become the true Prozac nation (. . .) and pills must not be a crutch for the wider issues in our society" (Woodward, 2008). According to Hamilton, consumer society on the whole is characterised by depression. Its clinical form aside, he says, the widespread incidence of low-level and episodic depression is an escape from the disappointment of the freedom and happiness promised by individualism (2008, 223). Close to a third of adult Australians depend on drugs or other substances to get them through the day, says Hamilton, adding that this "stands in contrast to their imagined identity as a nation of carefree people who take life in their stride" (2005, 118). It also clashes with marketers' images of customers who have found happiness by purchasing a particular product. Citing Tim Kasser (*The High Price of Materialism*, 2002), Hamilton says that psychologists are aware of the strong link between affluenza and psychological disorders: "Existing scientific research on the value of materialism yields clear and consistent findings. People who are highly focused on materialistic values have lower personal wellbeing and psychological health than those who believe that materialistic values are relatively unimportant" (2005, 119).

Pills may be a crutch for sufferers of depression and provide moments of 'ecstasy' (defined in 1959 by Schuon as "a 'departure' from terrestrial consciousness", p. 72), like the popular eponymous mood-enhancing drug, but the cost of socially sanctioned tobacco and alcohol use reveals a far greater problem, since alcohol in particular is an important feature of our culture, and excessive consumption tends to be regarded as the norm. In Australia, as a result of the major health and social risk this represents, a task force has been appointed to tackle the growing challenges caused by smoking and drinking, which cost the country $56 billion a year. A government report released by Health Minister Nicola Roxon shows that in 2004–2005 the social cost of alcohol was $15.3 billion, of tobacco was $31.5 billion and illicit drugs $8.2 billion. Alcohol and illicit drugs acting together cost another $1.1 billion (ABC News, 9 April 2008)—staggering figures revealing gross levels of consumption that suggest deep-rooted malady and a misguided pursuit of happiness.

'Grossness', in Sufi terms, is associated with *nafs*, or ego. Yet high self-esteem, assertiveness and strong sense of self are greatly valued in our culture. Whilst open to various interpretations, these concepts are generally understood to mean attributing greater importance to one's own individual ego than to others. Such egocentric reasoning is accompanied by the belief that one deserves more than one's fair share of resources (Epley *et al*, 2006). In light of *tawhid*, Sufism, on the other hand, aims to refine the ego since it causes conflict and "deprives the soul of its true bliss" (II, 25). Sufism distinguishes between the *rahmani* (attributed to God who is the Most Merciful) I, the greater self, and the *nafsani* (soul-derived, sensual, malignant) I, the individual, lesser self which prevents one from attaining the truth (Can, 2005, 258). It is the strident voice of the latter that will not harmonize until it is subdued. Sufi metaphor likens ego to the lion, sovereign among animals but slave to his passions and always unwelcome within his kingdom (II, 24). The ego is never sated and wants constant feeding.

Indulgence brings brief respite from ego's commanding voice but may result in the sense of self "developing into a monster", as Hamilton points out, with reference to the indulgence granted to children, which, he notes, has often been observed as "one of the greatest failings of Western society in recent decades" (2008, 181). According to Hamilton, today's 'me-generation' is afflicted by an unprecedented 'self-esteem epidemic' which has spawned an entire self-esteem and self-admiration industry whose aim is bolstering and selling notions of self. Over-indulgent parenting combined with a falling birthrate, educational trends reinforcing the importance of being seen, heard, recognised and rewarded, and com-

merce driving the new enchantment with self ('because you're worth it')
have contributed to what Hamilton refers to as a 21st century phenomenon—narcissism. It would be hard to find a better symbol of narcissism
than the 'Me-Ring', or as Hamilton believes, a better definition than the
following advertisement: "Your left hand says we, your right hand says
me . . . as brilliant and expensive as an engagement ring, symbolising independence, not alliance. It is a token of love from you to yourself" (Hamilton, 2005, 27). Like the mythical Narcissus who fell in love with his own
reflection and then died of thirst beside the pool rather than shatter his
image, we are seduced by our own form and its perceived importance.

The self-esteem movement has led its followers to believe that "lack of
self-esteem is the central cause of the world's problems", according to Associate Professor of Social Psychology at the University of North Carolina,
W. Keith Campbell (Campbell, 2008) and judging by the vast array of literature devoted to the subject, Campbell makes a valid point. It appears that
self-esteem (not to be confused with self-respect) must be unconditional,
which suggests that it just may, at times, be unmerited. In that case, the
University of Texas at Austin's Counseling and Mental Health Center suggests the following: "Rebut the Inner Critical Voice—Don't Be Critical of
Yourself", "Self-Nurture Even When You Don't Feel You Deserve It" and
"Fake It Until You Can Make It—when you treat yourself like you deserve
to feel good (. . .), slowly you'll come to believe it" (UTA, 1999).

However, the notion of suppressing the voice of conscience and making a deliberate attempt to believe what is false rather than endeavour to
correct the problem has serious repercussions. If, at the most fundamental level, truth is rejected in favour of the more convenient option of cling-
ing to falsehoods, personal responsibility is neglected and flourishing
compromised. The ego that is so fragile that setbacks such as "experiencing failures in sports or school" (*ibid.*) are sufficient to leave it battered
and bruised is more in need of truth than of deception. Rumi tells us that
truth (Law) dispels the darkness of ignorance:

> The Law is like a lamp: It shows the way. Without a lamp, you will not be
> able to go forward. (*SPL*, 10)

In his essay, *The Ethics of Belief*, William K. Clifford makes the moral
claim that rightness or wrongness of a belief is determined according to

how it was arrived at, not whether or not it happens to be true. "If it was arrived at dishonestly, it is wrong, even if it happens in the event to be true" (1876, as cited in Amesbury, 2007, 25). Clifford stresses the importance of forming beliefs "in the appropriate way", by which he means dispassionately considering the evidence, not suppressing doubts and reservations or acting with disregard for the consequences of possibly being wrong. Convictions, even if sincere, should not be come by carelessly and self-servingly according to Clifford, and believing that everything is fine does not absolve a person of responsibility for what happens, because the beliefs on which one acts (or which nourish one's inaction), even if sincere, may not be ones to which one is rationally entitled. Clifford emphasises that the right to believe a thing must be merited and that one may not be entitled to the right to believe a thing on the strength of the evidence before one.

We have a moral responsibility for our beliefs since belief is not a purely private matter (*ibid.*), or one that can be partitioned off from other aspects of life: one's beliefs have consequences for others, as well as for oneself. By denying this responsibility, Clifford argues, one depletes the cultural resources on which posterity will in turn rely, for culture is "an heirloom which every succeeding generation inherits as a precious deposit and a sacred trust to be handed on to the next one, not unchanged but enlarged and purified, with some clear marks of its proper handiwork". Clifford also maintains that "consistent neglect of one's epistemic obligations corrupts a person's own character, rendering one unfit to contribute positively to the creation of the world in which posterity will live" (*op. cit.*, 27). Self-deception aimed at boosting self-esteem would therefore be unethical and misguided. As long as we are deceiving ourselves, says Hamilton, we close ourselves off from the knowledge of what is in our long-term interests (2008, 38).

Entitlement, however, is clearly a component of narcissism. According to Campbell *et al* the awareness of psychological entitlement has existed for at least several generations, with the 1970s being referred to as the 'Me Decade', the 1980s as the 'Greed Decade', and the 1990s as the 'New Gilded Age' (Campbell *et al*, 2004, 30). The notion of entitlement has dramatically increased in society, and its impact is pervasive and harmful. According to Campbell it is a curse potentially affecting a wide range of individuals who feel that they deserve a disproportionate amount of resources, are more aggressive and selfish, competitive as opposed to cooperative and acquisitive rather than protective, even when dealing with a shared resource (*op. cit.*, 39). A strong sense of entitlement and of one's own needs is usually accompanied by a negative view of close others and of their psychological entitlement (*ibid.*).

3.2 Ego and the voices of others

The obese ego or inflated sense of self is the antithesis of the Sufi ideal since it perpetuates separation from the Beloved. Self-consciousness, says Mathews in similar vein, "deflects individuals from the Way" (2003, 9). Ultimately, the ego must be shed, she emphasises (*op. cit.*, 111). Conflict is an integral part of an egocentric relationship, coming to the fore whenever a threat to the ego is perceived. An egocentric approach adversely affects relationships, since the needs of the self are weighed against those of the other (Campbell *et al*, 2004). Outcomes of experiments conducted by Campbell *et al* on a group of couples reflect increased focus on own needs and less concern with partner needs, dismissing attachment—valuing self but not others, decreased accommodation, lower empathy and perspective taking; less respect for the partner, love associated primarily with game playing and "having fun" (*ludus*), selfishness (less *agape*) and significantly less loyalty.

Serving others has been replaced by serving self, says Farrelly, who believes that self-fulfilment, self-esteem, competitiveness and assertiveness have replaced selflessness and cooperation (2007, 148). "We're out there grabbing it, living our lives, as we should be" (*ibid.*), she says. Similarly, Mathews believes that chronic 'busyness' shields us from the failure really to register others and from "the meaninglessness of existence in the monological mode" (2005, 17). Believing that our feelings of deprivation might be alleviated materialistically, driven by a sense of lack rather than a realistic appreciation of what we actually have, says Hamilton, we tend to ignore the fact that quality of life and relationships are often sacrificed in our pursuit of money. Thus the 'sanctification of work' has become a phenomenon of our time (Hamilton, 2005), compromising wellbeing and the integrity of the family and of the community as people work long and irregular hours in an attempt to 'get ahead'. Increasingly competitive workplaces promote self-doubt and one-upmanship, according to Hamilton, rather than empathy or "fellow-feeling" (*op. cit.*, 190) between people working towards a common goal. People's mindsets are thus shaped, Hamilton believes, in such a way that "they feel their community is something they must protect themselves from rather than a resource from which they can draw and to which they can contribute" (*op. cit.*, 95).

"Career, business and industry not only relieve us of leisure to reflect on our condition; they also conveniently afford a modus vivendi oriented to a quantitative and abstract outlook. Organizing life in accordance with professional protocols and schedules, gauging supply and demand, calculating costs and profits, converting diverse environments into uniform 'resource bases', our daily attention is deflected from the qualitative and particular and hence from the danger of dialogical engagement" (Mathews, 2005, 17). Heart to heart, face to face communication has given way to electronic chat and twitter, mostly with strangers, and children are all too often parented by remote control or paid employees. We have hundreds of 'friends' in cyberspace but few in reality and share intimate details of our lives with people we will never know.

Northcott draws a distinction between good and bad work, referring to the latter as "the perversion of making" that has become commonplace and resulted in the destruction of small farms, local communities and ecosystems; bad work destroys social and natural capital, while good work builds up the relational nexus of friendships and partnerships in which true peace between peoples, between humans and the earth, and between creatures and Creator, is sustained (2007, 15). The builder who skimps on materials and cuts corners to complete the task quickly and cheaply for profit's sake does a disservice to the client, the client's family, the community and the environment. New Zealand's and Canada's 'leaky building syndrome' is exemplary of such work, where innocent families discover too late that the homes they purchased are leaking from above and rotting from below within ten years of construction (Leaky Homes Action Group, 2005). Bad work results in schools collapsing, killing thousands. A top Chinese official says shoddy workmanship and substandard building materials may have played a part in the collapse of more than 7000 schools during the earthquake that killed hundreds of thousands of children in China's Sichuan province. Grieving parents suspect officials accepted bribes to authorise inferior work. This is not a natural disaster, says Tania Branigan, this is the work of humans (Branigan, 2008). Bad work is characterised by the abuse of the earth's resources, or what Northcott refers to as "the profligate use of energy". Bad work, according to Northcott, redirects human life away from careful, embodied and skilful engagement with the natural world towards the alienated kinds of work of many industrial workers; work that involves shifting units of data around, staring at flickering screens, breathing artificially cooled or heated air in rooms devoid of natural light, at the service of "the great corporate economy" (2007, 207)—nameless, faceless and distant.

In a chapter titled *Can capitalism afford kids?*, Trinca and Fox explain how long hours at work have acted as a virtual contraceptive for a whole generation whose time and energy have been absorbed by their all-consuming jobs (Cited in Manne, 2008). While productivity is obviously necessary and beneficial, it is difficult to reconcile materialistic values with relationship building, particularly those involving life-partners and children. Hamilton emphasises that children need the time and attention of both their parents. He refers to what Barbara Pocock calls "parent-specific time-hunger" (2005, 98), and this, for most, means wanting to spend more time with parents who defer their own happiness in the belief that the long hours at work are justified by the benefits family members receive from the additional income. In the only study of its type in Australia, Pocock found that the majority of young people want more time with their parents, rather than more money from increased hours of parental work (Barbara Pocock & Jane Clarke, *Can't Buy Me Love? Young Australians' Views on Parental Work, Time, Guilt and Their Own Consumption*, 2004, cited in Hamilton, 2005, 98). Good work, says Northcott, pays attention to the needs of other persons and creatures and is prudential in its use of bodily and earth energy. Such attention, he emphasizes, is necessary for the proper nurture of children in the home, for good agricultural husbandry of animals, crops and soil (2007, 207). Good work is productive and beneficent in the place where it is practised and normalizes rhythm; bad work induces stress and destructive rhythm.

Materialistic priorities have led to the disintegration of traditional families. Changes to terminology, such as the widespread use of the word 'partner' instead of 'husband' or 'wife', reflect a reduction of the traditional spousal role and a shift towards a contractual arrangement based on shared financial interests, since the same term is used to designate a member of a business alliance. As the term is also used to designate members of same-sex couples, the nature of particular relationships becomes obscured. In Australia the divorced population increased by 172% between 1981 and 2001 and the number of single parents is continuously increasing. In 2001, 762 600 men and women were living as single parents, up from 552 300 in 1991, an increase of 38% (Australian Bureau of Statistics, 2002). About half of all American marriages end in divorce, according to Dr Larry Bumpass of the University of Wisconsin's Centre for Demography and Ecology (Cited in Hurley, 2005). As family units break down children's lives are diminished; the beauty of wholeness is replaced by fragmentation and disconnection. As forms disintegrate, meaning is lost.

Disintegration of families causes increased isolation and loneliness. As family members focus increasingly on fulfilment of their own desires, the needs of others, especially the elderly, are overlooked. The case of Sydney man Jorge Coloma, whose body was found more than a year after he died, received much publicity, but it is not an isolated case (Stafford, 2008). In 2007, 737 people's deaths in NSW and Victoria went unnoticed for between two and a half weeks and more than three months (*ibid.*). Gerry Naughtin, manager of the ageing policy for the Brotherhood of St Laurence, explains that isolation and loneliness are increasingly common among the elderly, and that the Brotherhood often finds itself organising funerals for clients who have no one else to do it. In parts of NSW, Red Cross workers are paid to call on the elderly daily, to prevent as far as possible people's deaths passing unnoticed (*ibid.*).

No generation has enjoyed the same level of wealth and opportunity as Generation X. Tertiary education was available at minimal or no cost, jobs were abundant and more secure thanks to protectionism, and housing was more affordable than today. Generation Y, on the other hand, is faced with the high cost of education, much greater competition, the daunting prospect of entering the property market while still, in many instances, repaying study loans, as well as paying a price for global warming. They will spend many more years repaying debts than previous generations. Furthermore, higher taxes are inevitable for Generation Y if the present level of social security and state pension funds is to be maintained, due to the strain the ageing population will place on available resources. If the financial scenario of Generation Y appears a little bleak, one might imagine that assistance from a privileged generation will bring relief. Not if the Commonwealth Bank of Australia has its way. "Retirement is payback time . . ." according to their advertisement depicting a carefree couple winging their way to a far-off destination, delighted to leave behind their dependent children, having discovered a convenient, novel income stream.

The CBA is just one of the many financial institutions advertising a product whose popularity is growing steadily—reverse mortgages, which allow older home owners to borrow money against the value of their property. The loan does not have to be repaid until a borrower moves, sells or dies. But CBA Australia's financial planning manager, Chris Benson, warns that there are several pitfalls involved in reverse mortgages. Asset-rich income-poor retirees could find themselves trapped, or even face losing their homes, under contracts that fail to offer a no-negative equity guarantee, he says. "With people living longer today, this scenario could see a 65-year-old take a loan and have nothing left by age 88, with the original borrowing well and truly spent," Benson says (Cited in Weekes, 2005). Nonetheless, the reverse mortgage product has been welcomed by retirees, though squandering resources on non-essentials shifts the burden of care to others, who are increasingly unable to provide support. Divorce may already have eroded assets, since it is a major contributor to financial stress, as well as depriving children of educational and other opportunities (Reed, **2008**). Washington philosophy professor, Martin Cook, sums up the relationship between poverty and divorce: "Many people are a divorce away from homelessness", he says (*ibid.*).

When traditional connections are severed, a void is created, demanding to be filled. We seek to fill it in unlikely places. Adler and Scelfo suggest that a generation raised on television looks to its celebrities for religious inspiration (Adler & Scelfo, 2006). So obsessed have we become with celebrity culture that as of 2009 seven year-olds in American primary schools are to receive formal guidance on "real world" living (Mansell, 2008) in a bid to interest the next generation in more than just the "fame formula" (Flanery, 2008). This formula applies to all areas of life, particularly when fame owes nothing to talent or achievement, as Hamilton points out (2005, 57), but is always attractively packaged. The quintessential, highly individualistic boomer religion, Scientology, makes a point of cultivating adherents in Hollywood, the home of their imposing Celebrity Center. Here the rich and beautiful recruit new members who hope to become like them, and endorse a 'religion' that promises transformation and total success. Adler and Scelfo cite the example of Bob Adams, a tight end with the Pittsburgh Steelers, who joined the church in 1973 because he was in search of assistance to become a better football player, teacher and parent. . . Says Adams: "Scientology was simple, precise, workable, and I saw effects immediately on the field".

Scientology teaches that human beings contain clusters of 'body thetans', or spirits, of aliens who died 75 million years ago in an intergalactic purge of overpopulated planets by the evil overlord Xenu. These thetans adversely influence thoughts and behaviour, and must be 'cleared' through 'auditing', a form of confessional therapy. Founder L. Ron Hubbard explained that unhappiness springs from mental aberrations ('engrams') and claimed that counseling sessions with the E-meter can knock out the engrams and improve a person's intelligence and appearance. Egos are boosted in self-admiration sessions and wealth and celebrity lifestyles lauded (Winter, 2005). But fulfilment comes with a hefty price tag in the Church of Scientology. In *Time Magazine*, Scientology has been called a "thriving cult of greed and power that poses as a religion but really is a ruthless global scam" (Behar, 1991, 50). Behar claims that "Scientology is quite likely the most ruthless, the most classically terroristic, the most litigious and the most lucrative cult the country has ever seen" on account of the amount of money it extracts from its members. At the Church of Scientology transformation is ostensibly for sale to those who can afford it as progression through its innumerable levels is extremely costly, making this church, not unlike the increasingly popular 'prosperity Christianity' (Chapter 2), the ultimate symbol of religious consumerism.

Some seekers, according to Adler and Scelfo, found gratification in the Unification Church, an organisation best known by the name of its founder, the Rev. Sun Myung Moon, who preaches that God's plan for the world involves uniting the races in Christianity through interracial marriage. Mass weddings of up to 2000 couples chosen by church leaders are conducted by Moon, the self-proclaimed "Messiah and Emperor of the Universe"—the "real Jesus". In *Bad Moon Rising* (2004), John Gorenfeld details the meteoric rise of Moon, "Scientology's L. Ron Hubbard of the East", convicted in 1982 of tax fraud and conspiracy, to land baron, media mogul and owner of the influential conservative newspaper, *The Washington Times* (Gorenfeld, 2004).

The restless impulse for self-transformation, which Todd Gitlin, author of *The Sixties*, describes as "a passion to find some new spiritual romance" (Cited in Adler & Scelfo, 2006) in, what sociologist Wade Clark Roof calls in the title of his 1993 book, *A Generation of Seekers*, finds an outlet in various movements whose pitch is utilitarian and self-serving rather than reverential and self-denying. Like Scientology's celebrity recruits, Madonna inspired an entire movement of Hollywood Kabbalists seeking, perhaps, to become more like her. The ancient eastern wisdom of Transcendental Meditation, taught by the Maharishi Mahesh Yogi, who as the Beatles' chosen guru automatically became the most celebrated Indian religious figure since Gandhi, enjoyed a surge of popularity in the West, fashionably repackaged as he was to appeal to the modern consumer. "Its benefits are immediate", testified one satisfied customer: "It gave me immediate experience of the unboundedness of my own nature" (*op. cit.*, 52). Pecuniary interests are not concealed and the movement widely advertises its related Iowa institution, the Maharishi University of Management, offering business degrees to seekers. The bridge from spiritual fulfilment to financial success appeals to the modern consumer in a materialistic world.

Contrived forms obscure their meanings, and as Naomi Klein says of the creators of brands in her book *No Logo*, they concentrate their efforts on creating and sustaining the intangible features that give them most of their value (cited in Hamilton, 2005, 38). Customers are encouraged never to shop primarily on price or to compare the features of branded products with non-branded equivalents, 'brand loyalty' ensuring that individual consumers develop an emotional relationship with the brand, a relationship based on trust and love (*op. cit.*, 39). Hamilton cites Kevin Roberts, head of Saatchi and Saatchi, on the nature of this love of brand: It is "beyond price, value, benefits, attributes, performance, distribution. You have to stay loyal to the idea of something because . . . because nothing. Because that's how you feel" (*ibid.*). These 'spiritual romances', like the "dream" of the "Family Romance" from which Mathews awakened

(2005, 167), were usually nothing more; they ran their course and left a void, yet the shared values of this generation have shaped the world we live in today. For most the experience was nothing more than a holiday romance—sweet but brief, followed by the longing for enduring love when it was over.

3.3 Ego and the Voices of Animals

Deafened by ego's commanding voice we fail to hear the soft voices of the creatures we have subjugated. The crude indifference of our culture, our fundamental attitude to reality, as Mathews describes it, manifests most clearly in our instrumentalisation of animals. Collectively mindless, unattuned to their plight, we ourselves have become a human herd, says former Bishop of Edinburgh, Richard Holloway—the most ferocious beast on the planet, inflicting depredation on animals we regard as commodities rather than meaningful beings (Holloway, 2009).

Sufism reminds us of the intrinsic unity of all things; in the rich diversity of all creatures the Sufi sees the divine reflection which inspires awe and reverence, yet the notion, supported by philosophy and science, as Mathews, Hamilton and Wheeler point out, that there is an existential difference between humans and world, has fostered supremacy of humans over other species and given rise to a moral scandal of far-reaching consequence. Kant declared "Man can have no duty to any beings except human", rendering all non-human beings mere means to human ends, as Hamilton points out. Cruelty to animals is not intrinsically wrong, said Kant; it should be condemned only because it deadens the feeling of sympathy for their suffering, and this callousness weakens the sympathy we may feel for other human beings (Hamilton, 2008, 211). "Modern Kantians, notably John Rawls, who privilege the rational above all else are caught in the same trap"—"a morality that treats animals only as means to human ends" (*ibid.*). Such views are convenient as they sanction our carelessness. But we fail as human beings when our self-serving actions cause harm; when commercial whaling threatens the survival of a species, when polar bears become endangered and seal, penguin and wild bird populations are in decline because of our thoughtlessness. We fail in our duty of care when we replace forests with palm oil plantations and allow our interests to constantly override the needs of other species.

In their facial and vocal expressions and body language Darwin found animal emotions to be clearly expressed, but this and similar work was criticised for being anecdotal, sentimental and anthropomorphic, says Masson (1996, 14); in other words, unscientific. It is of interest to note that Dr Jeffrey Masson, well-known author and researcher into the emotional lives of animals, studied under the eminent Sufi teacher Seyyed Hossein Nasr at Harvard. His awareness of *tawhid* enriches his worldview particularly with regard to understanding nonhuman species (Personal correspondence with Masson, 9 May 2008). According to Masson, the disciplines of comparative psychology and ethology, the more recent science of animal behaviour, still seek functional and causal, not emotive, explanations for behaviour. Konrad Lorenz, one of the main founders of ethology as a biological discipline (Brigandt, 2004, p 2), writes of 'crimes against animals' in an article entitled *'Tiere sind Gefühlsmenschen (Animals are Emotional People)* in which he asserts that anyone who has intimate knowledge of any individual higher mammal and does not believe that it has feelings similar to human feelings, is crazy (*Der Spiegel*, 1980, 47, p 251-262, cited in Masson, p 225). Yet we continue to deny, question or disregard their sentience.

Contrary to convenient, popular belief, fish do feel pain, and there is sufficient scientific evidence to support this view. Eminent animal physiologist, Neville Gregory, states unequivocally that neurological, pharmacological and behavioural studies indicate that fish feel pain. Furthermore, even simpler life forms such as gastropods share these features and like fish, they show pain responses analogous to those in vertebrates (Gregory, 1999). Yet we think nothing of dragging fish from the ocean depths, inflicting on them excruciating decompression, during which their internal organs often rupture. Finally we toss them on board where they slowly suffocate or are crushed to death. Others are still alive when their throats and stomachs are cut open (People for the Ethical Treatment of Animals (PETA), 2008).

In this connection one cannot but think of the ignominy of fishing as competitive sport (as of other activities which pit human against animal), where the purpose of the hunt is not survival but is accepted as an end in itself. Instead of constituting dialogical modalities, drawing us into deeper engagement with reality, such activities, "conducted in monological mode", Mathews believes, are the testimony of the block, "whose eyes are no longer for seeing the world, whose ears are no longer for hearing the voices of the world, and whose limbs are no longer for reaching out to it" (2005, 20).

Animal ethicist Peter Singer argues that humans and animals are in the relevant sense the same and their interests should therefore be given equal consideration (Hamilton, 2008, 208). Singer compares the pain and suffering we inflict on animals with that which resulted from centuries of tyranny by Whites over Blacks (Singer, 1975). Guilty of 'speciesism', a prejudice toward the interests of members of one's own species and against those members of other species, almost the entire oppressing group is directly involved in, and sees itself as benefiting from the oppression. According to Singer, the public believes it has an interest in the continuance of speciesist practices such as those of industrial farming and this allows people to accept reassurances that there is little cruelty. As Hamilton points out, accepting Singer's view has a number of ethical implications, including vegetarianism. Most people eat meat, buy what is cheapest, and have expectations of it being readily available and affordable. Furthermore the number of animals being consumed today is much greater than it was in the past, and growing prosperity in parts of the world is creating additional demand, increasing the scale of suffering as well as the burden on the environment. Powerful groups with vested interests combined with people's reluctance to know inconvenient truths means ignorance is perpetuated.

A substantial body of evidence suggests that human, animal and environmental interests are not being served by the international meat industry as we know it today. The full range of horrors to which animals are regularly subjected is revealed in, amongst many others, Peter Singer, *Animal Liberation* (1975); Wendell Berry, *The Unsettling of America* (1996) and *Life is a Miracle* (2000); Eric Schlosser, *Fast Food Nation: The Dark Side of the All American Meal* (2001); Karen Davis, *Prisoned Chickens, Poisoned Eggs*, (1996); Gail Eisnitz, *Slaughterhouse: The Shocking Story of Greed, Neglect and Inhumane Treatment Inside the U.S. Meat Industry* (2006). These and innumerable similar accounts tell of appalling suffering, first and foremost of animals, but theirs becomes a collective suffering for which animals, humans and the environment ultimately pay the price. Sufism reminds us that "with everything one eats one partakes of its spirit" (III, 53); the environment is not, as the word might have us believe, only around and beyond us, but absorbed within us and we into it in a continual, regular exchange. We are what we eat, and what we eat remakes the world, and as Michael Pollan elaborates in *The Omnivore's Dilemma*, we—a society of voracious, confused omnivores—are just beginning to recognise the profound consequences of our everyday food choices (2005). Eating meat might be considered pleasurable but, in the words of the Sufi: "for experiencing a passing joy, a joy that lasts only for a few minutes or for a few days, there will be a bill to pay; and the paying of that bill may take ten years" (VIII, 134), or more. Pollan alludes to that bill when he enumerates some of the unintended consequences that megaconsumption of fast, industrialised food, meat in particular, has had on the American diet, landscape, economy and culture.

Industrialisation entails long-distance transport for millions of animals before they are slaughtered. Over the last 30 years Australia's live export industry has exported over 150 million animals to the Middle East, to countries where there are no laws to protect them from acts of cruelty (Animals Australia Investigation, 2008). During this time, some 2.5 million have died en route to destinations as far away as Egypt, and according to Animal Australia investigators they may have been the lucky ones. Although the Egyptian live trade was suspended on animal welfare grounds by Australian Minister for Agriculture Peter McGauran in February 2006 after documentation of cattle having their tendons slashed and eyes stabbed in Cairo's Bassateen abattoir and the footage went to air on *60 Minutes* causing public outrage, trade has now been reinstated. The litany of disasters is well documented (*ibid.*) and condoning or ignoring the trauma these animals suffer at human hands on appallingly long journeys by ship, truck, squashed into car boots or tied on car roofs, regularly delayed, always distressed, haggled over and finally slaughtered, alive, without prior stunning, is immoral and indefensible.

Research indicates that by far the greatest source of human-inflicted suffering on animals has been found to be in the huge increase in animals kept confined on factory farms where overcrowding and unnatural social grouping prevent them from expressing any natural behaviour. Animals used in experiments are numbered in the tens of millions annually, but in one year ten *billion* birds and mammals are raised and killed for food in the United States alone and every year this figure grows. The increase alone from one year to the next, at around 400 million animals is, according to Singer, far greater than the total number of animals killed in the US by pounds and shelters, for research, and for fur combined (*op. cit.*). Gail Eisnitz provides a sobering account of the treatment of these animals that live their lives entirely indoors, never knowing fresh air, sunshine or grass in her book, *Slaughterhouse* (2006), which includes evidence of animals in major American slaughterhouses routinely being skinned and dismembered while still conscious.

Disregard for animals has serious consequences, as consumers of meat from distressed animals raised on inferior quality feed containing drugs, rendered animal products including animal waste experienced recently. Animal waste as an ingredient of animal feeds is mainly in the form of poultry and swine waste; in 2003 in Florida alone an estimated 350,000 tons of poultry litter were available for use in animal feed (Sapkota *et al*, 2007). Diseases such as Bovine Spongiform Encephalopathy (Mad Cow Disease) and Avian Flu were caused by meat- and waste-contaminated feed and resulted in mass-killings of cattle and poultry. In May 2008 a cull of the entire poultry population of Seoul was ordered by Korean authorities anxious to avoid the spread of Avian Flu (ABC news, 20 May 2008). Animals and birds are regarded as unclean and a potential source of disease, but in these instances it was human disregard for them that brought about these conditions. Production animals raised unnaturally with reliance on large quantities of pharmaceutical drugs cannot but deliver unnatural, chemically altered meat. In 2001/02, 547 tonnes of drugs were used in food-producing animals in Australia alone (Australian Pesticides and Veterinary Medicines Authority, 2005). Many of the drugs contained in animal feed are not degraded by the animals' bodies, but are excreted and end up in the environment. These drug residues may encourage the emergence of drug-resistant strains of micro-organisms, which constitute a further threat to health (Animals Australia, 2007).

The processes of animal raising and food production have become so alienated from nature that consumers, themselves disconnected from the natural environment, no longer associate food in general and meat in particular with the fecundity and natural rhythm of the earth. Food's life-giv-

ing properties have been overlooked and the moral aspect of our relationship with food forgotten. Instead of regarding the flesh of an animal
whose life is lost to the production process as a gift in which we discern
sacrifice and grace, we view it as another commodity to which we have a
right. Awareness of and gratitude for the gift of life might atone for the
harm inflicted and reduce the debt we incur in terms of mutual obligation.
Mostly, however, mindful eating has morphed into thoughtless consumption as food is consumed hurriedly, distractedly, carelessly and thoughtlessly. We accept the earth's gifts but without awareness of our obligation
to give thanks. Loving the Real, the Sufi reminds us, means giving thanks
for everything (Can 2005). In fact, the invocations with which he begins
a meal, *bismillâh* (In the name of God), and finishes the meal, *al-hamdu
li-llâh* (Praise be to God), "hold, just like the meal itself, our whole existence", explains Denis Gril in his interpretation of praise as thanks-giving,
and the "principal reason for the existence of the universe" (1997).

Similarly, Mathews describes the fundamental modality of panpsychist culture as 'grace' (2005, 21). Derived from the Latin *gratia*, grace
means favour or thanks (*ibid.*) and implies an attitude of gratitude for the
given, even if it is not that which one has sought. "In saying 'grace' before
a meal one offers thanks for sustenance rather than accepting it as one's
due". Grace on the part of the giver is giving for giving's sake, Mathews
explains; on the part of the receiver it is appreciation and gratitude rather
than expectation and demand (*ibid.*). Sufism teaches that the initiate can
do nothing without the initial grace of God (*tawfiq*, help of Allah)—freely given, pre-existing, the immutable cause of which is the Infinite
(Schuon, 1959, 90-91). Therefore Murat Çelebi urges us to be mindful
of the intricate processes that culminate in the storage of life-giving substances: "In your next meal, consider looking at the blessings on your
plate from the following perspective—'I am about to eat energy that was
heated approximately 100,000 years ago at 15 million degrees C in an
oven in the sun's center and later cooled and made appropriate for the
bodies of human beings'" (Çelebi, 2009).

An attitude of appreciation and gratitude transforms ordinary activities into "opportunities for communicative encounter with world"
(Mathews, 2005, 21). In Persian cuisine, in fact, recipes are often of a
poetic nature, reflecting awareness and cherishing of the one life in which

we all participate. The following is a translation of a Persian recipe for stuffed roast chicken, in which we discern respect and affection for the animal, and an essentially humble approach to preparation because the animal's intrinsic value is recognised:

> Your dead child. Prepare him for new life. Fill him with the earth. Be careful! He should not over-eat. Put on his golden coat. You bathe him. Warm him but be careful! A child dies from too much sun. Put on his jewels. This is my recipe (Fatima, cited in Sennett, 2008, 190).

As Northcott points out, the whole life-sustaining earth with its oceans, rivers and streams on which all forms of life are dependent represents the symbolic bread and wine of the flesh and blood of Christ and every meal is a partaking of it—a sacred communion (2007, 254). Humility is owed to *all* creatures, since all of them manifest divine qualities after their manner, says Schuon. "Man has no right to the things of creation except on condition that he respects them, that is to say on condition that he discerns in each one both its divine property and its spiritual language" (Schuon, 85). Northcott reminds us of "a moral and ritual continuum between the sacrality of the Lord's table and the profane household meal", where all meals have a "theurgic potential"; the boundary between *ecclesia* and *seculum* being determined by the spirit in which the blessing that food represents is received (2007, 255). The sensory experience of tasting which accompanies the ritual of eating that sustains the material body has its equivalent in the subtle realm of *batin*. 'Tasting' precedes 'unveiling', the awakening within the heart of mystical knowledge to which travellers on the Sufi path aspire. Ibn al-Arabi says:

> Knowledge comes only through tasting (. . .) I waited mindfully, not distracted, until there appeared to the eye the glory of His Face and a call to me, nothing else. I encompassed being in knowledge—nothing in my heart but God (*SPK*, 220-221)

Mostly distracted rather than mindful, however, we are often deaf to that call and blind to the glory of His Face as it appears in countless and unexpected forms. Animal abuse has many faces. Despite the efforts of international groups to stop the killing and exploitation of animals for their fur, each year over 50 million animals are killed for fashion, excluding rabbits, since no reliable data on rabbits killed worldwide for fur is available (Fur Free Alliance, 2007). According to Fur Free Alliance, Canada's annual commercial seal hunt represents the largest slaughter of marine mammals in which over 300,000 harp and hooded seals are killed for their pelts each year, many of which are skinned alive. In 2005, 98.5% of the seals killed were just two months of age or younger.

Consumer resistance and high prices have seen the development of an alternative to real fur—faux fur. But faux fur is not always fake. An investigation by The Humane Society of the United States (HSUS) exposed the widespread slaughter of companion animals, namely domestic dogs and cats, as well as raccoons, for the manufacture of 'faux' fur clothing, accessories and trinkets (2007). Because the 'faux' fur trade doesn't place as much emphasis on quality and uniformity, the quality of care given to furbearers is negligible. HSUS investigators witnessed the brutal slaughter of domestic dogs and cats in China and other Asian nations. Not only are these animals killed inhumanely, but their short lives are blighted by physical and behavioural abnormalities caused by the stress of caging conditions and neglect.

Fur is cut and dyed to look fake, so that unsuspecting consumers think they are getting faux fur. China, a country with no animal welfare laws (International Fund for Animal Welfare, Cited in HSUS, 2007), supplies half of all the finished fur products that are sold in the United States. An ongoing investigation by HSUS has found some of the biggest names in fashion selling raccoon dog fur trim on jackets that were mislabelled ('faux'), advertised as another species ('rabbit'), or not labelled at all (HSUS, 2007).

Animal suffering is widespread and occurs at every level. Born Free USA and the Animal Protection Institute (US) refer to pet shops as 'Little Shops of Sorrows' (2007) because of the unnatural, stressful and often unsanitary caging conditions the animals are made to endure. For some, suffering and risk do not end at the point of sale. Individuals who purchase animals in pet stores often act on impulse, without fully considering the commitment required to provide lifelong care for an animal. Every year thousands of reptiles, exotic birds, dogs and cats are sold to people who are unable to provide lifetime care and meet the unique needs of each animal.

Furthermore, we persist cold-heartedly in the belief that human life can be enhanced by sacrificing animals during scientific research. Guinea pigs, rabbits, hamsters, ferrets, rats and mice are among the animals still used in industry for widespread "product safety research" (Procter & Gamble, 2005, 11) during which "products (. . .) used in homes two billion times a day around the world" (*op. cit.*, 10) are tested. One of the many inhumane tests still being conducted, predominantly on rabbits, is the Draize eye irritancy test, which protects companies from potential lawsuits by their consumers but does not guarantee human safety. The Draize test is designed to show whether chemicals, especially those used on the face, hands and other parts of the body, can damage the eyes. Testing involves placing chemicals, which may be irritants to the eyes but which are designed for human use on the face, hands and other parts of the body, on the surface of the eyes of restrained animals (ANZCCART, 2006).

The list of injustices against animals is endless, but opposition to heartless practices is growing as more people learn to respect other species and to discern in each one both its divine property and its spiritual language, as Schuon suggests we should. On her farm outside Ravensthorpe in Western Australia, Julia Bell, "high priestess", has created a "pagan heaven" where "the orphaned, the runts, the surplus-to-requirements are taken in" (Mathews, 2005, 89), and "the discarded, the despised (and) the rejected" are forgiven, readopted and reclaimed (*op. cit.*, 91). Julia's farm is a "refuge from civilization" where camels, pythons, blowflies and spiders delight and enlighten in unexpected ways. In Julia's sacred world all things are in conversation, "in story", with the things around them—"just as things are in the 'state of nature'" (*op. cit.*, 98).

If we listen to their story attentively we discover that there is much we can learn and that what we learn can be adapted to improve the way we live. Wheeler's *Whole Creature* asserts the need for a return to a complex non-reductive semiotic biology (14), a need echoed by 'biomimics' such as Janine Benyus, who believes a wellspring of good ideas is readily available to us from our ten to thirty million planet-mates. The Creator has done everything human societies want to do technologically, biomimics point out, without mining the past or mortgaging the future. Spiders, for instance, Benyus explains, are "makers" of a true miracle fibre—silk, which is five times stronger, ounce for ounce, than steel (Benyus, *Biomimicry*, in Ausubel, p.10). Their raw materials are available locally and the manufacturing plant is the spider's body, so the fibre is created at body-temperature, a life-friendly temperature. The fibre is biodegradable and the spider can eat the web to make more of it (*ibid.*). Not only might these creatures awaken in us a certain compassion, as in Julia's case, but more especially respect for the elegance, simplicity and efficacy of their creativity, and awe for the genius that makes it possible. What if we could emulate spiders and figure out how to take carbon-based, abundant raw materials and allow them to self-assemble in a silent manufacturing process that operates in water at room temperature and produces a biodegradable fibre, Benyus muses (*ibid.*). Inspired by how efficiently other creatures do things, Benyus explains, industrial ecologists are finding new paradigms for their technologies—adhesion like a gecko, cooling buildings like a termite, growing ceramics like an abalone, making green plastics like a bacterium, and wicking water from air like a desert beetle. Or we might learn to treat our own illness, or prevent it as far as possible, and influence our fertility, as do chimpanzees (*op. cit.*, 11).

Contemporary Sufi scholarship clearly reflects this line of thought. Physicist Ahmet Uysal, for example, believes that even the tiniest entity inspires us to reflect on its Creator. Magnetotactic bacteria synthesize magnetite crystals from scratch and then put them in order like beads hitched on a string, he explains; a process whose basic principles we have yet to understand if we wish to mimic it. The more we understand the more highly we come to regard "the great craft of (the) Supreme Artist", Uysal believes (2010). Similarly, Sami Polatöz describes how research developments in fluid mechanics have been influenced by unique mechanisms in the movement of fish in water (2009). Soil-cleaning plants eliminate toxic substances from the environment or diminish their negative effects in the life-enhancing process of phytoremediation, according to Arif Ustaoğlu (2008). And highly sophisticated processes carried out by bees effectively preserve the ecological balance, explains Mahmut Veziroğlu; "if the bees become extinct, mankind will face many disasters, like erosion, desertification and the extinction of plants which are food for us and for the animals we raise" (2009). "Instead of seeing nature as warehouse, you begin to see her as teacher. Instead of valuing what you can extract from her, you value what you can learn from her. And this changes everything" (Benyus, *Biomimicry*, in Ausubel, p. 8).

Since "harmlessness is the essence of morality" (VIII, 92) we need to awaken to the intrinsic value of other species so that our coexistence becomes more ethical. We need to consider the lives of the animals that are sacrificed so that human living can be more comfortable, and reflect on how we receive their giving and what we give in exchange. "Fishes, which never dreamed of harming us, we catch in nets. We load burdens upon horses, camels and elephants, and we take from the calf its share in the form of milk and butter upon which our everyday's livelihood depends. What we have built up and have comforted ourselves with is nothing else than tyranny—of which we never stop to think for a while" (*ibid.*). The materialistic world is the state of being unaware of the One, says Rumi. We are masters of the material universe and have overpowered the strongest and most courageous animals, but are defeated by the animals within—the wolf of anger, the snake of lust and the dog of *nafs* (Can, 2005).

United in life the myriad forms from the simplest to the most complex display their meaning, in contemplation of which the voice of ego is stilled and listening occurs, in mystical awe and reverence.

3.4 Ego and the Voice of the Earth

"The world 'speaks' through symbolic constellations that are . . . uniquely apposite to the situation at hand" (Mathews, 2003, 66). "So, perhaps", says Mathews, "the world, if we are open to it, communicates with us via a poetic order", signaling to the self-aggrandizing ego the dissonance taking place in the wider fabric of the self (*op. cit.*, 67). Its signals are becoming impossible to ignore.

Like Mathews, Sogyal Rinpoche, author of *The Tibetan Book of Living and Dying* (2003), believes that societies have not developed the long-term vision necessary to restrain them from plundering the planet for their own immediate ends and from living in a way that could prove fatal for the future. Citing former Brazilian Minister for the Environment responsible for the protection of the Amazon rain forest, Jose Antonio Lutzenberger, he says: "Modern industrial society is a fanatical religion. We are demolishing, poisoning, destroying all life-systems on the planet. We are signing IOU's our children will not be able to pay . . . We are acting as if we were the last generation on the planet. Without a radical change in heart, in mind, in vision, the earth will end up like Venus, charred and dead" (Rinpoche, 8).

Environmental degradation has become part of life as we know it. Pollution, particularly irreversible "genetic pollution", referred to by Ausubel as "the vandalism of nature—graffiti in the book of life" (Ausubel, 2004, 141), drought, floods, climate change, rising sea levels, increased risk of bushfires, decimation of crops, decreasing water resources, desertification, damaged ecosystems—these and many more are a reality and impact on our quality of life. We seem no closer to eliminating the dire threats facing our planet and, according to Sir Martin Rees, may be on the brink of unwittingly triggering a global calamity (Rees, 2003). Indeed, according to Rees, the fact that human civilization survived the many threats of the 20th century is more due to luck than judgment. He warns of nuclear disasters resulting in the destruction of the biosphere, genetically engineered viruses causing an uncontrollable global pandemic, in short, the effect of information-based activity devoid of a vision of unity.

In April 2007 ANU Professor of Economics, Ross Garnaut, was commissioned by the Australian States and Territories, and subsequently the Commonwealth Government, to undertake a review examining the impact of climate change on the Australian economy. In a paper he presented on 29 November 2007 entitled 'Will climate change bring an end to the Platinum Age?' he exposes the 'inconvenient truth' of the side-effects of unprecedented global economic growth, which has exceeded in speed, magnitude and breadth that of the two beneficent post-war decades that came to be known as the 'Golden Age'. Garnaut describes the extension into the heartlands of the populous countries of Asia of the scientific, technological, industrial and commercial revolutions that had their origins in Britain and Northern Europe in the late eighteenth century. These changes spread through Western Europe and its regions of overseas settlement and to Japan through the nineteenth and early twentieth centuries, and to a number of smaller economies in East Asia in the third quarter of the twentieth century before reaching China, whose fast-growing economy now has a substantial impact on the global environment. Beijing is shrouded in the Gobi desert's fine, yellow dust that conceals the sky and gives the air a hazy, surreal density, yet as recently as 2007 the Chinese government was planning to multiply tenfold China's greenhouse gas production (Northcott, 2007).

Industrial development extends well beyond China, with high rates of growth being well established in India, and Vietnam with its economy that involves more people than any country in the European Union, growing as rapidly and consistently as India. According to Garnaut, the evidence is accumulating that the exceptionally high average growth rates of the early twenty-first century are not temporary phenomena, but, he reiterates, the unprecedented, rapid growth is not sustainable without major changes in the relationship between the environment and economic activity, since the latter is dependent on the utilization of fossil fuels, especially in the energy and transport sectors. Garnaut explains that global fossil-fuel carbon emissions from 2004 to 2006 grew at an annual rate of 3.1%, a rate in excess of that anticipated in many of the international climate change assessments, including the scenarios outlined by the Intergovernmental Panel on Climate Change (IPCC). Demand has increased in recent years, while limitations have been placed on expansion of production. This has lifted oil and other energy prices to exceptional levels, yet impending scarcity is unlikely to provide a substantial constraint on coal and total fossil fuel consumption for the foreseeable future, according to Garnaut.

Two highly emissions-intensive alternatives to oil—coal and synthetic liquid hydro-carbons (derived from coal, tar sands, shale or natural gas)—are expanding their global roles. The average amount of carbon per unit of energy used has actually been increasing in the large economies. Yet despite all the evidence, Garnaut states that "it is neither desirable, nor remotely feasible, to seek the removal of the risk of dangerous climate change through reduction in global ambitions for higher material living standards" (2008).

In the same paper Garnaut acknowledges that the reality of observed climate change in recent years represents "a worse and more urgent problem than we thought". The rate of emission increases has also exceeded that presumed in the most extensively discussed IPCC scenarios. He proposes three reasons for this: global economic growth, the intensity of growth and the carbon intensity of energy production that are all proceeding ahead of expectations. In a subsequent paper presented on 28 March

2008 entitled 'Climate Change and Australian Economic Reform', he makes the following point: "There are large uncertainties surrounding the science of climate change. Those of us who are not climate scientists must weigh intelligently reputed scientific opinion. The weight of scientific opinion advises, on a balance of probabilities, that, in the absence of effective mitigating policy, we face high risks of dangerous climate change. The prudent presumption is that unabated climate change could seriously disrupt modern economic growth".

Several points Garnaut makes require our attention. There exists a distinct possibility that strategies being considered may be flawed or inadequate, and potential outcomes miscalculated with dire results, since we are dealing with issues of utmost complexity, conflicting scientific opinion and incompatible vested interest groups. Science, Rumi reminds us, is a 'science of bodies'—a bird with one wing. Unless we take into account the moral significance of the earth, a satisfactory solution will not be found.

Despite its effects, economic growth is treated as the panacea for all our social ills, says Hamilton who, drawing on the new Economics Foundation in London, proposes a political manifesto for wellbeing—one devoted to restoring meaning to people's lives rather than committed to progress irrespective of the cost (2005, 217-224). "Australians are anxious about declining moral standards", he says. "We worry that we have become too selfish, materialistic and superficial and long for a society built on mutual respect, self-restraint and generosity of spirit" (*op. cit.*, 224). "The challenge of our age", Hamilton claims, "is to build a new politics that is committed, above all, to improving our wellbeing" (217). Hamilton's political manifesto, however, is included as a postscript and does not form part of his metaphysical-psychology which lends itself to application within the private sphere; like Sufism, it is apolitical and pertains to the heart, or as Anissian describes Sufism's role, to "the care of the soul" (2006, 19). "Governments can't legislate to make us happy", Hamilton acknowledges, "but many things they do affect our wellbeing. With time, they can change for good or ill the society and culture we live in" (2005, 218), he believes.

Governments and consumers appear reluctant to compromise higher material living standards, although it is the impact of consumption by the one billion most affluent humans on the planet that has far more negative environmental and societal consequences than that of the three billion poorest (Friends of the Earth Australia (FOTEA), 2005). According to FOTEA's position paper, *Immigration, Population and Environment*, Australia had in 2005 the highest per capita greenhouse gas (GHG) emission rates of any industrialized nation, at about 27.2 tonnes per person per year. This is twice the average level of other wealthy countries and 27% higher than emissions per person in the United States (21.4 tonnes). Our energy intensive economy and lifestyle are typical of the developed world, which has been responsible for over 80% of all GHG emissions from human sources on the planet. Australia, with only 21 million people, produces around 1.1% of global emissions. With this relatively small number of people we should not be producing more than 0.31% of global emissions if we were consuming a fair share.

Moreover, Australia is forecast to grow faster than any other industrialised nation over the next 40 years. A Washington survey predicts that Australia's population will grow by 55 per cent by 2050—to 35 million, faster than China or India (Berger, 2009). Politicians and business leaders welcome the population boom, but environmental groups and scientists warn of ecological overload and continuing growth, rather than cuts, in carbon emissions (*ibid.*).

The First World comprises only about 23% of the world's human population but consumes around 80% of the resources. Research (FOTEA, 2005) indicates that if everyone currently living on the planet were to live at the average First World consumption levels we would need to put all arable land into agricultural production, effectively meaning the loss of most of the planet's biologically diverse conservation reserves. However, we would require another two planets of the same size as the earth to meet everyone's needs. It is clear that such levels of consumption by affluent nations are neither sustainable nor ethical.

If it becomes a reality, deliberate planetary engineering will also have far-reaching consequences, the full force of which may only be experienced by future generations. Climate engineering, or the 'final solution' as it has grimly been referred to, has come out of the shadows and is being seriously considered by 'the world's top scientists and thinkers' as a means of counteracting climate change caused by rising CO_2 concentrations (Keith, 2008). While the scope of human impact is well and truly global, scientists have not yet made a deliberate attempt to transform nature on a planetary scale. This could however change in the foreseeable future, particularly given that geoengineering would, in the short term, be more cost- and time-effective than more conservative methods of cooling the earth. In some quarters, geoengineering is therefore being offered as an expedient solution to global warming. Nobel Prize winning scientist Paul Crutzen, for example, suggests various technologies to engineer a cooling effect. Aerosols could be added to the atmosphere to scatter sunlight back into space before the rays reach the earth and at the same time possibly also increase the lifetime and reflectivity of clouds. Alternatively, it might be possible to engineer giant shields in space to scatter sunlight away from the planet, according to Crutzen (*ibid.*).

Canadian atmospheric scientist David Keith is at the forefront of an international group of climate scientists calling for an honest debate about the risks and potential side-effects of what he calls 'the most dangerous techno-fix of all time' (*op. cit.* p 5). He draws our attention to occasions in the past where geoengineering in the form of cloud seeding—the use of aerosols dispersed from aircraft to induce cloud formation and produce rain—was utilised to produce unfavourable conditions for troops during the Second World War in spite of the far-reaching effects that the alteration of atmospheric chemistry entailed both to the nations involved and to the environment. He warns of the ethical and environmental implications of such intervention and the likely misuse of this power to suit human desires.

Keith poses the question whether the planet should be managed using all available tools so as to maximize human benefit here and now with little regard for the future, or whether we should rather seek to minimize human interference with nature. He cites advocates of active management such as Allenby (Earth Systems Engineering and Management, *IEEE Technology and Society Magazine*, 19:10-24, 2000) who argue that simple minimization of impacts is naive because the earth is already so transformed by human actions that it is, in effect, a human artifact. According to this view, the proper goal of planetary management is the maximization of the planet's functionality to humans. Allenby is of the opinion that it makes little sense to minimize impacts in order to let nature run free if there is no free nature left to protect (Keith, 2008).

Implementing sophisticated new technology to manipulate the earth's atmosphere, however, does not address the root cause of the problem, and may, in fact, make matters worse, as Kate Rigby explains in *Dancing with Disaster* (2009). "There is a very real danger", she says, "that we could become caught in a vicious circle, whereby our responses to the threat or impact of climate change engender further military conflict, exacerbate economic inequity, heighten political repression, and/or escalate habitat destruction" (Rigby, 132). With reference to Val Plumwood's *Feminism and the Mastery of Nature*, Rigby continues: "Climate change highlights the pitfalls of this standpoint of mastery by disclosing the blindness of assuming said nature to be a more-or-less passive background to human endeavour, fully knowable and infinitely manipulable" (*op. cit.*, 133). We overestimate the extent of our knowledge and control, says Rigby, and incomplete knowledge may lead to irrational actions: "What climate change discloses, then, in a particularly powerful way, and not without a potentially tragic irony, is the crisis of a way of thinking and acting that has long laid claim to the mantle of reason, not entirely unreasonably, but that can now be seen to constitute an ideological and ultimately irrational foreshortening of the promise of rational inquiry and reflection" (*op. cit.*, 135-136).

Climate change, says Garnaut, is a "diabolical problem". We know of course that this problem is very much of human making, nevertheless, Garnaut may just have put his finger on it. In his critique of neo-liberal economics, *A Moral Culture: The Ethics of Global Warming*, Northcott refers to social structures such as the global market economy as "structures of sin" since "they train us to act individually and disconnectedly" rather than aspiring to serve the common good (Northcott, 2008). According to Northcott, global warming is a moral and ethical issue and as long as our goals are short-sighted and self-serving and we lack awareness of the earth's intrinsic value, we will produce and perpetuate a culture of irresponsibility. "Global warming is the earth's judgment on the global market empire, and on the heedless consumption it fosters" he says (2007, 7), emphasising the importance of developing awareness, investing our relationships with knowledge and acting collectively so that the common good may be served.

Economist Kamran Mofid, born in Iran and educated in Canada and Britain, has been a pioneer in this field, establishing Globalisation for the

Common Good (GCG) in 2002 as an organisation aimed at "rekindling the human spirit and compassion in globalisation". Highly critical of post-enlightenment economic rationalism that has removed human needs concerns from economic equations by focusing on profit maximization, cost minimization and the highest returns to shareholders, Mofid is promoting an ethical, moral and spiritual vision that invests matter with meaning by adding love and compassion to our economic modelling. Having taught "secular, value-free" economics for over twenty years he is addressing the shortcomings of a system that he considers "hard of heart", since it undermines the very principles of needs fulfilment that it was originally designed to meet. "I told them to create wealth, but I did not tell them for what reason; I told them about scarcity and competition, but not about abundance and co-operation; I told them about free trade, but not about fair trade; about gross national product, but not about gross national happiness; I told them about profit but not about social consciousness, accountability to the community, sustainability, and respect for the creation and the Creator", says Mofid. "I did not tell them that without humanity, economics is a house of cards built on shifting sands" (Mofid, 2008).

Mofid's multicultural background and interdisciplinary work, drawing as it does on economics, politics, international relations, theology, ecology, ethics and spirituality, as well as the interfaith dialogue he conducts, give him a holistic view where he recognises commonality despite obvious differences and where all actions have consequences. His Common Good Initiative represents a coming together of diverse groups in celebration of their common humanity.

Similar thoughts are expressed by 2001 Nobel Laureate, Joseph Stiglitz, professor of economics at Columbia University and author of *The Three Trillion Dollar War*. He is critical of an economic system in which the major beneficiaries are the rich, while the gap between rich and poor notoriously widens. Globalisation, cutting trade barriers and opening markets does not necessarily generate development due to the asymmetrical nature of trade agreements that disadvantages poorer countries, he believes. 'Free' trade is never free and as with the animals in Orwell's *Animal Farm*, all are never equally free. Rich countries and large corporations dominate the global marketplace, creating unequal relations of power and information. As a result, trade is inherently unequal and instead of experiencing improved living standards, poor countries are likely to suffer increasing unemployment, poverty and income inequality (O'Shea, 2005). "The biggest mistake of the West was that it lacked love and mercy", says Şefik Can (2005, 279), with reference to an open letter written by the modern Turkish poet, Süleyman Nazif, telling of exploitation, oppression and injustice by Westerners towards weaker nations unable to protect themselves.

Stiglitz and co-author of *The Three Trillion Dollar War*, Linda Bilmes, claim that the true cost of the war in Iraq is being concealed by the Pentagon and that its infinitely greater and ever spiralling cost is a direct cause of the crisis in the economy. Accounting and reporting procedures which they claim lack transparency, hidden costs of long-term war that have been overlooked and payment of a war financed by deficits, lead the authors to conclude that it is "only a matter of time before the day of reckoning" (Stiglitz & Bilmes, 30 March 2008). As with climate change, the "day of reckoning" in the form of the cost of this extended war and its consequences, and failed economic policies will be borne predominantly by future generations.

Earth systems are interconnected in such a way that yesterday's actions, enjoyed today, must be confronted tomorrow. What is freely given carries no price, but debt incurred must be repaid and as past, present and future merge the notion of 'inherited sin' assumes new meaning for the generations that must make recompense. Though the idea of sin as inherited is offensive to the modern liberal mind because it suggests a fundamental lack of freedom, consequences are never lost within a system whose health depends on its interconnectedness. Citing Alistair McFadyen (*Bound to Sin*, Cambridge University Press, 2000, 27), Northcott says: "The denial of this situatedness is part of the pathology of global warming, resting as it does on the human refusal to *be* creature, and a refusal of responsibility for the welfare of other creatures" (2007, 182).

Pope John Paul II referred to global economic and governing ideologies that direct the path of human development away from the authority of natural and moral laws towards egotistic individualism as "structures of sin, originating in the sin of pride" (Pope John Paul II, *Sollicitudio Rei Socialis*, Libreria Vaticana, paragraph 36, cited Northcott, 153). Northcott suggests that this sin, which is a "prideful refusal of the creatures' dependence on the Creator", has the consequence of "destroying interdependence and solidarity between men and women, between them and other creatures and between humanity and God" (2007, 154). Fallenness is forgetfulness of the mystery, Heidegger tells us (1971). Russian theologian Sergei Bulgakov puts it as follows: "In the fall into sin humanity closes off the path to divine life, consequently nature appears under its aspect as created, no longer sophianic, as fallen or darkened Sophia, an image of non-being, sheer materiality" (Bulgakov, *The Lamb of God: On the Divine Humanity*, cited Northcott, 153).

Keith suggests an alternative view of climate policy that demands that we attribute intrinsic rights or values to natural systems independent of their utility. Under this view, we should minimize our impact on the natural world—for its own sake and because it has intrinsic value—not solely to reduce the risk that manipulation of natural systems poses for humanity (Keith, 2008). While Keith's comments are encouraging, the teachings of Sufism emphasise the inherent meaningfulness of all forms, so it is less a matter of attributing value to natural systems than of recognising their intrinsic value. Unless we still the voice of ego all forms will speak to us of commodity rather than of integrity. In Arendt's words, "the loss of all intrinsic worth begins with their transformation into commodities and values, for from this moment on they exist only in relation to some other thing which can be acquired in their stead" (1958, 157).

As climate change and fuel shortages bite, a global food crisis looms, warns John Vidal, environment editor of the *Guardian* (3 November 2007). Likewise the *Spiegel* informs us that around the world, rising food prices have made basic staples like rice, wheat and corn unaffordable for many people, pushing the poor to the barricades because they can no longer get enough to eat. But the worst is yet to come, it warns (14 April 2008). The UN World Food Programme compares the escalating global food crisis to a "silent tsunami" that could plunge more than 100 million people into hunger and poverty (ABC news, 23 April 2008). Prices for staples like rice, corn and wheat, which were relatively stable for years, have skyrocketed by over 180 percent in the last three years and global food reserves are at their lowest in 25 years (*Spiegel*, 14 April 2008). The price rises are reportedly the result of a combination of factors such as record oil prices, US farmers switching from cereals to biofuel crops, extreme weather conditions and growing demand from India and China.

The competition for grain between the world's 800 million motorists and its 2 billion poorest people is emerging as an epic issue, says Lester Brown, founder of the Washington-based Worldwatch Institute thinktank (*ibid.*). The outlook is widely expected to worsen as agro-industries worldwide prepare to switch to highly profitable biofuels, a practice which Jean Ziegler, United Nations' independent expert on the right to food, calls "a crime against humanity", saying it is creating food shortages and price increases that cause millions of poor people to go hungry (Lederer, 2007). According to Grain, a Barcelona-based food resources group, the Indian government seems committed to planting 14 million hectares of land with jatropha, an exotic bush from which biodiesel can be manufactured. Brazil intends to grow 120 million hectares for biofuels, and Africa around 400 million hectares in the next few years. Food shortages have already reached crisis point in these countries due to growing populations, extreme weather, ecological stress and political conflict, resulting not only in the abandonment or forced removal of formerly productive farms but in the escalation of forced migration more generally. Zimbabwe, for example, once the foodbowl of Africa, is now on the brink of collapse and those who remain there are starving, while one man's ego determines their fate (Buckle, 2002). In Haiti, where bread, corn tortillas and rice have become unaffordable luxuries, the poor survive on mud biscuits, whose main ingredient is clay. Combined with salt and vegetable fat, the baked clay numbs the pangs of hunger. According to World Bank President Robert Zoellick, exploding food prices threaten to cause instability in at least 33 countries, including regional powers like Indonesia, Pakistan and Egypt, where the crisis is helping radical Islamic movements to gain strength and terrorism's network to extend (Lederer, 2007).

In light of so much poverty, surfeit and ever-growing piles of waste represent not only an engineering problem but, more importantly, a moral problem, says Hamilton, who estimates that Australians spend a total of $10.5 billion every year on goods they do not use (2005, 101). According to Rob Jackson, director of the Centre on Global Change at Duke University, people generally view frugality as a negative thing. "The cultural norm is that if you save, or cut back, you're a bit eccentric", he says. "Unwrap it, use it, throw it out, forget it" is, according to Jackson, the prevailing mindset in a culture which rejects simplicity and prizes convenience and immediate gratification (Cited in Zane, 2007). In fact, things are made to be thrown away, and made in such a way that up to 90 per cent of the materials used in the process of making are wasted even before the end product appears in a store (McDonough & Braungart, M. *Cradle to Cradle: Remaking the Way We Make Things*, 2002, 27-28, cited Northcott, 114). Such a culture is entirely at odds with the regenerative and recycling patterns of natural systems (Northcott, 32-33) and the economy of the earth itself which is one of "no waste" (*op. cit.*, 132). According to McDonough and Braungart, modern humans are the only species to regularly take more nutrients from the earth than they return to it (*ibid.*), thereby destabilising and disrupting the fertile cycles and energy flows in the greater than human world.

The archaic understanding of fertility as an animating principle is central to both panpsychism and Sufism. Fertility depends on recycling, which, as Mathews explains, is not merely a prosaic practice—"a how-to-do-more-with-less philosophy of thrift and self-reliance" (2005, 91). "It is", as she says, "much deeper than this". At the heart of the notion of fertility is "a philosophy of reclamation, resurrection and renewal", "a 'recycling' at every level of life—the forgiveness of the degraded, the readoption of the rejected (and) the reclamation of the discarded", so that "the new can find its authentic form from within the shell of the old". "All aspects of life, unwanted as well as wanted, are part of life's sacred unity and must therefore be accepted . . . if the spirit is to grow", insists Mathews (*ibid.*).

With disregard for natural rhythms, no longer organised around the organic principle of fertility but rather around the industrial principle of production, "we condemn ourselves to living against the grain of things, missing the point of existence" (*op. cit.*, 96). Thus "modern societies have hijacked reality, overriding its inherent logic of unfolding" (*op. cit.*, 94). We have become alienated from "that perennial and substantial world in which we really do live . . . and in which we should accept our responsibilities again within the conditions of necessity and mystery" (Berry, 1983, 13). Slow to read the earth's signs of distress, our response is driven by rational self-interest, so that we turn outward to the powers of science and technology to undo our making rather than inward, as Rumi suggests we should:

Man is vision, the rest is skin; but only vision of the Friend is vision. Where there is no vision of the Friend, a man would be better off blind . . . Either vision of the Friend or love for Him—to what other end should a man employ this world? God's aim for man was vision and comprehension—oh, God's mercy never leaves vision and comprehension! (*SPL*, 295)

If we harnessed our insight and understanding we might, like Rumi, perceive the Beloved everywhere, His face veiled only by His dark tresses; its radiant beauty discernible in the clear light of day when sight is keenest, but obscured by the darkness of ignorance and ego, the heart's shadow. Lack of vision and comprehension produces thoughtless action, and the beauty of His face is violated as material progress, the guiding *telos* of human advancement, demands that the earth be subdued and transformed into human wealth and possession. As the increasing scale of destruction testifies, we have become heartless creators of a world in which progress is measured in terms of material goods—inferior, lifeless goods, mechanically produced, lacking the beauty and enduring qualities of the world we transform, actively supporting or passively endorsing the paradoxical reduction and simultaneous proliferation of 'the Good' to 'goods'.

The strident voice of ego must be stilled so that other voices might be heard. Rumi's tribute to his Beloved is a timely reminder that without "vision and comprehension" we will not see beyond the veils of form and meaning will remain concealed from us. "Either vision of the Friend (*marifa*) or love for Him (*ishq*)—to what other end should a man employ this world?"

CHAPTER FOUR

Finding Meaning (*Mana*)

Finding Meaning (*Mana*)

I n this chapter I will contrast the Sufi concept of *marifa* with the modern understanding of knowledge, the neoliberal association of knowledge with the economy, and the commoditisation of knowledge, making reference to Nasr's thought on the modern desacralisation of the *scientia sacra* and signaling affinities with Polanyi's account of tacit knowledge on which Wheeler draws. I will compare the Sufi concept of *amal*, knowledge in practice, as exemplified by Rumi's analogy of 'the Worker, hidden in His Workshop', with pragmatist Sennett's interpretation of craftsmanship. I will argue that the modes of knowing as elaborated by three contemporary philosophers, namely Mathews' understanding of 'encounter', Wheeler's of 'semiotic knowledge' and Hamilton's of 'moral certainty' are 'new' forms of a perennial, mystical concern with knowledge and meaning.

4.1 Knowing with the Heart

Weary and worn, the West is ripe for a meaningful, heart-centred approach to being which might allow for a glimpse of the Beloved's face in a world that hides it in its many forms. "In the area of meaning", claims John Carroll, "the modern West is in a state of crisis" (Carroll, 2008). Yet, he says, we are born craving meaning, and become depressed, neurotic, even suicidal, if we fail to find it. Trapped in a swiftly changing world of forms whose meaning eludes us, we are now more than ever in need of the kind of knowing that recognises and accommodates mystery and uncertainty; the kind of knowing that enabled Rumi to recognise in the unlikely figure of Shams the face of his Beloved and undergo an experience that transformed his life. This is the kind of knowing that is an attunement to the stillness of the heart; not one that imposes the ego's overwhelming voice on a defenceless world. Nor is it a negation of knowledge acquired rationally, but an understanding of its limitations. The values with which our culture bombards us have prompted deep dissatisfaction—potent agent of transformation initiating the *tawba* or 'turning' of the heart. The world has become a deeply troubled place where we, like the reed torn from the reed bed in the opening verse of the *Mathnawi*, experience the pain of separation. To restore unity we must move beyond the visible world of appearances governed by our preconceptions and our limited form of knowing, into the formless dimension and become attuned to its dynamic silence.

4.2 Knowing the Real

The nature of knowledge has been the subject of epistemological enquiry since the time of the early Greek philosophers, yet to date there is no single universally accepted definition of knowledge. Charles Taylor argues that all epistemic orders are imposed and that the epistemological construal is just another order. As such it has no claim to ultimate correctness, "not because it has been shown inadequate . . . but because all such claims are bogus. They mistake an act of power for an act of truth" (Taylor, 16). The theory of knowledge, epistemology, has been the main preoccupation of Muslim philosophers (Inati, 1998), and Ibn al-Arabi's comprehensive exegesis of knowledge is a testament to this. Taking the possibility of knowledge for granted, Muslim philosophers focus their epistemological effort on the study of the nature and sources of knowledge. Their intellectual inquiries, beginning with logic and ending with metaphysics are directed towards helping to understand what knowledge is (*ibid.*). To the Sufis, 'knowledge' (*marifa*) means 'knowledge of mysteries' (*'ulum al-asrar*); knowledge of that which in its all-comprehensiveness is unknowable—the 'coincidence of opposites' (*SPK*, 59; Mahmood, 2009) that has no opposite to 'make it clear', referred to in the Upanishads as *Neti-Neti*: 'not this, not that' (Mascaro, 1973, 26). Rumi says:

> He appears to be still and in movement, but He is neither this nor that; He manifests Himself in place, but in truth He has no place (*SPL, 23*).

He is ungraspable yet the Sufi recognises Him in all things. The search for *marifa* is the search for direct knowledge of God. To the Sufi all knowledge is knowledge of God in accordance with *tawhid*, the principle of oneness of Being—all things must be taken back to the One—and *wahdat al-wujud*, 'All forms are the forms of His Beautiful Names; everything is from Him'. Knowledge therefore concerns itself first and fore-most with the One. It is the realisation of the Qur'anic verses "Whither-soever you turn, there is the Face of God" (2:115), and "There is no god but God" (*SPK*, 147). A lack of knowledge (*marifa*) prevents us from see-ing beyond the veils, but those with knowledge know who He is. There-fore the veils, which portray either His mercy or His majesty but never His totality, reveal the divine attributes, from which knowledge of Him might be derived. All things must be known with a view of the totality and must therefore be taken back to the One by *tawil, the return to Source*. Recognition of the One in and beyond the veils of form, i.e. realisation of *wahdat al-wujud*, provides some understanding of the totality. Knowledge of divine unity provides the Sufi with a certainty of His reality which does not rely on proof.

At a time of great uncertainty and instability, the primacy of tradi-tional epistemology that privileges duality, as does the modern mechanis-tic worldview, is being challenged in some areas in favour of unifying modes of knowing such as those inspired by the mystical paradigm, known by the Sufis as *marifa*—knowing through unveiling, or recognis-ing (gnosis). Unveiling leads to transcendence of the divide between knower and known, in accordance with the traditional view of the nature of knowledge held by Aristotle, according to which when we come to know something, the mind (*nous*) becomes one with the object of thought, both being informed by the same *eidos* (Taylor, 1995, 3). Aris-totle's theory of knowledge has its origins in Plato's philosophy of forms, whose similarities with Rumi's understanding of 'form and meaning' we noted previously. According to Plato, unity is the greatest good; conse-quently knowledge which fosters a strong bond of unity is considered more valuable than that which fosters plurality (Plato, 1956, 415). Of course it might be argued that such a view could potentially embody "fun-damentalist proclivities" (Mathews, 2003, 7), and be used to homogenize and oppress 'others', a concern expressed, for example, by ecofeminist Val Plumwood ('Deep Ecology, Deep Pockets, and Deep Problems: A Femi-nist Ecosocialist Analysis', *Beneath the Surface: Critical Essays in the Philos-ophy of Deep Ecology, ed.* Eric Katz, Andrew Light and David Rothenberg, Cambridge, Massachusetts: The MIT Press, 2000) and there are indeed many examples to support her view. The issue might be best addressed by looking at the distinctive features of mystical knowing in the course of this chapter, (and in the following chapter at the nature of *ishq*, mystical love) to determine whether the oppressive conduct to which Plumwood refers bears any resemblance to the mystical approach.

Mystical knowledge, as recognition of unity, is not acquired from extraneous sources but awakened within the heart where it slumbers. As Plato described, it is not a product of mind but an attribute of soul (or heart), of which one partakes by recollection (Plato, 129). "Knowledge does not come by learning names and forms" (VI, 114). Unless meaning is experienced, it remains concealed by the veils of form, therefore Rumi says:

> The man more perfect in erudition is behind in meaning and ahead in form. . .
> A knowledge is needed whose root is upon the other side, since every branch leads to its root.
> Every wing cannot fly across the breadth of the ocean:
> Only a knowledge that comes directly from Him can take one to Him.
> (*SPL*, 25)

The 'science of bodies' (*ilm-i abdān*) is the study of the outer reality of things, and since it disregards essential *tawhid*, represents a bird with one wing. It is only when inherent meaning is recognised that the bird's integrity is restored and the freedom of flight becomes possible. The 'science of bodies', while useful to a point, cannot nourish the heart. Not 'outer' language but the formless language of the heart, the 'language of the birds' (Qur'an, XXVII 16), is the language of the divine mysteries, the expression of the birds of the spirit which fly in God's presence. Mystical knowledge, or what Nasr calls "principial knowledge", "which can penetrate into foreign universes of form and bring out their inner meaning" (Nasr, 1981, 291), renders forms intelligible and transparent, allowing the cosmos to reveal its meaning as a vast book whose pages are replete with the words of the Author. Like the words of the Qur'an, it has multiple levels of meaning, of which innumerable interpretations exist, but Sufis insist that "The All-Merciful taught the Qur'an", therefore people should "listen to its exegesis from God". Listening to any other is "the exegesis of the speaker's state, not the exegesis of the Koran" (Chittick, 2004, 152):

Whoever attains to vision has no more need for hearsay.
When you sit together with your beloved, you can send away the go-
betweens. (Rumi, *SPL*, 126)

Rumi tells us that the 'go-betweens' or 'science of bodies' masquerade
as knowledge but represent the limitations of discursive knowledge and
rational thought, the products of the partial as opposed to the universal
intellect in its full radiance. They represent outer knowledge or the literal
aspect, *Zahir*, and concern names and facts, opinion and hearsay, and are
given form by languages that conceal true meaning. The hidden meaning,
Batin, is accessible only to the heart and has no need for intermediaries or
outer language. In stillness the receptive heart responds to the universal
language, sounding continuously—the "speech of the existent things
which God let the Folk of Allah hear" (Ibn al-Arabi, *SPK*, 246) in which
meaning might be found. Knowledge of this language helps us to overcome the disconnectedness reinforced by a materialistic culture in which
forms of knowledge are limited by self-interest. Such knowledge enables
one to recognise unity within diversity, i.e. the "Unity of manyness", and
to "know the nature of being" (*op. cit.*, 437).

'Opinion' about 'appearances' (Plato) or forms (Rumi) does not constitute mystical knowledge. Those who see only plurality but fail to recognise unity are said to have opinion (*doxa*) but not knowledge (Plato,
441). Knowledge of the mystery of being can be attained experientially
only, by means of vision or tasting. Emphasising the unifying nature of
mystical knowledge, Plotinus explains that discursive knowledge divides
or separates its objects in order to make them intelligible, therefore the
One cannot be known through the process of discursive reasoning (Emilsson, 1998). Knowledge of the One can only be achieved through the
experience of its 'power' (*dunamis*) whose nature it is to provide a foundation (*arkhe*) and location (*topos*) for all existents. This 'power', he says,
is capable of being experienced only through contemplation (*theoria*) or
'vision'. Such a non-cognitive union or vision transcends analysis. Knowledge by way of vision or tasting, tasted philosophy or wisdom ('sapience'
from *sapere*, meaning to taste) (*SPK*, 203), provides access to truth which
is otherwise inaccessible. Ibn al-Arabi tells us:

Man has no access to the domain of Absolute Unity, that station in which
God is One in every respect and no other can be conceived or imagined.

The Essence remains inaccessible and unknowable to every created thing always and forever *(SPK,* 364).

Therefore while the Unity of manyness might be known, the unity of the One remains inaccessible. In a vast body of work on the subject of knowledge, Ibn al-Arabi elaborates on its countless aspects, with the infinity of knowledge being one of the most frequent themes. As a divine attribute of all-encompassingness, its essential nature cannot be delineated nor its bounds determined, since it embraces all bounds (*SPK,* 148). He leaves us in no doubt that Reality in its all-comprehensiveness is unknowable, since "None knows God thoroughly but God" (*SPK,* 153). All knowledge is knowledge of God, but God in Himself, in His Essence, cannot be known by other than Himself. Nothing can be known of God except what He discloses of Himself. He discloses His names and the entities—the creatures—which are the properties and effects of His names and attributes. But He never discloses Himself as Essence (*ibid.*). So "He who supposes that he possesses knowledge of Self has supposed wrongly, for (this) would limit Him, while His Essence has no limits. This is a door which is locked toward engendered existence and cannot be opened. The Real alone has knowledge of it" (*SPK,* 155). As Peter C. Coleman argues more recently, ours is an 'ungraspable' reality that cannot be definitively known with any epistemological or ontological security (2007, 43).

Though Reality is unknowable in its essence, knowledge is considered one of the greatest goods and should always be sought because, as the most all-encompassing of the divine attributes, (God being "Knower of all things"), it provides access to Him (Qur'an IV:176). "God never commanded His Prophet to seek increase of anything except knowledge, since all good (*khayr*) lies therein" (Ibn al-Arabi, *SPK,* 148). Hence the Prophet's instruction to the people to pray, "My Lord, increase me in knowledge!" (Qur'an XX:114). The search for knowledge is therefore central to Islam and Sufism. We know that Sufis such as Rumi and Ibn al-Arabi were deeply committed to their search for knowledge in diverse fields, a tradition upheld to this day, as Mustafa Tabanlı (2009) notes, with particular reference to the high level of erudition attained by Nasr, not only in the wide field of Islamic studies, but in the natural sciences, his academic qualifications including a Master's degree in geophysics. "God created the cosmos only for knowledge of Him", writes Ibn al-Arabi, and to this end the cosmos displays the signs of Him and points to Him so that we might gain knowledge of Him. The search for knowledge is endless, since the objects of knowledge are endless; the thirst for knowledge is never quenched as reality unfolds continuously and the creation renews itself from instant to instant.

"In the beginning", explains Nasr, "Reality was considered to be at once being, knowledge, and bliss" (*qudrah*, *hikmah*, and *rahmah* which are among the Attributes of Allah in Islam, or the *sat*, *chit*, and *ananda* of the Hindu tradition) "and in that ever-present 'in the beginning,' knowledge continues to possess a profound relation with that primordial Reality which *is* the Sacred and the source of all that is sacred" (1981, 1). Although knowledge has become separated from being and bliss, and "nearly completely externalised and desacralised" in the course of modernisation, "the root and essence of knowledge continues to be inseparable from the sacred" (*ibid.*), for its substance is the knowledge of that reality which is the Sacred as such, he says, with reference to the following citation from the *Atma-Maya*: "The substance of knowledge is Knowledge of the Substance; that is, the substance of human intelligence, in its most deeply real function, is the perception of the Divine Substance" (*op. cit.*, 50). Finding meaning entails rediscovering sacred unitive knowledge and the basic function of the heart as the means of access to that which Nasr calls the central and essential Reality.

Following the 'tasting' of the fruit of the tree of Good and Evil, things came to be seen as externalised, in a state of "otherness" and separation (Nasr, 2). The "'participation mystique' of primal un(self)consciousness" has given way to "the anxiety and fragility of individual self-consciousness", says Mathews (2003, 94). Knowledge has been so thoroughly depleted of its sacred character and the primacy of the sapiential dimension within various traditions so forgotten, according to Nasr, while the claims of rationalism so emphasised that mystical knowledge has been widely discredited (Nasr, 1981). Nasr reminds us of the *sapientia* (as understood by Plato in the *Republic* and *Laws*) of the wisdom teachings relating to the Divine Intellect and the Origin of all that is sacred—a reminder that mystical knowledge can make meaning accessible. As indicated in Chapter One, Sufism's unifying vision is reflected in the *scientia sacra* of the oldest wisdom traditions, and Nasr reminds us of some of these and the primacy they accord to knowledge of unity. The Hindu tradition, for example, places the sacred character of knowledge at the heart of its perspective and sees in the innate ability of humans to discern between *Atman* and *maya* the key to deliverance. The Sacred, insofar as it might be found within the human heart, is attainable most directly through knowledge which pierces the veils of *maya* to reach the One which alone is (op. cit., 7). In this sense, Nasr believes, knowledge of the Divine should properly be called autology rather than theology (*ibid.*).

Other traditions, such as Buddhism, also emphasise the primacy of knowledge. Nasr explains that the beginning of Buddhism, *Boddhisatt-vayana*, means "birth of awareness that all things are void" (*op. cit.*, 7). "At the heart of Buddhism, therefore, lies knowledge that was to lead later to the elaborate metaphysics of the Void which is the foundation of the whole of Buddhism and which was championed by Nagarjuna" (*ibid.*). The *paramitas*, the virtues of the Bodhisattva, culminate in wisdom or *pra-jna* (*ibid.*). Within the Chinese tradition, in both Confucianism and Taoism, "the role of knowledge as the central means for the attainment of perfection (also) reigns supreme" (*op. cit.*, 8). This is most evident in Taoism, says Nasr, where perfect man is believed to be one who "*knows* the Tao and lives according to this knowledge which means also that he lives according to his own 'nature'". Sacred knowledge allows him to "see God everywhere, to observe harmony where others see discord, and to see light where others are blinded by darkness" (*ibid.*).

The Islamic tradition, perhaps more than any other, is entirely based on the primacy of knowledge concerning the nature of Reality, its ultimately sacred character and the sapiential perspective in the spiritual life, a perspective which, according to Nasr, remains faithful to and aware of the function of knowledge and the nature of intelligence as a precious gift which becomes the most important means of gaining access to the Sacred, intelligence being itself ultimately of a sacred character (Nasr, 1981). Although the process of desacralisation of the instrument of knowing has also taken place to some degree in the case of Islam, though not to the same extent as in Judaism and Christianity (Nasr, 1981), the sacred nature of all forms of knowledge is truly preserved within Sufism. Sufi poetry itself is primarily a means of knowing God, a pathway to the Real; the Arabic word for poetry (*al-shir*) is related to the root meaning 'consciousness' and 'knowledge', as opposed to 'making' as is the case with *poiēsis* (*op. cit.*, 12). In Sufi poetry, language becomes a way of showing the way to harmony and peace that passes understanding, says Aahlia Khan (2009). "Words do not strain, slip and crack here. They are meaningful, not illusory nor simulacra. They create meaning: meaning is not endless regression here. . . Functioning as a therapy, Sufi poetry. . .reanimates and brings dead hearts to life". Not only is the mystical experience of Sufi poets liberating, so is their language, "promoting human well being, rather than being constrictive as Derrida, the philosopher of language, claims it to be" (*ibid.*).

Recourse to the radical individualism and rationalism which characterise modern European philosophy (*op. cit.*) marks the final stage of the gradual process of desacralisation of knowledge and language constriction. It was Descartes, not proponents of ontological unity such as his contemporaries, Spinoza (1632–1677) and Leibniz (1646–1716), who has been called the father of modern philosophy, and he epitomises "the reduction of knowledge to the functioning of individual reason cut off from the Intellect, in both its microcosmic and macrocosmic aspects", according to Nasr (*op. cit.*, 41). His self-centred *cogito ergo sum* shifted the main concern of Western philosophy from metaphysics to epistemology. Unlike eleventh century Sufi Mansur al-Hallaj who was put to death in Baghdad for uttering "I am the Truth" (*ana'l-Haqq*), Descartes was not referring to the divine I when he said 'I think' (*ibid.*). It was Descartes' individual, therefore limited, self placing its own limited experience and consciousness of thinking as the foundation of epistemology, ontology and source of certitude, explains Nasr. The individual ego became the centre of reality and foundation of knowledge.

Recognising the Real, or indeed admitting of its existence, is problematic given current materialistic assumptions of duality, according to which deanimated matter, devoid of meaning, cannot belong to the fundamental nature of physical reality, the exclusive domain of mentality, as the Cartesian perspective would have mind as interiority and matter as sheer externality. When matter is envisaged in this way, its reality cannot be grasped conceptually or epistemologically, according to Mathews (2003, 29), who argues that only by adopting a nondualistic perspective can such an account be provided of the reality of things. "Realism is an indispensable presupposition of everyday life", she says, and with reference to philosophy's preference for "the skeptical or de-realist end of the epistemological spectrum", "any philosophy that cannot accommodate this primal intuition is to that extent in debit" (*ibid.*). Endeavouring to bridge the "epistemological gap" at this time of ecological crisis, Mathews' "argument from realism" (*op. cit.*, 36) draws once again on the thought of proponents of ontological unity.

Knowledge, in Sufism, concerns only the Real. As Ibn al-Arabi, expounding at length on the reality of the Real, asserts: "Every possible thing is in the grasp of a divine reality" (*SPK*, 37), and we noted in Chapter 1 that the Supreme *Barzakh*, the entire cosmos, is a manifestation of the Real. Although its trajectory differs, proceeding as it does in the form of an argument as opposed to the poetic approach of the Sufis, Mathews' "argument from realism", countering the "pervasive skeptical legacy in philosophy" which would have the world as "facade"—"ideal or phenomenal or socially constructed" (2003, 31)—and altogether unreal, culminates in the same unifying vision of meaningful matter held by the Sufis. Although this difference in approach is important, it is not fundamental, culminating as it does in a similar vision of reality. Whilst the forms may differ, their meaning is one.

Mathews rejects the argument which relies on God as the guarantor of the reality of things, advanced most notably by Descartes, whose notorious separation of mind from matter led to "a turning away from . . . questions concerning the nature of a world that lies beyond our epistemic reach, and a turning towards questions concerning the scope and limits, the very possibility, of knowledge itself" (*op. cit.*, 37). Yet as we noted previously, Mathews and Hamilton both find inspiration in the work of Leibniz and Spinoza, who, in their different ways, sought to capture "the intuition that everything is woven from the same skein" (*op. cit.*, 3).

However, "(t)he word 'God' means different things today", says Tacey (37). "God is no longer conceived as a distant powerful figure who intervenes in human affairs from 'above'", he says, but rather "a mysterious moral force" which we might recognise as "the still-small voice within" (*ibid*)—the "moral self" as Hamilton describes it. Differences regarding meanings associated with names (particularly the name 'God') remind us of Rumi's exhortation to 'escape from names', and demonstrates the veracity of Ibn al-Arabi's words: ". . . the disagreement lies in the names, not in the meaning" (*SPK*, 149). Therefore al-Arabi says "I have a Beloved whose name is that of all who have a name" (*Diwân al-ma'ârif, in Addas, 2002*). The "God hypothesis", advanced by Descartes and examined by Mathews, is found to be "antiquated" and "anachronistic" in a contemporary context (Mathews, 2003, 34), replete with the dualistic limitations of an anthropomorphic deity. Spinoza's God, on the other hand, is the Real—"the seed of every religion", "the self-conceiving infinite 'being', the immanent substance preceding all manifestations in the universe" (Hamilton, 2008, 107). The Sufi's certainty regarding the Real requires no proof as it is true and valid for him once and for all and not for a particular age or mentality, able to be validated directly by his own unitive experience, and not, therefore, in any sense, in need of 'evolving' (Oldmeadow, 2007).

Confusing the concept of God, as we tend to do, with the reality, we should, perhaps, re-imagine the meaning of the name, or escape altogether from it, as Rumi recommends; a Western invention, used reductively, it has been the source of much misunderstanding and disagreement. Like the name 'mysticism' to which it relates, it is fraught with hazards and tarnished with careless usage. It evokes a "naive metaphysics" (Hamilton, 2008, 106), one which implies transcendence (designated by the prefix *meta*) but not immanence, therefore a metaphysics quite different from metaphysics as the ultimate 'science of the Real' which Nasr considers identical with *scientia sacra* (Nasr, 1981, 132). Mathews refers instead to "the great sea of namelessness to which every last thing returns" (2005, 164); similarly, the Sufis speak of the ocean of infinitude into whose depths the ebbing wave invariably returns. They insist that no name is appropriate to designate the Unknowable and Incomparable since "All names are His names, (because) everything is from Him". As "Nothing is like Him" (*SPK*, 122), Ibn al-Arabi advises us to reflect on all things, but not to reflect on the divine Essence whose meaning cannot be found:

> . . . the Essence has no name . . . nor is It known by anyone. There is no name to denote it without relationship, nor with any assurance. For names act to make known and to distinguish, but this door is forbidden to anyone other than God, since "None knows God thoroughly but God". So the names exist through us and for us. They revolve around us and become manifest within us. Their properties are with us, their goals are

toward us, their expressions are of us, and their beginnings are from us .
. . If not for us, they would not be (*SPK*, 62).

Knowledge of the world in its essence is, therefore, according to Ibn
al-Arabi, clearly unattainable via rational process. In the manner of the
mystic who recognises the Real in all things, Mathews questions whether
we have a right of unlimited epistemological access to things, whether the
world *must* be known, and whether, simply by existing, it invites us to
investigate it (2003, 75). Mathews signals the inappropriateness of the
"Western knowledge project" in its attempt to expose the structure of
reality—"seeking to lay bare its internal mechanisms, to penetrate its mysteries", to expose its secrets (*op. cit.*, 76). "Subjecting the world to an epistemological probe", Mathews concludes, does indeed constitute a moral
and spiritual affront to the world (*ibid.*).

Mathews', Hamilton's and Wheeler's approach is by way of argument, which is not the mystic's approach, but is deemed necessary at this
time of denial of the *scientia sacra*. The station of gnosis, however, can be
defined only by its results and never by argumentation and dialectic
(Corbin, 1969, 230). Without awareness of *tawhid*, particular forms such
as theories, dogmas and doctrines that separate and cause conflict might
be embraced, whereas only the heart transmutes dogma by disclosing its
limits. Those who cling to the limits of form seldom convince others of
the superiority of their preferred form: "Each particular dogma is no better or worse than any other concept elaborated by the rational intellect;
essentially limitation, it looks upon every other dogma as a contradiction;
reduced to analyzing, to decomposing the whole into parts . . ." (*ibid.*).

Mathews' argument from realism is supported by the findings of
quantum mechanics but may still not convince skeptics. Making the leap,
as she does, from classical physics' "substantival view of space, and a
geometrodynamic view of physical process" whereby "the universe may
be conceived of as a unified, though internally differentiated and dynamic, expanding plenum" (2003, 47), to knowledge that "the world, as One"
(op. cit., 61) is profoundly sacred, calls for a different kind of knowing,
unconcerned with scientific validation. It is this kind of intuitive knowing
which is more likely to lead to the realisation that the world in its entirety, as it appears here and now, is sacred, and to kindle the kind of passion
in whose grip the ego is willingly surrendered. Analytical rationality, no

matter how useful a tool, will never, in itself, provide access to full under-standing. For this reason Sufis have, throughout the ages, developed other faculties in order to find meaning, as "knowing demands the organ fitted to the object" (Plotinus, Cited in Oldmeadow, 2007, 11), a princi-ple to which modern philosophy has, according to Oldmeadow, been largely indifferent. From his perennialist perspective, Oldmeadow asserts that the "grotesqueries" of modern philosophy, often bred by scientistic ideologies, are revealed in the refusal to acknowledge the boundaries beyond which reason has no competence or utility (Oldmeadow, 12).

Finding meaning entails a different kind of knowing; not only the knowing of the intellect, sterile and cold, "that takes you to the threshold, but doesn't take you in" (Rumi, cited in Chittick, 2004, 48). Indeed, Mathews envisages that the role of reason would be up for renegotiation (2003, 6) if her philosophy were accepted as a premise for our thought. Liberated into a larger field of metaphysics from the materialist premise to which it has been tied in the framework of modern thought, reason, says Mathews, can "take its proper place, as the friend of all our human faculties, in our endeavour to become part of the world's unfolding" (*ibid.*). It should "clarify our intuitions as to the limitations of the old premise . . . and bring to light the true scope and limits of rational delib-eration" (*ibid.*).

However, in view of the primacy accorded to knowledge as a means of increasing our understanding of reality, the validity and usefulness of all forms of knowledge for particular purposes must be acknowledged. Sufism is a celebration of knowledge "all of whose forms (are), in one way or another, related to the sacred, extending in a hierarchy from an 'empir-ical' and rational mode of knowing to that highest form of knowledge (*marifa*)" (Nasr, 1981, 12). Scientist and mystic do not operate in two different worlds, as emphasised in Chapter 1—empirical and mystical knowledge are not mutually exclusive, and in reality scientists and mystics share the same desire to discover the secrets at the heart of the One mys-terious being. For pragmatist Dewey, finding out what there is is a mat-ter of finding out what descriptions of things will best fulfil our needs. Finding out what needs we should fulfil then becomes a task for reflection about what human beings might become (Rorty, 2004). While both empirical and pragmatic knowledge serve certain purposes, unifying knowledge is needed to discern which purposes are proper. Rowan Williams, Archbishop of Canterbury, addressed this issue recently at a le*cture at Rikkyo Gaukin University in Japan:*

> A "reasonable" or "rational" human being . . . is one who seeks not first and foremost to master and control a passive universe, but one who looks for the ways in which he or she can discover the rhythms and patterns of reality and so understand themselves more fully. Certainly it implies that this kind of knowledge will be useful: it is better to work with the grain of reality in what we do than to work against it. But if the very first question is always 'What is the use or the profit of this?' we are training ourselves to ignore everything that lies outside our own immediate practical questions. That is not the spirit in which great discoveries are made; and it is certainly not the spirit in which great human beings are made". By allowing "mind and heart to be shaped by the flow and complexity of what is around, not prejudging what the important questions are but letting (our)selves be carried along by a certain degree of wonder and uncertainty, (we are more likely) to arrive at innovative and creative insight" (Williams, 2009).

Mary Evelyn Tucker expresses similar sentiments when she explains the importance of both religion and science at this time of environmental crisis. Science can make us aware of issues relating to sustainability and to think through problems with a sense of creating solutions, she believes, noting that "an immensely inspiring, moving, sustainable sense of well-being is emerging from the sciences". And religions, Tucker believes, are "awakening to their ecological aspect, to their commitment to life, its aesthetic beauty, and the intrinsic value of other species; they are taking on a sense of commitment for the future generations of all species". Religions can awaken us to "a sense of gratitude and awe in the face of the great mystery of life". Religion and science share the role of reigniting what Tucker calls "a critical component to our environmental and ecological sensibility", namely, wonder. Science awakens it and religion confirms it with the great mystery of life systems, Tucker believes (Tabanlı & Tucker, 2010).

As Ibn al-Arabi explains, reason and logic are extremely important in the search for knowledge, for the purpose of discernment, but he emphasises that the most real and useful knowledge is bestowed by the Real rather than acquired through ratiocination. While the latter is useful in establishing the Unity of the many, it is not conducive to understanding it. The Prophet Muhammad, "most knowledgeable of all people" (*SPK*, 135), we remember, was the "unlettered Prophet" (Qur'an VII: 158) whose knowledge came directly from God. And Rumi reportedly cast aside his books and fell at Shams' feet, renouncing his religious teachings when Shams told him that knowledge was of no use unless it emanated from the heart and "liberated the self from the self" (Vaughan-Lee, 2000, 12). As Oldmeadow points out with reference to Frithjof Schuon's work, *Understanding Islam*, (149), thought can become increasingly subtle and complex without approaching any nearer to the truth—"an idea can be subdivided into a thousand ramifications, fenced about with every conceivable qualification and supported with the most intricate and rigorous logic but, for all that, remain purely external and quantitative for 'no virtuosity of the potter will transform clay into gold'" (Oldmeadow, 2007, 12).

Like Ibn al-Arabi, Rumi nonetheless emphasises the importance of intellect in pointing the way to knowledge by monitoring the voice of ego. Discernment is essential in order to distinguish the ego's divisive manifestation from the heart's unifying capacity, the essential function of human intelligence being discernment between the Real and the illusory, the Permanent and the impermanent. Such discernment is essential to prevent what Mathews describes as "separation of self from world", which occurs when "products of humanity convers(e) only with itself" (2003, 88). Discrimination terminates in the awareness of the nondual nature of the Real (Nasr, 134). This awareness, says Nasr, is the heart of gnosis and represents not human knowledge but the Real's knowledge of Itself—the "consciousness which is the goal of the path of knowledge and the essence of *scientia sacra*" (*ibid.*).

When reason does not lead to a vision of unity it is "a chain around the feet", but when the lover breaks this chain, the path leading to the Beloved becomes perfectly clear (Rumi, in Can, 2005, 186). Only by way of unifying vision is the partial, individual intellect able to overcome the limitations of its form:

> Without the key of the intellect, knocking upon God's door is a result of self-will, not sound motives. . . Whoever possesses a partial intellect is in need of instruction. . . .. Come into the heart, the place of contemplating God! Though it is not now, it can be made so (Rumi, *SPL*, 125)

'Intellect', in Sufi usage, is a reality with many dimensions, the lower of which, the partial intellect, (*aql-i juzwī*) is intimately connected with the ego (*nafs*), but the higher intellect, which might be likened to the power of discernment, is connected to the Universal Intellect (*aql-i kullī*). The lower intellect is veiled by the dross of ego, ('clogged with the pollutions of mortality', according to Plato (Plato, 379)), resulting in partial intellect which requires nourishment from outside itself. Through intellect the 'science of bodies' can be acquired by learning (*SPL*, 220). Rumi says:

> The acquired intellect is like a stream led into a house from outside. If its way should be blocked, it is helpless. Seek the fountain from within yourself! Be well aware of the discrepancies among intellects, which extend in degrees from earth to heaven! There is an intellect happily flickering like a lamp, and another like a spark of fire. . . Partial intellect has disgraced the Intellect; desire for the world has deprived man of the Object of his desire (*ibid.*).

Though we find similar, seemingly dualistic terminology in Plato, we should remember that when Rumi speaks of 'desire for the world' he is not opposing two separate worlds, one human the other divine, but rather referring to the failure to recognise the One in a world of manyness. Mathews makes the same distinction in references to the "rich materiality of the real" (2003, 60) which is not constituted exclusively of externality, but of "the interiority of matter", of which, she says, only some selves are aware (*ibid.*). Similarly, Plato speaks about "discrepancies among intellects", resulting in the many being seen but not known and the One being known but not seen (1954, 435-441). Few are capable of recognising the One in a world where manyness tends to conceal it:

> Such a one who recognizes the existence of absolute beauty and is able to distinguish the idea from the objects which participate in the idea. . . may we not say that the mind of such a one has knowledge?
> Those who see the many beautiful, and who yet neither see absolute beauty, nor can follow any guide who points the way thither, such persons may be said to have opinion but not knowledge. But those who see the absolute and eternal and immutable may be said to know, and not to have opinion (*ibid.*).

The form of Mathews' and Hamilton's philosophies—well-constructed, logically argued and rigorously defended—assumes an appearance which veils a distinctly mystical heart. For beyond the appearance of rationality and logic is, above all else, an appeal to the heart; an appeal which would have us "kneeling tenderly" at the feet of "our beloved" (Mathews, 2003, 1), "the sacred ground", "our sovereign, our solace", "awaiting *its* command, trying to divine *its* will" (*ibid.*). Relinquishing our command of the world in order to "resacralize the ground beneath our feet" (*op. cit.*, 5) or attaining unmediated access to truth such as Hamilton describes (2008, 244), the certainty of "life in the noumenon", calls for total humility and ultimately surrender of the individual will. Such an approach, we know, is utterly alien within the Western context with its focus on individualism, self-promotion and freedom of expression. The spirit of submission is, however, epitomised by Islam, the word 'Islam' itself being synonymous with 'surrender', and the richly symbolic act of prostration (*sujud*), in which the forehead is placed on the ground in recognition of the source of life in an act of supreme humility.

If God is understood as the only Reality, everything is dependent on God for its reality, therefore all things are 'submitted' to God, explains Chittick in *The Vision of Islam* (4). Submission to the Real involves effort and struggle (*mujahada*); the mystic does not, as Mathews suggests, "surrender to the status quo" (2003, 114), which implies blind acceptance of it. Sufi nonconformism is well documented (e.g. Rice, 1964; el-Khazari, 2006), and Rumi himself did not surrender to the status quo but took control of his destiny when he fled his homeland. Surrender, for the Sufi, is to the One, and always involves recognition of the infinitely greater reality in relation to his individual, relatively insignificant, will; the greater good in relation to individuated good, and Mathews does in fact promote this kind of attitude, making reference to 'surrender' in the opening pages of both her books. Ibn al-Arabi explains the need for *sujud* as follows:

> When a thing is diverted from being a root by being a branch, it is said to it, "Seek that which is absent from you, your root from which you have emerged". So the thing prostrates itself to the soil which is its root. The spirit prostrates itself to the Universal Spirit from which it has emerged. . . All roots are unseen. Do you not see how they become manifest in trees? The roots of trees are unseen, for the act of bringing to be is unseen (*SPK*, 152).

Thus the Sufi is constantly mindful of his emergence from that root, and the ground which nourishes him does, in fact, assume that sacred reality for which Mathews appeals.

Since panpsychism also entails "a pervasive spirituality" (2003, 88), it calls for the transformation of all human praxes, and to this end Mathews proposes "practices of invocation and response—ritual practices" recovered and adapted from traditional religious forms (*ibid*.). It is precisely to such practices that the Sufi dedicates himself. They entail invocation and remembrance (*dhikr*), and prepare the heart to be 'opened up' to the unseen world and to the infusion of knowledge, so that all actions might become meaningful. 'Opening' is, as Chittick explains, a near synonym for several other terms such as 'unveiling', 'tasting', 'witnessing', 'divine self-disclosure' and 'insight', each of which designates a mode of gaining direct knowledge of the unseen without intermediary (*SPK*, xii). In this regard, it should be noted that Ibn al-Arabi provides many criteria for distinguishing among different types of 'incoming thoughts' as these might not all be useful, depending on their source. They might, for example, be *nafsani* or ego-centric (*SPK*, xii-xiii), therefore the ability to discern between unifying and non-unifying thoughts is vital.

Mathews' suggestion that practices from 'traditional' religious forms be recovered invites us to reflect briefly on the Sufi understanding of 'tradition', a word not to be confused with custom, habit or inherited pattern of thought. "Tradition", Nasr explains, "is at once truth and presence", and comes from the Source from which everything originates and to which everything returns (1981, 68). The Arabic near-equivalent, *al-din*, (as in the form of Rumi's name as Chittick uses it 'Jalāl al-Dīn') is inseparable from the idea of "permanent and perpetual wisdom", the *Sophia perennis* which can be identified with the *philosophia perennis* as understood by Coomaraswamy (*ibid*.). Tradition, says Nasr, means "truths or principles of a divine origin revealed or unveiled . . . through various figures envisaged as messengers, prophets, avatars, the Logos or other transmitting agencies, along with all the ramifications and applications of these principles in different realms including law and social structure, art, symbolism, the sciences, and embracing Supreme Knowledge (*scientia sacra*) along with the means for its attainment" (*ibid*.). "It also implies an inner truth which lies at the heart of different sacred forms and which is unique since Truth is one" (*op. cit.*, 71). For this reason the doctrine of unity is seen not only as the essence of the Islamic tradition, says Nasr, but the heart of every religion. Revelation, understood in this way, means the assertion of *tawhid*, itself considered to be of divine origin, which is why, according to Nasr, Muslims did not distinguish between religion and paganism but between those who accepted unity and those who denied or ignored it (*ibid.*).

Leibniz, in whose work Mathews finds inspiration, had sympathy with 'traditional' ideas (Nasr, 71) such as Nasr interprets them. In the Western, antitraditional world, characterised by the "nearly total eclipse and loss of that reality which has constituted the matrix of life over the ages" (*op. cit.*, 66), Mathews seeks a recovery of "traditional treasures", so that "the One might be a party to all our undertakings" (2003, 88). The usage of the term 'tradition' itself, Nasr explains, emerged only at the moment of the final phase of the desacralisation of both knowledge and the world which surrounded modern humanity (Nasr, 65-66). With the demise of tradition, sacred knowledge has been forgotten, and, in a secu-larised world, the sacred itself has assumed the appearance of the "totally other" (Nasr, 75).

In recognition of the sacred Reality from which all life emerges, the Sufi encounters all things with humility and all human praxes assume a sacred dimension. Hazrat Inayat Khan refers to such meaningful praxes as "the art of being" (VIII, 56). However, as Mathews notes, such praxis stands in deepest contrast to the praxes of modernity, characterised by the imposition of our will, and the impossibility of 'encounter' under such con-ditions. Being nonintrusive yet attentive to the response of the other yields insights into their nature; in this sense encounter is likely to result in a cer-tain degree of knowledge without constituting a transgression or violation of their essential being (Mathews, 2003, 78). "Knowledge" (as understood within the Western context) "seeks to break open the mystery of another's nature; encounter leaves that mystery intact", says Mathews (*op. cit.*, 78). She continues as follows: "When I believe I have revealed the inner myster-ies of another . . . my sense of its otherness in fact dissolves . . . But where I respect its opaqueness, I retain my sense of its otherness . . ." (*ibid.*).

By 'otherness' we should understand, in this context, 'mystery' or 'unknowability', unlike the meaning of 'essential difference' or 'foreign-ness' applicable to the word as Nasr (2 & 75) and Hamilton (2008, 149) use it—as in 'othering', which involves objectification and instrumentali-sation stemming from the failure to recognise the 'inner mysteries' of a thing and the belief that its nature can be revealed. Such a thing is destined to remain 'other' as no commonality is established. In scientific research, for example, animals are often subjected to extreme cruelty in the course of experimentation precisely because they remain essentially 'other', irrespective of the amount of information obtained about them. On the other hand, when essential unity is recognised, 'otherness' becomes secondary to commonality and the inclination to probe wanes. In Nasr's words, when we recognise the mysterious One in all things, we realise that "all separation is union, all otherness is sameness" (1981, 214). "Discover(ing) one another's subjectivity and establish(ing) the mutuality that is the foundation for sympathy and respect" (Mathews, 2003, 78), i.e. recognition of the One in all things, must surely dispel notions of otherness (foreignness). Hamilton refers to such recognition as "fellow feeling" (2008, 190) or "metaphysical empathy", which, he says, is "the awareness of participation in the being of others that arises from identification of self with the universal essence" (*op. cit.*, 146-147).

Such recognition of the One, i.e. knowledge of a sacred reality, is a divine gift, of which Ibn al-Arabi says:

> God never commanded His Prophet to seek increase of anything except knowledge, since all good lies therein. It is the greatest gift . . . By knowledge I mean only knowledge of God, of the next world, and of that which is appropriate for this world, in relationship to that for which this world was created and established . . . It is the most excellent bounty of God. (*SPK*, 148)

It is a divine 'bestowal', the greatest of "the favours of the Beloved upon us" (Cited in Can, 2005, 128) which must be earned through acts of spiritual struggle (*mujāhada*) (*SPK*, 148). This inward struggle is against one's own negative tendencies, one's likes and dislikes, as well as against the pressure of society to conform to the crowd (Chittick, 1994). The seeker applies himself to the mirror of his heart and polishes it with divine recollection so that it consistently reflects divine light and dispels the darkness of ignorance distorting reflections of forms. This, Rumi tells us, is self-sacrificing work, "warrior's work", "not for brittle, easily-broken, glass-bottle people" (Cited in Vaughan-Lee, 2000, 60).

Knowledge resides in the heart since it alone has the capacity to perceive the divine self-disclosure without limitations:

The heart is His throne and not delimited by any specific attribute. On the contrary, it brings together all the divine names and attributes, just as the All-Merciful possesses all the Most Beautiful Names (Rumi, *SPK*, 107).

The heart is a mirror of God, says Rumi:

These things are all delimited and defined, but the heart's mirror has no limits—know that! Here the intellect must remain silent, for the Heart is with Him (*SPL*, 38).

The heart, locus of knowledge, like the 'moral self' envisioned by Hamilton, emerging from the noumenon, is recognised by Sufis as that fixed point Archimedes was seeking, which is believed to provide certainty—"the arbiter, the inner judge, who speaks to us with an immediacy and authority no external legislation or contract can possess" (Hamilton, 2008, 147). The moral certainty it is thought to provide contradicts postmodern theories of moral relativism, such as Bruno Latour's social constructionist theories, according to which there is no such thing as objective or absolute truth, all facts being inherently contingent. Such theories imply that we can have no "natural, unmediated, unbiased access to truth", meaning being discernable only through 'deconstruction' (*op. cit.*, 122). However, with extensive reference to unifying Eastern philosophies, Hamilton concludes that the expression of the moral self requires no mediation in the form of church, state or science, since moral autonomy is invested in each individual, implicated by virtue of the universal Self in one all-encompassing reality.

Reason (*'aql*) and heart (*qalb*) are not two different entities, but different modalities of knowing. The root meaning of *'aql* is 'that which limits the free and ties down the unconstricted', while *qalb* means 'fluctuation', and refers to the constant transmutation the heart undergoes in keeping with the never-repeating self-disclosures of God (*SPK*, 159). Both the analytical and discursive functioning of the mind and the intuitive functioning of the heart constitute the fullness of human intelligence, and together make possible the reception and communication of the Real (Nasr, 151). The heart 'knows' through letting go of all restrictions; its 'eye' transcends duality. Knowledge acquired by the heart is therefore not irrational but beyond the rational—supralogical, based on symbolism and analogy, and therefore descriptive rather than ratiocinative (Schuon,

1959, 8); the kind of knowledge Mathews believes is lacking in our world when she suggests that the problem with modern thought is not that it is *too* rational, but that it is not rational enough (2003, 6). Expanding on the association of mysticism with the irrational, Schuon claims "it is a grave error to suppose that metaphysics has any right to irrationality" (as cited in Oldmeadow, 12), a view endorsed more recently by Aahlia Khan (2009). As Schuon remarks, the equating of the supernatural with the irrational is characteristic and amounts to claiming that the unknown or the incomprehensible is the same as the absurd. The rationalism of a frog living at the bottom of a well is to deny the existence of mountains: logic of a kind but distinct from reality (*ibid.*).

When the roots of knowledge extend only as far as the mind, stopping short of penetrating the heart, knowledge is unlikely to be of a unitive nature and therefore may well be inappropriate. Without heart-knowledge (vision and insight), the well-being of the whole is jeopardized. Physicist David Bohm, whom Mathews names as one of several thinkers who might be considered as anticipating panpsychism (2003, 185) and on whose *Wholeness and the Implicate Order* (1980) both Hamilton and Wheeler draw, calls knowledge which does not take into account the "super-implicate order" "knowledge of endarkenment" (Bohm, 2002, 261-289), which leads to entrapment rather than freedom.

The appropriateness of knowledge is determined by the fruit it bears. Appropriateness demands that knowledge (*marifa*) be actualized through good works (*amal*). Ibn al-Arabi tells of the Sufi Junayd who, when asked about the nature of gnosis, replied, "The water takes on the colour of its cup". "In other words, the gnostic assumes the character traits of his Beloved, to the point where it seems as if he is He. He is not He, yet he is He" (*SPK*, 149). Knowers who mirror divine attributes when actualising knowledge become makers of the world as it should be. They actualise the *scientia sacra* in their being (Nasr, 1981, 145). 'Theopraxy', defined by Michael Benedict as the practice or realisation of God in our actions, in *God is the Good we do* (2008), reflects a similar perspective.

Similarly, in *God is a Verb* (1997), Rabbi David Cooper highlights the active nature of God within the context of a constantly unfolding creation, an ongoing process in which the Creator is revealed at every moment of the creation's unfoldment. The dualistic, fixed timeline notion of historic creation does not take into account creative activity occurring from moment to moment in the timeless present. Since everything is in motion and change is continuous, 'matter' should be a verb, suggests Cooper, rather than a noun which gives it the appearance of stability and inactivity. This interpretation closely resembles Mathews' description of the universe as a dynamic, expansive, self-actualizing plenum, a locus of subjectivity to which *conatus*—will or purpose—is attributable. Knowledge, as the supreme attribute of the One, is active, mindfully, and the knower participates meaningfully in its activity. It is not an intellectual acquisition and has no value independent of practice. David Bohm expresses this perspective as follows: "By loosening the restrictions of matter on consciousness dominated by knowledge, we may begin to discern our inherent link to the holomovement—the unknown, timeless present, the infinity of nature at the experiential level. In this way we embody true individuality, manifesting our creative potential through participation in—rather than objectification of—a total field of experience" (Bohm, 253-254).

Finding the Real entails 'shedding' or 'unknowing', referred to as 'emptying the cup' of inappropriate (i.e. divisive) information and opinion, assumptions and prejudices, and turning away from the ego towards the deeper mystery of the heart. 'Unknowing', the aim of which is a loving, non-conceptual knowledge of a sacred reality, setting aside images and concepts deriving from our language-formed way of thinking, is also a feature of the apophatic tradition or *via negativa* of Christian mystics such as Thomas Aquinas and John of the Cross, and the subject of the fourteenth-century work *The Cloud of Unknowing* (Braine, 1998). Similarly Lao-Tzu says: "In the pursuit of learning, every day something is acquired. In the pursuit of Tao, every day something is dropped" (cited in Nasr, 1981, 51). Rumi tells us to wash away the polluting clay of outer knowledge so that the heart can be filled with the revivifying water of *marifa*:

> Where should we seek knowledge? In the abandonment of knowledge (*SPL*, 175).

Mystical knowing is creative and unifying. By listening (*samā*) to the universal language when ego's voice has been stilled, unveiling can begin as knowledge of unity (*tawhid*) illuminates the heart and the unseen world is glimpsed with the eye of the heart (*ayn al-qalb* or *chashm-i dil*). Unveiling is "the cause of knowledge of the Real in the things" (Ibn al-Arabi, *SPK*, 225), and for Ibn al-Arabi it is knowledge that provides vision of the Real, while for Rumi love is the intoxicating wine that provides a taste of the Real. The divine attributes of mystical knowledge (*marifa*) and love (*ishq*) are intimately connected as prerequisites for finding the Real.

4.3 Knowledge as Commodity

> There is many a fool who seeks the luminous sun in the desert with a lamp
> in his hand (Shabistari, cited in Nasr, 1981, 159)

Devoid of the quality of the sacred, secularised knowledge is, in Nasr's view, directly related to the desacralisation of the cosmos (*op. cit.*, 45). Secularised reason, as the sole instrument of knowing, has "killed the gods", leaving a world in which there is no wholeness because holiness has ceased to be of central concern (Nasr, 1981, 48). Sufism's mystical knowledge and ancient wisdom teachings such as those of Plato, Confucius, Lao-Tzu and Aquinas have been marginalised by ideologies which privilege particular forms of knowledge such as those embodied in the natural sciences and economics (Giroux, 1984), as postmodernism problematises their ancient "metanarrative" (Lyotard, 1984, 33)—the mystery of life and Imagination's creativity in shedding light on it.

Knowledge has come to represent "cultural capital" (Giroux, 36) and as such reflects and promotes only the dominant culture of society. Instead of reflecting the entire spectrum, this form of knowledge takes on the same shade as its legitimating authority. Hegemonic discourses are promoted, and eventually accepted, as the truth. In the eighteenth century Adam Smith, father of modern economics, had already identified self-interest as the driver of economic activity and education's role in furthering the economic cause. Like the concept of freedom to which knowledge is closely tied, it is reduced by the narrow concerns of national, political and economic interest. In the 21st century, "knowledge is no longer the subject but in the service of the subject, and legitimized through the autonomy of the will, is neither neutral nor objective as it embodies particular interests, prejudices and cultural assumptions" (Lyotard, 36). It might be legitimate but it is not 'true' (Giroux, 1984).

The emergence in the 1960s of neoliberal ideologies rapidly led to domination on a global scale, keeping non-western nations with traditional forms of knowledge in a state of servile dependency. According to dominant neoliberal ideologies based on a particular conception of knowledge and 'free' trade, globally imposed, together with assumptions of rationality, individuality and self-interest, those bodies of knowledge deemed useful are promoted while others are consigned to oblivion (Giroux, 1984). Knowledge is power, as Foucault proclaimed, but when the concept of power is reduced to political or economic power, knowledge becomes "lodged in the ethos of instrumentalism and a self-serving individualism" (*op. cit.*, 37). In his analysis of the knowledge-power nexus, Foucault exposes the technologies of domination and indicates how knowledge, in the sense of discursive practices, is generated through the exercise of power in the control of populations. Such knowledge, embodying dominant Western ideologies, has effectively been imposed on the world for the past four decades, disregarding cultural differences and reinforcing an almost unbridgeable economic divide. Eight centuries ago it was the Mongols from the East and the Crusaders from the West who attempted to impose their ideologies on Rumi's people; the ideologies have changed but the ego's willful imposition remains. Forms of knowledge are used to control while purporting to emancipate (Peters & Wain, 2002). As Mathews explains, this kind of knowledge enables us to "uncover and adjust the mechanisms underlying 'the appearances' in order to manipulate the course of events"; "by removing the unnerving mystery of things and abolishing their unpredictability" we are able to better control them and advance our own interests (2003, 97). Now, as wealth and power are threatened or lost, and a beleaguered earth increasingly communicates its distress, the assumptions behind ideologies shaping economies, education, societies and politics must be challenged. Those forms of knowledge, regarded most recently as reliable, must be reassessed to evaluate whether they are truly meaningful. The current global crisis indicates that the 'rational' processes which brought us to this point may have been irrational.

In the 21st century 'knowledge economy', knowledge not only becomes a commodity, but the key commodity. A Trade and Industry Committee (U.K.) paper entitled *Progress towards the Knowledge Driven Economy* (2005) provides insight into prevailing neoliberal expectations of knowledge as a commodity. In a knowledge economy, the authors say, "the generation and exploitation of knowledge have come to play the predominant part in the creation of wealth . . . It is about the more effective use and exploitation of all types of knowledge in all manner of economic activity". The idea that knowledge is intimately linked to prosperity is not new; what is new, however, is the commodification of knowledge for the sole purpose of creating wealth and the scale on which this is occurring. Denied its inherent value when it is 'promoted' to creator of wealth, knowledge is paradoxically reduced to a form devoid of intrinsic meaning. Knowledge has become more and less important, simultaneously (Johnston, 1998). On the one hand its profound and privileged status as truth and representation of reality has been significantly challenged while, on the other, it has become the basic form of capital, the implication of the knowledge economy being that there is no alternative way to prosperity than to make knowledge-as-commodity and knowledge-production of prime importance.

When knowledge is in the service of the subject, it becomes a tool; in the hands of the novice, the tool is likely to be used inappropriately, resulting in a defective product. In the above citation, 'effective' use of knowledge aligns itself with 'exploitation', and raising more questions than it answers about the nature of activities in which such exploitation might result, the phrase 'all manner of economic activity' does little to allay the suspicion that the sole purpose of such knowledge is to procure wealth, irrespective of the appropriateness of such activity. Moreover, in the neoliberal knowledge economy there is no synthesizing or neutral master discourse to reproduce the speculative unity of knowledge or adjudicate between competing views, claims, or discourses (Giroux, 1984).

Instead of turning the 'eye of the soul' to the 'divine eternal patterns bound together by the Idea of the Good', as Plato recommended (1956), education today, according to Standish, encourages unhealthy fragmentation, and its concern with the image of quality rather than quality itself means that substance is often sacrificed while the focus is on method and presentation (Standish, 1995). With reference to postmodern "educational malnutrition", Standish points to the need for a "balanced diet and whole food" (*op. cit.*, 122) to restore the system's health. Such wholeness could be restored by an over-arching discourse, he suggests; a richer metanarrative so that education might once again fulfil its proper role in educating "the whole person" (Smeyers, 1995, cited in Standish, 124). Moral certainties, problematised by postmodernism, having been abandoned, ethics has become largely "a matter of individual discretion and chronic uncertainty" (Halpin, 1992, cited in Standish, 125).

More and more we have come to rely on the ever-changing stream of information as our elemental knowledge, our basic awareness or "primal intuition" of what is "appropriate" (Mathews, 2003, 29) is eroded, and we become incapable of answering the most fundamental human questions; indeed, we become forgetful of the questions themselves, and unable to imagine solutions to the most mundane problems. Postman (1992) argues that all forms of cultural life willingly submit to the sovereignty of technique and technology, undermining certain mental processes and social relations that make human life meaningful. Increasingly we find ourselves turning for guidance to the successful purveyors of knowledge, the 'experts' or 'Modern Professionalists' (Day, 2008) in whom we place our trust.

In addition to the fragmentation of knowledge and its replacement by information, there is the socio-economic question of access. In a knowledge economy knowledge is pivotal; one might therefore expect it to be a common good, available to all who wish to partake of it for the sake of the economy so that all might benefit, rather than a commodity whose price makes it inaccessible to many. Knowledge is said to be "a non-rival good"; once produced, its use by one person does not preclude its availability and use to others (Callon, 1994). In practice, this is of course not the case. In the 2008 budget, for example, Commonwealth funding to the tune of approximately $6.5 billion dollars was allocated to private schools, compared to $3.5 billion for public schools (Moore, 2008). One wonders what the advantages might be of perpetuating the disparity between public and private schools by investing less in the sector that serves the majority. The outcome of such skewed investment must surely be increased disparity between those who can afford to buy knowledge and those who cannot, continued intellectual and social snobbery and a weakened public system. The usefulness of reinforcing competition between public and private schools must be questioned when it might be more meaningful to use public funding to bring the two rival sectors closer together in the spirit of unity.

During what Michael Sandel, Reith Lecturer 2009, calls the age of market triumphalism, without quite realising it, he says, and without ever deciding to do so, we drifted from having a market economy to being a market society and the concept of the public good has become outdated. If goods are to be valued correctly, argues Sandel, moral and spiritual questions cannot be overlooked. Public institutions, he says, are only partly for the sake of looking after those who could not afford those services on their own. They are also traditionally sites for the cultivation of a common life, so that people from different walks of life are able to encounter one another and so acquire a sense of a shared life. It is in this way that we can meaningfully think of one another as citizens in a common venture.

The Sufi understanding that all action should promote the flourishing of the One is also supported by Wheeler's and Mathews' accounts of the self as an essentially relational entity that maintains itself through continuous exchange with other similarly relational entities. As Mathews explains, focusing not so much on the private good of the individual as on the common good, which might be conceived of as the unfolding of the One in the matrix of the Many, and safeguarding its integrity by way of "*mutualistic* relations" based less on competition than on "mutually sustaining interaction", relations are promoted that favour individual flourishing by promoting the flourishing of the many who contribute to it (2003, 56-57).

Knowledge as a commodity, however, comes at considerable cost and affordability often entails debt which compromises flourishing. Valued for its wealth-generating potential, knowledge is dearly purchased by the consumer eager for wealth and its accoutrements. As a consumer good, it must have immediate, popular appeal; regular rebranding gives it a fresh new look to enhance its desirability. It must appear useful here and now; in other words, its link to wealth production must be direct. Repackaging begins with a semantic shift as 'information' and 'opinion' are promoted to 'knowledge'. In a short period of time old words with deep-rooted meanings have new meanings imposed on them. 'Memory', for instance, as Berry (2001) reminds us, is no longer stored in the heart but has become purchasable; we plug it in or out, lose or discard it. 'History' is a website visited a moment ago. Redefining value-laden words occurs without our being taken by surprise since the old words still look the same, says Berry, and we are unaware of the implications of their old meanings becoming irrelevant and the appearance of meaning being mistaken for meaning. Information and opinion have a use-by date, sometimes only moments away or perhaps already passed. Packaged as a commodity, and not immune from "block logic" (Mathews, 2005, 18), knowledge must be organised into discrete disciplinary blocks, managed and controlled by assessing, filtering, interpreting, modifying, rejecting or storing. It requires frequent repackaging to ensure not only its appeal but also its safety and saleability.

So a need has been perceived, within our 'market society', to transform the ancient mystical teachings into "a truly contemporary idiom" (Mathews, 2003, 7). Insights derived from inspirational traditions must be "rendered adaptively" (*ibid.*) so that they might once again find appeal. Hamilton, for example, repackages the mystical concept at the heart of his philosophy as a form of psychology, albeit a metaphysical one. In his review of Hamilton's *Affluenza*, entitled *The Mystic Social Scientist* (2005), Andrew Norton sheds light on what he believes was Hamilton's need to repackage his mystical theme in a more appealing format. According to Norton, Hamilton's earlier work, *The Mystic Economist* (1994), lacked broad interest and appeal. 'Mystic' writers, Norton believes, cannot easily convince people who want evidence or logic, who are reluctant to "accept intuition and to acknowledge their feelings as guides to action". The Fairfax online database in fact records no mention of *The Mystic Economist* in 1994. Hamilton knew he had a problem, says Norton, and admitted that "the arguments of this book run counter to the underlying principles of academic discourse" (preface), but in 1994 had no solution. Over the next decade, however, Hamilton kept his basic ideas but changed his tactics, Norton explains. "To persuade people with no nostalgia for the pre-modern world, and no felt need to transcend any division with the universe, he repackaged his argument in more familiar terms. In subsequent work God retreated into the background, replaced by the more acceptable idea that there can be differences between our short and long-term interests, between what we are doing now and what we should be doing, between our inauthentic and authentic selves". Cleverly, says Norton, Hamilton cites comments on the issue by left-liberals such as John Rawls and right-liberals such as F.A. Hayek, to show that he is entering the intellectual mainstream and to criticise neoliberals for creating economies and societies in which the 'true self' is continually trumped by the untrue self.

Repackaging traditional teachings requires their less attractive aspects be occluded; mystical concepts such as surrender of the ego and cultivation of an attitude of humility and submission are alien within the neoliberal context within which individual liberty is most highly valued. Holding little appeal to the modern consumer, mystical goals need to be concealed within the new forms, the forms themselves simply reflecting the conditions from which they emerge. Truth is one but enunciations of it are many, some more direct and others less so. Be that as it may, explains Schuon, "the thing which matters is not the form but the meaning of the enunciations; that one enunciation may be less direct in its form than another is no proof whatever of a lesser wisdom but solely of a lesser receptivity on the part of a particular environment" (Schuon, 1959, 68). As Carl Ernst (2009, 18) points out, long before the commodification of knowledge, Sufi masters, particularly those of the Chishti order, were aware that the ongoing challenges of each age should be met with responses suitable to the needs of the time. Hazrat Inayat Khan, for example, himself of the Chishti order, presented Sufism to Europeans and Americans as a spiritual path that was not necessarily tied to Islam because, as Ernst believes, he "grasped the depth of the enormous prejudice against Islam in Europe and America".

"Sufism for Westerners" (Hammer, in Westerland (Ed.), 2004, in Ernst, *op. cit.*) downplays the Islamic connection and mystical aspects while emphasising more popular ones. Less attractive features such as 'annihilation' (*fana*) and 'surrender' to the 'master' tend to be occluded. Ernst notes that in modern interpretations Rumi has become "the touchstone for modern rethinking of identity in a non-authoritarian mode" (2009, 9).

Furthermore, new technologies have spawned a profusion of 'Sufi teachings' in a process which Ernst refers to as "the publication of the secret" (*op. cit.*, 10). "The apparent paradox of publicizing an esoteric tradition is nowhere more apparent than on the Internet, where the open secret of mysticism must be reconfigured in terms of what are basically advertising paradigms", says Ernst (*op. cit.*, 14). Its authors may well be 'nameless and faceless' like the *sheikhs* of old, but unlike them, are neither known nor loved. Mystical teachings, previously cautiously dispensed to the devotee by the trusted *sheikh*, are now universally disseminated in a bewildering array of forms. Discerning meaning beyond the veil of words is therefore of particular importance, and involves now, as it did then, effort and struggle (*mujahada*). For as al-Qushayri (d. 1074) observed, and Ernst reminds us, "The vocabulary of Sufism is designed both to facilitate understanding among Sufis and to frustrate it for outsiders . . . to conceal and to display, to show and to hide". Sufi esotericism, carefully guarding its secrets, is designed to prevent "wild misunderstandings on the part of people who have no access to the underlying experiences of encounter with God" (Ernst, 2008). The novice is unlikely to recognise the face of his beloved wherever he turns, as Rumi did, or know, like Ibn al-Arabi, that "God possesses . . . faces . . . without limit" (*SPK*, 156), and that not all of them have a divine appearance. As Rumi tells us, not all knowledge leads to a vision of mercy and gentleness:

> When knowledge is revealed to the heart, it becomes an aid; but knowledge acquired by the body is a heavy load. Like an ass carrying books: knowledge not from Him is a burden. Knowledge not immediately from Him will soon vanish like paint on a woman's face (*SPL*, 129)

In the modern teaching arena we are told: "Our changing knowledge and learning contexts are axiomatic . . . Everything is going digital. *The end user is gaining control* . . . and everything seems to be *speeding up*" (emphasis in original) (Siemens, 2006). Siemens explains that because problems are becoming increasingly complex, each 'user' (as opposed to knower) will only 'know' in part. "Certainty is for a season, not a lifetime", says Siemens. Contrasting sharply with principial knowledge, of which Nasr says "it can penetrate into foreign universes of form and bring out their inner meaning" (1981, 291), knowledge represented as relative, transient and fragmented, though useful for contingent ends, cannot possibly be instrumental to the 'user' gaining control. While it may give control, to a degree, of physical phenomena, and enable certain interventions, divorced from principial knowledge, its harmlessness cannot be guaranteed. The speeding up which Siemens considers a boon is a key factor contributing to the accelerated globalisation of economic activities, conducted by unknown people in faraway places, whose motivation is profit and growth, at the expense of local economies which evolved from an intimate knowledge of people and place and which conferred on its members the freedoms implicit in familiarity, mutual respect, affection and support (Northcott, 2007; Berry, 1993). 'Knowledge' as it is understood within this context has become a wolf in sheep's clothing and as such it contributes directly to a loss of control.

As a commodity, knowledge has no inherent value. It is of human creation and therefore "may reside in non-human appliances" (Siemens, 2006). This suggests that inanimate objects may 'know' more than humans, and that tools may 'know' more than their makers. Such an understanding has serious implications. Not all knowledge is important, according to Siemens, so the user, who is presumably not a knower, would need to discriminate between 'important' and 'unimportant' knowledge; 'new' being important ("altering the landscape") while "decisions made yesterday" are irrelevant (Siemens, 2006). According to Siemens, our understanding of knowledge requires continual adjustment to keep abreast of changes to business and academic environments "in order to ensure that we are basing our decisions on an accurate foundation" (Siemens, 2006). A reliable foundation must surely be knowledge that is true and enduring—'knowledge of the Real' (Ibn al-Arabi, *SPK*, 225); a fixed standard, unlike the shifting sands that give rise to the vicissitudes of so much human enterprise. Plato specifies that knowledge must "show the eternal nature not varying from generation and corruption" (1956, 443). "While there is a right answer now", says Siemens however, "it may be wrong tomorrow due to alterations in the information climate affecting the decision" (*op. cit.*). When such transient and fragmented 'knowledge' serves as the foundation of our activity, it must surely compromise the safety of the earth and the wellbeing of its inhabitants.

Modern societies' commitment to the new derives, as Mathews explains, "from a wholesale embrace of discursivity that is a corollary of materialism, of disenchantment with the concrete dimension of reality", and combines with the commitment to increase the "standard of living" indefinitely, in the name of progress (2005, 11). Chronic dissatisfaction with the given results in the current regime of perpetual change, "a perpetual quest to improve the world, to make it over in accordance with our own latest designs" rather than to let things be, respecting the natural cycles of creation, decay and regeneration (*ibid.*).

In the knowledge economy, however, "Nature and history will play a much smaller role while human ingenuity will play a much bigger role", according to Lester Thurow (*New Tools, New Rules: Playing to win in the new economic game*, 1991, cited in Houghton & Sheehan, 2008). In their guide to the knowledge economy for people in business and government, Professors John Houghton and Peter Sheehan of Victoria University's Centre for Strategic Economic Research explain that the forces driving the knowledge economy are fundamentally reshaping the world. The knowledge economy, they say, emerges from two defining forces: the rise in knowledge intensity of economic activities, and the increasing globalisation of economic affairs (2008). In light of globalisation, local communities must compete on a global scale as traditional boundaries shift, and scale and time become increasingly important to ensure competitiveness, "a key aspect of value—essentially a new factor of production" (*op. cit.*, 8). Since these processes are proceeding rapidly and their impact is already considerable, Houghton and Sheehan propose that each nation find its appropriate response to the new economic realities which, they point out, will polarise people and nations into different strata of economic activity and of living standards rather than promote convergence as standard neo-classical growth theories suggest about economies subject to market forces (*op. cit.*, 15).

We have seen in the market's response a rebranding of knowledge as a desirable consumer good, whose advertisers promote its indispensability to progress and economic growth. Its mass production has delivered vigorous growth of dubious quality, and distribution via an extensive network has ensured it is widely available. Houghton and Sheehan suggest that programs be introduced to ease the burden of adjustment on individuals, families, communities and regions on which the costs of becoming internationally competitive fall especially heavily, and to help them make the transition to the new environment's competitive industrial structure. While failing to suggest what form such programs might take and who would be responsible for their creation, they do, however, draw attention to the potential dangers of basing our activity on flawed knowledge. Suggesting 'programs' might offer solutions to such fundamental issues trivializes the new order's impact.

Unrestrained, unsustainable economic growth is one example of not knowing (Berry, 1993 & 2001). If we want to succeed in our aims and hopes as a people, Berry advises, "we must understand that we cannot proceed any further without standards, and we must see that ultimately the standards are not set by us" (1993, 12). In a climate of uncertainty where knowledge is at continual risk of becoming obsolete, however, standards and values are not inviolable as they too must satisfy the needs of the market, prompting Berry to remind us that "it is foolish, sinful and suicidal" to destroy the health of the world for the sake of a financial system which is "unnatural, undemocratic, sacrilegious and ephemeral" (1993, 13).

Berry has found that local economies in harmony with the laws of nature, based on intimate knowledge and love of place, are sustainable because what is known and loved is taken care of, while the unknown and distant are more likely to be exploited. Mathews believes that indigenous societies have this kind of knowledge of their environment, and while it enables them to work in partnership with the natural world, it prevents them from dismantling their world and rebuilding it according to their own abstract designs (2003, 79). Theirs is an encounter with the "world-as-it-is", on which their survival depends, and in relating to it, they respect its subjectival dimension (*ibid.*). Thoughtfulness should direct even the smallest action, says Berry, so that the whole is taken into account at every moment. "The true source and analogue of our economic life should be the economy of plants", he believes, "which never exceeds natural limits, never grows beyond the power of its place to support it, produces no waste, and enriches and preserves itself by death and decay. We must learn to grow like a tree, not like a fire", he concludes (1993, 13).

'Subsistence' (*baqa*) in the Real (Ibn al-Arabi, *SPK*, 219) is the Sufi's preferred mode of being in the world. It follows the final step of 'annihilation' (*fana*) of ego (*nafs*) when divine self-disclosure takes place. 'Subsistence', at best, entails sufficiency to maintain life and minimise harm, though hazard and hunger are undeniably part of its reality. This model, depending as it does on relinquishment of personal control, trust that one's needs will be met, and gratitude for the given, whatever its form, represents, by Western standards, extreme hardship and misfortune. The first step on the meaningful path, we remember, is *islām*, submission of the knower to the Known, or as Rumi experiences it, of the lover to the Beloved. The Sufi path is one of surrender—the mystic gives up his own will for the sake of the mystery to which he is ineluctably drawn. It is this spirit of humility which would have us "kneeling tenderly at (the world's) feet, awaiting *its* command, trying to divine *its* will", as Mathews envisions (2003, 1).

Because of his awareness of the relative nothingness of his ego, the Sufi surrenders to what he knows and loves. His own humility reflects the "divine humility", the "humility" of God being the simplicity of His essence (Schuon, 1959, 87). "[Symbolically] the Lord who gets up from His throne and takes one hundred steps to meet His servant, who need take only one" (*Hadith of the Prophet,* cited in Schuon, 87), reveals not only his greatness but above all his humility (*ibid.*). He turns the mystic's heart (*qalb*) and calls him back to Him. Those who identify only with their own effort and will have forgotten His primal need for them in order to know Himself. The ninth-century Sufi, Bistami, expresses this understanding as follows:

> At the beginning I was mistaken in four respects. I concerned myself to remember God, to know Him, to love Him and to seek Him. When I had come to the end I saw that He had remembered me before I remembered Him, that His knowledge of me had preceded my knowledge of Him, that His love towards me had existed before my love to Him and He had sought me before I sought Him (cited in Vaughan-Lee, 2000, 7)

Dissatisfaction with the world-as-it-is and our knowledge of it appears to have triggered what Nasr calls a "quest for wholeness" (1981, 117), which, in his view, is inseparable from the quest for holiness. Through the study of ecology, he believes, the sacred has reentered into the world view of contemporary science. Moreover, the emergence of and growing interest in ecophilosophy might be interpreted as a response to an awareness, more recently awakened, of a unified, orderly, meaningful reality, and philosophies such as those of Mathews, Wheeler and Hamilton, which penetrate into the very heart of material manifestation, contribute to piercing the veil that distorts and divides. Similarly, in a world perceived too long as fragmented, we witness the surge of interest in Rumi's poetry, a celebration of unity through love. According to Nasr, the search for wholeness has manifested itself also in the concern with

holistic medicine, whole foods, in short—a "desire to return to that primordial harmony of man with the natural environment" (*ibid.*). Two
decades later Tacey enumerates countless and diverse sites in Australia,
ranging from Aboriginal reconciliation to workplace relations and youth
culture, that appear to be giving rise to a new spirituality that "is primarily about connectedness" (2000, 15). But in a world "hungering for anything that might break the confines of a stifling materialistic ambience"
(Nasr, 1981, 119), in the absence of principial knowledge, discernment is
not always possible.

4.4 Meaningful Expression

"Assuming the character traits of God—that is Sufism", says Ibn al-Arabi
(*SPK,* 283), therefore just as the Real "gives each thing its creation", the
human must "give each thing its due" (*ibid.*). Mystical knowing leads to
meaningful creativity—"Making Him manifest in His creation" (*SPK,*
219)—which entails giving each created thing its due. Knowledge of
divine Reality presupposes or demands moral conformity to this Reality,
"as the eye necessarily conforms to light", Schuon explains; "since the
object to be known is the sovereign Good, the knowing subject must cor-
respond to it analogically" (1991, 86).

"On the basis of His knowledge He makes the things properly and
well", says Ibn al-Arabi (*SPK,* 298). Knowers participate in the making,
"creating in this earthly abode through good work (*amal*), not through
saying 'Be!'" (al-Arabi, *SPK,* 178). The latter is the task of the divine Creator to whom the knower submits and in whose name the knower conducts good works. Acting 'properly and well' and 'giving each thing its
due' constitute the responsibility of the knower and therein resides the
inherent value of knowledge. Such knowledge prevents what Berry terms
"the perversion of making" (2001, 15). Without knowledge, we are
unaware that we are actors; we fail to act meaningfully and to give each
thing its due.

Making 'properly' involves what Berry refers to as thinking and acting with "propriety" (2001, 13); a term which, like the value it denotes,
has become something of an anachronism. According to Berry, the value
of propriety is in its reference to the fact that we are not alone; that our
life inescapably affects other lives. We are being measured, he believes, by

a standard that we did not make and cannot destroy, although various crises and most notably the environmental crisis testify to our attempt to defy this standard. Propriety is the antithesis of individualism, argues Berry, since individual wishes can never be the ultimate measure. Similarly, Rowan Williams emphasises that being reasonable means understanding our place and being in proper *relation* to reality, and developing mind and heart and imagination capable of right relation with others, with the environment and with the ultimate truth of God (2009). Propriety and restraint call for an examination of our relation to reality, and in order that this might be harmonious, the voice of ego must be stilled. Questions of propriety do not call for specialised answers if this means providing answers that are uniform and universal—the same styles, explanations, routines, tools, methods and models for everybody, everywhere, says Berry. Professionals and experts too often "subscribe to the preeminence of the mind and of the career", and submit to the laws of professionalism, politics and profit rather than to the dictates of propriety (Berry, 2001, 15).

Not making things properly and well has consequences not always commensurate with the act of omission that gives rise to them. "These things then direct a claim" against their makers (*ibid.*), says Berry, reflecting the Sufi understanding that within each action is embedded consequence. Sufi teachings are quite explicit in this regard—not only science, technology, economics or the law should set the standards by which we measure our actions, but heart-knowledge, intimate and unchanging, which is essential to make our creativity meaningful. Failure to make properly and well has consequences that some might interpret as punishment meted out by an anthropomorphic God. A vengeful God perhaps, or vengeful Mother Earth as in James Lovelock's *Revenge of Gaia* (2006).

'The Almighty Teacher', who is also 'The Worker', sets the standard through self-disclosure (*SPL*, 213). In the 'workshop of nonexistence' the divine Maker is hidden in the making. Nameless and faceless, inaudible and invisible, He dwells beyond the veil of His work:

> The Worker is hidden in the workshop—go to the workshop, see Him face to face! Since the work has woven a veil over the Worker, you cannot see Him without it. The workshop is His dwelling place, so enter into it, that you may see the Worker and the work together! (Rumi, *SPL*, 178)

The work has rendered the Worker invisible. Only the work appears to be existent whereas the one who created it appears to be nonexistent. This Worker, Rumi tells us, is the 'Almighty Teacher' who teaches us through self-disclosure (*SPL*, 213). Since the Prophet Muhammad was "the greatest locus of divine self-disclosure" (*SPK*, 240), a close imitation of his actions is binding for every faithful Muslim (Schimmel, 1975) and Sufism itself is an endorsement of the *silsila*—the initiatic chain whose origins Sufis trace back to the Prophet, and following his death, to the 'Friends of the Prophet', who live in constant remembrance of the Divine Names and in turn teach disciples who are able to pass on the wisdom teachings (Anissian, 2006). By constantly remembering the Almighty Teacher in all their actions, devotees aspire to meaningful expression. Direct experience is essential and knowledge is often passed on by non-explicit means, therefore the Sufi poet Kharaqani says: "The heir of the Prophet is he who follows the Prophet with his actions, not he who blackens the face of paper" (Schimmel, 1975).

By observing the master and then working under the master's guidance, the apprentice picks up the rules of the art, including those which are not explicitly expressed. In similar vein, Polanyi (1969), on whose interpretation of tacit knowledge Wheeler bases her 'intimations of knowing', argues that positive knowledge is unarticulated and that such 'tacit' knowledge is passed on by apprenticeship. As Plato had already argued in the *Meno* (Wheeler, 64-65), and Polanyi more recently explained, intimations of a hidden reality guide the pursuit of discovery. Human creativity proceeds via tacit knowledge and our sense that we are in contact with a complex reality of which there is more to be known, and in which "what is comprehended has the same structure as the act that comprehends it", says Wheeler (*ibid.*).

Sufi teachings are often conveyed wordlessly; the 'opening' of the 'eye of the heart' does not depend on speech. Van Stolk provides a vivid account of the transmission of unarticulated knowledge from master to pupil in his recollection of Hazrat Inayat Khan's own apprenticeship. He recounts how every day the eager pupil would appear before his Sufi master, but more than six months passed before the latter broached the subject of Sufism. When the young Inayat opened his notebook, his teacher immediately stopped. "I understood what that meant" Inayat wrote later;

"it meant that the teaching of the heart should in the first place be assimilated in the heart. The heart is the notebook for it . . ." (Van Stolk, 21). And of the reluctance of his teacher to speak about spiritual matters, he wrote: ". . . all knowledge comes in its own time . . . there is nothing in the whole world more precious than the presence of the master. His teaching may not be given in theories, but it is in his atmosphere. That is a living teaching which is real upliftment" (VI, 76). Conversely, Yasin Ceran emphasises that a good teacher understands "the silent words that pour from their students' tongues of disposition", their facial expressions, and their voice levels and tones. "Educators who do not carefully observe these signs are like those who close their eyes during the bright daylight and wonder why they cannot see" (Ceran, 2010).

The master, eminently skilled and having reached the pinnacle of his craft, is best placed to teach the apprentice who in turn aspires to create meaningfully. Meaningful making as the expression of knowledge in action had its philosophical home in the classical Greek tradition, with Plato regarding expert craftsmen as having *episteme*, knowledge, imbued with an awareness of the Ideas, i.e. *technē*, which made its epistemic status unsurpassable (Craig, 2005). Like the lover and mystic who lose themselves in the being of the beloved, the craftsman attains true insight by becoming one with the craft. It is that state of oneness, not the exclusive activity of thinking about reality, which provides the experience of egoless immersion in the world—the 'taste' of reality.

Sufis emphasise the indispensability of the teacher's guidance, and Maulana and Maizebhandari remind us that Rumi fulfilled his potential only after Shams came into his life (2010). "When the master demonstrates the proper procedure, the apprentice absorbs the lesson by osmosis" (Sennett, 2008, 181). Disclosure—the manifestation of the unknown, and demonstration—showing the way, fundamental aspects of 'good' teaching (Clifford, 2008; Renich, 2007) and meaningful making, remain the most effective—and natural—way of teaching, and we see this particularly in regard to the teaching of language. The babe in its mother's arms absorbs her tongue uncritically. The Japanese violin teacher, Dr Shinichi Suzuki, was so inspired by the way children appear to absorb language automatically that he developed his now famous 'mother tongue' method to teach not only violin but other instruments as well. In light of *tawhid*, knower and known are lover and beloved, making theirs a relationship based on trust and love, quite different from modern teacher/learner relationships which, according to the Vinson Report (2002) into Public Education, are often marred by student aggression and a refusal to cooperate, making the day-to-day business of teaching distressing and difficult for Australian teachers. Similarly, a New Zealand Educational Institute study found that one in seven primary school teachers were hit by their students in 2006, and that more than 50 per cent of teachers and more than 25 per cent of school support staff reported aggressive verbal confrontations with their students (NZ Herald, 28 July 2007). The Sufi relationship with the teacher, on the other hand, is enriched by quiet surrender; in the process of stilling the voice of ego a concentrated listening can occur so that meaning might be discerned.

The view that "good action is nothing but a glimpse of beauty" (VIII, 111) and that human beings are enriched by the skills and dignified by the spirit of meaningful making can be traced back to Homer's hymn to Hephaestus, builder of all the houses on Mount Olympus, coppersmith, jeweller and inventor of chariots. Similar insights guided Confucianism throughout several thousand years (Sennett, 2008, 286). Plato's *aretē* designates above all goodness in action since the *aretē* of a soul enables it to perform its function, namely living, successfully. Aristotle's conception of *aretē* is founded on the analogous idea that the human function can be performed better or worse, and that happiness is most likely to ensue when virtue is active. Socrates identifies *aretē* with knowledge used wisely (Sedley, 1998). Nothing is valuable unless used wisely; hence wisdom is the only underivatively valuable thing, he claimed (*ibid.*). Because it must be awakened within, Plato also emphasises the importance of being "guided aright" (1956, 377).

Making meaningfully implies making wisely. More recently meaningful making finds its philosophical home within pragmatism, the movement which has, for more than a century, dedicated itself to making sense of concrete experience (Sennett, 286). The first wave of pragmatists included Charles Peirce, John Dewey, F.C.S. Schiller and William James who hoped to construct an alternative to the anti-religious, science-worshipping positivism of his day. In his essay *The Will to Believe* (1896), James attempts to reconcile science and religion by viewing both as instruments useful for distinct, non-conflicting purposes (Rorty, 2004). The second and current wave of pragmatists includes Hans Joas in Germany and the Americans Rorty, Bernstein and Sennett. The animating impulse of pragmatism remains to engage with ordinary, constructive human activities (Sennett, 287). Sennett uses the term 'craftsmanship' to name that basic human impulse to do a job well for its own sake.

For Dewey, in particular, pragmatism is about anchoring creativity in action. In *Art as Experience* he argues that "knowledge is instrumental to the enrichment of immediate experience through the control over action that it exercises" (cited in Joas, 1996, 132). Knowledge "liberates and liberalizes action" (Dewey, *The Need for a Recovery of Philosophy*, 1917, 63, in Joas, 133) by imbuing each step with meaning, so that within each action reflection and purpose are embedded, unlike the Cartesian interpretation of action, which conceives of perception and cognition as preceding action (Joas, 158). Work that disregards consequences is nothing more than drudgery (Dewey, *Democracy and Education*, 1916, 241, in Joas, 155)—activity as means, carried out under external or self-imposed compulsion. Work is meaningful only when it is permeated with regard for consequences, *as part of itself*. For Dewey the crucial issue is the difference between goals that are external to the action and prescribed, and goals which emerge from within the action itself. In *Art as Experience* Dewey says: "In a better-ordered society than that in which we live, an infinitely greater happiness than is now the case would attend all modes of production. We live in a world in which there is an immense amount of organization, but it is an external organization, not one of the ordering of a growing experience, one that involves, moreover, the whole of the live creature, toward a fulfilling conclusion" (cited in Joas, 140).

Action, in the first instance, concerns itself with expression, which in humans mostly takes the form of speech. Referring to the alienated labour of capitalist productivism and portraying the worker as *animal laborens*, whose mind engages only when labour is done, Hannah Arendt asserts that "A life without speech . . . is literally dead to the world" (1958, 55). Speech, however, as we have seen, too often reveals the kind of making to which Arendt refers—making that is not meaningful, though it might be elaborately crafted, or simply thoughtlessly spewed "like a cuttlefish spurting out ink" (Orwell, 1945, 137). If by 'world' we understand 'locus of the Real', we should seek a life with less speech but more meaningful expression where our own voice falls silent and we listen with 'the ear of the heart'. I would argue that less speech, less thoughtless, mechanical language production, less artifice and squandering of words in favour of more prudent use of linguistic resources might allow meaning to come to the fore. Knowing the Real means longing for authenticity—words, inherently precious, used truthfully, so that meaning might become clear.

Acutely aware of the power of language to manipulate people and conceal truth, Orwell provides several useful pointers to counteract what he calls "the debasement" of language, the most important of these being to "throw your mind open" (*ibid.*). Mindful of the word's worth, Orwell recommends using the fewest and shortest words to convey meaning. In fact, for the sake of truth he suggests refraining from words altogether until sufficient reflection has taken place. Similarly the Bhagavad-Gita teaches the harmony of "right words": "words which give peace, words which are good and beautiful and true" (Mascaro, 1973, 30). The harmony of words, 'Right Speech', which reflects the ideal of truth, constitutes the third stage of the Path to Perfection for the Buddhist apprentice. Lack of control of the ego inclines us to act too hastily, without sufficient reflection or knowledge, explains Hazrat Inayat Khan (XI, 78). 'Thinking clearly' and silently reflecting on the intended use of the resource at hand and on the seeds of consequence that will take root as a result of action, for which responsibility will have to be taken, will result in more honest expression. Built into the beat of life and the living heart is rhythm, determinant of outcomes, and as we have seen, actions are likely to live on in the same rhythm from which they spring. Therefore establishing a *sattvic* (harmonious) rhythm before acting or speaking is important since "the impulse that comes to a person who is in the rhythm of *sattva* is inspired and in harmony with the rhythm of the universe" (XIV, 83). In stillness, the *sattvic* rhythm can best be cultivated so that actions undertaken are not marred from the outset by the chaotic rhythm of ego.

We have seen that wealth is considered this age's highest good and since the production of wealth is often dependent on speed, the two have come to be regarded as incomparable goods. Paralleling Heidegger's critique of technology, Paul Virilio, in *Speed and Politics: An Essay on Dromology*, 1977, argues that speed, not class or wealth, is the primary force shaping our civilization. Armitage and Graham trace the source of conflict back to speed, concluding that "speed, disposable time, surplus production and a devotion to wealth constitute one side of the two interdependent and contradictory extremes of the political economy of speed: trade and war" (Armitage *et al*, 2003). According to Sufi teachings, the chaotic rhythm of speed, known by its Sanskrit name *tamas*, is the source of failure, disease and destruction; in short, the source of all pain and sorrow (IV, 28).

The focus on speed prevents the maker from dwelling in the reality of the thing he is making, of anticipating its coming into existence, of guiding its every stage from non-existence to face to face encounter. Making a thing function, says Wheeler, "we incorporate it in our body", "so that we come to dwell in it" (2006, 63). Only by dwelling in the thing do we come to understand it, she says. Dwelling involves stillness so that listening can occur to ensure that one's response, in time, will be appropriate. Sennett describes the relationship with the thing being made as a dialogue during which resistance is encountered, followed by "opening up" the problem, questioning, suspending resolution and decision, and listening before resuming action in a new form. None of these processes occur instantly or simultaneously. The regular rhythm of action-rest characterises the development in time of the craftsman's complex skills (Sennett, 279). The capacity to open up a problem, Sennett explains, draws on intuitive leaps, specifically on the ability to draw together unrelated domains. "Opening up" means observing more closely, hearing the other voice, stilling one's own, being open to see and make differently.

However, the demand for speed and the 'reality' of time constraints encourages superficiality and guesswork rather than reflection. Dwelling in a problem so that insight might be gained is often not possible and is actually discouraged by testing regimes that determine success not according to evidence of reflection or depth of understanding, but according to the superficial criterion of speed. The often cryptic nature of multiple-choice questions in particular invites creative students to puzzle over possibilities and to make connections between unrelated elements instead of hurriedly ticking boxes to gain the better score. Berube (2004) advocates that tests should measure understanding, analysis and synthesis, and evaluate the depth of students' understanding. Instead, she says, teachers spend valuable time training students to master the mechanics of testing, and it is often this mastery that determines their success. The reality of having to 'beat the clock' means tests are unreliable, unrealistic indicators (Kellow, 2008), particularly of the capacity for *amal*—good work, the fruit of knowledge. Sennett maintains that the capacity to work well is shared fairly equally among human beings (285), an observation which is not born out by the results of superficial testing.

Finding meaning entails, most importantly, the art of stillness and concentration (Schuon, 1959, 89). Schuon explains that pure concentration is less a fixing of the mind on an idea or object than the elimination of every distraction; the divine presence, or grace, as Mathews envisions it, or intellect according to the perspective, must be allowed to act without hindrance, "like a leaven" (*op. cit.*, 90). This 'spiritual technique' is at the heart of Sennett's interpretation of craftsmanship, according to which the craftsman is fully responsive to and focused on his making, gaining intimate knowledge in the process. This means rising above chaotic motion (Sennett, 295) and adopting a harmonious rhythm that enables reflection and allows skills to evolve through the routines of repetition and practice, enabling *animal laborens* to develop skill from within through a slow process of metamorphosis. In the process of giving form, the maker is transformed, working on the thing as well as on the instrument, since the quality of the instrument ultimately determines the quality of the thing. "It is not enough for a viol to be played well", says Schuon, "its wood must also be of a noble quality" (1959, 90). Both body and mind must be cared for, developed and refined as a defective instrument causes discord.

In light of the importance of the art of stillness and concentration one might question the current approach of medicating the increasing number of children who experience learning difficulties because of their inability to be still, in a culture which appears not to value stillness, let alone regard it as an art. One might question the value of constant exposure to sensory stimuli, much of it electronic, and perhaps also reflect on the possible effect unlimited freedom of expression, as of right, virtually from birth, might have on a child. Children diagnosed with Attention Deficit Disorder typically display "distractable, disruptive and inattentive behaviours", a condition most commonly treated with Ritalin (T.M.) (Hurd, 1996). Such an approach may be convenient because medication takes immediate effect and requires no fundamental change of behaviour, but a more natural approach, though slower to take effect and requiring greater effort, might be more meaningful in the long-term. The process of acquiring knowledge is slow and painful, and calls for struggle, patience, perseverance, right guidance, trust and love (Schuon, 1959).

'Good work', Orwell emphasises, involves effort so that we might avoid the many bad habits which, in his opinion, blight spoken, and particularly, written English. One such habit, he says, is lack of creativity, evidenced by increasing recourse to worn-out metaphors which have lost all evocative power and are merely used because they save people the trouble of creative thought. He draws our attention to two fundamental requirements for all forms of meaningful making: effort and imagination, without which our language is devoid of meaning—nothing more than noises emanating from the larynx. Effortless and convenient, thoughtless usage of language exemplifies the mass-production of low quality goods promoted by materialistic societies forgetful of meaning. Unaware of what we are saying we resort to the same clichés, banalities and untruths; inferior goods churned out effortlessly by an unimaginative production line.

4.5 Creativity of the Heart

He provided causes to make us from a drop of sperm. It had neither ears, nor awareness, nor intellect, nor eyes, neither the attribute of kingliness nor that of servanthood; it knew neither heartache nor joy, neither abasement nor greatness. He gave that unaware drop a home in the womb and made it into blood through a subtle process. Then He coagulated and congealed that blood and, in that private house, made it into new flesh without head or organ. He opened the door of the mouth, the eyes, and the ears. He provided a tongue and then, behind the mouth, the treasury of the breast. Within it, He placed the heart, which is both a drop and a world, a pearl and an ocean, a servant and a king. Whose intellect could have comprehended that He would bring us forth from that lowly and unaware region to this one? He says, "You have seen and heard from whence to where I have brought you. Now I tell you that I will take you out from this earth and heaven to an earth finer than raw silver and a heaven that cannot be contained in imagination or description because of its power and subtlety. . .

If you do not believe His words, then think about that drop of sperm: Suppose you had said to it, "There is a world outside of this darkness, within which are a heaven, a sun and a moon, countries, cities and gardens. In it are His servants, some of whom are kings; some are wealthy, some healthy, some afflicted and blind. So fear how you leave this dark house, oh drop of sperm! Which one will you be?" That sperm drop's imagination and intellect would not have believed this story. How could it accept that other than darkness and bloody nourishment another world and food exist? Be sure that it would be heedless and deny. Yet it could not escape. It would be pulled and dragged outside. (*Rumi, Maktūbāt, SPL*, 76)

Dwelling "between two fingers of the All-Merciful" (Ibn al-Arabi, *SPK*, 107), the heart reflects the unlimited nature of Divine Possibility (Schuon, 1959, 2). The heart is the undisputed link between ourselves and God. Rumi repeatedly reminds us not to go outward but to return within ourselves to satisfy our deepest needs:

> Do not look for God, look for the one looking for God. But why look at all? He is not lost, He is right here, in the heart (Rumi, Cited in Star, 85) There is a force within which gives you life—seek That. In your body lies a priceless gem—seek That. O wandering Sufi, if you want to find the greatest treasure, don't look outside, look inside, and seek That (*ibid.*)

Only in the subtle organ of the heart can contradictory dimensions become complementary, so it is in the heart that duality can become unity. It is the specific function of the active imagination, whose locus is within the heart, to effect this union. "He who does not know the status of imagination has no knowledge whatsoever" says Ibn al-Arabi (Chittick, 1994, 11-12). In fact, he establishes imagination as the fundamental constitutive element not only of the mind, but of the cosmos at large (*ibid.*). According to al-Arabi, the forms that fill the cosmos are related to God as dream-images are related to a dreamer, and our own individual imaginations are streams in an infinite network of interlocking imagery. In his study of al-Arabi's teachings, Henry Corbin introduces the terms *imaginal world* and *mundus imaginalis to draw a clear distinction between itself as the world of 'Divine Epiphany' and the imaginary world, the latter being the product of the rational mind, which identifies its imaginings simply with the unreal (Corbin, 1969), more commonly referred to as fantasy. James Hillman, a student of Jung's, denotes* imagination as "the authentic voice of the heart", not the "reflective broodings of the mind" (Cited in Anissian, 17). Yet in our materialistic culture, says Berry, "we appear to have unleashed fantasy but curtailed imagination" and in doing so have "sealed ourselves in selfishness and loneliness, fantasy being of the solitary self and unable to lead us away from ourselves" (1993, 63). It is by recourse to imagination that we bridge the differences between ourselves and other beings and in doing so acquire the traits necessary to make our expression meaningful.

Mystical insights with their power to transform have had a strong influence on the practice of psychology and in particular on depth psychology and its most famous practitioner, C G. Jung. Jung's thinking was deeply influenced by Eastern religion and mysticism, and to this several of his publications attest, such as his *Symbols of Transformation* (1952), *Mysterium Coniunctionis* (1955), *The Holy Men of India* (1958) and *Concerning Rebirth* (1958). J. Marvin Spiegelman's *Sufism, Islam and Jungian Psychology* (1991) draws a direct parallel between Sufism and Jung's work on the inner world of archetypal images and was written with the assistance of Pir Villayat Inayat Khan. Henry Corbin's work on Ibn al-Arabi, known as "the pole of knowledge" for the depth of his insight, continues to influence depth psychologists today, such as James Hillman, who has become one of the most influential post-Jungian psychologists, reflecting Sufi thinking in his work (Anissian, 12).

Rumi reminds us of the Reality of the imaginal world, which Plotinus refers to as nous—'primary reality', the domain of intelligence and intelligible beings, emanation of the ineffable One, the ultimate principle of everything:

> Why do you wonder that the true beloved's Image should bestow strength upon the lover, both in his outward form and in the Unseen World? But how can we speak of 'imagination'? That is the very soul of Reality; that is not called 'imagination'. (Rumi, *SPL*, 256)

The One is perceived as three seemingly separate worlds: the spirit world, the material world and the luminous world of Idea-Images, the world of apparitional forms and of bodies in the subtle state (*'alam al-mithal*)—the Imagination. This world is the intermediary between the world of pure spiritual realities, the world of Mystery, and the visible, sensible world (*SPK*, ix). "It is the realm where invisible realities become visible, corporeal things are spiritualized and essential expression becomes audible. It is more real and subtle than the physical world, but less real and denser than the spiritual world, which remains ... hidden and cannot be known as such" (*ibid.*). In the Imagination, however, all the essential realities of being are manifested in real Images and these are projected to the heart (*qalb*), the subtile organ of perception where mystical knowledge resides and intuition and *marifa* arise. Of heart's sovereignty Rumi says:

> You are both the paradise and the hell and the pool of Kawthar. O heart, you are out of these two worlds, you are a universe, everything is in you and you are above and beyond everything (Cited in Can, 2005, 132)

The mystic's heart, its surface polished so that no trace of ego remains, functions like a gleaming mirror when the Image from the World of Images, the microcosmic form of the Divine Being, is projected on to it. The mirror of the heart reflects that Image, thus producing an imaginal representation of the Image's true 'mode' of being (Corbin, 1969). Rumi explains:

> Everyone sees the Unseen in proportion to the clarity of his heart, and that depends on how much he has polished it. Whoever has polished it more, sees more—more Unseen forms become manifest to him. . . .. (*SPL*, 162-163)

The imagination, by virtue of its creativity, provides access to the world of mystery. When the image reflects into the heart of the mystic, it is the mystic's active imagination which creates that image into a representation of the Image itself, thus reproducing the Image in a purely 'imaginal' way. As Ibn al-Arabi reminds us, the heart's creativity is not *ex nihilo*; it merely causes something to appear which already exists. "The Imagination does not construct something unreal, but *unveils* the hidden reality; it's action is, in short, that of the *tawil*" (Corbin, 29). "The Imagination is the organ of theophanies, because it is the organ in which Creation is perceived and because Creation is essentially theophany" (Corbin, 221). The imagination provides knowledge by realising the essential unity, *tawhid*, behind the appearance of multiplicity. It therefore carries out the divine intention; the intention of the hidden treasure yearning to be known. The imagination enables recognition of the Divine Face as it is veiled by the multitude of forms, and of the Divine Voice, the *Logos* of the world, as it resonates in all things.

The concept 'Imagination', as interpreted by Corbin, is not designated as such by Nasr, who uses the term 'Intelligence' instead. Accordingly, Intelligence is a divine gift which pierces veils and is able to know reality: "It is a ray of light which pierces through the veils of cosmic existence to the Origin and connects the periphery of existence, upon which man lives, to the Center wherein resides the Self" (1981, 146). Its function is 'intellection' (*op. cit.*, 148) and its focus *scientia sacra*.

Theophany is not a denial of science but, as Nasr explains, a "view of the cosmos and the forms it displays with such diversity and regularity as reflections of divine qualities and ontological categories rather than a veil which would hide the splendour of the Beloved's face" (1981, 197). "To contemplate the cosmos as theophany", he concludes, "is to realise that all manifestation from the One is return to the One, that all separation is union, that all otherness is sameness, that all plenitude is the Void. It is to see God everywhere" (Nasr, 214).

Light (*nūr*), as the agent of the Imagination (or Intelligence), dispels the darkness of ignorance by making visible the hidden meaning of things 'as they are'. Thus knowers "stand upon a clear sign" to receive knowledge from Him and from what has come from Him (Ibn al-Arabi, *SPK*, 202). Without Imagination, "we know the world only as we know shadows" and we are ignorant of the One projecting the shadow (Corbin, 217). The intermediate world of *mundus imaginalis* is instrumental to the mystical hermeneutic that is the cornerstone of Sufism, *tawil*—the 'carrying back' of a thing to its principle, of a symbol to what it symbolises. The imagination is the 'organ' (Corbin, 14) which at once produces symbols and apprehends them. Because every thing that manifests to the senses or the intellect reveals only its outer form (*zahir*) and because it carries a meaning which transcends the simple data and makes that thing a symbol, all things seen in this world must be carried back (*tawil*) to their real or hidden form (*batin*), in order that "the appearance of this Hidden form may manifest it in truth" (Corbin, 242). The capacity that concerns itself with meaning, which re-imagines things as symbols and which has as its field the intermediate world of subsisting images is variously referred to as Light or Knowledge. Nasr compares this Light to a ray which emanates from and returns to the Absolute, and suggests that its miraculous functioning is itself the best proof of that Reality which is at once absolute and infinite (Nasr, 2.). For this reason the Prophet instructed the people to say "My Lord, increase me in knowledge!" (Qur'an XX: 114) and submitted everything that came his way to *tawil*—the heart's understanding of the symbol.

Mental vision progresses through 'verification' (imaginative witness-ing vision) to vision of the heart, the inner eye (*basirah*), 'the eye of God'. It is this visionary capacity that frees the mystic from the limitations of form, allowing recognition of the divine in the multiplicity of forms. The material world presents itself to the inner eye as the treasure itself and an infinite source of knowledge of the ever-present giver in all his metamor-phoses. Therefore, mystical knowledge is lived; it is personal, profound and intimate. It enables us to envision the life of the earth and lives of beings different from ourselves: animals, plants, people of other countries and other races, people with conflicting ideologies. In the imagination arises the ability to see commonality in spite of obvious differences. In the imagination, knowledge of meaning becomes possible. Such knowledge is vital if we hope to overcome differences and promote wellbeing.

Yearning to return to its source whose essence it recognises as its own, the heart of the mystic responds: "Here I am! Enter my Paradise" (Qur'an, in Corbin, 132). Mystical knowledge, *marifa*, is the heart's knowledge of itself:

> When you have entered into my Paradise, you have entered into yourself, and you know yourself with another knowledge, different from that which you had when you knew your Lord by the knowledge you had of yourself, for now you know Him, and it is through Him that you know yourself (Ibn al-Arabi, in Corbin, 133)

To enter paradise means to contemplate that Reality which Nasr calls "completely other and yet none other than the very heart of the self, the Self of oneself" (1981, 3). In the heart the experience of simultaneity, not of contradictories, but of complementary opposites, or what Corbin refers to as *coincidentia oppositorum* (1969, 209) becomes possible. Experiencing this essential aspect of the One is instrumental in illuminating our limited understanding. When the strictures of form are overcome and opposing dimensions merge, wholeness is restored through *mysterium coniunctionis*. The realisation or 'actualisation' (Schuon, 1959, xiii) of knowledge con-sumes the whole being. Having reached that station, Rumi says: "I was immature, I matured and I was consumed" (Cited in Nasr, 154). The journey of the heart opens up a new dimension of being, based on com-munity of essence. He can then be likened to a 'Qur'an', of which God said: "We have neglected nothing in the Book, for it synthesises that which has happened and that which has not happened. But no one will understand what we have just said except for him who is himself, in his person, a 'Qur'an', for to him discernment will be given" (Ibn al-Arabi, in Corbin, 211).

When we have no 'visionary' knowledge and merely 'think' with the 'brain' instead of seeing with the heart, our reasoning is likely to be deficient. At this time of crisis, the awakening of *marifa* and the power to imagine the lives of people, animals, plants, sea, soil and air in our oneness is vital so that in our expression we are not harming them. Our Western culture may bombard us with materialistic values, but Rumi's current popularity suggests a longing for the taste of the real, for knowledge of the mystery of things and for a mysterious love affair of the heart rather than of the ego. The path of knowledge, as it weaves into the path of love, leads the spiritual wayfarer home.

CHAPTER FIVE

Being Meaningful

Being Meaningful

In this chapter I will introduce mystical love, *ishq*, and elaborate its centrality to *fana* and *baqa*, Sufi concepts which, I will argue, also resonate with Mathews' panpsychism and Hamilton's metaphysical-psychology. I will refute Mathews' claim that mystical love pacifies, and both Mathews' and Wheeler's claims that the mystic's path is a refuge from the developmental journey of life. I will also address Plumwood's interpretation of the unitive self as a potentially incorporative self by elaborating the reductive and creative aspects of Eros from a Sufi perspective.

5.1 Coursing through the Arteries of the World

By not making clear distinction between love's different forms, any feeling from the most fleeting of fancies to the deepest, most selfless form is given the same name. Sufi poetry, however, as language of the heart, invites us to witness mystical love's deeper truths by providing access to a world of meaning well beyond the limitations of the name:

> Love is the treasury of divine secrets, love is the music of the divine instrument; love peoples the abode, love makes the slave free; love is the harvest of our existence, love is our adornment and decoration (Dard, Cited in Shah, 1979, 107)

> It is love that teaches man: Thou, not I; Love that ends, is the shadow of love: True love is without beginning or end (Khan, 1960, 117)

> Love is truly God's Attribute: that One who is unique,
> Who is your beginning and your end.
> When you find that one,
> You'll no longer expect anything else:
> That is both the manifest and the mystery (Rumi, *SPL*, 132)

"The manifest and the mystery, the seen and unseen worlds, both come to be through love, the cause and the effect of all life" (IV, 54). Love, source and goal, brings all things from the world of unity to the world of diversity, and takes them back again to the world of unity. All things lead back to God, but not necessarily to the same face of God, since God has as many faces as He has attributes (*SPL*, 46).

Knowledge leads to meaningful activity (*amal*) but love is the creative energy generating all forms and as such all things have their origin in it. It is, as Suzan Khoromi claims, the "energy" or "glue" that holds the universe together. With reference to Maghsoud Angha's argument that "the electrostatic force holding together the two strands of DNA could be considered a form of love", Khoromi points to "an awakening" within the medical scientific community about the "need to learn more about the neurophysical and chemical underpinnings of love" because of its centrality to life (Khoromi, 2010). Love (*ishq*), in the Sufi tradition, is the creative spirit itself, coursing through the arteries of the world, the soul or spirit, *Ruh*, being its dwelling place. In this respect Platonic wisdom supports mystical thought: "Love walks not upon the earth, nor yet upon the skulls of men, but in the hearts and souls of . . . men; in them he walks and dwells and makes his home", says Agathon in the *Symposium* (Plato, 360). The word 'love' can be traced back to the Sanskrit word *lobh*, meaning 'desire' and 'wish', impulses which come together and culminate in the highest station in the soul's development, *Shuhud*, the realisation of love. Sufis believe that it is the soul's desire to arrive at this station (V, 143).

Love's desire manifests as longing. We are told that in Essence God is beyond all need, but at the level of His Attributes He said, "I desired (or loved) to be known, so I created the world" (*Hadith Qudsi, SPK*, 197). Longing is the soul's primal cry of separation, revealing its desire to return to its source. "Love is longing constantly" (Khan, 1960, 117). Longing, experienced as dissatisfaction, is regarded as a gift because it reminds us of our purpose. Though "rancorous and disruptive", the social discontent we are currently witnessing could be understood as a "holy discontent" because of its potential to lead to "a new stability and unity to society" (Tacey, 2000, 7). The journey Home is a reaching out to make contact with Reality, and begins when the heart is awakened and infused with divine love. This is the moment of *tawba*, the "turning of the heart", which awakens the memory of our state of oneness and makes us aware that we have become separated from the One we love (Vaughan-Lee,

1997, 31). The exile remembers Home and begins the difficult journey back to the Beloved:

> . . . in Love, there are union and separation—on the road there are ups and downs . . . You still must travel a long journey before you reach the place you seek in your madness (Rumi, *SPL*, 325)

The *Mathnawi* begins with the plaintive song of the reed lamenting its separation from the reed-bed. Although the reed's secret is contained within its song, "ear and eye lack the light whereby it should be apprehended" (Rumi, tr. Nicholson, I, 7-9). Most interpret their dissatisfaction at a material level, but the Sufi, whose "heart has been pierced" (*ibid.*) by the strains of the reed, recognises the divine soul awakening in him the longing to return home.

5.2 *Ishq*—'Dying for Love'

The mystic's love of the Real—"a love for which our modern languages lack words"—is like the love of matter, with its rich interiority, described by Mathews; "an aching love", unlike other loves, it holds us, encompasses us and breathes life into us (2005, 7). There is little recognition or articulation of this kind of love in modern Western thought, she notes, yet its reality is so intensely felt that the urge to respond by "dropping to (her) knees and kissing the ground" is overwhelming (*ibid.*). Its reality is mostly unrecognised, and since it is nameless, says Mathews, we treat it as of little consequence, never suspecting how we ourselves are diminished by our thoughtlessness (*op. cit.*, 8).

Nor does *Ishq*, the Arabic word for intense, passionate love, 'dying for love' (hence, *fana*, annihilation of ego), have an English equivalent. Gülen explains that the mystic's real, intense love is "a wing of light granted to us by Him so that people can use it to reach Him". Feeling such love can be described as being drawn like a moth toward the Light, the essence of existence (Gülen, 2001), and in this regard we remember the fate of the moth in Attar's famous poem (see end of chapter), which undoubtedly inspired the title of Vaughan-Lee's *Love is a Fire*. Because *ishq* demands union, the love experienced by the Sufi is that of Eros, though more subtle since it seeks spiritual union when ego is effaced, rather than physical union while ego remains intact.

The path of the One and the Many is, for both ecophilosopher Mathews and for the Sufi, the path of Eros. However, the erotic nature of Sufi love appears to have been overlooked by Mathews, but love poet Rumi makes it abundantly clear that his love is that of Eros, and Anissian's thesis, *Eros in Sufism* (2006), for example, is just one of several works on the subject. Erotic love demands the annihilation of the ego—Rumi repeatedly speaks of 'naughting' the self; in order to become 'all heart' ('One'), the ego must be sacrificed, as Taoism teaches that "in the quest for the *dao* one must let go, lose and be silent" (Tu, 1998). Serving Eros takes the mystic on an all-consuming journey; responding to the Beloved's call does not lead only to encounters with His Gentleness. As Ibn al-Arabi reminds us, all names are His names (*SPK*, 95), and on the journey to egolessness His many names are encountered, and these include Severity as well as Wrath. This does not imply that the One is a vengeful god imposing his will or punishment on us, but rather that we are bound to encounter the many faces of reality on our journey through life. And as Mathews says, "there is no end-state of plenitude, no final cure for suffering and uncertainty", life being mysterious and its goal potentiation, "not release from suffering, not salvation nor redemption" (2003, 111), nor indeed happiness (Hamilton, 2008). Naughting the ego entails radical transformation, accompanied by the longing, grief and heartache of separation after the taste of union, so the mystic's path is not, as Mathews suggests, a refuge from the all-encompassing nature of life but the life-changing experience of its reality. Mystical union is not a "retreat" that "short-circuits the project of life" (2003, 107), nor does mystical love "induce social impotence" (2003, 114) or "pacify" (107) the mystic. Wheeler also interprets mysticism as "an escape from difficult realities" and is therefore anxious not to "slip into, or naively to avow (it)" (2006, 80). Creative Eros seeks increase but always by way of reduction, and those, like Rumi, who follow him, burn in love's fire. Rumi's poetry is a testament not to a pacifying, comforting love to which he retreats, but to the electrifying nature of Eros to whose harsh demands he submits.

It draws him, like the moth, irrevocably, into the simple oneness that underlies the multiplicity of life:

> The dead man has been annihilated in one respect through loss of life, but the Sufis have been annihilated in a hundred respects (Rumi, *SPL*, 190)

For Rumi, Love is all that matters:

> My religion is to live through Love . . . The school is Love, the teacher the Almighty. Our books and lessons are His Face. Choose Love, Love! (*SPL*, 221)

For Mathews, 'eros' describes intersubjective, rather than merely sensuous, contact, and entails a particular "panpsychist awareness"— "awareness of the interiority of matter" (2003, 60), and in this regard her interpretation of eros as it defines the panpsychist approach is consistant with the mystical understanding. She explains: "In reaching out to the world . . . and seeking to participate as deeply as possible in it, the self will necessarily seek to connect not merely with the materiality of things, but with their subjectivity" (*ibid.*). We remember the primal impulse of the One was love, manifesting as wanting, wishing and longing for self-realisation, the primal impulse shared by the many. *Orexis*, from the Greek *orektos*, meaning 'longed for' or 'stretched out for', says Mathews, embraces three functions: desire, spirit, and wish, and connotes a condition of longing for contact with reality (2003, 61). "Orexis may be expressed via many modalities", Mathews explains, "ranging from the strictly appetitive to the intersubjective, the subtleties of eros", and it is through *orexis* that members of the Many realise themselves, "eros (being) the path of the self that affirms both the Many (including itself) and the One" (*ibid.*). Realising themselves through orectic contact, which is the goal of eros, "poses daunting psychological difficulties for the self", says Mathews (2003, 114), explaining that the self must be "melted down" and "beaten into shape in the fires . . . fires that destroy delusions and create . . . durability and strength" (2003, 108). This process cannot, of course, in any way, be regarded as an escape from difficult realities. Yet Mathews continues: "The unitive self avoids the orectic" (and therefore erotic) "engagement that would exacerbate its vulnerability to suffering" (2003, 114). Both these claims, I believe, are inaccurate and as such, I will in the course of this chapter expand on the orectic and erotic nature of the mystic's embrace of Reality in its all-encompassingness.

Eros' parentage sheds light on the contradictories which define his nature (Plato, 369-371). Born of Penia (Poverty), who was poor and foolish, and Poros (Plenty), who was wealthy and wise and the son of Metis (Discretion), Eros embodies these opposing states, so that he is flourishing at one moment and perishing at another. "First in the train of gods", born after Chaos and Earth, he is "neither fair nor good" nor "evil and foul", but "fertile in resources" and "keen in the pursuit of wisdom" (Plato, 341). Seduced by his softness, overwhelmed by his power, the mystic lives for erotic love which enriches as it reduces him to a state of poverty. Vaughan-Lee expresses the contradictory nature of erotic love as follows: It is "real and endless, a place not for the fainthearted, not for those who like security or safety. . . . This love abuses our sense of self, destroys our patterns of control, violates our deepest beliefs, and takes us back to God. In this love there is neither form nor limit, only a completeness beyond our dreaming, a sweetness beyond imagining, and a terror that belongs to the absolute. Love takes us into the infinite emptiness of His presence, into the vastness that is hidden within our own heart" (2000, 111). Reaching that infinite emptiness, "Oblivion, the Nothingness of Love" (Attar), entails a journey of the heart, a journey at once painful and ecstatic, from separation to union—from ego to heart.

According to Sufi teachings, all love emanates from the divine and as such serves a purpose (VIII, 259). Rumi says "By journeying on the path of love you will arrive in the presence of the Sovereign of love" (VIII, 260). The metaphor of love as rays of light, brightest at their source, weakest when furthest from it, is a common one in Sufi literature. One might therefore distinguish, as Rumi does, between two kinds of love—love of the Real, *ishq-i haqīqī*, and love devoid of knowledge of the Real, *ishq-i majāzī* (metaphorical love). They appear to be different, yet to the Sufi all love is love for God, since all forms are a manifestation of Him, while others believe in the independent existence of various objects of desire and so turn their love only toward them (*SPL*, 201). The unity of all things being the cornerstone of Sufism, the Sufi is the lover of the one Beloved no matter the object of his or her love. Love courses through the arteries of the world, and all beings participate in it, therefore all beings are lovers (*op. cit.*, 198):

> It is He who is manifest within every beloved to the eye of every lover—and there is nothing which is not a lover. The cosmos is all lover and beloved, and all of it goes back to Him . . . The gnostics never hear a verse, a riddle, a panegyric, or a love poem that is not about Him . . . (Ibn al-Arabi, *SPK*, 181)

5.3 Love and Beauty

'Meaning' (*mana*) is sometimes interpreted as beauty, in the Platonic sense of Absolute Beauty—an unchanging aspect of the noumenon as it manifests in the phenomenon. As a divine attribute, beauty pertains to innerness rather than outerness, and as such has moral significance. "Beauty is a function of meaning", says Mathews, "not only of abstract aesthetics" (2005, 52). "God is Beautiful", said the Prophet, "and He loves beauty" (Cited in Schuon, 1959, 118), and His incomparable beauty should elicit from us incomparable love, one of the greatest inducements of love being beauty. "There is one object of praise, the beauty which uplifts the heart of its worshipper through all aspects from the seen to the unseen", says Hazrat Inayat Khan (1960, 297). Initially attracted by outer beauty and our need and desire for union, we start out on the path of love by loving beautiful forms. As inner beauty is discovered in a particular form, it may be recognised more widely, and so love of the particular may lead to love of similar and, in time, perhaps, differing forms. "The one whose eyes are focused on beauty in time will join the good" (VIII, 257). In this regard Sufism aligns itself closely with Platonic and Neoplatonic insights, in particular with thoughts expressed in the *Symposium* (Plato, 376-382). Image becomes reality, says Plato, when God is "befriended", and while the sober rationality of his tribute to love lacks the passion of Rumi's unbridled voluminous outpourings inspired by his Beloved, he is generous in his praise of beauty as it leads to love:

> For he who would proceed aright in this matter should begin in youth to visit beautiful forms; and first, if he be guided by his instructor aright, to love one such form only—out of that he should create fair thoughts; and soon he will of himself perceive that the beauty of one form is akin to the beauty of another; and then if beauty in general is his pursuit, how foolish would he be not to recognize that the beauty in every form is the same!. . . He will become a lover of all beautiful forms . . . (Plato, 377).

We remember that Rumi's all-consuming love for the Beloved was born of his love for his spiritual teacher Shams-i Tabrizi, who disappeared from his life mysteriously, leaving the tormented lover to search for him far and wide. The void left by Shams was later filled by Husamuddin, and Rumi recognised the divine aspect of both these "Perfect Men" (Nicholson, I, 5). From the unbearable pain of outer separation and loss emerged an inner union as he discovered the Beloved in his own heart. Refined by love's fire, he reassures lamenting lovers that 'derivative' love is a divine gift (*waridat*) and favour (*mawhiba*):

> Consider it a blessing that you have suffered loss in the lane of love: Leave aside derivative love; the goal is love for God (*SPL*, 214).

The dualistic appearance of Sufi (and Platonic) metaphor invites us to confront our own lack of insight as we experience the 'He/not He' of form. By not recognising the innerness of things we fail to discern meaning and overlook the unlimited potential inherent in all forms. Precisely because of her awareness of "the interiority of matter" (2003, 60) and the fact that matter is not "sheer externality" (2003, 29), Mathews recognises meaning and is able to value, infinitely, the particular. Mystical knowledge enables us to delve deep beneath the surface, so that we might find the Beloved hidden in the heart of matter and recognise its meaningfulness. If, through lack of struggle (*mujahada*) and knowledge (*marifa*) we "take up residence on the lowest rungs of the ladder" (Rumi, *SPL*, 206) i.e. the surface of things, we will not recognise their true potential or experience enduring love for them. Conversely, *marifa*, by enabling recognition of deeper meaning, opens up forms' sacred dimension and transforms our superficial relationships into more meaningful ones. "Derivative love" and "love for God" therefore both involve love of forms, the difference between them being one of knowledge; the "lover of God" recognises the sacredness of all forms and knows that everything is meaningful—"all is from Him", while the others have not awoken to His all-encompassing reality. Similarly, the Many as Mathews conceives of them, are sacred by virtue of the One in whom they participate. Therefore when Mathews, in speaking of mystical love, says that "the unitive self is unable to experience connection with finite others, or the energization and potentiation that such connection affords" (2003, 113-114), she appears, in this instance, to have adopted a dualistic perspective. For where else can the Beloved be if not in the heart of forms?

Since meaning—absolute beauty—resides deep within all forms, all forms lend themselves to being loved meaningfully, provided their inner dimension is recognised. As Mathews says, ". . . I am not dependent on the erotic favour of my human peers . . . because erotic possibilities are omnipresent. The world in its entirety is available for congress" (2003, 111). It is preoccupation with externality and the failure to recognise forms' hidden meaning which prevents us from loving meaningfully, and which might account for the common misunderstanding of the nature of mystical love. Rumi exhorts us to recognise forms' inner dimension, *batin* within *zahir*—"the eternal light of Love" (*SPL*, 221) as it radiates from within all forms, so that our superficial relationships might be deepened. The well-known Sufi story of Layla and Majnun illustrates this point, as only Majnun, who loved Layla absolutely, recognised her beauty. Rumi is critical of those who see nothing but externality because they have not 'polished the mirror of their hearts' and lack *marifa*, thus making meaningful love impossible. The 'eye' of their heart has not been opened. It is to this eye that Plato alludes when he asks:

> What if man had eyes to see the true beauty—the divine beauty, I mean, pure and clear and unalloyed, not clogged with the pollutions of mortality and all the colours and vanities of human life? (Plato, 379)

Similarly, Rumi urges us to look carefully and discern meaning within form so that love is not indiscriminate:

> Your beloved is not form, whether your love is from this world or that . . .
> Oh lover, look carefully! Who is your beloved? (*SPL*, 215)

If we had eyes to see inner beauty we would see all things 'face to face'. The Sufi looks beyond the veils of externality and encounters inner reality:

> All the hopes, desires, loves, and affections that people have for different things—fathers, mothers, friends, heavens, the earth, gardens, palaces, sciences, works, food, drink—the saint knows that these are desires for God and all those things are veils. When men leave this world and see the King without these veils, then they will know that all were veils and coverings, that the object of their desire was in reality that One Thing. All their questions will be answered. They will see all things face to face (Rumi, *SPL*, 98)

Without insight, we fail to recognise beauty beyond veils—both metaphorical and literal, thus the concept of veiled beauty both as an attribute of form and cultural phenomenon is particularly poorly understood within the western context, the veil itself having become the most powerful symbol of 'otherness'. Symbol of concealment of the most sacred (Nursi, 1995, 258), the veil has become, in a culture preoccupied with externality, a symbol of oppression and male dominance—the most visible evidence of "structures of patriarchy" (Cudworth, 2005, 94). However, drawing on fieldwork-based ethnography, anthropology, history and original Islamic sources, Fadwa El Guindi (2000) elaborates the rich and nuanced sociocultural phenomenon of veiling and its long and complex history, of which, she believes, most western commentators are not fully aware. Western feminists and secularists who have been most vociferous in decrying the veil, El Guindi says, fail to realise that veiling has been actively embraced by many Muslim women as both an affirmation of cultural identity, the veil representing liberation from colonial legacies, and a strident feminist statement. Contemporary veiling, she explains, is as much about modesty and privacy as it is about resistance in Islamic societies. Often a bottom-up movement, veiling represents a form of activism which reaffirms Islamic identity and morality and rejects western materialism, consumerism, commercialism and values. Veiling as a movement condemns exhibitionism in dress and behaviour; reserve and restraint symbolise a renewal of cultural identity rather than female suppression, El Guindi believes (*ibid.*).

Having herself made the choice to adhere to 'modest dress', Eren Tatari points out that the veil (*hijab* or *burqa*) frees women from the pressures of society to conform to a particular physical type or to fashion: "Knowing that (we) are not being judged as feminine 'objects' helps to enhance (our) self-esteem. When we dress and act modestly, others value us as human beings based on character and intelligence" (2008). This does not mean that only women must watch the way they act and dress, says Tatari; as the Qur'anic verse 24:30 states, men are obligated to "lower their gaze" and adopt modest dress and behaviour as well (*ibid.*).

Veils, like *mashrabiyya* (lattice woodwork screens and windows in Arabo-Islamic architecture), embody the essence of traditional notions of privacy, "because 'seeing' is more than a physiological act" (El Guindi, 2000, 93). Veils guard women's right to privacy in the same way that *mashrabiyya* guard families' right to privacy—that is the right to 'see' and the right not to be seen—and are not about seclusion and invisibility, according to El Guindi, drawing on Gilsenan (*Recognizing Islam: Religion and Society in the Modern Arab World*, 1982). Gilsenan says: "(Women) are publicly 'not there' *because* they are so significant" (emphasis in original, cited in El Guindi, 95). Similarly, Tatari says: "The underlying principle is to keep your beauty to yourself . . . so that you will not be viewed as an 'object'. . . valued only for (your) physical beauty" (2008). While *mashrabiyya* are stationary, veiling is mobile, carrying women's privacy to public places. A woman carries 'her' privacy and sanctity with her, says El Guindi, much the same way as when a Muslim worships in any space, converting it to sacred and private (*ibid.*).

Marifa pierces veils, enabling recognition of beauty:

> She is the radiance of God . . . (*SPL*, 169)

At the phenomenal level (*zahir*), the creative principle manifests most fully in the form of woman, and Rumi pays the highest tribute to her, but it is the hidden aspect, *batin*, for which the Sufi searches. Together with the dynamic masculine principle, most perfectly embodied in man, unity of being can be restored, sexual union symbolising the wholeness inherent in the human state at the physical level. At the noumenal level (*batin*), however, complementary opposites coincide. Within the heart the dual aspects of feminine and masculine come together, and although quite different, they are of equal value. El Guindi emphasises that the Arabo-Islamic linguistic construction affirms their equality and encapsulates the "heterosexual complementarity of two autonomous persons, which is culturally considered the basis of society" (2000, 72). Arabic words referring to one of a pair, two as a pair, partner, and spouse, as used for example in *Sura* 51: 49 "All things were created in *zawjayn* (pairs)", are ungendered, and in *Sura* 49: 13 ". . . we have created you a *thakarun* (male) and *untha* (female) . . .", capture a nuance of completeness which is lacking when gender is denoted (*ibid.*). She explains that the Qur'anic reference to the creation of neutral-gendered Adam states that out of the same single soul the *zawj* (pair) was created—simultaneously. Arabic linguistic structures emphasise gender mutuality and the completeness of a heterosexual pair that reproduces humankind, reflecting the absence of gender primacy in the sacred Islamic imagination (*ibid*; Fulya Çelik, 2008).

> He teaches by means of opposites, so that you have two wings to fly, not one (Rumi, in Vaughan-Lee, 2000, 82)

"Femaleness and maleness permeate through the articulations of being . . . (They) are two conjoined, simultaneous, mutually corresponding principles, sharing one act", explains Souad al-Hakim with reference to Ibn al-Arabi's interpretation of woman, an interpretation which al-Hakim describes as "a new vision of woman in the history of Islamic Culture . . . a vision worthy of inspiring contemporary Muslims, of acting as a foundation for the reassessment of their notions and concepts about women in Islam, and of propelling the wheel of cultural change in the proper path" (al-Hakim, 2006, 14).

The two wings of love take us into a reality that is eternally present, yet hidden. Everything that comes into life has a dual aspect, according to the Sufi perspective. Even the primal energy of love, says Vaughan-Lee, has a 'masculine' side and a 'feminine' side; the former seeks to make itself known, the latter is naturally hidden. But in an extrovert culture which tends to reject the invisible, we run the risk, on our journey through life, of not embracing both the sacred feminine and masculine aspects of the path. Cultural conditioning has led us to repress much of the feminine. Instead, says Vaughan-Lee, we live primarily masculine values; we are goal-oriented, competitive, driven; we seek to be better, to improve ourselves and to 'get somewhere'. We have, he believes, forgotten the feminine qualities of waiting, listening, responding and nurturing. Our natural tendencies may have been overshadowed, Vaughan-Lee believes, and so we see many women for whom the masculine focus is easier, and many men who find themselves more in touch with their feminine self. As Vaughan-Lee points out, in the spiral dance of love we need to embrace both masculine and feminine qualities, to breathe in and to breathe out, to contract and to expand, in the continual process of movement and change in which each aspect has its time and purpose. The real limitation, he says, is to remain caught in one stage, in the masculine dynamic of contraction (*qabz*) or the feminine quality of expansion (*bast*).

In its attempt to preserve the integrity, unity and stability of the traditional family as the key social unit and to prevent what are perceived as the ills associated with its disintegration, Islam has defined most clearly the special role of each highly valued family member (Tatari, 2008). What is most important, however, is that fundamental differences be respected and preserved. In this regard, Nasr draws our attention to the modern erosion, in the name of egalitarianism, of qualitative differences between the sexes, an insensitivity which, he believes, does not take into account the sacred nature of these real differences (1981, 188). Contrary to negative stereotyping which depicts the majority of Muslim women as victims of male dominance, Islam reinforces the equality of men and women and of their complementary roles, and failure to respect this equality should not be attributed to Islamic teachings but to individual shortcomings (to which Sufism applies itself), or what Ahmed refers to as "Muslim male tyranny" (1992, 43). Islam itself is regarded as the most 'egalitarian' religion, where each person is his or her own priest, and all people are equal before God in light of their immortal soul, this characteristic taking precedence over that of diversity of qualifications (Schuon, 1959, 141; Algül, 2009). The levelling outlook of Islam with its great emphasis on learning, love, promotion of family life and assistance of the less privileged is too often overlooked.

Vaughan-Lee elaborates on the difficulties confronting women in our western culture, whose material values in themselves might be experienced as a violation of the feminine. Entering the patriarchal workplace, he says, women are often forced to adopt masculine attitudes and goals (2000, 83). In Islamic tradition, on the other hand, women are guardians of the sanctity of the home, a role to which great importance is accorded because of its influence on the integrity of the whole community, and ideally the family seeks to protect a woman from 'indignity', as culturally defined, but this would include accepting employment in which she may not be valued (El Guindi, 2000). The stigma is not from work *per se* but from being unprotected by a family that can afford to support its members but doesn't (*ibid.*). As the family in Islamic culture is considered of primary relevance to individual lives, its members are entrusted with protecting it in clearly defined ways. In a simpler, less materialistic world, where the quest for meaning took on a different form, and the portion of 'daily bread' (*rizq*) allotted by God was deemed sufficient (Rumi, tr. Nicholson, I, 12), this would entail men taking care of the 'outer' dimension (*zahir*) and women taking care of the families' more subtle needs (*batin*). Vaughan-Lee traces the emptiness that many people feel in today's material culture to the fact that the sacred feminine aspect has been rejected and forgotten, resulting in collective impoverishment from which we all suffer (2000, 97).

Al-Arabi's own spiritual teacher (*shaykha*) was a woman from Seville, Fatima bint al-Muthanna. In several passages in the *Futuhat* he relates the depth of her knowledge and the influence she had on him when he surrendered to her guidance (al-Hakim, 2006). And as Khaleb el-Khazari reminds us, one of the great early Sufi teachers was Rabia al-Adawiyyah (d. 801), a woman and former slave, a situation which would have been an affront to the *ulema* (body of scholars) at the time (Khazari-El, 2006). Still today, as al-Hakim points out, "this is very much a contemporary issue, which no Islamic scholar in the twenty-first century would dare to agree with" (2006). Yet, as Carl Ernst notes, women hold prominent positions in Sufi groups throughout the western world (2009). Al-Hakim concludes that the vision of Sufis has the potential to "restore truly Islamic principles, which have been banished by the passage of years and masked by personal interests" (2006, 27).

Vaughan-Lee likens our embrace of both masculine and feminine qualities within us to the "spiral dance of love" that is our journey home (2000, 84). "A spiral has both a circular and a linear movement", he explains. "The 'masculine' takes us in a linear direction, towards a goal, which can appear to be upward or downward but in truth is inward". This course demands a focus of intent and a conscious commitment to persevere regardless. The 'feminine', he says, is the spiral's circular movement, which is inclusive. It "requires us to be flexible and continually changing, responsive to the inner oscillations of the path" (*ibid*.). Sufism teaches the strength of focus and the softness of vulnerability, lessons of detachment and the fullness of life's embrace. "The danger is to remain caught in one aspect and the failure to embrace both within ourselves" (*ibid*.). As Rumi insists, life is sacred in its entirety, because "everything is from Him".

The two wings of love take us into a reality that is eternally present, yet hidden, says Vaughan-Lee. They help us make the journey to the root of the root of our own being where we can glimpse the beauty of our own nature and come to experience that same beauty within all life. Above all else, says Gülen, we should love Him, and love all others because they are manifestations and reflections of His Beautiful Names and Attributes. Each encounter, he says, reveals to us the hidden face of creation and allows us to experience oneness with the Beloved. For those who can decipher, every creature is a shining mirror and a eulogy written in great verse, and every face a reflection of Mercy (Gülen, 2007). As Rumi says:

> The universe displays the beauty of Thy loveliness! The goal is Thy Beauty—all else is pretext (*SPL*, 209)

If indeed he had eyes to see such beauty, he would be able to "bring forth, not images of beauty, but realities, for he has hold not of an image but of a reality" (Plato, 378). If we had eyes to see divine beauty we would see all things face to face, said Rumi, and be able to bring forth realities. We think again of the worker, hidden in the workshop, the craftsman and poet, who, like Rumi, lovingly give form to Him. In the verses of the *Mathnawi,* described by the celebrated poet Jami from Persia as a Holy Book (Esirgen, 2007), Rumi brings forth not images of beauty—images, being unreal, are forbidden in Islam, but rather realities which, in Schuon's words, give form to what lies Beyond Form, to the Uncreated, and to the language of Silence (1959). Rumi's poetry, exemplifying the finest sacred art, gives form to the formless and a voice to the silence, not through the personal aims and inventiveness of the individual, but through his humility which makes of him an instrument of divine creativity—"It is love that teaches: Thou, not I" (Khan, 1960, 117). When he says, "Listen to the reed" in the opening line of the *Mathnawi,* he is alluding to the fact that he is only a vehicle for words placed in his mouth. As Aahlia Khan emphasises, Sufi poets only ever saw themselves in the role of translators, who "transfer, reconstitute and interpret divine truths from the transcendental domain to the context of this physical world" (2009, 14). Sacred art communicates an intelligence which is not individuated or limited in any way, explains Schuon, but rather incommensurable and transcendent, and with its own precise rules, which may not be infringed, regarding content, symbolism and style (1959, 106)—aspects which, like the Beloved himself, are both terrible and merciful. Though they appear restrictive, these rules confer qualities of depth and power such as the individual has little chance of drawing out of himself, says Schuon (*ibid.*). "Beauty itself has no need of innovation, although the poet's knowledge, love and effort enable him to find inexhaustible variations within the framework laid down by the sacred tradition" (*ibid.*). "The inexhaustible richness of reality is already given", says Mathews; "it does not need to be invented, only embraced" (2005, 67). Genius attains perfection, depth and power of expression almost imperceptibly, says Schuon, "by means of the imponderables of truth and beauty ripened in that humility without which there can be no true greatness" (1959, 108).

Art is sacred, Schuon emphasises, not through the personal aims of the artist, but through its content, its symbolism and its style. By its content: because the subject is largely prescribed by the tradition; by its symbolism: because the sacred is adorned in a given manner, and by its style: because its truth must be expressed in a particular hieratic formal language and not in an invented style (*op. cit.*, 107). Rumi himself called the *Mathnawi* "the roots of the roots of the roots of the (Islamic) Faith", emanating directly from God; the essence of the Qur'an, and many passages indicate his belief that it is nothing less than an inspired exposition of the esoteric content of the Qur'an (Nicholson, Commentary I: 3). Therefore Rumi, in effect, would have been acutely aware that his poetry would lose all right to existence if he infringed the precise rules governing its form, and he would have had the greatest interest in observing, most faithfully, these seeming restrictions of a highly complex poetic form.

Bringing forth realities entails, above all else, self-sacrificing love (*ishq*). Love creates beauty in order that it may be able to love, says Hazrat Inayat Khan (II, 11). 'Grasping' the Beloved and creating the perfect abode for Him in both heart and verse would have entailed the most intense form of "erotic engagement with matter"—a passionate encounter with His reality defined by the contradictory nature of Eros and the joy and pain of finding/ not finding which cannot in any way be described as "a refuge from the developmental journey of life" (Mathews, 2003, 109). On the contrary, the mystic's way *is* arguably the ultimate developmental journey in the course of which he *becomes* the very thing he loves as form and meaning become one. And so, in a sense, Rumi has become his poetry, and in his poetry love, lover and Beloved live on, united in perfect harmony, forever free from the limitations of time and place: "Thy Love has transformed every one of my hairs into a verse and a *ghazal*[1]" (*SPL*, 271), he says.

---

[1] The *ghazal* is a complex poetic form, but it is also a gazelle or deer, and Hazrat Inayat Khan explains the symbolic significance of the gazelle as follows: "When it is thirsty, the deer runs about in the forest looking for water and is delighted to hear the sound of thunder, but sometimes there is only thunder and no rain after-

Struggling (*mujahada*) to incorporate meaning within the materiality of words, rhymes and rhythms, Rumi reveals the utmost humility and self-deprecation, and contempt for the inadequacy of his poetry, comparing it to "the lowest of goods" (*SPL*, 270) in the market-place. "My poetry is like Egyptian bread: night passes, and you cannot eat it" (*ibid.*), he says. His is a monumental struggle culminating in the creation of no fewer than 70,000 verses in which he endeavours to give form to his Beloved, a struggle which attests to his love of enformed meaning, and his willingness to suffer, at times, the anguish of not finding—"God gave me no heartache but to seek out rhymes for my verses" (*SPL*, 271), and in despair he cries out: "What have I to do with poetry? Oh God, I detest poetry. In my eyes, there is nothing worse . . . Let a torrent take away these rhymes and specious words! They are skin! They are skin! Fitting only for the brains of poets!" (*ibid.*). Constantly aware of forms' limitations and the ambiguity of words, he advises: "Take this poetry and tear it up, for meanings transcend words and wind and air" (*ibid.*).

Yet he continues to craft his poems, relentlessly, revealing his self-sacrificing love for the infinite beauty and variety of words and their unlimited potential to convey meaning. The ecstasy of finding compensates for the heartache of not finding, so, despite Rumi's protestations, there are indications that the *Mathnawi* is more than his mere words and that Rumi himself has become the Beloved's flute, animated by His breath. Longing for union with his Beloved, Rumi experiences the heartache of separation, a pain that transforms his reed-like heart into a flute to be used by God as the instrument for the music that He constantly produces. Stripped of his ego, Rumi's perception of his poetry as impoverished reflects his own impoverished state; empty of self, his being infused with divine music, his heart is opened to the God of love. The poetry that comes as a cry from the heart brings a message—His message, words of truth, Rumi says, that emanate from God's description of His own uncreated Word: "This noise

---

wards, and so the deer remains thirsty. And so is the thirst of a fine soul in this world. The soul is constantly thirsty, looking for something, seeking for something; and when it thinks it has found it, the thing turns out to be different, and so life becomes a continual struggle and disappointment. And the result is that instead of taking interest in all things, a kind of indifference is produced; yet in the real character of this soul there is no indifference, there is only love" (I, 181).

of the reed is fire . . . It is the fire of Love that is in the reed" (Nicholson, I, 7-9). Anissian writes in her thesis that her relationship with her research is like her relationship with the Divine (2006, 53); in light of *tawhid*, I would argue that they are one and the same, and that Rumi's relationship with his poetry *is* nothing less than an aspect of his relationship with his Beloved, the endlessly communicative beloved Real whose ungraspable simplicity, the "Nothingness of Love" (Attar), leaves the lover ever-struggling to give Him form:

> Whatsoever I say in exposition and explanation of Love, when I come to Love itself, I am ashamed of that (Rumi, in Nicholson, I, 113-114).

> If I should continue my explanation of Love, a hundred resurrections would pass before I could complete it; but the date of resurrection has a limit—where are limits when it is a question of God's Attributes? (Rumi, *SPL*, 46)

> How shall I describe His Beauty? For those exotic birds avoid the snare of my words (Rumi, *SPL*, 275)

5.4 Bringing forth Images

Having considered the nature of some of our making in previous chapters, I shall now look at contemporary forms of 'love making' to establish whether we are creative with our hearts or only our bodies—whether our love is of true Beauty, simple and unadorned, its rhythm harmonious. Can we say, like Ibn al-Arabi, that the object of our love is Sophia, whose beauty is 'without ornament' and when she speaks she does so in silence, because only Silence can 'speak' and indicate transcendences? Does our love bring forth realities or is it dimmed by ego's dross?

These fundamental ideas, we noted previously, have been reduced to their most superficial level within popular culture, with postmodern thinkers such as Roland Barthes and Jacques Derrida declaring that a universal source of significance or value is an impossibility (Hamilton, 2008, 237). Furthermore, within a market society, concepts of beauty and the forms of love it induces are mere market constructs with the focus on ego rather than heart, appearances rather than realities, surface rather than depth. "There is nothing beneath the surface", declared Andy Warhol, "making money is art . . . good business is the best art" (*op. cit.*, 236). Superficiality has come to be the hallmark of popular culture, which, according to Hamilton and

Mathews, has no intrinsic value. The contemporary 'cult of the body' is presided over by secularised eros, modern society no longer requiring an intermediary between the divine and human realms.

"Your beloved is not form" said Rumi to the body-worshipper who could not discern his head from his feet (*SPL*, 333). "Are we indeed unawoken", asks Mathews, "for the major part of our lives, so estranged from animating contact with reality that we look exclusively to our sexual relations to deliver to us the vividness of the moment"? "We sexualise our bodies, our personalities, our occupations, our cars and household appliances, our very culture, in an increasingly desperate bid to recapture the existential essence we have lost", says Mathews (2005, 22). Sexualisation fills the gap left by secularisation, according to Hamilton, who suggests that current unhealthy sexual activity will continue until avenues are found for a more balanced and pure expression of the noumenal energy (2008, 201). The word 'love' itself, perhaps because of its association with mystery, has taken on a quaint appearance. Historian Peter Stearns documents the 'cool' trend of disdaining love and describes the emotional frustration, alienation and sexual promiscuity that go hand in hand with essentially heartless human relations, which look with suspicion on mystery and love, and cultural trends within materialistic, consumer-oriented societies that have combined to produce a "general coarsening and flattening of the sensibilities" (2001, 117). "Cultural bankruptcy" is how Ahmed describes the elevation of sex into the single most important human activity in a society "obsessed with the material, the trivial and the immediate" (1992, 246).

Sexologist Leonore Tiefer refers to the "McDonaldization" (2004, 3) of sex—overexposed, processed, supersized, accessible and cheap, and in the words of Eberstadt, "If your appetite is stimulated and fed by poor-quality material, it takes more junk to fill you up" (2008, 8). Like the Golden Arches, giant billboards in city streets scream crass messages from on high, making the assault of in-your-face sexual imagery and language an inescapable part of our constructed world. We are suffering the ill-effects of bingeing on sexual junkfood whose obese form eclipses any vestige of meaning.

Reflecting on the meaning of sex, Hamilton identifies three aspects—bodily pleasure, procreation and union, the latter in turn having two forms—emotional and metaphysical (2008, 196-197). Metaphysical union is a direct expression of our noumenal selves, says Hamilton; it is the aspect of sex that is least acknowledged and therefore worthy of most attention. Through metaphysical intimacy, "loving sexual partners 'know' each other in a way that cannot be had by other means", which is why, he believes, 'free love' and intimacy are incompatible. The true value of sex, says Hamilton, lies in the timelessness of the noumenon, in the metaphysical aspect of sexual union, in that the subtle essence of two humans can merge in the most intimate way. At its best, he continues, the ecstatic nature of sex reflects the dissolution of one manifestation of the universal essence into another, so that they become one; the word 'ecstasy' is derived from the Greek word *ekstasis*, meaning to stand outside of one's conscious self (2008, 201). According to Hamilton, "the orgiastic character of modern sexual expression is a manifestation of an elemental human urge for metaphysical reconciliation" and the intimacy that comes from it. The portrayal of sex as playful and pleasurable in popular culture while ignoring its esoteric significance is unsatisfactory, even dangerous, he says. Similarly Gülen says "If knowledge about the inner aspects is lacking, then there are no means for an everlasting connection", and explains that "love always blooms in direct relation to the refinement of the soul, as well as to the sensitivity and profundity of perception" (2009).

Contemporary relationships appear to reflect little of such intimate merging where the strictures of form may be overcome and wholeness restored through *mysterium coniunctionis*. Uncertainty, anonymity and a lack of intimacy are characteristic of much contemporary sexual activity, which may explain the popularity of cyberdating (Hardie, 2006). Its appeal lies in its convenience; its terms determined by self-interest. Casual sexual encounters often include elements of violence, as Lynn Phillips outlines in *Flirting with Danger* (2000), in which thirty women give accounts of being pushed, hit and verbally abused, yet they describe the encounter as having been 'good'. 'Love' sometimes ends in death at the hands of the 'beloved'. Being murdered by a male partner is the leading cause of death for American heterosexual women under forty, according to Phillips (*ibid.*). Multiple sexual partners, experimentation and risk-taking in the form of frequent, casual coupling (Beadnell, 2005) further diminished by the increasing use (Wilkins, 2007) of (legal) party-pills (Sheridan, 2007), alcohol and other stimulants (Hegna, 2007) have reduced 'love making' to pure mechanics, a topic of huge interest if the surfeit of 'How-to' sex manuals is anything to go by. One hundred and sixty thousand titles relating to the mechanics of sex were available from Amazon Kindle at Amazon.Com in 2008.

Common consequences of casual sex include a dramatic increase in sexually transmitted diseases (*ibid.*). Casual sex, or what Berry refers to as "instinctual coupling" (1993, 21), is neither 'recreational' nor 'safe'. Genital herpes is one of the most common sexually transmitted diseases in Australia; it has no cure and about eighty percent of people infected with it don't know they have the virus (Australian Herpes Management Forum, 2008), consequently pregnant women with STDs risk harming their babies (*ibid.*). Two out of three pregnancies in Australian women are unplanned and one out of every three Australian women will have an abortion in her lifetime, despite the availability of contraception (Haigh, 2008).

According to clinical psychologist Wendy McCord, twenty percent of babies born in the United States are born to mothers using drugs, tobacco or alcohol, and sixty percent of babies born are conceived unintentionally. She explores the implications, for both child and parent, of thoughtless conception and unplanned, unwanted pregnancies in *Earthbabies: Ancient Wisdom for Modern Times* (2003), based on her research in pre-and perinatal psychology. The 'preventive psychology' she advocates—the steps that should be taken *before* conception and during pregnancy to improve a child's chances of healthy emotional development—is based on ancient wisdom teachings which resonate with those of Sufism, such as the notion that actions are likely to live on in the same rhythm from which they spring. Preparation of mind and body is therefore considered of greatest importance. "Just by hoping and believing", says Hazrat Inayat Khan, "good things do not necessarily come"; it takes effort, persistence and patience to accomplish things (VI, 225). "One should make preparation, as for a journey, and know what to take, so that the journey does not become too arduous and one fails to accomplish one's goal. Preparation makes the way easier, smoother, better", he explains; "since life has no end of difficulties from the time one opens one's eyes, one might wish to choose the smoother way" (I, 27). Consistent with this line of thought is McCord's belief that prevention of problems in infancy, insofar as this is possible, begins prior to conception, and that children who are truly wanted by their parents are healthier, stronger, happier and brighter (McCord, 2003).

Introducing a financial incentive to encourage population growth for the sake of the economy, as Australian Treasurer Peter Costello did in 2004, not only increases the load on all natural systems—earth, air and water—the elements of life, but also the likelihood that even more children will be born into families where their subtle needs will not be met. With economic growth clearly the priority, the 'baby bonus' scheme does not take into account the full reality of raising a child to fulfil its potential, an ongoing challenge requiring total, not merely financial, commitment and self-sacrificing love. It devalues the creative function, as does the idea of 'maternity leave', to the extent that it suggests a vacation or hiatus from meaningful employment. Rumi accords greatest priority to creativity, which, in its highest, procreative, form, is priceless, and therefore to woman as "creator". Paradise, he tells us, has been placed not under the father's feet but under those of the mother, whose qualities should be treasured by her family as a divine gift (Can, 2005, 198). Rumi says: "Externally man is superior to woman, just as water is superior to fire. But in reality, he is taken over by her" (Can, 199). Perhaps the enormity of the task of creating life is not fully appreciated by women themselves; its unparalleled creative and transformative potential is often overlooked while opportunities for greater fulfilment are sought in other avenues.

The sexual revolution of the Sixties was intended to liberate and empower women, but according to Hillier male-female relations are still a combat zone, with the sexual relationship being a site in which the exercise of power and resistance is played out and 'performance anxiety' is an issue for both females and males (2008). Mathews goes much further, claiming that *all* aspects of our interactions are laden with sexual consequence, and that spontaneous self-expression is increasingly checked, a situation she describes as "an unbearable heaviness, this necessity always to calculate our effects" (2005, 22). Women may strive for sexual autonomy, but it is a state which young women in particular rarely achieve, Hillier continues. Yet research also indicates that more than half of men experience feeling emasculated and believe that they have lost their traditional role in society (Womack, 2008). The ideal of the 'gentle man' appears outmoded (Berry, 1993), and with the demise of the ideal comes the removal of many expectations of courtesy and consideration. According to Womack, many men 'feel handcuffed' and only 33 percent feel they can speak freely and say what they think, whereas two thirds find it safer and easier to keep their opinions to themselves. Asked what it means to be a man in the 21st century, more than half think that society is trying to feminise them, and boys, particularly those raised by single mothers, are at a loss as to their role (Lashlie, 2007). "A man has to feel embarrassed about being a man", says Mansfield (2006, 21). Men are singled out, Ahmed believes, and riven with doubt, still looking for a role—"which varies in its extremes from gentle, caring New Man to the cannibal with a palate for female flesh" (Ahmed, 244).

Being male has, in effect, come to imply a potential for predation, according to Lashlie (2007). We think particularly, in this regard, of paedophilia, and the horror it evokes, but Hamilton makes the point that it is difficult to reconcile the "social panic about paedophilia" with "society's apparent indifference to the far more widespread practice of 'corporate paedophilia'", a widely accepted marketing method which aims at the sexualisation of children (2008, 203). Olfman enumerates the consequences of children developing sexual awareness at younger and younger ages, and concludes that American culture with its focus on sexuality is failing its children. In a culture of promiscuity and wastefulness, she says, the question becomes not 'Why?', but 'Why not?' (2005). Being 'active', however, entails conforming to a stereotypical ideal of beauty constructed by the market, and striving for the all-important 'look' leads to body image anxieties increasingly accompanied by eating disorders (O'Dea, 1999). Biology becomes secondary to the size, shape and colour of various parts of the body.

Our obsession with appearances has unleashed a new paradigm of 'self-making', not the slow remaking of the heart, but the instant transformation of the body. The reinvention craze sweeping all aspects of contemporary society is nowhere better dramatized than in cosmetic surgical culture, which epitomises our dissatisfaction with the given and our determination to recreate our selves in accordance with a market constructed ideal, in the belief that the transformation of facial or bodily features will improve our lives. Sociologist Anthony Elliott attributes this obsession to unprecedented socio-economic pressures and our celebrity culture's love affair with appearances, which, he suggests, introduces anxieties that are increasingly resolved by individuals at the level of the body (2008). Living up to the beautiful images constitutes a "seductive but tyrannical trap—the painful beauty trap" (Ahmed, 247), in which many people and particularly women find themselves, as looking ordinary is not good enough and looking old quite unacceptable. Never before have bodies been pumped, pummelled, plucked, suctioned, stitched, shrunk and pierced at such an astonishing rate as the obsession to look young and beautiful reaches new heights.

Brides-to-be increasingly turn to cosmetic surgeons to achieve the desired level of perfection for their wedding day look. According to Dr Niamh Corduff of the Australian Society of Plastic Surgeons (ASPA), the rate of brides and members of the bridal party having non-surgical enhancement is growing by more than 25 per cent each year, while surgical procedures are increasing by more than 15 per cent. In the United States, one in three brides reportedly has some form of cosmetic enhancement for their wedding and, according to Dr Corduff, Australia is mirroring this trend. The most popular pre-wedding procedures, he says, are rhinoplasty, breast enhancement, liposculpture, botox and 'fillers' to plump up the lips (Elliott, 2008). Rumi's message is a timely reminder that the veil should not obstruct our vision, and that we should seek hidden potential rather than be obsessed by form, whose ephemeral nature, sooner or later, will disappoint.

Transformation, at times, involves a drastic remaking of the body's subtle physiology. Since the introduction of oral contraceptives less than fifty years ago, dosages of synthetic hormones, which thwart the body's own mechanisms and replace naturally occurring estrogen and progesterone, have been markedly reduced, so much so that they now contain only one-tenth the amount of medication used in the first pills (Brown University Health Education, 2008), which indicates that the science behind the pill is itself still evolving. Its potential side-effects are many and varied (McGraw-Hill, 2008); moreover, it offers no protection against sexually transmitted diseases which have spread significantly since its introduction (*ibid.*). Of course unwanted pregnancies must be prevented, and medication undeniably serves a purpose, but when women globally and for the long term, en masse, choose to entrust the working of their innermost rhythm to a purchased product, of which most have little or no knowledge of the pharmacokinetics, far-reaching consequences must be anticipated. Reinventing the body's rhythmic structure by substituting a natural rhythm for an artificial one in the name of 'lifestyle choice' devalues the form and appears to be a form of self-deception in which the body's own expression is stifled. Respect for the integrity of the body and for natural rhythms, and their power to communicate particular truths once we become aware of their reality, might lead to an overall healthier approach.

Increasingly, 'Women's Health' has become an arena for medical intervention, and procreation of technological intervention, the implication being that the medical professional and medical treatment are largely responsible for general wellbeing and foetal flourishing. Feminists such as Maria Mies draw our attention to the ever-increasing medicalisation and technologisation of procreation, and historian of the body, Barbara Duden, traces back to around 1800 the tendency to construct, in medical and juridical discourses, women's wombs as a public space (Beinssen-Hesse & Rigby, 1996, 59). And as Erika Cudworth reminds us, some radical and ecological feminists have drawn parallels between the control of animal fertility and the application of reproductive technology to women (2005). Similarly, according to Eberstadt, pregnant women have become comparatively insignificant—"bystanders in babymaking" (2008).

Technology has changed childbearing for 'routine' pregnancies but more spectacularly for women employing cutting-edge medical techniques (Howard, 2006). As biotechnology constantly explores new ways to enhance, produce, select or destroy embryos (and human clones are rumoured), it has become possible for women of all ages to have babies, with or without the father's involvement (Hall-Schwarz, 2006), though it may not be the optimal time to ignite the fragile spark of life. This unprecedented level of medical intervention may satisfy individual desires, but when considered holistically, is more difficult to justify. A more holistic approach might be preferable to the current, highly interventionist approach, not only in "creating" new life and maintaining health, but at the opposite end of life's spectrum, by not artificially extending, at great financial and emotional cost, to the individual, to society and to the environment, the lives of the sick and frail aged who are desperate to be allowed to die with dignity. Heart knowledge may be considered unscientific and therefore unreliable, but would lead to a more natural approach to natural processes, which, if balanced with medical intervention when necessary rather than as the norm, would arguably be more humane.

Love, says Rumi, must be practised—like the Beloved, it cannot be known any other way. The public language of Love, he says, is meaning-less:

> Whatever you have said or heard is the shell: The kernel of Love is a mystery that cannot be divulged (Rumi, *SPL*, 79)

What would Rumi then have made of the public discourse today, which addresses all aspects of sexual practice except for the practice of love? "Public discourse today", Berry says, "addresses issues such as contraception, sexual harassment, pornography, rape and (the oxymoron of) 'safe' sex and how it should be practised, but remains silent about self-control, responsibility, commitment and trust" (1993, 45). The very public language of sexuality is a form which distorts, talking only about the *feeling* of love and its physical expression and always in the context of autonomy, of choice or of the economy. "It is language diminished by subjectivity and lack of accountability and commitment, of word-giving and word-keeping"—of what Berry calls "fidelity to the word" (1983, 71).

Berry argues that the devaluation of sexuality destroys its correspondence to other values, and so all of its communal forms such as courtship, marriage, family life and household economy have been eroded. "Although essentially private, sex as a necessary, precious and volatile power is commonly held and can never be merely the private concern of the individual" (1993, 48), reflecting, as it does, principles which are ultimately of "meta-cosmic significance" (Nasr, 1981, 177). Traditional mechanisms such as marriage and family structure are in place to preserve its energy and beauty and to reduce its volatility, says Berry. Its power thus preserved and clarified, it joins not only husband and wife to one another but parents to children, families to the community and the community to the environment. Sexual love, Berry believes, is the force that in our bodily life connects us most intimately to all the earth's creatures, to the care of animals, land, air and water, to the fertility of the world. It joins all beings in the one dance of life:

The creatures are set in motion by Love, Love by Eternity-without-beginning; the wind dances because of the spheres, the trees because of the wind (Rumi, *SPL*, 197).

5.5 Bringing forth Realities

Oh God, show to the spirit that station where speech grows up without words . . . (Rumi, *SPL*, 251)

Arriving at the station where every form speaks of meaning and where 'nothing' reveals everything entails an arduous journey using "the feet of the heart" (Nursi, 1920, 41). Then we will understand the divine language (lisān al-Haqq), the "speech of mute things" (ibid.), communicated by virtue of shared essence. Mathews describes panpsychic awareness as an "attunement to the world", an ability to decipher cryptic messages in the most improbable places, to the point of being drawn into an "utterly engrossing poetic dialogue" with the world (2005, 55). Vaughan-Lee speaks of "catching the subtle hints that are given"; "living the mystery that calls us—the mystery of the Beloved's imprint within the heart" (2000, 55). But first the veils of dust must be stripped away from its neglected surface so that the reflection in the mirror is true.

'Polishing the mirror of the heart' is lovers' work in the course of which the ego is effaced and the heart is transformed so that things are revealed 'as they are in themselves'. The rich imagery of Sufi poetry depicts the devotee's heart in all its stages from dull surface soiled with the rust of worldliness and self-regard to brightly polished mirror, free of all impurities, clearly reflecting the divine attributes. Since the heart or 'eye' is the 'organ' through which the divine is revealed to us, it is our task to cleanse the heart, to polish it, and ultimately to make of it a perfect mirror reflecting Him (*SPL*, 37). Longing to hear the Beloved's voice and see the Beloved's face in all forms, the Sufi applies himself to the purifying process called *Suluk*, the cultivation of the heart. *Suluk* consists of ten stages: 'Turning' (to God) (*Tawba*), Detachment from the Outer (*Zuhd*), Poverty (*Riyada*), Piety (*Wara*), Contentment (*Qana'a*), Trust in God (*Tawakkul*), Patience (*Sabr*), Thankfulness (*Shukr*), Satisfaction (*Rida*) and Love (*Ishq*) (Valiuddin, 1980, 121).

The rigorous practices of *Suluk* offer guidance on that most challenging of paths of 'naughting the self'—the annihilation of the ego, the heart's shadow, so that the lover might experience fully the unity of life rather than merely possess knowledge of it. Then darkness is illumined by the light of His embrace, life renewed by drawing in His simple essence, and love sealed with a kiss—the "kiss of His mouth" (Nasr, 1981, 19) symbolising the transmission of sacred knowledge in a state of perfect intimacy. The secrets of the heart shared in this way are infinitely precious though freely given. Yet there is a hidden cost, to which Mathews alludes: "We have to face enigmas, difficulties, mortal perils. We have to risk ourselves" (2005, 21). This is a price the Sufi gladly pays to experience the Beloved's touch, the intoxicating beauty of His presence. For, as Sufi poets tell us, love is an ocean, an ocean whose currents flow fast and strong, washing away all defenses. It is no sweet romance; its burning intensity demands everything. All-consuming, like a fire, it annihilates the ego. Only the "idiots of God" give themselves to what they can never grasp, and can only wonder at (Vaughan-Lee, 2000, 62). Reason and logic turn us away from a path which holds such risk, so Rumi urges us to "Keep away, keep away from the lane of love" (*op. cit.*, 60) because there is neither safety nor security on this journey, only the intensity of our own devotion to that mysterious One, to hold us.

Ishq compels the devotee to walk on the path till duality disappears, effacing personal will in His will (Can, 2005, 136-137). *Fana fi'llah* (annihilation in God) does not designate the destruction of personal attributes. It symbolises the passing away of the appearance of separateness of forms and leads to *baqa*, their perpetuation or subsistence in the One that is pluralised in its epiphanies (Corbin, 202). Each creation is the beginning of the manifestation of one form and the occultation of another, the latter being the *fana* of the forms in the One divine being. Citing Shabestari (1978), Anissian interprets *fana* as the disintegration of negatives (liberation from sociointellectual consciousness and removal of the small i of identity) and *baqa* as restoration of wholeness or birth in the cosmic or universal self (2006). In egolessness, the self is not lost but amplified, therefore the term 'no-self', when used in the context of mysticism, is a misnomer. We are not dealing with a 'no-self' as Mathews suggests, but rather a fully potentiated one, its wholeness having been restored. ". . . He has become all my being" (Rumi, cited in Can, 2005, 274). Gülen describes *fana* as an "indescribable and all but unattainable state of pleasure, in which the transience of existence gives way to permanence". Such a feeling, he says, is akin to that where a drop admits what its origin, capacity and end really is with respect to the ocean (2007, 27). "In ceasing to exist separately, it reclaims its beauty—it exists yet it does not exist" (VI, 53).

Baqa (subsistence) denotes that nothing can come into existence or maintain its existence without being dependent on Him (Gülen, *op. cit.*). The transience of forms is in contrast with the permanence of the Self-Subsisting One, and Gülen explains that when the devotee experiences this essential difference, the Self-Subsisting One extends His permanence to him. This favour, he says, is called *Fana fi'llah* (annihilation in God) and *baqa bi'llah* (subsistence by God's Self-Subsistence). Those who have attained subsistence with God, says Gülen, always feel and think of Him, are always with Him, and see Him everywhere.

Because the heart is the 'eye' with which we see God, the eye is a particularly powerful symbol in Sufi literature. Absorbed in each other, gazing into each other's eyes, lovers lose sight of themselves. They see themselves not narcissistically but as singular beings, separate and smaller than the being they "create" together. In contrast, "eye contact, once the signature of our humanity, has become a danger", says Berry (1993, 142). Without vision, material man is the 'deprived soul' of whom Rumi says:

> For him 'reality' is the genitalia and the gullet, speak less to him about the mysteries of the Friend! (*SPL*, 112)

Insofar as *Suluk* entails purification of the heart in the spirit of humility and sincerity, the mystic's approach is conducive to minimising harm though personal risk and loss are inevitable aspects of this process. For this reason the mystical approach does not lead to oppression. Therefore the concept of unity, as understood by the Sufis, is not a key ideological construct underpinning oppressive projects, such as Plumwood suggests might be the case in the Deep Ecological interpretation. The 'use' of unity made by 'the incorporative self' in the act of self-imposition and appropriation in Plumwood's description bears no resemblance to the mystical goal of dissolution of self in the Ocean of Being. The self of her description is an accumulative self rather than one whose aim is shedding ('emptying the cup') as it merges with the simple essence. Plumwood writes:

The incorporative self uses unity in a hegemonic fashion to absorb the other or re-create them as a version of the self. To the extent the colonizing project is one of self-imposition and appropriation (literally "making self"), the incorporative self of the colonizing mind is insensitive to the other's independence and boundaries, denying the other's right to define their own reality, name their own history, and establish their own identity. This insensitivity extends to include the other's epistemic boundaries; it often assumes that the other is transparent—that they can be grasped and known as readily as the self—or that they are too simple for anything to be hidden, to outrun the colonizer's knowledge. To the incorporative self, the other can be taken (appropriated) for a benefit expressed exclusively in terms of the self, of the one, about whose beginning and end we are encouraged to be unclear (2000, 61).

The self of Plumwood's description is, essentially, an egotistic self, not one on the journey of the heart.

Ishq is of such a nature that it transforms the lover into the thing he loves. Sufi poets, drunk with the wine of love, reveal to us the wonder of oneness, the innermost union of lover and Beloved. The transformation of self is the essential aspect of *tawil*, the return journey, in which the heart, like other forms, requires continuous unveiling. Consummation can occur only when through effort and grace the lover, consumed by love, no longer surrenders to the ego's demands. Restoring the heart to its original state is a painful, hazardous process and few succeed, as the Sufi poet Attar illustrated so poignantly in his *Conference of the Birds* (*Mantiq-ul-tair*) to which Rumi frequently alludes. Of the several thousand birds that set out on the tortuous journey across seven valleys and mountains to find their king, most abandon the search; they turn back, make excuses and many die. Only thirty birds complete the journey, and in doing so, discover their own divine nature. Only mad lovers fly to the spheres, says Rumi, the others die in the depths of the blaze (*SPL*, 218). 'Love cleans rust from mirrors', Rumi tells us (*ibid*). As Eros was born of Chaos, the re-making of the self occurs in the fertile soil of bewilderment, pain and suffering.

Mathews speaks of "daunting psychological difficulties for the self" (2003, 114) that are inevitable on the panpsychist path of eros. She is unequivocal that this is a path which demands selfhood be surrendered (*op. cit.*, 106)—"the erotic self", says Mathews, "has ultimately to shed her ego" (*op. cit.*, 111). The self must be "melted down and beaten into shape in the fires" (*op. cit.*, 108). Fires reduce all things to their essential essence and leave nothing of individual forms. This, I have argued, is the mystic's goal, yet Mathews is emphatic that the path she envisages is not the mystic's path of no-self (*op. cit.*, 61). As explained previously, the term 'no-self' is misleading; 'egoless self' or 'fully potentiated self' might be more appropriate and might clarify what Mathews perceives as a difference between mysticism and panpsychism. "Self-abnegation", she says, "is the corollary of a view of the One that negates the Many" (*ibid.*). But mysticism is not one of those "unitive spiritual traditions" that spurn the Many as "an illusion, a meaningless contingency or a tragic accident or mistake" (*op. cit.*, 56). The Sufi's recognition of the One *affirms* the Many by restoring wholeness—it does not negate it, as indeed recognition of the One has enriched Mathews' view of the Many. Explaining that "Eros is the path of the self that affirms both the Many and the One" (*ibid.*), there appears to be some inconsistency regarding the need, on the one hand, to shed the ego, while on the other, assiduously avoiding association with mysticism, while the path Mathews describes is consistent with the mystic's path, the goal of which is annihilating the ego in order to affirm the One/Many via engagement with the Real.

Annihilating the ego, 'dying before death' is the price of 'tasting'—a price most of us are unwilling to pay. In our death-denying, death-defying culture (Kübler-Ross, 1969), the idea of 'dying before death' holds little appeal. However, through 'tasting', direct knowledge is acquired, because the self is consumed in the process of becoming consummate. Knowledge that is personal, profound and intimate is revealed only to the lover. As the ego's voice is stilled, other voices can be heard in a state of mystical union which makes possible knowledge of the deep flesh of the universe, unfettered by veils of form. "The whole of your body will become a mirror, all will become eye . . . and the ear will stir up an image that becomes the go-between for union with the Beloved", says Rumi (*SPL*, 259). Separateness of form melts away and "awareness of the work of the world" (Rumi, Chittick, 2004, 130) grows from the silence.

As the Sufi, his heart transformed, becomes one with the simple essence of his Beloved, so too the poet, who acquires consummate skill by becoming one with his craft. Reflecting this mystical perspective, Dewey asserts that the realisation of goals emerging from within the action itself demands a remaking of the whole of the live creature (Cited in Joas,

1996, 140). Through patient, disciplined practice, organised repetition, self-criticism and reflection, skill is developed in the course of time; "the *coup de foudre* or sudden inspiration usually being a narcissist's fantasy" (Sennett, 2008, 37). Hazrat Inayat Khan, himself a consummate musician, refers to this process as 'tuning', since it involves sensitizing the whole being. As we have seen, the unitive self, as exemplified by Rumi, mystic and poet, does not in any way avoid the orectic (and therefore erotic) engagement that would "exacerbate its vulnerability to suffering", as Mathews suggests (2003, 114). Sennett enumerates the many steps that need to be taken when developing any skill, and refers particularly to the development of the musician's 'intelligent hand'. First the fingertips must be sensitized, "enabling (the hand) to reason about touch", so that hand, wrist and forearm can be integrated. Then the hand can work with the eye to coordinate perfectly, to anticipate and to sustain concentration (*op. cit.* 238). The tone produced must satisfy the ear, while the heart reflects the rhythm. Each stage, like the stations of *Suluk*, is a challenge and grounds the next. Each stage involves the heart. Most abandon the task because the process of transforming the whole being is too slow and painful. Uncovering the heart, turning dust to gold, requires total commitment, effort and time. The Sufi, however, thirsting for the taste of love's intoxicating wine, never turns back. Dwelling in the moment of being in a thing, acquiring knowledge that is intimate and real, totally absorbed in that thing, the Sufi becomes the thing itself, as Rumi illustrates in the *Mathnawi*. "We are the lyre which thou pluckest" (Nasr, 1981, 257), he says—the Supreme Artist in whom he subsists and expresses his own divine creativity.

Art is the child of the Intellect, says Plato in *Laws* (cited in Nasr, 1981, 253), and traditional or sacred art is an imitation of the art of the Creator of forms (*Al-Musawwir*) (*op. cit.*, 257), reflecting directly the creativity of the Master. According to Nasr, traditional art, such as Sufi poetry, is inseparable from sacred knowledge, and is at once based upon and is a channel for *scientia sacra*. "It has a sacramental function and is, like religion itself, at once truth and presence" (*op. cit.*, 253), the expression of knowledge and love acquired in a slow process of personal transformation inevitable when learning something of the divine 'art'. Technical training in the crafts was always combined with spiritual instruction, and the close nexus between craft guilds and Sufi orders has survived to this day in certain Muslim cities, according to Nasr. "Man is fashioned by what man makes", he says of a process which implies a return to essence and as such is closely related to the refinement of ego and the cultivation of heart (*op. cit.*, 259).

As Rumi was 'fashioned' by his making, his many readers worldwide, who increasingly turn to his poetry for the insights it offers, are not left untouched by its beauty. Refraining from speech so that Rumi can speak to us in the language of the heart, we too might surrender to the beauty of his poetry whose complex form and distinctive otherness we do not fully comprehend. Those who listen to him, in meditative fashion, with the ear of the heart, find themselves expand beyond the limitations of their prosaic world, into the sacred world which Rumi leads them. As Rumi surrenders to his Beloved's beauty and gives it life in an elaborate new form, they too are humbled by the power of love to transform dust into gold. Listening attentively, they might be opened to the meaning of Rumi's experience and be extended too, both by the beauty of his poetry and by their own efforts to understand it more fully. The struggle to find the Beloved, simple and unadorned, beyond the veils of complexity, must surely change readers in ways unimagined at the start of their search for meaning.

As Hamilton says of great art, it guides us to the noumenon as the artist provides "a bridge from the everyday world of phenomena to the noumenal world of meaning, to the unitary reality that is the substrate of all things, to the transcendence and the immanence" (2008, 236). The poet, according to Emerson, may rightfully be called "the Sayer, the Namer, the Language-Maker", as he "can penetrate into that region where the air is music" and we find ourselves not critically engaged but in a holy place. This musical air is the universe's own expression; a sacred communication audible to poets and mystics whose hearts are attuned to its fine vibration, its "primal warblings composed before time was" (1907, 16). Born of *ishq* and *marifa*, Rumi's creation invites us to partake of the mystery of the world, and be transformed by it.

5.6 Submitting to Quietness

Starkly contrasting the contemporary paradigm of physical transformation is the mystical motif of naughting the self, the supreme expression of passion, as a necessary condition for any wholeness that an individual might realise. Rumi employs various terms to designate the station of nothingness and those who have attained it, such as 'poor man', 'fakir', 'dervish' and 'Sufi', implying "one who has nothing of his own and is empty of selfhood (*nafs*/ego)" (*SPL*, 187). From the Sufi perspective, the poor man's state is the most desirable since he has progressed furthest on the path of knowledge and love: "Of all the different kinds of knowledge, on the day of death only the science of poverty will supply provisions for the way" (Rumi, *SPL*, 188).

In the 'tavern of ruin', intoxicated lovers abandon everything that separates them from the Beloved:

> Drunk on the wine of selflessness, they have given up good and evil alike. Drunk, without lips or mouth, on Truth, they have thrown away all thoughts of name and fame, all talk of wonder, visions, spiritual states, dreams, secret rooms, lights, miracles (Rumi, Vaughan-Lee, 2000, 187).

In the 'nothingness' of love with its endless potential, the voice of ego finally falls silent. Loving the Real, its rivers and oceans, soil and air (Gülen, 2009), its 'others' whose "exotic" (Mathews, 2003, 7) appearance veils their reality, calls, above all else, for a radical transformation of the heart so that we might, in a state of stillness, hear its voice and respond appropriately, despite the inevitable cost to ourselves.

Rumi's exhortations to seal the lips are innumerable:

> Refrain from speaking . . . Abandon life and the world, that you may behold the Life of the world (Rumi, Nicholson, 169)

> Be silent that the Lord who gave you language may speak . . . (Nicholson, 191)

> Be silent and free from the pain of speech . . . (Nicholson, 195)

> If you want every one of your parts to speak and compose poetry, then go, silence your speech! (*SPL*, 271)

In stillness we might become attuned to the sounds and letters of the universe. French philosopher Merleau-Ponty argues that the whole visible, sensual world is the deep flesh of language. As flesh of its flesh, "pregnant with all possibles", all forms participate in language: "the *logos* of the

world is not the *logos* of anyone . . . it is a revelation of Being" (1962, 23).
In keeping with the phenomenological tradition, Merleau-Ponty is mindful of Husserl's injunction to "return to the things themselves"—to let the
forms speak for themselves, since "language has us and it is not we who
have language" (*op. cit.*, 35). We should not therefore be deceived by the
muteness of forms, or postmodernism's repudiation of what it calls "the
dream of an innocent language" and the universalist vision of a noise-free,
transparent sphere of communication (Lyotard, 1984), but, like poets and
mystics throughout the ages, be attentive to the universe's expression that
dispels all notions of dualism. In a universe of 'things', the divine aura
breathes through forms. Muffled by the ceaseless din and clamour of
human activity, its expression is subdued and hidden among the strident
voices on the surface. Yet it is the music of the Absolute, the bass, the
undertone, of which Hazrat Inayat Khan says "it is the loudest and the
softest, the highest and the lowest; all gradually merges into it; it always
is and always will be" (II, 58).

We should listen to it with the ear of the heart:

> What is the *Samā*? A message from those hidden within the heart.
> The heart finds peace in their missive.
> It is a wind which causes the branches of the intellect to blossom,
> a sound which opens the pores of existence.
> At the time of *Samā*, the Sufis hear another sound, from God's throne.
> You cannot perceive the clapping of the leaves—you need
> The ear of the heart, not the body's ear. (Rumi, *SPL*, 328)

"We have no knowledge of Him except through the knowledge that
He gives to us, and His giving of knowledge takes place through His
Speech" (al-Arabi, *SPK*, 212), the language of the manuscript of Nature,
the Supreme *Barzakh*, addressing the heart. For Rumi, it speaks of the
oneness of love, lover and Beloved, of beauty, of harmony, of rhythm, of
gentleness and might, of mercy and severity. Languages, like all forms,
come to pass but the language of the universe remains ever-present. While
variously interpreted, it has been heard throughout the ages by people of
different cultures and creeds because it speaks eternally, with clarity and
simplicity.

Language lives from the silence, as the void does the holding and the
Absolute Being works in nonexistence. "Silence is there to make us hear",

as Claude Lefort, Merleau-Ponty's protégé, says; "speech is between two silences and as speech goes from one to the other, speech does not abolish silence". "Silence is the horizon and the depth of speech" (Evans & Lawlor (Eds.), 2000, 73). In Taoism, the inconceivable stillness is the Mother of the Universe—Tao, and like Rumi's Beloved, it is the integrating principle behind all things:

> The root is called Quietness;
> What has submitted to Quietness has become part of the always-so.
> To know the always-so is to be illumined; to become part of the always-so
> (Cited in D'Adamo, 163)

Submission to quietness necessitates an adjustment of our chaotic rhythm so that every activity becomes an expression of devotion and love, carried out—as Mathews says—"with attentiveness to . . . the fidelity and communicativeness of form", in order to counter the "crude indifference" of modern cultures (2005, 20). Far from simply utilitarian in intent, she says, daily activities are opportunities to celebrate the One and give thanks for the gift of life. This is consistent with the Sufi understanding that every activity should be conducted 'prayerfully', remembering the One who makes all things possible. Cultures premised on such an attitude do not seek affluence in material terms, but are infinitely rich in spirit, and "abundant in graces" (*op. cit.*, 21).

To be able to say "O world, I am in tune with every note of thy great harmony," knowing "that all is order . . . that oneness of feeling exists between all the parts of nature, in spite of their divergence and dispersion" (Aurelius, 68-69), that same natural order, rhythm and harmony must be reflected in the heart. This should be in tune, not with the 'course vibration of matter', but with the 'fine vibration of spirit', so that the heart is tuned, not to its surroundings, but in spite of its surroundings, to its natural pitch. The Sufi therefore aims for a natural as opposed to an artificial rhythm. "What is spirituality but to be natural?" asks Hazrat Inayat Khan (IV, 71), and similarly, Mathews asserts "Nature knows best", which, she explains, "does not mean a 'return to nature' in the sense of restoring lost attributes, but rather a stepping back, a letting-be, so that we cease intervening and making things over in accordance with our decontextualised designs" (2005, 31). Though such an approach might entail individual hardship, the greater whole is likely to fare better than when things are subject to our arbitrary interventions, she argues.

From the metaphysical point of view there are different rhythms describing the condition of the heart—*sattva, rajas* and *tamas*. *Sattva* is its harmonious rhythm, *rajas* is a rhythm which is not in perfect harmony with nature, and *tamas* is chaotic and destructive. Activities conducted while a person is in a chaotic rhythm are likely to be of a destructive nature, less so if conducted in the rhythm of *rajas*. However, the impulse that originates from a *sattvic* rhythm is inspired because it is in harmony with the rhythm of the universe (IV, 70). *Sattva* is comparable to the Taoist notion of inaction, *wu wei*, which, as Mathews explains, is "not mere inactivity, but activity that is undertaken with rather than against the grain of conativity". "One who is acting according to this rhythm might seek to overcome oppression, disturbance and malaise not by confronting them head on . . . but by attuning and joining herself to the conative dynamics of self-increase" (2005, 45).

"The silent life experiences on the surface through activity" (II, 16). Awakening initially an awareness of, but ultimately union with, that silent life, the immanently eternal as opposed to the relative and transitory, is the Sufi's goal. "When our lips are sealed, God begins to speak" (Khan, 1960, 93). In quietness he hears the language of the universe and his heart adopts its rhythm: "I hear Thy music, my Beloved, and my soul speaks of its joy in song" (*op. cit.*, 88). According to Hazrat Inayat Khan, this divine music is the natural inclination of all things; they have their origin and resolution in it (VII, 39). Its rhythms and patterns determine "the self's unique dance with the universe", as Mathews envisages it in its most potentiating orectic-erotic form, since "the state of desire is not merely appetitive in nature"; the primary cathexis is the immature self's initial psychic reaching out and establishment of a bond with one who is primally present to it (Mathews, 2005, 118). It is via this primal psychic investment that the self comes fully into being, she says (*ibid.*). Its psychic energies are activated and begin to flow outward, she continues, explaining that only through such contact does the self feel "the finitude and boundaries, and hence the reality, of its own existence" (*ibid.*). "The self's dance with the universe", as Mathews describes this contact, is most dramatically symbolised by the whirling associated with the Sufi order founded by

Rumi, the Whirling Dervishes, whose ecstatic 'dance', representing the simultaneous abandonment of self and perfect discipline are a metaphor for the Sufi path of love. "To whom or what the primary cathexis is made, matters", says Mathews, explaining that it should be an enabling and encompassing other in whose responses the emerging self can discover itself (*op. cit.*, 119).

The reality of the individual's finitude and boundaries becomes apparent in the face of the infinite whose absolute reality renders the individual's reality relative, therefore the Sufi, having reached *fana*, is aware of his own transience and subsistence (*baqa*) in His permanence and boundlessness. But the primacy of the 'Real', and the importance of our desire for it, is irrevocably asserted by both the Sufis and by Mathews, who argues that maximum potentiation occurs when the state of desire is not merely appetitive, but rather when the erotic impulse directs itself to "world" (*op. cit.*, 120), whose reality she affirms in her argument (2003, 25-44). In cathexis with the Real, the self's integrity is not compromised; inner being, says Mathews, will not require suppressing or reprogramming in accordance with social expectations (2005, 120). The "primary sense of self, that particular constellation of out-reaching psychic energies with which (a person is) born", is retained in such a relationship (*ibid.*). This relationship with the Real therefore forms the self's "energic foundation" on which "discursive layers of identity may be contingently overlaid", "but they will not replace it", and "sexual relations will be a subset of erotic relations", the self's innate rhythm and pace and pattern of engaging with Reality, Mathews explains (*ibid.*).

Similarly, Hamilton addresses the self's desire for the noumenon, which, he explains, can only be achieved "by giving up the self, by relinquishing the attachment to our ego-self and, ultimately, annihilating it" (2008, 170). Just as the Sufi recognises that the turbulence of the external world with its pleasures and pains is the shadow of the real life that it veils, Hamilton makes numerous references to the silent life from which everything comes and to which everything returns. In sublime union with its quietness, "when the phenomenal form of the world is dissolved", he says, with reference to Wordsworth's poem *Tintern Abbey*, the pure life force that pervades all things, the 'thing-in-itself', might be apprehended. Then the 'illusion' of our independent existence falls away, he says, because the individual self 'owes' its origin to the noumenon or universal Self whose will should guide its actions (2008, 94).

Hamilton's interpretation is also consistent with the Sufi understanding of *fana* and *baqa*—annihilation and subsistence in the Beloved, though it lacks Sufism's passion. Exceedingly rational and abstract, his metaphysical-psychology evokes little of the "purity of passion" (226) he argues are necessary for a life of meaningful participation in the world. Sufism itself is sometimes referred to as a psychology, but 'heart' is always at its centre. Idries Shah, for example, says: "We view it (Sufism) not as an ideology that moulds people to the right way of belief or action, but as an art or science that can exert a beneficial influence on individuals and societies . . . Sufism is a psychology" (1968, 21). Hazrat Inayat Khan repeatedly refers to the importance of understanding the "psychology of life and of the situation". He explains as follows: "I do not mean by psychology what is generally understood by this word; I mean the understanding of the self, the understanding of the nature and character of the mind and of the body" (X, 251). "Real psychology", he says, "is the understanding of a law working behind the scenes. It is the understanding of cause and effect in everything, in every action, in every aspect. It is a stepping-stone towards esotericism" (XI, 74).

When the self acts in accordance with the will of the universal Self, with its essence in the noumenon which is "at the heart of our existence", says Hamilton, it becomes detached from the "external" aspect of things, their influences and coercions (2008, 219). This is not indifference, he explains, but rather intentional participation in the world (*op. cit.*, 226). Similarly, the panpsychist may appear "strangely halfhearted in her social endeavors" (Mathews, 2005, 124), since her exclusive allegiance is not to the discursive system of culture, "but to reality" (*op. cit.*, 126). Through their groundedness in the Real rather than in a set of discursive ideals socially imposed, such unitive selves are relatively free from the strictures of the world, strictures which, Rumi says, can be overcome if only the bird of spirit chooses flight. Analogously, the form of the 'whirl', with its well-defined boundaries, offers the dervish the possibility of ecstasy and freedom as he submits to the Real's eternal, infinite quietness that potentiates and holds.

The Real, however, manifests in multiplicity; its expressions are infinite and never-repeating so we may not recognise its face in all its many forms. In order for the One/Many to flourish, forms in which we do not recognise the Real (through lack of knowledge and effort) should nevertheless be respectfully encountered, their communication heeded and their boundaries observed. Perhaps this entails not so much that the self "alter her overt behavior in accordance with social expectations, without suppressing and reprograming her inner being", as Mathews suggests (2005, 120), but rather, if at all possible, a recovery of the Real within forms we perceive to be 'unreal'. Mathews' own patient "naturalisation" of a soulless industrialised 'block', I believe, illustrates the potential inherent in all forms, including those we perceive least attractive, to provide a locus in which the Real might unfold if only we let it be. "Letting-be", as Mathews explains, "is not synonymous with letting-die, but rather with healing, in a synergistic sense, drawing on forces or powers already present within the existing state of things to restore . . . dynamic equilibrium" (2005, 41). By reaching out, in a spirit of acquiescence in the given, to the 'unreal' form with all its perceived limitations, rather than abandoning, remaking or destroying it, the process of life can begin anew. At the heart of such an approach are gratitude and grace; the one who gives and the one who receives both acknowledge dependence on each another, and on the larger than human world.

Embracing the given presupposes not only gratitude for potential, but fidelity that extends to the limitations of the form. Berry's remarks, in this regard, on faithfulness to forms, particularly the forms of marriage and language, are pertinent. Unlike sexual love which is natural, he says, marriage as a form is artificial and therefore initially arbitrary, but once chosen and entered into, its form is no longer arbitrary. Like that of language, once adopted, it imposes its own discipline. Only by understanding the form's subtle meaning can sense be made of its strictures. "Breaking the form by escaping its strictures does not lead to freedom but simply to the limitations of a different form as all forms impose their particular form of authority on those who adopt them" (1983, 203).

The meaning of marriage, Berry explains, begins with the *Logos*—the giving of words:

. . . not impulsive, hurried and abstract or diminished by subjectivity, but words that are accountable, particular and truthful. We join ourselves to another by giving our word. And this giving of the word must be an unconditional, full and generous giving, for in giving it we join past, present and future. We join ourselves to the unknown and the term that is set to the responsibility for the consequences of such joining is 'until death', at which time it may be said to be fulfilled. We do not know and cannot determine the road, but we commit our lives to it, and the form itself sets the definitions and limits of that road. It is these formal bounds that turn us back from fantasy, from wishful thinking and self-pity when the road appears unnavigable . . . Zen scholar Aitken Roshi says: 'Sometimes one gets stuck and must stay there for a while'—form joins us to time, to the consequences and fruitions of our actions . . . Not everything that we stay to find out will make us happy, but by staying we learn something of the truth, the truth that is good to know, that sets us free, and that is always both different and larger than we thought (1983, 206).

Unlike the romantic who is often in flight from the troubles of duration, the Sufi finds his Beloved in all forms despite their limitations. Commitment to meaning involves staying (*sabr*) when it would be more convenient to leave. Then His reality becomes clear: "Thou art revealed by every atom" says Rumi (Nicholson, II, 189). Seeing His face in all forms brings joyful liberation:

From the time I first saw Thy Face, wherever I sit I am joyful, wherever I go I dwell in the midst of roses. Wherever the Beloved's Image may be, that is a garden and place of contemplation; whatever station I enter, I am wrapped in pleasure (*SPL*, 298).

The purpose of meditation, contemplation, the essence of religion, mysticism and philosophy is, according to Hazrat Inayat Khan, "the attainment of that depth that is the root of life" (VII, 42). Stilling the restless mind so that it can intuitively apprehend reality is therefore an integral part of the mystical tradition. Probably best known for their stilling techniques and meditative practices are the Zen Buddhist schools, which emerged in China as a reaction against the increasing scholastic complexities of the Tiantai and Huayan schools, which some Zen practitioners believed was more of an obstacle than an aid (Lusthaus, 1998). Heraclitus speaks of the eternal unchanging stillness that abides within the world of change as early as the sixth century BCE, and Plato affirms the power of silence to restore and replenish. The proper object of enjoyment, he believes, is a process which is perceived to restore the body's silence by removing the clamour of the mind (Marshall, 1998). Similarly, Aurelius recommends finding renewal in the untroubled retreat of the soul (1964). For Plotinus, contemplation is the single thread uniting all existents; "the power uniting the One, the Intelligence, and the Soul in a single all-productive intellectual force to which all existents owe their life" (Moore, 2006).

Meditation, according to Vaughan-Lee, awakens us to what is always present, "love's eternal now" (2000, 28). This love may fill us with bliss, saturate us with longing, touch us with silence, or just open a door to emptiness, he says. Coming out of meditation we bring with us a subtle knowledge of another dimension and a different way of being which becomes an invisible foundation to our consciousness. Meditation refines, while 'constant remembrance' (*dhikr/zikr*) allows us to attune ourselves to His reality and align ourselves with His rhythm as each breath becomes alive with His name. As the fifteenth century Indian mystic Kabir said, "The breath that does not repeat the name of God is a wasted breath" (Cited in Vaughan-Lee, *ibid.*).

Essentially methods such as the Sufi *dhikr*, the Buddhist *nembutsu* (recollecting the Buddha), Hindu *mantras* (chanting the holy names) and Christian meditative prayer have the same goal, and their value has been widely acknowledged. Nicholls and Gray, for example, focus in their research particularly on the cognitive processes that are facilitated when the mind is stilled (2007). Their research indicates that the entire nervous system can be slowed down so that a person can access calm emotions and form new neural networks and patterns which in turn influence perceptions, emotions and cognitions. Periodically slowing down mind and body enhances mindfulness and equilibrium. Citing Claxton (1999, 111), Nicholls and Gray describe mindfulness as the ability to see, to observe patiently and to notice without comment whatever is happening in the moment. From this patient observation insight develops into what is helpful, misguided or harmful. Insight—seeing from within, "seeing with the heart" (IV, 36)—gradually replaces "moral blindness, the darkness of ignorance and narrow vision" (Venkatesananda, 7).

The practice of stilling the mind is common to traditions whose goal is to foster peace and harmony by cultivating the silence within so that other voices might be heard. Rumi compares a person's own voice to a disruptive intruder whose arrival in a company creates embarrassment and checks the flow of conversation:

> . . . in the presence of the King, had there not been an intruder in the company, Jesus would have revealed to thee the mysteries, point by point (Nicholson, I, 157)

At a time when many voices are not heard, it is particularly important that we learn to listen. But stilling the mind and the voice of ego is exceedingly difficult, and the unruly mind and restless body are bars of the cage that imprisons us. Trapped by our thoughts, emotions and senses, "we are not masters but slaves" (VII, 16). Reminding us that the word 'man' is derived from the Sanskrit words *Mana, Manu, Manushya*, etymologically equating human beings and mind, product of mind, and also controller of the activity of mind (*ibid.*), Hazrat Inayat Khan explains that it lies within our own mind whether we will be masters of our minds or slaves. If we choose to escape from the closed cage of our minds, we need to follow a path that does not lead to slavery. Rumi shows the way:

> I have closed the passage of the lips, and opened the secret way; I am free in one moment from the desire of speech (Nicholson, I, 158)

When we open 'the secret way' we no longer "strive to perform deeds that would flesh out a narrative" in terms of which one's life might be defined, as Mathews explains, pursuing fulfilment by "getting the most out of life", but "awaken to the world, to its vastness, its beauty, its endless communicativeness", so that life assumes a poetic structure (2005, 68). Closing the passage of the lips, stilling the commanding voice of ego, represents 'the secret way' of which Rumi speaks, but is, as Sufi poetry illustrates so poignantly, the most difficult thing to do. Attaining 'poverty' (of ego) is the prerequisite for meaningful being and as such is a recurring theme in Sufism. It is also the purpose of the Buddhist path of perfection which culminates in the silence of Nirvana (Mascaro, 1973). Similarly, in the *Tao Te Ching,* the path that leads to Nothing is the path of the Infinite: "Go far into the Void and there rest in quietness" (*op. cit.*, 27).

5.7 *Baqa* and the Economy

In contrast with the frenetic striving of the conscious world on the surface, where materialistic pleasures hold modern consumers in their thrall,
the centre, to which the Sufi journeys, is a place of peace, where meaning
can be found in *baqa*—subsistence in the One. Subsistence entails trust
that one's needs will be met, gratitude for the given, contentment, and
frugality (Nursi, 1920); it is essentially a life of simplicity, which is not a
privation of what is necessary, but a refusal of whatever is superfluous
from the point of view of physical need (Schuon, 1959, 162). Its opposite, luxury ('high standard of living'), which envisages only material
acquisition and keeps adding to it fresh needs, is a "theft from nature"
(*ibid.*), the inevitable consequence of an "extractive profit-driven economics, an ideology of progress, an ethos of consumerism and an international regime of colonialism" (Mathews, 2005, 9).

Poverty, in the mystical sense, is an inner state that does not depend
on one's outer situation or presuppose the abandonment of material
things. The Sufi is not a recluse surviving on meditation and alms. On the
contrary, achieving poverty of self, the Sufi is enriched, fully embracing
the One's plenitude. The *sattvic* rhythm of his heart, unimpeded by ego,
is in harmony with the rhythm of the universe; its laws become his own.
Through loving surrender to these laws of creation (*shariah*), he participates in the natural economy, which is a life-sustaining 'gift' economy,
and knows that the earth will provide in accordance with her nature and
rhythm. This knowledge springs from the Sufi's intimate love of the
earth's divine nature as opposed to a love of money.

The non-accumulative subsistence economy such as hunter-gatherers
practise might be considered the economic paradigm of *baqa*, insofar as
they adhere to traditions of a primordial character, where meaning is
directly related to natural forms which are known intimately. Subsistence
economies are founded on principles of allegiance and what Mathews
describes as faithfulness to place, "as sovereign, solace, beloved . . . its will
our command" (2005, 8), in other words, the attitude of letting-be which
she advocates. Economics, thus conceived, constitutes an opportunity for
encounter, says Mathews. Such relationality and the certainty that derives
from it cannot be found in any other economy, including the 'free' market economy by which we are all bound, which thrives on exploitation and

waste. Since its complex workings cannot be fully understood, even by 'experts', it cannot be relied on to keep poverty at bay. Although the physical risk associated with subsistence is extremely real, scarcity being an ontological constant rather than a man-made anomaly (Salleh, 2009), it is familiar to those who have knowledge of natural patterns ("Nature's patterned parsimony", Wheeler, 28), and can therefore be taken into account. As such it might be preferable to the unfamiliar risks presented by a world in which many elements of beauty and so also of well-being have been crushed in the name of progress and of raising the 'standard of living', invented and imposed on all peoples, says Schuon (*op. cit.*, 163).

Thus the "native self" of Mathews' description "dwells within the parameters of the given", "attuning herself to the inner rhythm" of an inexhaustibly deep and poetic reality. "She adjusts her own inner curvature to that of the world, and in gratitude she lets the waves plot her course" (2005, 129). Mathews believes that implicit in nativism is the custodial ethos which, according to Salleh, might be ascribed to all those whose capacities to subsist derive from traditional knowledge and practices which do not contribute to the ecological debt notched up by industrialised societies as main contributors to climate change (Salleh, 2009).

With reference to ecofeminist and former quantum physicist, Vandana Shiva, Salleh describes how eco-sufficiency is achieved by meta-industrial workers in north India. These workers respect the integrity of ecological and human cycles. Their daily round, protecting natural sustainability and human sustenance is, Salleh believes, an exemplar of scientific complexity in action. Aboriginal Australians too, she points out, traditionally make the seasonal walk through country with deliberation and disciplined harvesting to ensure renewal. Three hours' work a day suffices in this bioregional economy where no more is extracted than what is needed for maintenance. In regions where communal land is undisturbed by development, self-managed indigenous economies are "both sovereign and synergistic", satisfying many needs at once. Citing Chilean economist Manfred Max Neef, she says: besides subsistence, they foster learning, participation, innovation, ritual, identity and belonging (*ibid.*).

Salleh lists some of the features of subsistence which, she believes, are paradigmatic of sustainability science: The consumption footprint is small because local resources are used and monitored daily with care. Autonomous local economies imply food and energy sovereignty. The scale of production is intimate, maximising responsiveness to matter/energy transfers in nature, so avoiding entropy. Lines of responsibility are transparent, and with social organisation less convoluted than in urban centres, synergistic problem solving can be achieved. This economic rationality distinguishes between stocks and flows—no more is taken than is needed. The work process is empowering and without division between workers' mental and manual skills. The labour product is enjoyed or shared whereas the industrial worker has no control over his or her creativity. Such provisioning is eco-sufficient because it does not externalise costs on to others as debt. Multi-criteria decision-making is simply common sense; judgments are built up by trial and error, and a cradle to grave assessment of ecosystem health prevents risk-taking associated with short-termism (*ibid.*), with regard to which the Prophet's injunction is particularly relevant: "Work for your worldly life as if you were going to live forever, but work for the life to come as if you were going to die tomorrow" (Rice, 1999, 349).

Recently we have become all too familiar with the high cost of risk taken by people worldwide who neither understood nor had the capacity to bear it. The global financial system's extreme complexity is used as "a tool to fool" according to Johnson and Kapoor (Orr, 2009), in order to maximise profitability and avoid regulation, and the strategy's effectiveness depends partly on the practice of misnaming its instruments, they claim, arguing that the whole system needs reform to bring about simplicity. The global financial crisis is, according to Joseph Stiglitz, recipient of the 2001 Nobel Prize in Economics, "the fruit of dishonesty and incompetence" (2008, 12). The collapse of trillion dollar companies AIG, Lehman Brothers, Merrill Lynch, Fannie Mae, Freddie Mac and countless others, affecting people worldwide, exposes an industry built up on unmanageable debt, and whose complexity is designed to disguise the dubious nature of its transactions and the sliding value of its assets. "It was all done in the name of innovation", says Stiglitz, "but not in ways that made the economy stronger" (*ibid.*). Speculative 'short-selling' is just one example of the type of hazardous practice that has made this economic model a 'broken' one—the practice of borrowing stock from a bank or a broker at a certain price, selling it on (although there is no prior ownership) and then buying it back at either a lower price at a profit or at a higher price at a loss (Long, 2008). Precarious practices such as this, and that of incurring further debt as a solution to the problems caused by unmanageable debt, have turned the economy into a "house of cards" (Stiglitz, *op. cit.*). Furthermore, in what is the biggest bail-out in history (*ibid.*), public money is being used to rescue commercial financiers. Profits are privatised while losses are socialised, which would appear to be extremely unethical.

With unprecedented levels of debt at both household and national levels throughout the western world, including national bankruptcy in Iceland (October 2008) and Greece (May 2010), and several European countries and North American states teetering on the brink (June 2010), there is increasing evidence that the global financial crisis might well trigger radical changes in the free-market economy, possibly even a shift of financial power, followed by a shift in real power, to other parts of the world, such as resurgent Asia, increasingly powered by China, with different ideologies. Though aspects of Western ideologies may have been adopted by those cultures, traditional values have not been entirely rejected. Sinologist Gloria Davies describes the re-emergence of Confucianism in modern Chinese thought (2007), and historian Anthony Milner attributes rapid economic growth in many parts of Asia to Confucian commitment to "hard work, thrift and filial piety" (Milner, 2000). It has been widely acknowledged that the binge by Western nations has largely been on Asian credit (James, 2008). Political analysts, such as Colin James, believe we are on the brink of a new world order, the current one being mired in wastefulness, self-indulgence and greed (*ibid.*). Moreover, fundamental instabilities at the heart of the system do not appear to have been addressed, and problems caused by unsustainable levels of debt are being tackled by incurring yet more debt (Orr, 2009).

The market mayhem we are witnessing is not unprecedented. Financial institutions have collapsed before, even the most well-regarded, previously considered "pillars of the establishment" (Maiden, 2008). Just two days before Wall Street began to crash in 1929 heralding the Great Depression, US banker Thomas Lamont told President Hoover reassuringly that "the future appears brilliant; we have the greatest and soundest prosperity, and the best material prospects of any country" (*ibid.*). For all his expertise, Lamont was blind to reality and perhaps that blindness is as prevalent now as it was then. The difference between the current economic meltdown and previous collapses is one of scale. With Wall Street reported to have seen $US4 trillion vanish in a year (Maiden, 2008), the scale is unprecedented; inconceivable figures become stripped of meaning. Maiden traces this and previous economic collapses back to a lack of restraint and the illusory foundations of burgeoning debt on which unsustainable growth is built.

Economist Steve Keen claims that virtually every aspect of conventional economic theory is intellectually unsound and concludes that any policy recommendation in economics is as likely to be harmful as helpful. Long before the 2008 collapse he raised the alarm at the growing debt binge promoted by a financial system capitalising on speculation and greed, which feeds enormous amounts of debt on to people unable to take on that level of debt. Economics and economic theories have been preserved, not via greater knowledge, as their advocates might have us believe, but by ignorance, argues Keen. He explains that many economists are simply unaware that the foundations of economics have been disputed, let alone that these critiques have motivated prominent economists to profoundly change their views and to themselves become critics of economic orthodoxy. Prominent economists such as Irving Fisher, John Hicks, Paul Samuelson, Robert Solow, Alan Kirman and Joseph Stiglitz have to varying degrees distanced themselves from conventional economics after coming to understand, for a range of reasons, that economic orthodoxy harboured fundamental flaws (*ibid.*).

With the global financial crisis we witnessed the unravelling of an immoral economy whose deceptive demeanour and irresistible powers of seduction held us in its thrall. Like frenzied moths we were drawn to its light in a daze, our wings engulfed by the blaze as we ardently wooed its flame.

> Every sensual desire in the world, whether property, position, or bread, can make you drunk. Then when you do not find it, you become winesick. This winesickness—which is heartache—is proof that you were drunk with your desire (Rumi, *SPL*, 324).

Intoxication caused by alcohol and other substances, or by wealth, power or success which temporarily dull the mind and offer brief visions of flight, followed by heartache, is in stark contrast with mystical intoxication experienced by Sufis. Theirs is a state of utmost lucidity; "it heralds the unfoldment of the soul, the opening of the intuitive faculties, the awakening of the heart to all beauty within and without, uplifting and bringing that perfection for which every soul yearns" (II, 9). Therefore Rumi advocates drinking the "wine of the spirit", the "wine of gnosis" (*SPL*, 318):

> When you escape from this awareness through constant drinking and intoxication, the Wine-seller's generosity will give you a hundred other awarenesses. Take this other wine, not that red or amber one. This one will make you the master of meaning and deliver you from outward forms! (*SPL*, 312)

Winedrinking and its resultant intoxication is a recurring image in Sufi poetry, representing as it does the annihilation of form's limitations. The transformation of grapes into wine is symbolic of *fana* and *baqa*; the grape, when turned into wine, loses its individuality but lives on and is much enhanced—as a grape it would soon have perished. In selflessness, the self is not lost but amplified. Rumi's poetry is replete with images which could be mistaken for wanton sensuality and recklessness but which are metaphors expressing love's intoxication. God is the *Saki*—the cup as well as its content, the wine or nectar of love, and losing himself in the body and spirit of the Beloved, the lover becomes totally 'drunk'. Thus understood, intoxication brings freedom from 'winesickness', the enchainment of form:

> Begin the toasts! Uproot sobriety! Deliver unveiled pleasure from the chains of existence! Rise up, for we have been delivered and have broken the chains! Rise up, for we are drunk, free of winesickness for all eternity! (*SPL*, 324)

5.8 Freedom

Oh, Thou bestowest a thousand freedoms upon the world! (Rumi, *SPL*, 303)

Yet, when we are trapped by beliefs, by prejudices, by thoughts and desires of a divisive rather than unitive nature, the concept of freedom is reduced to mere abstraction. As long as we seek freedom only in forms, endeavouring to free ourselves of everything except the strictures of ego, giving little thought to inner freedom, we are caught in the greatest captivity of all—the trap of self, where we remain like birds in a cage. The desire for self-fulfilment and freedom from spouse, authority and 'others' simply leads to a different form of servitude. As Arendt says, "man cannot be free if he does not know that he is subject to necessity, because his freedom is always won in his never wholly successful attempts to liberate himself from necessity" (1958, 121). The quest to free life and labour from biological laws, from effort and pain, has the paradoxical outcome of subverting human life to the necessity of ceaseless activity and ultimately to more extreme forms of ecological necessity as the earth is consumed to the point of collapse.

"To be free we must submit", says Hamilton; this is "the antinomian quality of freedom" (2008, 219). Not self-aggrandizement but poverty of self brings freedom from the strictures of form. This freedom does not require defeat of the other, which would sooner or later require another battle; it is the freedom at the heart of our existence which preserves the harmony and beauty of the whole. Enriching ourselves through forms' unlimited potential does not exempt us from respecting their limitations—pushing out their boundaries merely distorts their form. Unrestrained freedom of markets, we noted, led to their collapse, but all forms of freedom are reduced when their boundaries are not observed.

Democracy is arguably the ideal political form, since unlike other political forms, it promotes liberty and equality and recognises certain basic rights. Amartya Sen calls the rise of democracy the pre-eminent development of the 20th century, and claims that in the general climate of world opinion democracy has achieved the status of being taken to be "generally right" (Sen, 1999). In this acceptance of democracy as a universally relevant system, which recognises it as a universal value, there is a major revolution in thinking, and this is one of the main contributions of the 20th century, according to Sen. While undoubtedly offering many benefits, the limitations of its form should not be overlooked in the West's ambition to impose it universally.

One of its achievements, Sen argues, is bringing about economic development. He attributes financial crises in some economies (including South Korea, Thailand, Indonesia) to undemocratic governance, "closely linked with the lack of transparency in business and the lack of public participation in reviewing financial arrangements" (*ibid.*). "Democratic capitalism is the best financial system", affirms George Bush in the wake of the biggest financial crisis to date. Yet Warren Buffett, ranked by *Forbes* (March 2008) as the richest person in the world, refers to these same systems as "financial weapons of mass destruction" (Buffett, 2008). The markets did not regulate themselves as economists claimed they would; the notion of self-regulation is an illusion when meaning is not understood.

Whilst not advocating Plato's ideal form of rule by philosopher kings, or suggesting democratic ideals be relinquished, I believe his awareness of the limitations of the democratic system (a system which failed his teacher), might be noted. "Knowledge of beauty and goodness", the result of "trial in the refiner's fire", he says (1956, 468-469), is the single most important requirement of a ruler. Only when the ego has been refined will knowledge be fully awakened and a person be ready to guide others. Such rulers would be "true lovers of knowledge" (*ibid.*) who would be guided by the higher good rather than by a desire to be popular and would not be susceptible to corruption. In this regard one thinks of great leaders like Mahatma Gandhi, Nelson Mandela and the Dalai Lama, "avatars of virtue" (Hamilton, 2008, 166), who exemplify the purest characteristics of the moral self—*adl* and *ihsan*, balance and compassion, *marifa* and *sabr*, knowledge and patience, central features of Sufism. At the source of the message of these moral exemplars is "a goodness of heart that transcends the decency of others," says Hamilton—a presence of goodness that "makes the heart so large that it embraces the world, so that everything lies within it" (Schopenhauer, cited Hamilton, 167). In a democracy, on the other hand, those whose language is most persuasive will eventually dominate politics, rather than those striving to govern well (Plato, 434).

As we have seen, beauty resides in the heart of forms, and this is certainly true of democracy, but the strident voice of ego is most likely to produce discord where harmony could prevail. And so there has been little evidence recently of the transparency and reviewing of financial arrangements by citizens which Sen considers one of the strengths of democracy, and no evidence to suggest that the interests of non-stakeholders and non-human stakeholders in particular are well represented. Ahmed draws our attention to the plight of minorities, tyrannised by the majority using democracy as its vehicle. As long as the majority group stays united along sectarian or ethnic lines, Ahmed believes, democracy could mean perpetual rule (1992). When power is jealously guarded and responses lack imagination and compassion, and tolerance and fairness are not universally practised, minorities become vulnerable. Lyotard reminds us that the state resorts to the "narrative of freedom" every time it assumes direct control of people, under the name of "the nation", in order to "point them down the path of progress" (1984, 32). He explains that modern liberal democracies construct political identity on the basis of a series of binary oppositions (we/them, citizen/noncitizen, legitimate/illegitimate), which effectively excludes or "others" some groups of people. Western countries grant rights to citizens—rights being dependent on citizenship—and regard noncitizens, that is, immigrants, those seeking asylum, and refugees, as "aliens" (Peters, 2002).

Neo-liberals argue that any way of organising a large and powerful democratic state is likely to produce serious inefficiencies. They infer that one ought to transfer many of the current functions of the state to the market and limit the state to the enforcement of basic property rights and liberties which can be more easily understood and brought under the control of ordinary citizens (*ibid.*). Evidence suggests, however, that the common good is not served by such a system. Large concentrations of private wealth and power imposed on populations without their consent are forces no more benign than other forms of governance. Capitalism's freedom is exploitative unless it is tempered by a sense of responsibility or curtailed by regulation and legislation. Legal mechanisms are not always in place to safeguard the common good, nor are they always effective, as we have seen.

Like political forms, forms of law often fall short of their purpose and as such are inadequate substitutes for moral law, which has no need of form to affirm its being. Not Moses who represents the outer law but Khidr[2], the 'Green prophet', the voice of the universal Self, is the archetype of the Sufi guide (Vaughan-Lee, 1997, 170). Khidr is not an abstract mystical figure, but an archetype of something hidden within ourselves—a natural aspect of our own divinity, something so ordinary that we overlook it. Yet to follow the way of Khidr, says Vaughan-Lee, is to awaken to our own natural way

---

[2]   Khidr (or Khadir) literally means green or a place with abundant green plantation. According to a hadith Khidr was named so because he sat over a barren white land and it turned green with plantation after (his sitting over it) (*Bukhari*, Anbiya, 29). It is also reported that since Khidr drank from a fountain in Paradise, every place he stepped on turned green (*Makdisi*, III, 78).

of being with God and with life (*ibid.*). Self-centred individual freedom as promoted by various forms of public entertainment, the commercial world and contemporary liberation movements (Berry, 1993) ignores this more important law and its prescription of mutual respect and assistance, which grow from knowledge and love. Dualistic thought has given rise to a perception of difference between the inner and outer law, but "the Sufi lives by the highest ethics" (Vaughan-Lee, 2000, 54) and understands that one law, whose operation he can observe throughout the cosmos (Nasr, 1981, 194), embraces all orders of creation.

The most important function of ratiocination, we remember, is discernment, its focus always on that which unifies rather than divides. So, finally, in this study advocating submission to the enriching potential of Quietness, it is appropriate to reflect on the importance of discernment in our expression, rather than accept freedom of speech and expression as our right. As Lyotard points out, uttering the word is an act of submission to the authority beyond the physical form with its forgotten history and its unknowable future, and in both respects the word will go beyond the knowledge and control of the user (1984, 131). Like all forms, it is never fully known or in our control; the Sufis have shown us that wine-drinking leads to intoxication, not to quenching. In the absence of discernment, 'free' speech leads to division and discord; in the absence of discernment, empathy and compassion are likely to be lacking.

Draw back your tongue, for your tongue is harmful (Rumi, *SPL*, 63)

We think, for example, of the turmoil surrounding Rushdie's *Satanic Verses*, and contrast it with the unifying effect of Rumi's sacred verses, now stronger than ever, despite the passage of time. At the time of the controversy, many in the West had little insight into how dearly Muslims revere the Prophet, the *insan-i-kamil* (the perfect person), the very mention of whose name elicits gestures and expressions of reverence, while radical Muslims did not fully appreciate the value attributed by the West to freedom of speech, expression and movement. The full impact of the book, the *fatwa* against the author and the burning of his book were also underestimated, according to Ahmed (1992). Deeply significant actions on both sides touched the rawest of nerves. There was little sign of dialogue, of balance and compassion. Egos on both sides were too great, issues too complex and bitterness too deep, says Ahmed. In our attempt to "make a life" for ourselves, and to make it "as exciting or impressive as we can make it", as Mathews believes moderns are inclined to do (2005, 63), we should be mindful of the consequences of our expression, and the power of words to harm or heal.

Words, like acts, born from spirit and body, cling to your skirt like your child, says Rumi (*SPL*, 106). For this reason, Hazrat Inayat Khan is said to have advised his students to reflect, before speaking, on the nature of the words they might use, and to refrain from words that did not reflect humility, charity and truthfulness. Schuon explains the reason for such an approach: "One has to be humble because the ego tends to think itself more than it is; one has to be charitable because the ego tends to love only itself, and one has to be truthful because the ego tends to prefer its own tastes and habits to the truth" (1959, 86). Without love and knowledge, words ring hollow, creating nothing but noise. Because our knowledge is always incomplete and the potential to cause harm exceedingly real, from a Sufi perspective, freedom of speech should never be regarded as a right, only ever as a gift, of words—sacred words, at the heart of which is the *logos*, the everlasting cosmic order whose contrasting aspects disclose an underlying unity; *kalam*, God's Word, the Word from which all life emanates (Rumi, *SPL*, 269). Rumi reminds us to look beyond the veils of form—"Take this poetry and tear it up, for meanings transcend words and wind and air" (*SPL*, 271)—and in seeking meaning we find that it is not revealed primarily by words with their potential for discord, but by the simplicity and quietness from which all words emerge. Only when the lips are sealed can we hear the Beloved speak. As we listen, separateness melts away.

Forms of knowledge, like forms of love, are veils concealing the reality of the impulse that inspired them, and this impulse, unlike its outer form, is ineffable. Despite Rumi's 70,000 impassioned verses, he is unable to capture fully the all-encompassing essence, the power and glory of what it is that he knows and loves. The Beloved can be reached only through the heart, when the wine of *fana* has been drunk and the intoxicated lover surrenders to His embrace. Only then does His face become real in the brightly polished mirror of the lover's heart. In his poetic account of the moth's seduction by the flame in *The Conference of the Birds*, Farid ud-din Attar conveys most poignantly many of Sufism's central themes; above all that form's hidden meaning cannot be conveyed but must be awakened in the heart:

> Moths gathered in a fluttering throng one night
> To learn the truth about the candle's light . . .
> A moth more eager than the one before
> Set out and passed beyond the palace door.
> He hovered in the aura of the fire,
> A trembling blur of timorous desire,
> Then headed back to say how far he'd been,
> And how much he had undergone and seen.
> The mentor said: 'you do not bear the signs
> Of one who's fathomed how the candle shines.'
> Another moth flew out—his dizzy flight
> Turned to an ardent wooing of the light;
> He dipped and soared, and in his frenzied trance
> Both Self and fire were mingled by his dance –
> The flame engulfed his wing-tips, body, head;
> His being glowed a fierce translucent red;
> And when the mentor saw that sudden blaze,
> The moth's form lost within the glowing rays,
> He said: 'He knows, he knows the truth we seek,
> That hidden truth of which we cannot speak.'
> To go beyond all knowledge is to find
> That comprehension which eludes the mind . . .
> No creature's Self can be admitted here
> Where all identity must disappear . . .
> Be nothing first! And then you will exist,
> You cannot live whilst life and self persist –
> Till you reach Nothingness you cannot see
> The Life you long for in eternity . . .
> Be still in selflessness and pass beyond
> All thoughts of good and evil; break this bond,
> And as it shatters you are worthy of
> Oblivion, the Nothingness of love.
> (Attar, 1984, 3987-4020)

Conclusion

At a time of widespread dissatisfaction despite affluence, general discord and division instead of harmony and cooperation, and thoughtless defacement of the manuscript of creation instead of creative interpretation of its signs and symbols so that its message of unity might be understood, we are reaching the point of *tawba*, the turning of the heart, and must consider the journey home. I have argued that this journey, 'going beyond form', as Rumi urges us to do, entails submission to the quietness from which a deeper understanding of reality might emerge. The commanding voice of ego must be stilled so that meaning can come to the fore.

Having critically analysed the fertile ground that has given rise to the recent surge in Rumi's popularity, and concluded that our obesogenic way of life is not only meaningless but harmful, I have argued that we need to recover an ethical ethos, an ethos inspired by heart rather than ego, so that we might progress beyond our romance with externality, which would have ego transform the entire world but not itself, to a deep, abiding love of simplicity. I have argued that the mystical approach, poetically rendered by Sufis centuries ago and more recently given new life, new names and forms as new needs arise and hearts are turned, has the potential to address the modern disconnect from the natural, the alienation from and exploitation of the body of the earth, which is an important aspect of our reality. In this connection I have explored Mathews' argument from realism, notwithstanding differences of form. I have elaborated Sufism's defining principle of *tawhid,* and while extensive reference to Rumi's 'Beloved' may, at first glance, also "evoke a naive metaphysics", I have emphasised, as Rumi does, that we should not be deceived by the limitations of names, since all names pertain only to certain aspects of one sacred reality. In an era of growing ecological awareness which has given rise to distinctive ecophilosophical forms, I have explained that Sufism entails knowledge of reality, Rumi's Beloved being the all-encompassing

Real, or, as Hazrat Inayat Khan claimed almost a century ago, 'all-inclusive nature', not in a pantheistic or panentheistic sense, but in accordance with *tawhid*'s unity of being. I have therefore argued that Sufism, with its meaningful approach to life, is indeed the message of the day, illuminating the complex issues of the day, as Pir-o-Murshid believed it did.

The issues of the day, I have claimed, are moral issues requiring an ethical response, such as is only possible when unselfconscious listening occurs so that intimate knowledge is gained and common ground established. Climate change is undoubtedly the issue of deepest concern, as well as, potentially, the strongest uniting force, offering unlimited opportunity for listening and for vision, for immersion in the harsh reality confronting others—for heartfelt 'encounter'. I have argued that finding an appropriate response requires us first to examine our own thoughts, actions and words, to consider the consequences of our choices and to accept responsibility for them. It requires us to distinguish between our wants and needs, to recognise those of others, and to temper our greed with humility and gratitude. I have urged that we re-imagine our response so as to minimise the harm we cause. Reimagining, I have insisted, means seeing with the eye of the heart since its unifying perspective accommodates all views, hence shedding of prejudice and assumption is necessary, creating a space in which 'fellow-feeling' and love might grow. Such re-imagining, I have said, must be deeply rational—'supralogical', as Schuon suggests; it will entail neither inventiveness nor fantasy, such as mysticism's critics suggest it might, but a recovery of meaning emerging from submission to the quietness concealed beneath the chaos on the surface. Responding appropriately, I have argued, will entail above all, the recovery of heart. Only when ego is stilled and we tune in to the soft voice within will the cooperation on which the flourishing of our interconnected systems depends become a reality.

I have argued, as Hamilton does, that we ignore this moral voice at our peril. Unlike Hamilton, however, I have not suggested that we need a new political philosophy or indeed a new philosophy, and have emphasised that all forms, including legal and political ones have their limitations which must be observed. Instead, I have advocated the *tawil*—the return of all things to the heart, as its infinite capacity alone can provide us with a glimpse of truth and a taste of the freedom we appear to crave.

I have argued that *tawil* transforms ordinary activities, making them meaningful acts of remembrance of the One's sacred reality, and that the Sufi way therefore exemplifies the meaningful life Hamilton envisages. *Tawil* transforms ordinary activities into "practices of invocation and response—ritual practices" that Mathews too believes we need, transforming existence into the 'art of being' and Art, thus conceived, as Coomaraswamy explains, is not about individual genius, but about effort and love. Every person therefore has the potential of becoming an artist, expressing love in every activity. Love and simplicity, not artifice, transform our activities into works of art in which rhythm, regularity and cooperation create harmony. The art of being, I have emphasised, is about maintaining harmony, first and foremost within one's own mind and body, so that flourishing, more generally, will not be compromised, or in Hazrat Inayat Khan's words, so that "the symphony of life can be preserved, a symphony whose beauty depends on rhythm, regularity and cooperation, and participation in which necessitates learning the art of life" (VIII, 56).

Becoming an instrument whose tone enhances the beauty of that symphony is, I have argued, a painful process and does not in any way constitute a refuge from the developmental journey of life, as Mathews and Wheeler suggest. I have insisted that annihilating the ego entails radical transformation in the course of which the heart is finely tuned, so that its creativity might contribute to harmony. I have argued that mystical union is not a retreat that short-circuits the project of life, nor is it a key ideological construct underpinning oppressive projects, such as Plumwood suggests it might be, and that mystical love neither induces social impotence nor pacifies, as Mathews claims, but rather enables the fullest potentiation that connection affords, as is reflected in Rumi's own creativity.

I have introduced, but not developed more fully, the process of *suluk*, the tuning of the heart. Its comprehensive pedagogy falls outside the scope of this book, but insofar as it has the potential to revitalise educational practices and in doing so, facilitate a reformation of society, it merits much greater attention, particularly in view of the pressing needs of the time, needs to which the Archbishop of Canterbury, Rowan Williams, refers in his address at *Rikkyo Gaukin University*. He makes the following point: "Just at the moment, in the wake of last year's financial crisis, people throughout the world are asking about what kinds of behaviour are life-giving and sustainable, now we have seen the effects of greedy, individualistic, self-absorbed and obsessional practice. More than ever we need educational practices and educational communities that open the door into other possibilities" (Williams, 2009). Religiously grounded educational institutions, he explains, have at their basis clear doctrinal commitments, and particular beliefs. Whilst recognising fully the valuable contribution made by these institutions, and the fact that "what distinguishes a Christian institution is not so much the doctrine as the outworking of it in the style and ethos of a community", I believe that non-doctrinal Sufism, which is a heart-centred system of mental culture could be a particularly powerful unifying force with a great gift to offer in that it too "rests its hopes and visions on the ultimate definition of love". Further research might reveal how Sufi teachings could best be fostered within education specifically and in society generally so that its vision of unity might be realised.

I have explored love's creative and reductive aspects, and since 'shedding' is central to the Sufi path, I have acknowledged that the journey home is fraught with risk as hazard is encountered. And though the outer form of Rumi's path of love holds exceptional appeal given its fashionable new look, and has been eagerly embraced, modern consumers may find its deeper meaning and the struggle and effort the search for it demands far less attractive. In a world that hides the face of the Beloved behind innumerable veils which it treats as realities, meaning may easily be overlooked. The meaningful life has few advocates, says Hamilton; perhaps too, as my observations would indicate, it has few followers, because those who persist in their search for meaning do not only experience the joy of finding, but suffer the heartache of not finding and the bewilderment of knowing yet not knowing. Like Sufis, longing to grasp the nothing at the heart of everything, they too must surrender, not to the ego with its strident voice and limited vision, but to the heart, whose single eye reveals the hidden face of creation that cannot be contained by any form. Answering the Beloved's call, they too must 'die for love' and become all heart, for the sake of the world.

Bibliography

ABS. (2002). Marriages and Divorces, Australia. Retrieved 17 April 2008 from http://www.abs.gov.au/Ausstats/abs

ABS. (2008). Australian crime: facts and figures. Retrieved 23 December 2008 from http://www.aic.gov.au/publications/facts/2006/01

Abu-Sway, M. (1998). "Towards an Islamic Jurisprudence of the Environment". Retrieved 6 April 2010 from http://www.iol.ie/~afifi/Articles/environment.htm.

AC Nielsen. (2006). "Shopping becomes hot pastime in China". *China* Daily, 21 September 2006. Retrieved 17 January 2008 from http://www.chinadaily.com.cn/china/2006-07/21/content_646678.htm.

Addas, C. (2002). "The experience and doctrine of love in Ibn 'Arabî". *Journal of the Muhyiddin Ibn 'Arabi Society XXXII*. Retrieved 2 March 2010 from http://www.ibnarabisociety.org/articles/addas1.html.

Adler, J., & Scelfo, J. (2006). "Finding and Seeking; Born in affluence, the baby-boomers were driven to ask Big Questions about fulfillment and the meaning of life. How their legacy has changed us". *Newsweek*, 18 September 2006, 148, 52.

Ahmed, A. S. (1992). *Postmodernism and Islam: Predicament and Promise*. London and New York: Routledge.

AHMF. (2008). "The Facts About Herpes". Retrieved 30 August 2008 from http://www.thefacts.com.au/?OVKEY=sti&OVRAW=sti&OVKWID=106296215041

Algül, H. "Islam as a Religion of Love and Peace". *The Fountain Magazine*, (70), July-August 2009. Retrieved 4 March 2010 from http://www.fountainmagazine.com/article.php?ARTICLEID=1038.

al-Hakim, S. (2006). "Ibn 'Arabî's Twofold Perception of Woman: Woman as Human Being and Cosmic Principle". *Journal of the Muhyiddin Ibn 'Arabi Society XXXIX*, 1-29. Retrieved 3 March 2010 from http://www.ibnarabisociety.org/articles/women.html.

Altay, K. "Muhammad: A Prophet for Our Time". *The Fountain Magazine*, (66), November-December 2008. Retrieved 2 March 2010 from http://www.fountainmagazine.com/article.php?ARTICLEID=975.

Amara, F. ABC Radio National News Broadcast. 15 August 2009.

Amesbury, R. (2007). "The virtues of belief: toward a non-evidentialist ethics of belief-formation". *International Journal for Philosophy of Religion* 63:1, 25-37.

Animals Asia Foundation. (2008). "Bear Bile Farming". Retrieved 18 May 2008 from http://www.animalsasia.org/index.php?module=2&menupos=7&lg=en.

Animals Australia. "Water, Drought and Animal Production". *The Voice for Animals*, May 2007. Retrieved 10 May 2008 from http://www.animalsaustralia.org/features/water_animal_production.php#_ftnref7.

———"Investigation: Live Animal Exports". *The Voice for Animals*. Retrieved 19 May 2008 from http://www.liveexport-indefensible.com/investigations/.

Animals' Voice. (2007). "Animals as Commodities". Retrieved 17 May 2008, from http://www.animalsvoice.com/sites/AniRitesAgenda/commfacts.html.

Anissian, Mahnaz. (2006). *Eros in Sufism: Journey to mystical love* (Unpublished PhD thesis). Pacifica Graduate Institute, US.

ANZCCART. (2006). "Draize Eye Irritancy Test". *Humane Science*. Retrieved 23 April 2008 from https://www.adelaide.edu.au/ANZCCART/humane/Draize.html.

Arberry, A. J. (1942). *An Introduction to the History of Sufism*. London: Longman Green.

———(1961). *Discourses of Rumi*. London: John Murray.

Arendt, H. (1958). *The Human Condition*: Chicago: Chicago University Press.

Armitage, J., & Graham, P. (2003). "Dromoeconomics: Towards a Political Economy of Speed". Retrieved 17 July 2008 from www.philgraham.net/Dromo.pdf.

Aslandoğan, Y. "Fasting in Ramadan and Developing Self-Control". *The Fountain Magazine*, (65), September-October 2008. Retrieved 5 March 2010 from http://www.fountainmagazine.com/article.php?ARTICLEID=946.

Astin, A. W. (2004). "Academic Spirituality". *Spirituality in Higher Education*, I, 1, 8-12.

Athar, S. (2009). "Human Longing for Spirituality". *Sufism Journal* IX, 3. Retrieved 6 March 2010 from http://www.sufismjournal.org/psychology/psychologylonging.html.

———(2010). "Inner Jihad—Striving Toward Harmony". *The Sufism Journal* X, 3. Retrieved 7 March 2010 from http://www.sufismjournal.org/practice/practicejihad.html.

Atlas Society. (2007). "The Virtue of Selfishness". Retrieved 25 March 2008 from http://www.objectivistcenter.org/cth-406-FAQ_Virtue_Selfishness.aspx.

Attar, F. (1984). *The Conference of the Birds*. Darbandi, A. & Davis, D. (Trans.). London, Penguin Classics.

Aurelius, M. (1964). *Meditations*. Staniforth, M. (Trans.). London: Penguin.

Aydın, H. "Connection, Always and Everywhere". *The Fountain Magazine*, (71), September-October 2009. Retrieved 1 March 2010 from http://www.fountainmagazine.com/article.php?ARTICLEID=1062.

Aydın, N. "Infinity: A Window on Divinity". *The Fountain Magazine*, (70), July-August 2009. Retrieved 5 March 2010 from http://www.fountainmagazine.com/article.php?ARTICLEID=1044.

Barks, C. (3 September 2007). "Tribute to Rumi". ABC National Radio.

Barlow, J. P. (2001). "The Pursuit of Emptiness: Why Americans Have Never Been A Happy Bunch". Retrieved 4 April 2008 from http://forbes.com/asap/2001/1203/096.html.

Beadnell, B., Morrison, D., & Wilsdon, A. (2005). "Condom Use, Frequency of Sex, and Number of Partners: Multidimensional Characterization of Adolescent Sexual Risk-Taking". *Journal of Sex Research*, 42, 192-202.

Beaver, E. E. (1998). "The adjustment of overseas students at a tertiary institution in New Zealand". *New Zealand Journal of Educational Studies*, 33, 167-179.

Behar, R. (1991). "The Thriving Cult of Greed and Power". *Time Magazine*, 6 May 1991, 50.

Beinssen-Hesse, S., & Rigby, K. (1996). *Out of the Shadows: Contemporary German Feminism*. Carlton South: Melbourne University Press.

Benedikt, M. (2007). *God is the Good we Do: Theology of Theopraxy*. New York: Bottino Books.

Bennett, J. B. (2004). "Academic Spirituality". *Spirituality in Higher Education*, I, 1, 7.

Benyus, J. "Biomimicry". In *Nature's Operating Instructions - The True Biotechnologies*. Ausubel, K., & Harpignies, J. P. (Eds.). San Francisco: Sierra Club Books, 2004

Berger, C. "Australia Takes Gold in Population Growth". *The World Today*, 23 September 2009, 13.

Berry, W. (1977). *The Unsettling of America: Culture and Agriculture*. Berkeley: University of California Press.

_____(1983). *Standing by Words*. San Francisco: North Point Press.

_____(1993). *Sex, Economy, Freedom & Community*. New York: Pantheon Books.

_____(2001). *Life is a Miracle - An Essay Against Modern Superstition*. Washington, D.C.: Counterpoint.

Berube, C. T. (2004). "Are Standards Preventing Good Teaching?". *The Clearing House,* Washington, 2004, 77 (6), 264-268.

Bohm, D. (2003). *The Essential David Bohm*. Nichol, L. (Ed.). London: Routledge.

Born Free USA. (2007). "Little Shops of Sorrows". Retrieved 17 May 2008 from http://www.api4animals.org/a5a2_facts.php.

Bosco, H. (1976). *Le Reel et l'Imaginaire dans l'Oeuvre d'Henri Bosco*. Nice: Jose Corti.

Brady, V. "How to reinvent the world: The hope of being true to the earth". *Monash Colloquy*, November 2006 (12), 103-113.

Braine, D. (1998). "Negative theology". *Routledge Encyclopedia of Philosophy*. E. Craig (Ed.). London: Routledge. Retrieved 5 February 2010 from http://www.rep.routledge.com/article/KO53SECT1.

Branigan, T. (13 May 2008). "This is not a natural disaster - this is done by humans". Retrieved 21 May 2008 from http://www.guardian.co.uk/world/2008/may/13/china.naturaldisasters3.

Brennan, A. (1998). "Environmental Ethics". In *Routledge Encyclopedia of Philosophy*. E. Craig (Ed.). London: Routledge. Retrieved 10 March 2010 from http://www.rep.routledge.com/article/LO20SECT.

Brennan, T. (2002). "Forms, Platonic". In *Routledge Encyclopedia of Philosophy*. E. Craig (Ed.). London: Routledge. Retrieved 6 October 2009 from http://www.rep.routledge.com/article/A131SECT1.

Brewer, S. "Respect for 'these people'". *Denver Post*, 13 July 2002, 5.

Brigandt, I. (2004). "The Instinct Concept of the Early Konrad Lorenz". Retrieved 8 May 2008 from http://www.ualberta.ca/~brigandt/instinct.pdf.

Brown University Health Education. (2008). "BCPs". Retrieved 1 September 2008 from http://www.brown.edu/Student_Services/Health_Services/Health_Education/sexual_health/ssc/bcps.htm.

Bruthiaux, P. (2000). "In a nutshell: persuasion in the spatially constrained language of advertising". *Language & Communication*, 20, 297-310.

Buckle, C. (2002). *African Tears: The Zimbabwe Land Invasions*. Johannesburg: Jonathan Ball Publishers.

Buffett, W. ABC Radio National News Broadcast. 25 September 2008.

Burns, D. J. (2007). *Self-Construction through Consumption Activities: An Analysis and Review of Alternatives*. Wilmington, US: ISI Books.

Burnside, J. (2005). *Word Watching: Field Notes from an Amateur Philologist*. New York: Avalon Publishing Group Inc.

Burris, J. "Society is cursed with four-letter words". *McClatchy - Tribune Business News*. Washington, 26 November 2007, 11.

Bush, G. W. ABC Radio National News Broadcast. 25 September 2008.

Callon, M., & Bell, G. (1994). "The Changing Nature and Forms of Knowledge: A Review". *STI Review*, 14, 59-117.

Campbell, W. K., Bonacci, A. M., Shelton, J., Exline, J. J., & Bushman, B. J. (2004). "Psychological Entitlement: Interpersonal Consequences and Validation of a Self-Report Measure". *Journal of Personality Assessment*, 83, 29-45.

Campbell, W. K., Manne, A., & Mackay, H. *Narcissism*. ABC Radio National. 6 April 2008.

Can, S. (2005). *Fundamentals of Rumi's Thought*. Saritoprak, Z. (Trans.). New Jersey: Light.

Cardoso, S. H. (2007). "Hardwired for Happiness". *Cerebrum 2007: Emerging ideas in brain science*, 169-184.

Carone, G. R. (1998). "Plato and the Environment". *Environmental Ethics*, 20(3), 115-133.

Carroll, J. (2008). "Ego and Soul with John Carroll". La Trobe University (Melbourne) podcast.

Çelebi, M. (2009). "The Tale of a Photon". *The Fountain Magazine* (71), September-October 2009. Retrieved 11 March 2010 from http://www.fountainmagazine.com/article.php?ARTICLEID=1060.

Çelik, F. (2009). "Women and the Qur'anic Prescriptions". *The Fountain Magazine* (66), November-December 2008. Retrieved 17 March 2010 from http://www.fountainmagazine.com/article.php?ARTICLEID=961.

Center for Reduction of Religious-Based Conflict (2007). Retrieved 14 July 2007 from http://www.center2000.org/.

Ceran, Y. (2010). "Renewers". *The Fountain Magazine* (74), March-April 2010. Retrieved 3 May 2010 from http://www.fountainmagazine.com/article.php?ARTICLEID=1116.

Chittick, W. C. (1983). *The Sufi path of Love: The Spiritual teachings of Rumi*. New York: State University of New York Press.

_____(1989). *Ibn al-Arabi's Metaphysics of Imagination: The Sufi Path of Knowledge*. New York: State University of New York Press.

_____(1994). *Imaginal Worlds - Ibn al-Arabi and the Problem of Religious Diversity*. New York: State University of New York Press.

_____(2003). "Mysticism in Islam". Retrieved 1 June 2009 from http://meti.byu.edu/mysticism_chittick.html.

_____(2004). *Me & Rumi: The Autobiography of Shams-i Tabrizi*. Louisville, Kentucky: Fons Vitae.

Choueiri, Y. (1998). "Islamic Fundamentalism". In *Routledge Encyclopedia of Philosophy*. E. Craig (Ed.). London: Routledge. Retrieved 16 August 2007 from http://www.rep.routledge.com/article/H007SECT2.

Chryssavgis, J. "The Earth as Sacrament: Insights from Orthodox Christian Theology and Spirituality". In *The Oxford Handbook of Religion and Ecology*, Gottlieb, R. S. (Ed.), 2006, New York: Oxford University Press, 92-114.

Cixous, H. *Encounter: Franz Kafka*. ABC Radio National. 21 November 1999.

Clark, J. (2001). "Fulfilling our Potential: Ibn 'Arabi's understanding of man in a contemporary context". *Journal of the Muhyiddin Ibn 'Arabi Society XXX*.

Retrieved 29 April 2010 from http://www.ibnarabisociety.org/articles/clark.html.

Cliath, A. G. (2007). "Seeing Shades: Ecological and Socially Just Labelling". *Organization and Environment*, 20, 413-439.

Clifford, R. (2008). "What Is 'Good' Teaching?" *Foreign Language Annals*, 41.

Clyne, M. (2008). "In the beginning was the word". Retrieved 8 November 2008 from http://www.languageseducation.com/newsl080619.pdf

Coates, P. (1999). "Ibn 'Arabī and Modern Thought". *Journal of the Muhyiddin Ibn 'Arabi Society XXV*. Retrieved 29 April 2010 from http://www.ibnarabisociety.org/articles/ibnarabimodernthought.html

Coleman, P. C. (2007). *Ungraspable Nature - An Eco-Exploration of Indefinition* (Unpublished PhD thesis). Melbourne: Monash University.

Coomaraswamy, A. K. (1969). *Introduction to Indian Art*. Delhi: Munshiram Manoharlal.

Cooper, D. (1997). *God is a Verb: Kabbalah and the Practice of Mystical Judaism*. New York: Riverhead Books.

Corbin, H. (1969). *Creative Imagination in the Sufism of Ibn 'Arabi*. Manheim, R. (Trans.). London: Routledge & Kegan Paul.

Cornell, V. (2004). "Practical Sufism: An Akbarian Foundation for a Liberal Theology of Difference". *Journal of the Muhyiddin Ibn 'Arabi Society XXXVI*. Retrieved 11 March 2010 from http://www.ibnarabisociety.org/journals.html.

Cudworth, E. (2005). *Developing Ecofeminist Theory:The Complexity of Difference*. University of East London, UK: Palgrave Macmillan.

D'Adamo, A. (2004). *Science Without Bounds: A Synthesis of Science, Religion and Mysticism*. Retrieved 3 August 2008, from http://www.AdamFord.com.

Dağlı, C. K. (2007). "The Time of Science and the Sufi Science of Time". *Journal of the Muhyiddin Ibn 'Arabi Society* (41). Retrieved 6 November 2009 from http://www.ibnarabisociety.org/articles/timeofscience.html.

Dastur, F. "World, Flesh, Vision". In *Chiasms: Merleau-Ponty's Notion of Flesh*. Evans, F., & Lawlor, L. (Eds.). SUNY Press, New York, 2000, 31-72.

Dawkins, R. (1989). *The Selfish Gene*. UK: Oxford University Press.

Day, E. (2008). "Legal drug craze is new killer". Retrieved 4 April 2008 from http://www.guardian.co.uk/world/2008/feb/10/usa.

De Botton, A. (2000). *The Consolations of Philosophy*. London: Penguin.

Dewey, J. (1917). *Creative Intelligence: Essays in the Pragmatic Attitude*. New York: Holt.

Dhir, C. C. (2005). "The value of language: Concept, perspectives, and policies." *Corporate Communications*, 10(4), 358-382.

Dittmar, H. (2007). "The cost of consumers and the 'cage within': The impact of the material 'good life' and 'body perfect' ideals on individuals' identity and well-being." *Psychological Inquiry,* 18(1), 23-31.

Eberstadt, M. (2008). "The Vindication of Humanae Vitae". *First Things,* 2008, 185, 35-42.

Eckersley, R. (2004). *The Green State: Rethinking Democracy and Sovereignty.* Cambridge, Massachusetts: MIT Press.

El Guindi, F. (2000). *Veil: Modesty, Privacy and Resistance.* New York: Berg.

Eliade, M. (1987). *The Sacred and the Profane: The Nature of Religion.* London: Harcourt Brace.

El-Khazari, K. "Sufism and the Struggle within Islam". *Sufi News and Sufism World Report,* 7 July 2006. Retrieved 18 November 2009 from http://sufinews.com/2006/11/sufism-and-struggle-within-islam.html.

Elliott, A. (2008). *Making the Cut.* Chicago: University of Chicago Press.

Elliott, E. J., Payne, J., & Morris, A. (2008). "Fetal alcohol syndrome: a prospective national surveillance study". *Archives of Disease in Childhood,* 93, 732-737.

Emerson, R. W. *Essays (Second Series) 1, The Poet.* Retrieved 21 September 2009 from http://www.uvm.edu/~hag/eng330/rwemerson_poet.html.

_____*Nature,* 1. Retrieved 11 March 2008 from http://www.vcu.edu/engweb/transcendentalism/authors/emerson/essays/naturetext.html#Int

_____(1907). *Addresses and Essays.* London: Watts & Co.

Emilsson, E. K. (1998). "Plotinus". In *Routledge Encyclopedia of Philosophy.* E. Craig (Ed.). London: Routledge. Retrieved 10 July 2008 from http://www.rep.routledge.com/article/A090SECT3.

Epley, N., Caruso, E., & Bazerman, M. H. "When Perspective Taking Increases Taking: Reactive Egoism in Social Interaction". *Journal of Personality and Social Psychology,* November 2006, 91(5), 872-889.

Ernst, C. (2008). "Mystical Language and the Teaching Context in the Early Lexicons of Sufism". In *Mysticism and Language,* Katz, S. T. (Ed.). New York: Oxford University Press, 189-200.

(2009). "Rumi on the Sound of the Human Voice". *Sacred Spaces: A Journey with the Sufis of the Indus,* 21-40. Retrieved 28 April 2010 from http://www.unc.edu/~cernst/articles.htm.

(2009). "Sufism, Islam, and Globalization in the Contemporary World: Methodological Reflections on a Changing Field of Study". *In Memoriam: The 4th Victor Danner Memorial Lecture, Bloomington.* Retrieved 18 March 2010 from http://www.unc.edu/~cernst/pdf/danner.pdf.

Esirgen, O. (30 March 2007). "UNESCO's International Rumi Year Celebrates the Great Poet/Thinker". Retrieved 16 August 2008 from http://www.observercyprus.com/observer/NewsDetails.aspx?id=1349.

Farrelly, E. (2007). *Blubberland The Dangers of Happiness*. Sydney: New South.

Flanery, P. D. (24 October 2008). "The Fame Formula". *The Times Literary Supplement* 5508, 24 October 2008, 31.

Foltz, R. C. "Islam". In *The Oxford Handbook of Religion and Ecology*, Gottlieb, R. S. (Ed.), 2006. New York: Oxford University Press, 207-219.

FOTEA. (2005). "Immigration, Population and Environment". Friends of the Earth Australia position paper, 14 May 2005.

Frankl, V. E. (1984). *Man's Search for Meaning*. New York: Washington Square Press.

Fur Free Alliance. (2007). "Facts about the Fur Trade". Retrieved 11 May 2008 from http://infurmation.com/facts.php.

Gaita, R. Interview with Raymond Gaita. ABC Radio National, 5 March 2008.

Garnaut, R. (2007). "Will climate change bring an end to the Platinum Age?". Retrieved 30 March 2008 from www.garnautreview.org.au.

_____(2008). "Climate Change and Australian Economic Reform". Retrieved 30 March 2008 from www.garnautreview.org.au.

Gioia, D. (2008). "Critical Convictions: The Impoverishment of American Culture". *American Record Guide*, 71, 45-48.

Giroux, H. A. (1984). "Rethinking the Language of Schooling". *Language Arts*, 61, 33-40.

Gluek, M. (2009). "Eco Asceticism". *Encounter*. Retrieved 8 December 2009 from http://www.abc.net.au/rn/encounter/ /2009/2640219.htm#transcript.

Gorenfeld, J. (2008). *Bad Moon Rising*. California: PoliPoint Press.

Gottlieb, R. S. (Ed.). (2006). *The Oxford Handbook of Religion and Ecology*. New York: Oxford University Press.

Graham, P. (2006). *Hypercapitalism: New media, language, and social perceptions of value*. New York: Peter Lang.

Gregory, N. (1999). "Do fish feel pain?". Retrieved 17 May 2008 from http://www.adelaide.edu.au/ANZCCART/.

Griego, T. (2002). "Why do words divide people?". Denver Post, 15 July 2002, B, 1.

Gril, D. (1997). "There is no Word in the World that does not Indicate His Praise". *Journal of the Muhyiddin Ibn 'Arabi Society XXI*. Retrieved 30 September 2009 from http://www.ibnarabisociety.org/articles/indicatehis-praise.html.

Gülen, F. (2001). *Sufism-1, Emerald Hills of the Heart*. (E-book). Retrieved from http://en.fgulen.com/sufism-1.

_____(2007). *Sufism-2, Emerald Hills of the Heart*. (E-book). Retrieved from http://en.fgulen.com/sufism-2.html.

_____"Our World and Its Inherently Exquisite Mystery". *The Fountain Magazine* (72), November-December 2009. Retrieved 20 March 2010 from http://www.fountainmagazine.com/article.php?ARTICLEID=1071.

_____"Fleeting Storms, Perennial Breezes". *The Fountain Magazine* (73), January-February 2010. Retrieved 12 May 2010 from http://www.fountainmagazine.com/article.php?ARTICLEID=1091.

Haigh, G. (2008). *The Racket*. Carlton South, Victoria: Melbourne University Press.

Hakim, S. (2004). "Unity of Being in Ibn 'Arabî - A Humanist Perspective". *Journal of the Muhyiddin Ibn 'Arabi Society, XXXVI*. Retrieved 2 April 2010 from http://www.ibnarabisociety.org/articles/unityofbeing.html.

Hall-Schwarz, R. "A qualitative study of the lived experiences of women with advanced degrees who delayed marriage and motherhood until the age of 35 and older". Dissertation Abstracts International Section A: Humanities and Social Sciences, 66 (12-A), 2006, 4557.

Hamilton, C. (2008). *The Freedom Paradox: Towards a Post-Secular Ethics*. Sydney: Allen and Unwin.

Hamilton, C., & Denniss, R. (2005). *Affluenza: when too much is never enough*. Sydney: Allen & Unwin.

Hamilton, C. (2010). *Requiem for a Species: Why we Resist the Truth about Climate Change*. London, Washington D.C.: Earthscan.

Hardie, E., & Buzwell, S. (2006). "Finding Love Online". *Australian Journal of Emerging Technologies and Society*, 4(1), 1-14.

Hawley, J. (2003). "Crowded Land of Giants". Retrieved 16 January 2008 from http://www.smh.com.au/articles/2003/08/26/1061663776473.html.

Hegna, K., & Rossow, I. "What's love got to do with it? Substance use and social integration for young people categorized by same-sex experience and attractions". *Journal of Drug Issues*, 37(2), Spring 2007, 229-256.

Heidegger, M. (1959). *On the Way to Language*, Hertz, P. (Trans.). New York: Harper & Row.

_____(1971). *Poetry, Language, Thought*, Hofstadter, A. (Trans.). New York: Harper & Row.

Hick, J. (1993). *God and the Universe of Faiths*. Oxford: Oneworld Publications.

Hillier, L., Harrison, L., & Warr, D. (1998). "Negotiating competing discourses about safe sex". *Journal of Adolescence*, 21, 15-29.

Holgate, S. (2005). "Persian Poet Rumi Conquers America". Retrieved 22 November 2008 from http://www.america.gov/st/washfile-english/2005/March/20 050315183204ndyblehs0.8505365.html.

Holloway, R. (2009). *Between the Monster and the Saint*. Edinburgh: Canongate Books.

Houghton, J., & Sheehan, P. (2000). "A Primer on the Knowledge Economy". Centre for Strategic Economic Studies, Victoria University. Retrieved 27 June 2008 from http://www.cfses.com/documents/knowledgeeconprimer.pdf.

Howard, A. R. (2006). "In Moral Labor". *First Things*, 161, New York, 4.

Humane Society US. (2007). "Fur-Free Campaign". Retrieved 11 May 2008 from http://www.hsus.org/furfree/news/fur_labeling_bill_introduced.html.

Hurd, G. (1996). "A.D.D. The Natural Approach". *Total Health*, 18 (5), Woodland Hills, 11.

Hurley, D. (2005). "Divorce Rate: It's Not as High as You Think". Retrieved 17 April 2008 from http://www.divorcereform.org/nyt05.html.

Inati, S. C. (1998). "Epistemology in Islamic philosophy". In *Routledge Encyclopedia of Philosophy*. E. Craig (Ed.). London: Routledge. Retrieved 23 June 2008 from http://www. rep.routledge.com/article/H019SECT1.

James, C. (2008). "Wisdom needed to face new world order". Retrieved 15 October 2008 from http://www.nzherald.co.nz/business/news/article. cfm?c_id=3&objectid=10537314

Jameson, F. (1990). *Postmodernism, or, the Cultural Logic of Late Capitalism*. Durham: Duke University Press.

Joas, H. (1996). *The Creativity of Action*, Gaines, J. & Keast, P. (Trans.). Oxford: Polity Press.

Johnston, R. (1998). "The Changing Nature and Forms of Knowledge: A Review". Retrieved 25 June 2008 from http://www.dest.gov.au/archive/highered/eippubs/eip98-16/98-16.

Jones, J. M. (2006). "From Racial Inequality to Social Justice". *Journal of Social Issues,* 62(4), 885-909.

Kafka, F. (1964). *The Diaries of Franz Kafka*. Brod, M. (Ed.). London: Penguin.

Keen, S. (2001). *Debunking Economics - The Naked Emperor of the Social Sciences*: Sydney: Pluto Press.

Keith, D. W. "Climate Engineers", ABC Radio National, 6 April 2008.

_____(2008). "Engineering the Planet: Climate Change Science and Policy" Retrieved 6 April 2008 from http://www.ucalgary.ca/~keith/papers/89.Keith. EngineeringThePlanet.p.pdf.

Kelley, D. (2007). "I bet you look good on the salesfloor". *Journal of Strategic Marketing,* 15(1), 53-63.

Kellner, I. (2007). "Americans' real national pastime is shopping". Retrieved 5 May 2008 from http://www.marketwatch.com/News/aspx?guid={DE69A406.

Kellow, J. T. "Does a college degree matter? Tests, surveys are unreliable, unrealistic". *Atlanta Journal*, 12 May 2008, 11.

Khan, A. S. "Translation of Sufi Poetry". *The Fountain Magazine* (69), May-June 2009. Retrieved 15 May 2010 from http://www.fountainmagazine.com/article.php?ARTICLEID=1020.

Khan, H. I. (1960). *Gayan, Vadan, Nirtan*. London: Barrie and Rockliff.

_____(2004). *The Sufi Message, Volumes I - XIII*. Delhi: Motilal Banarsidass Publishers

Khan, M. M. (1971). *Pages in the Life of a Sufi*. Surrey: Sufi Publishing Company.

Khoromi, S. (2010). "The Neurochemistry of Love". *The Journal of the Sufi Psychology Association*, 7 (2), 2010, 11-17.

Kinney, J. (1994). "Pop and Circumstance". *Gnosis Magazine* (32), Summer 1994, 9-12.

Kohn, R. (2007). *The Spirit of Things* . Retrieved 12 November 2007 from http://www.rachaelkohn.com/.

Koran, L. (2003). "Antidepressant helps alleviate compulsive shopping disorder, Stanford researchers find". Retrieved 17 January 2008 from www.eureka-lert.org/pub_releases/2003-07/sumc-aha071603.php.

Kübler-Ross, E. (1969). *On Death and Dying*. New York: Macmillan.

Lampman, J. (2007). "Sufism may be powerful antidote to Islamic extremism". *The Christian Science Monitor*, 5 December 2007, 13.

Lashlie, C. (2007). *He'll be OK: Growing Gorgeous Boys into Good Men*. Auckland: Harpercollins.

Leaky Homes Action Group. (2005). "Toxic rot in homes linked to sickness". Retrieved 13 May 2008 from http://www.leakyhomesactiongroup.org.nz/.

Leckey, M. "The Sufi Heidegger". Paper presented at the Sufi Movement Winter School, July 2009, Melbourne.

Lederer, E. M. (2007). "UN Expert Calls Biofuel 'Crime Against Humanity'". *Live Science*, 27 October 2007, 11.

Lings, M. (1975). *What is Sufism?* London: George Allen & Unwin Ltd.

Long, S., ABC Radio National Report, 19 September 2008.

Lonsdale, T. (2007). "Pet Food Kills Pets". *Nexus*, October-November 2007, 5.

Lovelock, J. (2007). *The Revenge of Gaia: Why the Earth is Fighting Back and How We Can Still Save Humanity*. London: Penguin Books.

Lusthaus, D. (1998). "Chinese Buddhist Philosophy". In *Routledge Encyclopedia of Philosophy*. E. Craig (Ed.). London: Routledge. Retrieved 16 March 2008 from http://www. rep.routledge.com/article/G002SECT9.

Lyotard, J.-F. (1984). *The Postmodern Condition: A Report on Knowledge*. Bennington, G. & Massumi, B. (Trans.). Minneapolis: University of Minnesota Press

Macauley, D. (Ed.). (1996). *Minding Nature: The Philosophers of Ecology*. New York: Guilford Press.

Magonet, J. ABC Radio National interview, 15 July 2007.

Mahmood, S. B. "The Holy Qur'an and Dirac's Theory of Pairs". *The Fountain Magazine* (68), March-April 2009. Retrieved 29 April 2010 from http://www.fountainmagazine.com/article.php?ARTICLEID=1000.

Maiden, M. "Amid the market mayhem, lessons must be learned". *Quarterly Essay* September 2008, 31.

Manne, A. "Love & Money: The Family and the Free Market". *Quarterly Essay*, March 2008, 29.

Mansell, W. "Guidance for over-7s to combat allure of celebrity". *The Times Educational Supplement*, (4808), October 2008, 8.

Mansfield, H. (2006). *Manliness*. New York: Vail-Ballou Press.

Margenau, H., & Varghese, R. A. (Eds.). (1992). *Cosmos, Bios, Theos*. Illinois: Open Court.

Marker, R. L., & Smith, W. J. (2004). "Words, Words, Words". Retrieved 31 January 2008 from http://www.internationaltaskforce.org/fctwww.htm.

Marshall, G. (1998). "Theories of Pleasure". In *Routledge Encyclopedia of Philosophy*. E. Craig (Ed.). London: Routledge. Retrieved 16 March 2008 from http://www. rep.routledge.com/article/VO25SECT2.

Mascaro, J. (Trans.). (1973). *The Dhammapada: The Path of Perfection*. London: Penguin.

Masson, J. (1996). *When Elephants Weep: The Emotional Lives of Animals*. London: Vintage.

Mathews, F. (1998). "Ecological Worldviews". In *Routledge Encyclopedia of Philosophy*. E. Craig (Ed.). London: Routledge. Retrieved 10 April 2008 from http://www. rep.routledge.com/article/NO17SECT3.

_____(2003). *For Love of Matter: A Contemporary Panpsychism*. Albany: State University of New York Press.

_____(2005). *Reinhabiting Reality: Towards a Recovery of Culture*. Sydney: University of New South Wales Press.

Mayo Clinic Report. (2006). "Wrinkle creams". Retrieved 11 September 2008 from http://www.cnn.com/HEALTH/library/SN/00010.html.

McCord, W. (2003). *Earthbabies: Ancient Wisdom for Modern Times*. Gilbert, Arizona: Epona Publishing.

Mcgee, P. (2007). "U.S. kids learn parents' language". McClatchy-Tribune Business News, Washington, 20 December 2007, 5.

McGraw-Hill. "Oral Contraceptives - Adverse Effects". *Access Medicine*, September 2008: 40.

Merchant, C. (1992). *Radical Ecology: The Search for a Livable World*. New York, London: Routledge.

Merleau-Ponty, M. (1962). *Phenomenology of Perception*. London: Routledge.

Miller, D. T. (1999). "The norm of self-interest". *American Psychologist* 54, (12), 1053-1060.

Milner, A. (2000). "Asia Consciousness and Asian Values". Retrieved 20 October 2008 from http://www.anu.edu.au/asianstudies/data/Asia_Consciousness_and_Asian_Values.pdf.

Mofid, K. "Globalisation for the Common Good". ABC Radio National, 2 March 2008.

Montaigne, M. d. (1991). *The Complete Essays*. Screech, M. A. (Trans.). London: Penguin.

Moore, E. (2006). "Plotinus". Retrieved 17 March 2008 from http://www.iep.utm.edu/p/plotinus.htm#SSH2c.iii.

Moore, T. (22 May 2008). "A Real Education Revolution". Retrieved 26 May 2008 from http://www.abc.net.au/education/s2252365.htm.

Morris, M. N., Misra, S., & Sibary, S. (2008). "Global Fattening: Designing Effective Approaches to Reducing Obesity". *Journal of American Academy of Business*, (12), 2, 249-256.

Moulana, S. S. & Maizebhandari, S. (2010). "The Purpose of Sufi Training". *The Sufism Journal*, 9, 4.

Muhaiyaddeen, M. R. B. (2002). *Islam and World Peace*. Philadelphia: Fellowship Press.

Murata, S., & Chittick, W. C. (1994). *The Vision of Islam*. St. Paul, Minnesota: Paragon House.

Mutlu, S.. "The Carrot: A Source of Healing". *The Fountain Magazine*, (73), January-February 2010. Retrieved 18 April 2010 from http://www.fountain-magazine.com/article.php?ARTICLEID=1098

Nash, J. D. (1999). *Binge no more: Your guide to overcoming disordered eating*. Oakland, California: New Harbinger Publications.

Nasr, S. H. (1968). *Man and Nature: The Spiritual Crisis of Modern Man*. London: George Allen & Unwin.

———(1981). *Knowledge and the Sacred: The Gifford Lectures*. New York: Crossroad

———(1998). "Mystical Philosophy in Islam". In *Routledge Encyclopedia of Philosophy*. E. Craig (Ed.). London: Routledge. Retrieved 17 August 2007 from http://www. rep.routledge.com/article/HOO4SECT6.

Nicholls, V., & Gray, T. (2007). "The role of stillness and quiet when developing human/nature relationships". *Australian Journal of Outdoor Education*, (11) 1, 21.

Nicholson, R. A. (1952). *Selected Poems from Rumi's Divani Shamsi Tabriz*. Cambridge: Cambridge University Press.

_____(2003). *The Mathnawi of Jalalu'ddin Rumi, Translations & Commentary*, 3rd ed. (I-VI). New Delhi: Adam Publishers.

Nietzsche, F. (1996). *Human, All Too Human*. Hollingdale, R. J. (Trans.). Cambridge: Cambridge University Press.

Northcott, M. "The Ethics of Climate Change". ABC Radio National, 26 March 2008.

_____(2007). *A Moral Climate: The Ethics of Global Warming*. London: Darton, Longman & Todd.

Norton, A. (2005). "The Mystic Social Scientist". Retrieved 22 September 2009 from http://www.cis.org.au/Policy/spring05/polspr05-8.htm.

Nursi, B. S. (1920). *The Flashes: Letters, Seeds of Reality*. (E-book). Retrieved from http://www.risaleinur.us/.

O'Dea, J. A., & Abraham, S. (1999). "Onset of disordered eating attitudes and behaviors in early adolescence: Interplay of pubertal status, gender, weight, and age". *Adolescence*, 34, 136, 671-679.

Oldmeadow, H. (2003). "The Firmament Sheweth His Handiwork: Re-awakening a Religious Sense of the Natural Order". Introduction to *Seeing God Everywhere: Essays on Nature and the Sacred*, McDonald, B. (Ed.). Bloomington, World Wisdom, 1-22.

_____(2007). "The Comparative Study of Eastern and Western Metaphysics: A Perennialist Perspective". *Sophia: International Journal for Philosophy of Religion, Metaphysical Theology and Ethics*, 46(1), 49-64.

Olfman, S. (Ed.). (2005). *Childhood lost: How American culture is failing our kids*. Westport, Connecticut: Praeger Publishers.

Oneill, J. (2001). "Self-interest". In *Routledge Encyclopedia of Philosophy*. E. Craig (Ed.). London: Routledge. Retrieved 3 May 2008 from http://www. rep. routledge.com/article/L141SECT2.

Orr, A. "Too complex to regulate?". Economic Policy Institute, 8 June 2009. Retrieved 15 September 2009 from http://www.epi.org/analysis.

Orwell, G. (1945). *Politics and the English Language, Collected Essays, Journalism & Letters of George Orwell*. Retrieved 31 January 2008 from http://www.k-1.com/Orwell/index.cgi/work/essays/language.html.

O'Shea, C. (2005). "Joseph Stiglitz Speaks on Globalization". *Global Policy Forum*. Retrieved 1 April 2008 from http://www.globalpolicy.org/globaliz/econ/2005/0411stiglitz.htm.

Özalp, M. "The Fundamental Spiritual Benefit of Fasting". *The Fountain Magazine* (65), September-October 2008. Retrieved 28 April 2010 from http://www.fountainmagazine.com/archive.php?ARCHIVEDETAIL&ARCHIVEID=65.

Payne, S. (1998). "The Nature of Mysticism". In *Routledge Encyclopedia of Philosophy*. E. Craig (Ed.). London: Routledge. Retrieved 17 August 2007 from http://www. rep.routledge.com/article/KO51SECT2.

Perry, G. (2008). "The Power of Our Words: Teacher Language That Helps Children Learn". *Young Children*, 63 (1), 96.

PETA. (2008). "Fishing Hurts". Retrieved 30 September 2008 from http://www.peta.com/FishFeelPain.asp.

Peters, M., & Wain, K. (2002). "Postmodernism/Post-structuralism". In *The Blackwell Guide to the Philosophy of Education*, Blake, N., Smeyers, P., Smith, R., & Standish, P. (Eds.), 1 (3).

Phillips, L. (2000). *Flirting with Danger*: New York: SUNY Press.

Plato. (1956). *The Works of Plato*. Jowett, B. (Trans.). New York: The Modern Library.

Plumwood, V. (1993). *Feminism and the Mastery of Nature*. London: Routledge.

Plumwood, V. (2000). "Deep Ecology, Deep Pockets, and Deep Problems: A Feminist Ecosocialist Analysis". In *Beneath the Surface: Critical Essays in the Philosophy of Deep Ecology*, Katz, E., Light, A. & Rothenberg, D. (Eds.). Cambridge, Massachusetts: The MIT Press.

Polanyi, M. (1969). *Personal Knowledge: Towards a Post-Critical Philosophy*. London: Routledge & Kegan Paul.

Polatöz, S. (2009). "Fish: A Source of Inspiration for Efficient Energy Production". *The Fountain Magazine* (69), May-June 2009. Retrieved 10 May 2010 from http://www.fountainmagazine.com/article.php?ARTICLEID=102

Pollan, M. (2006). *The Omnivore's Dilemma: A Natural History of Four Meals*. New York: Penguin.

Postman, N. (1992). *Technopoly - the Surrender of Culture to Technology*. New York: Knopf, Inc.

Prabhupada, B. S. (Ed.). (1972). *Bhagavad-Gita, As It Is*. London: Bhaktivedanta Book Trust.

Procter & Gamble. (2005). "The Fifth World Congress on Alternatives and Animal Use in the Life Sciences". Retrieved 17 May 2008 from www.pg.com./science/Brochure_print.pdf.

Ramacharaka, Y. (1904). "The Hermetic Principles". *Journal of the Muhyiddin Ibn 'Arabi Society*, IV. Retrieved 12 January 2008 from http://www.ibnarabisociety.org/articles/hermetic.html.

Rand, A. (1957). *Atlas Shrugged*. New York: Random House.

Rauf, B. (1987). "Concerning the Universality of Ibn 'Arabi". *Journal of the Muhyiddin Ibn 'Arabi Society*, VI. Retrieved 10 March 2010 from http://www.ibnarabisociety.org/articles/universality_ibnarabi.html.

Razer, H. "It's where we go". *The Age*, 26 December 2007, 15.

Reed, B. "Back from the brink". *McClatchy - Tribune Business News*, Washington, 2 February 2008, 2.

Rees, M. (2003). *Our Final Hour: A Scientist's Warning*. New York: Basic Books.

Regan, L. "Turning back the clock", SBS Television, 23 December 2007.

Renich, B. I. (2007). "The Transmission of Knowledge: Perspectives on the Change from Traditional to Modern Settings in Papua New Guinea". (Ed.D dissertation), Northern Illinois University, U.S.

Rice, C., O. P. (1964). *The Persian Sufis*. London: Allen & Unwin.

Rice, G. (1999). "Islamic Ethics and the Implications for Business". *Journal of Business Ethics*, (18), 345-358.

Rice, W. (2007). "The Dangers of Food Additives". Retrieved 23 January 2008 from http://www.vaccinetruth.org/junk_food.htm.

Rigby, K. (2009). "Dancing with Disaster". *Australian Humanities Review*, (46), 131-144.

Rinpoche, S. (2003). *The Tibetan Book of Living and Dying*. London: Rider.

Robinson, N. (1998). "Ibn al-'Arabi, Muhyi al-Din". In *Routledge Encyclopedia of Philosophy*. E. Craig (Ed.). London: Routledge. Retrieved 17 August 2007 from http://www. rep.routledge.com/article/HO22SECT1.

Robinson, P. (2002). "The Philosophy of Punctuation". Retrieved 25 September 2008 from http://www.press.uchicago.edu/Misc/Chicago/721833.html.

Rorty, R. (2004). "Pragmatism". In *Routledge Encyclopedia of Philosophy*. E. Craig (Ed.). London: Routledge. Retrieved 11 July 2008 from http://www. rep. routledge.com/article/NO46SECT1.

Rumi, J. (1995). *The Essential Rumi*. Barks, C., Moyne, J., Arberry, A. J. & Nicholson, R. A. (Eds.). San Francisco: Harper.

_____(2006). *Rumi: Spiritual Verses*. Williams, A. (Ed.). London: Penguin.

Ruskin, J. (2004). *The Poetry of Architecture*. Birch, D. (Ed.). New York: Oxford University Press Inc.

_____(1912). *The Works of John Ruskin* (V). Cook, E. T. & Wedderburn, A. (Eds.). London: George Allen

Salleh, A. (Ed.) (2009). *Eco-Sufficiency and Global Justice: Women Write Political Ecology*. London, New York: Pluto Press.

Sallis, E. (2007). In *Translating Lives: Living with Two Languages and Cultures*. Besemeres, M. and Wierzbicka, A. (Eds.). Brisbane: University of Queensland Press.

Sandel, M. (2009). *2009 Reith Lecture Series: A New Citizenship*. Retrieved from http://www.bbc.co.uk/programmes/b00kt7rg

Sanigorski, A. M., Bell, A. C., Kremer, P. J., & Swinburn, B. A. (2007). "High childhood obesity in an Australian population". *Obesity*, 15 (8), 1908-1912.

Sapkota, A. R., Lefferts, L. Y., McKenzie, S., & Walker, P. (2007). "What Do We Feed to Food-Production Animals? A Review of Animal Feed Ingredients and Their Potential Impacts on Human Health". *Environmental Health Perspectives*, (115), 663-670.

Sayoran, B. "The Good, the Bad, and the Happy". *The Fountain Magazine*, (70), July-August 2009. Retrieved 3 February 2010 from http://www.fountain-magazine.com/article.php?ARTICLEID=1045

Schimmel, A. (1975). *Mystical Dimensions of Islam*. Chapel Hill: The University of North Carolina Press.

Schlosser, E. (2001). *Fast Food Nation: The Darker Side of the All-American Meal*. New York: Houghton Mifflin Company.

Schuon, F. (1959). *Language of the Self*. Madras: Ganesh & Co.

_____(1991). *Roots of the Human Condition*. Bloomington, Indiana: World Wisdom.

_____(1997). *The Eye of the Heart: Metaphysics, Cosmology, Spiritual Life*. Bloomington, Indiana: World Wisdom Books, Inc.

Sedley, D. (1998). "Parmenides". In *Routledge Encyclopedia of Philosophy*. E. Craig (Ed.). London: Routledge. Retrieved 15 November 2007 from http://www. rep.routledge.com/article/A079.

Sen, A. "Confronting the Challenges to Democracy in the 21st Century". *Journal of Democracy*, July 1999. Retrieved 25 September 2008 from http://muse. jhu.edu/demo/jod/10.3sen.html

Sennett, R. (2008). *The Craftsman*. London: Penguin.

Shah, I. (1968). *The Way of the Sufi*. London: Penguin

_____(1978). *Learning How to Learn—Psychology and Spirituality in the Sufi Way*. London: The Octagon Press.

_____(1979). *The World of the Sufi*. London: The Octagon Press.

Sheridan, J., Butler, R., & Wilkens, C. (2007). "Legal piperazine-containing party pills—A new trend in substance misuse". *Drug and Alcohol Review, Australasia* (26), 335-343.

Siahpush, A. (2009). "Energy". *Journal of the Sufi Psychology Association*, 8. Retrieved 11 December 2009 from http://sufipsychology.org/en/page_spaJournal.htm.

Siemens, G. (2006). "Connectivism: Learning and Knowledge Today". *Global Summit 2006: Technology Connected Futures*. Retrieved 26 June 2008 from http://www.educationau.edu.au/jahia/webdav/site/myjahiasite/users/.

Singer, P. (2002). *Animal Liberation*. New York: Harper Collins Publishers.

Singh, R. (Ed.). (2001). *The Path to Tranquility*. London: Rider.

Solana, T. (2009). *Catalan Crime Fiction*. Paper presented at Monash University, Arts, Melbourne.

Spiegel Staff. (14 April 2008). "Global Food Crisis: The Fury of the Poor". Retrieved 22 April 2008 from http://www.spiegel.de/international/world/0,1518,547198,00.html.

Stafford, A. "Isolated and lonely, the unnoticed deaths of the elderly". *The Age*, Melbourne, 12 April 2008, 7.

Standish, P. (1995). "Postmodernism and the Education of the Whole Person". *Journal of Philosophy of Education*, 29 (1), 121-135.

Star, J., & Shiva, S. (1992). *A Garden Beyond Paradise, The Mystical Poetry of Rumi*. New York: Bantam.

Stead, C. (1998). "Logos". In *Routledge Encyclopedia of Philosophy*. E. Craig (Ed.). London: Routledge. Retrieved 12 January 2008 from http://www. rep. routledge.com/article/AO65SECT1.

Stearns, P. (2001). *American Cool: Constructing a Twentieth-Century Emotional Style*. New York: SUNY Press.

Stiglitz, J. "Crisis the fruit of dishonesty and incompetence". *The Age*, Melbourne, 18 September 2008, 13.

Stiglitz, J., & Bilmes, L. (2008). *Three Trillion Dollar War: The True Cost Of The War In Iraq*. New York: Penguin.

Sylvester, R. "Church, Man and Morality". *The Age*, Melbourne, 22 September 2007, 4.

Tabanlı, M. "On Nature, Beauty, and Transcendence: An Interview with Seyyed Hossein Nasr". *The Fountain Magazine*, (69), May-June 2009. Retrieved 17 February 2010 from http://www.fountainmagazine.com/article. php?ARTICLEID=1022.

Tabanlı, M, & Tucker, M. E. "Protecting of Life Forms Is a Moral Responsibility". *The Fountain Magazine*, (74), March-April 2010. Retrieved 3 May 2010 from http://www.fountainmagazine.com/article.php?ARTICLEID=1115.

Tacey, D. (2000). *ReEnchantment: The New Australian Spirituality*. Sydney: HarperCollins.

Tatari, E. (2008). "Modest Dress in Abrahamic Traditions". *The Fountain Magazine*, (66), November-December 2008. Retrieved 8 November 2009 from http://www.fountainmagazine.com/article.php?ARTICLEID=971.

Taylor, C. (1995). *Philosophical Arguments*. Cambridge: Harvard University Press.

_____(2007). *A Secular Age*. Cambridge, Massachusetts: Belknap Press of Harvard University.

TIC. (2005). "Progress towards the Knowledge Driven Economy". Trade and Industry Committee, London. Retrieved 25 June 2008 from http://www. publications.parliament.uk/pa/cm200405/cmselect/cmtrdin.

Tiefer, L. (2004). *Sex is Not a Natural Act and Other Essays*. Boulder, Colorado: Westview Press.

Toffler, A. (1970). *Future Shock*. New York: Bantam Books

Tu, W. (1998). "Self-cultivation in Chinese philosophy". In *Routledge Encyclopedia of Philosophy*. E. Craig (Ed.). London: Routledge. Retrieved 12 February 2009 from http://www. rep.routledge.com/article/GO14SECT6.

Tucker, M. E. (2006). "Religion and Ecology: Survey of the Field". In Gottlieb, R. S. (Ed.), *The Oxford Handbook of Religion and Ecology*. New York: Oxford University Press, 398-418.

Twenge, J., & Campbell, W. K. (2009). *The Narcissism Epidemic: Living in the Age of Entitlement*. New York: Simon & Schuster, Inc.

Twinch, C. (2006). "The Circle of Inclusion". *Journal of the Muhyiddin Ibn 'Arabi Society XL*. Retrieved 15 July 2009 from http://www.ibnarabisociety.org/journals.html.

Ustaoğlu, H. A. "Soil-Cleaning Plants". *The Fountain Magazine*, (66), November-December 2008. Retrieved 29 December 2009 from http://www. fountainmagazine.com/article.php?ARTICLEID=972.

UTA. (1999). *Better Self-Esteem—Counseling and Mental Health Center booklet*. Retrieved 12 April 2008 from http://www.utexas.edu/student/cmhc/booklets/selfesteem/selfest.html.

Uysal, A. "The Tiniest Captains of the Ocean". *The Fountain Magazine*, (74), March-April 2010. Retrieved 23 May 2010 from http://www.fountain-magazine.com/article.php?ARTICLEID=1124.

Valiuddin, M. (1980). *Contemplative Disciplines in Sufism*. London, The Hague: East-West Publications.

Van Stolk, S. & Dunlop, D. (1967). *Memories of a Sufi Sage, Hazrat Inayat Khan*. The Hague: East-West Publications.

Vaughan-Lee, L. (1997). *Sufism: The Transformation of the Heart*. California: The Golden Sufi Center.

_____(2000). *Love is a Fire: The Sufi's Mystical Journey Home*. California: The Golden Sufi Center.

Venkatesananda, S. (1967). *Yoga*. Durban: Sivananda Press.

Veziroğlu, M. "Tiny, With a Great Mission: Seeds and Bees". *The Fountain Magazine*, (68), March-April 2009. Retrieved 3 January 2010 from http://www.fountainmagazine.com/article.php?ARTICLEID=1002.

Vidal, J. (3 November 2007). "Global food crisis looms as climate change and fuel shortages bite". Retrieved 22 April 2008 from http://www.guardian.co.uk/environment/2007/nov/03/food.climatechange.

von Heyking, A. (2004). "Ties that bind? American influences on Canadian education". *Education Canada*, (44), 30.

Wainwright, M. (2005). "Threat to IQ". The Guardian, 22 April 2005, 9.

Wallace, A. D. (1993). *Walking, Literature, and English Culture*. Oxford: Oxford University Press.

Watson, D. (2003). *Death Sentence: the Decay of Public Language*. Sydney: Random House.

Watson, D. (2009). *Bendable Learnings: The Wisdom of Modern Management*. Sydney: Knopf.

Weekes, P. "Reverse mortgages gain traction". *The Age*, 3 September 2005, 11.

Werbner, P. (2005). *Pilgrims of Love: The Anthropology of a Global Sufi Cult*. Bloomington & Indianapolis: Indiana University Press

Westerland, D. (Ed.). (2004). *Sufism in Europe and North America*. London: Routledge Curzon.

Wheeler, W. (2006). *The Whole Creature - Complexity, Biosemiotics and the Evolution of Culture*. London: Lawrence & Wishart.

Williams, R. (1961). *The Long Revolution*. London: Chatto and Windus.

Williams, R. (2009). "Education Based Only on Reason is Incomplete". *Pelican Web's Journal of Sustainable Development*. Retrieved 1 November 2009 from http://www.pelicanweb.org/solisustv05n10page4rowanwilliams.html.

Winter, J. "Mystery Scientology Theater". *The Village Voice*, 50 (26), 2005, 30.

Witteveen, H. J. (1997). *Universal Sufism*. Dorset: Element.

Witteveen, H. J. (2003). *Sufism in Action*. The Hague: East-West Publications.

Womack, S. "Survey finds men have lost their role in society". *The UK Telegraph*, 7 January 2008,12.

Woodward, W. (2008). "Clegg warns of 'Prozac nation' Britain as pill-taking soars". Retrieved 4 April 2008 from http://www.guardian.co.uk/politics/2008/feb/08/uk.liberaldemocrats.

Wright, A. (2000). *Spirituality and Education*. London: Routledge

Yeşilova, H. "Social Reform and Fethullah Gülen: the Cairo Perspective". *The Fountain Magazine*, (72), November-December 2009. Retrieved 7 January 2010 from http://www.fountainmagazine.com/article.php?ARTICLEID=1074.

Zane, J. P. (2007). "What happened to thrift? Prosperity and technology have fed decades of consumerism". *McClatchy-Tribune Business News*, Washington, January 2007, 7.

Zhou, M., & Kim, S. (2006). "Community Forces, Social Capital, and Educational Achievement: The Case of Supplementary Education in the Chinese and Korean Immigrant Communities". *Harvard Educational Review*, 76 (1), 1-31.

INDEX

A

Aboriginal, 13, 36, 63, 170, 233
Abraham, 25, 42, 262
Abu-Sway, 15, 16, 249
ACNielson, 55
Adams, 107
Adler, 106, 107, 108, 249
Afghanistan, vii, viii, 4
Aflatun, 28
Africa, 129
Agathon, 190
Ahmed, 15, 201, 207, 211, 212, 239, 241, 242, 249
al-Hallaj, 143
alienation, xvii, 82, 207, 245
Allah, 8, 16, 23, 114, 139, 141
Allenby, 124
amal, xxiii, 135, 156, 170, 178, 190
Amazon, 119, 209
Andersons, 59
Anissian, 24, 122, 172, 180, 181, 192, 206, 216, 250
annihilation, xxiii, 24, 38, 49, 57, 164, 168, 191, 192, 215, 216, 217, 227, 237
anorexia, 70
anthropomorphic, 27, 110, 145, 171
anti-Semitism, 20
anxiety, 19, 68, 76, 77, 82, 97, 141, 210
Aquinas, 157, 158
Arabic, vii, viii, x, xiii, 6, 8, 12, 24, 142, 152, 191, 199
Archimedes, 31, 155
Arendt, 57, 97, 128, 175, 238, 250

Aristotle, xvi, 28, 35, 137, 174
arkhe, 139
Armstrong, 22
art of being, 153, 247
asbab, 48
Aslandoğan, 70, 250
Attar, 44, 191, 194, 206, 218, 242, 243, 250
Attention Deficit Disorder, 178
Attributes of God, 27
Aurelius, 32, 37, 43, 224, 230, 250
Australia, xiv, 30, 58, 66, 67, 82, 97, 99, 104, 105, 106, 112, 113, 117, 123, 170, 209, 212, 249, 250, 251, 256
Australia Institute, xiv
Ausubel, 117, 118, 120, 251
Avian Flu, 113
awareness, viii, xi, xv, xix, xxii, 3, 5, 10, 18, 64, 65, 68, 77, 101, 110, 114, 125, 142, 146, 149, 154, 161, 169, 173, 179, 193, 196, 211, 215, 219, 225, 237, 239, 245
ayat, 44, 53

B

Baghdad, 143
Balkans, 22
Balkh, vii, 4
baqa, xxiii, 168, 189, 216, 217, 226, 227, 232, 237
baqa bi'llah, 217
Barks, viii, 66, 251, 264
Barlow, 97, 251
Barramunga, 60, 65, 72

Barthes, 206
Barzakh, 32, 44, 144, 223
basirah, 184
batin, 28, 44, 48, 115, 183, 197, 199, 201
BBC, 73
Beatles, 108
Beaver, 82, 251
Behar, 107, 251
Beijing, 120
Bell, 117, 252, 265
Beloved, vii, ix, xii, xiii, 4, 5, 6, 7, 9, 16,
    20, 21, 25, 26, 27, 29, 41, 44, 53,
    57, 70, 71, 89, 102, 131, 135, 145,
    149, 154, 156, 169, 183, 191, 192,
    194, 195, 196, 202, 203, 204, 205,
    206, 214, 215, 216, 218, 219, 221,
    222, 223, 224, 225, 227, 229, 237,
    242, 245, 248
Benedict, 156
Bennett, 18, 251
Benson, 106
Benyus, 117, 118, 251
Bernstein, 175
Berry, ix, xiv, xv, 33, 66, 88, 111, 130,
    162, 163, 166, 168, 170, 171, 180,
    209, 210, 214, 217, 228, 241, 251
Berube, 177, 251
bewilderment, 4, 218, 248
Bhagavad-Gita, 23, 25, 26, 45, 176, 263
Bible, 35, 46, 61, 73, 93
biosemiotics, vii, xiii, xv, xix, xxii, xxiii, 3,
    13, 34, 40, 53, 80
Birch, 42, 43, 264
Bohm, xxii, 3, 38, 39, 156, 157, 251
Botton, 86, 254
Bradsher, 64
Branigan, 104, 252
Braungart, 130
Brennan, xvii, 28, 252
Britain, 98, 120, 125, 268
Bruthiaux, 78, 79, 80, 252
Buddhist, xx, 13, 30, 36, 46, 71, 176,
    229, 230, 231, 259

Buffett, 239, 252
Bumpass, 105
Burnside, 86, 87, 252
Bush, 238, 252

C

Cairo, 15, 112, 269
Campbell, 100, 101, 102, 252, 253, 267
Canada, 103, 116, 125, 268
Canterbury, 19, 148, 247
Capitalism, 240, 258
Capra, xxii, 3, 38, 39
career, 82, 171
Cartesian, xxii, 3, 33, 143, 175
cathexis, 225, 226
Catholic, viii, xi
Caucasus, 22
Çelebi, 114, 253
Çelik, 199, 253
Ceran, 173, 253
Chadstone, 55
China, 25, 55, 103, 116, 120, 121, 123,
    129, 229, 235, 249
Chishti, 164
Chittick, vii, viii, x, xi, xiii, 4, 7, 8, 10, 11,
    32, 65, 138, 147, 151, 152, 154,
    180, 219, 253, 261
Christ, 9, 72, 74, 115
Christian, xv, 9, 23, 25, 28, 61, 62, 74,
    157, 230, 248, 253, 259
church, 55, 72, 73, 74, 107, 155
civilization, 59, 117, 120, 177
Cixous, 96, 253
Claxton, 230
Clegg, 98, 268
Clifford, 100, 101, 173, 254
cogito ergo sum, 143
Coleman, viii, 140, 254
Coleridge, xx, 33
Coloma, 105
Commonwealth, 106, 120, 161
comprehension, 131, 243
Confucianism, 142, 174, 235

consciousness, xvii, 6, 9, 10, 29, 31, 32, 34, 37, 39, 57, 95, 98, 102, 126, 141, 142, 143, 149, 157, 216, 230

consumerism, vii, 54, 56, 64, 81, 107, 198, 232, 269

contentment, 48, 57, 232

Coomaraswamy, xii, 72, 73, 74, 152, 247, 254

Cooper, 156, 157, 254

Corbin, 24, 42, 146, 180, 181, 182, 183, 184, 185, 216, 254

Corduff, 212

Cornell, 17, 254

cosmos, 7, 8, 21, 32, 41, 138, 140, 141, 144, 158, 180, 183, 194, 241

Costello, 210

creativity, 36, 118, 158, 170, 171, 172, 175, 179, 182, 203, 210, 220, 234, 247

Creator, 16, 24, 38, 103, 117, 118, 126, 128, 156, 170, 220

Crusades, 23

Crutzen, 124

D

D'Adamo, 7, 40, 41, 62, 224, 254

Dağlı, 41, 254

Danner, 6, 256

Darmon, 67

Darwin, 95, 110

Davies, 235

Davis, xv, 111, 250

Dawkins, 95, 254

Denniss, xiv, 257

Derrida, 143, 206

dervish, vii, 222, 227

desacralisation, xxiii, 135, 142, 143, 153, 158

Dessalles, 79

Dewey, xii, 147, 174, 175, 219, 254

Dharma, 26

Dhir, 81, 255

dissatisfaction, ix, 19, 135, 166, 190, 191, 211, 245

Dittmar, 56, 255

diversity, xvii, 5, 27, 87, 109, 139, 183, 190, 201

divine, ix, x, xii, 4, 9, 12, 14, 15, 17, 20, 23, 26, 27, 28, 32, 34, 41, 53, 61, 76, 83, 85, 89, 109, 115, 117, 128, 137, 138, 140, 143, 144, 145, 150, 151, 152, 153, 154, 155, 156, 158, 160, 165, 168, 169, 170, 171, 172, 178, 182, 183, 184, 189, 190, 191, 194, 195, 196, 197, 203, 205, 207, 210, 215, 216, 218, 220, 223, 225, 232

Divine Epiphany, 180

divine self-disclosure, 152, 154, 168, 172

divinity, 9, 27, 41, 240

Drewnowski, 67

dualism, xxii, 3, 30, 32, 33, 223

dualistic, 28, 29, 32, 145, 150, 156, 196

Duden, 213

dying before death, 219

E

ecofeminism, xvii, xviii

Ecology, xii, xvi, xviii, 105, 137, 253, 256, 260, 261, 263, 265, 267

ecophilosophy, vii, xvi, xviii, 169

ecosemioticians, 33

ecstasy, 97, 98, 205, 208, 227

Edinburgh, 109, 258

egalitarianism, xvii, 201

ego, xxi, xxii, xxiii, 6, 9, 10, 19, 24, 29, 35, 38, 46, 49, 58, 63, 70, 90, 96, 99, 100, 102, 109, 119, 128, 129, 131, 135, 143, 146, 149, 150, 152, 157, 159, 164, 168, 169, 171, 174, 176, 182, 185, 191, 192, 194, 205, 206, 215, 216, 218, 219, 221, 222, 226, 231, 232, 237, 239, 242, 245, 246, 247, 248

egolessness, 192, 216

Egypt, 11, 15, 22, 112, 129

eidos, 28, 35, 137

Eisnitz, xv, 111, 113

Eliade, 10, 255

Elliott, 211, 212, 255

Emerson, 221, 255

encounter, xxiii, 3, 10, 11, 20, 60, 64, 65, 114, 135, 153, 162, 165, 168, 177, 192, 202, 204, 208, 232, 246, 256

Engels, xix

England, 33

Enlightenment, xix, xx, xxii, 3

Ernst, xiii, 14, 23, 75, 164, 165, 202, 255

eros, 193, 207, 218

esoteric, x, xi, 14, 20, 164, 204, 208

Essence, 7, 21, 24, 25, 140, 145, 190

essentialism, xviii

Ethiopia, 22

Europe, 23, 120, 164, 268

European Union, 121

euthanasia, 81

existence, vii, xvi, xx, xxi, xxii, 7, 8, 9, 21, 24, 25, 30, 39, 40, 44, 48, 49, 65, 81, 89, 95, 102, 114, 130, 140, 143, 150, 156, 177, 182, 189, 191, 194, 204, 217, 223, 225, 226, 227, 237, 238, 247

exoteric, vii, 17, 20, 24, 26

F

fakir, 222

fana, xxiii, 6, 164, 168, 189, 191, 216, 226, 227, 237, 242

Fana fi'llah, 216, 217

Farrelly, ix, xiv, 18, 33, 55, 58, 62, 63, 66, 72, 73, 84, 85, 102, 256

Farsi, viii, x

fasting, 70

Fethullah Gülen, 15, 47, 269

Fisher, 236

Foltz, xii, 16, 17, 256

Fountain, xiii, 249, 250, 251, 253, 257, 259, 260, 261, 263, 265, 266, 267, 268, 269

Frankl, 47, 48, 57, 256

freedom, ix, 12, 62, 63, 64, 98, 127, 138, 151, 156, 158, 178, 227, 228, 237, 238, 240, 241, 242, 246

G

Gaita, 38, 256

Gandhi, viii, xvii, 108, 239

Garnaut, 120, 121, 122, 125, 256

Generation X, 105

Generation Y, 105, 106

Germany, 175

ghazal, 204

Gilsenan, 198, 199

Gitlin, 108

globalisation, 14, 18, 126, 165, 167

global warming, 105, 124, 125, 127

gnosis, 9, 137, 146, 149, 156, 237

Gobi desert, 120

God, v, x, 4, 6, 7, 8, 9, 11, 12, 14, 16, 17, 21, 22, 23, 24, 25, 26, 27, 32, 35, 40, 42, 44, 62, 63, 66, 72, 73, 97, 99, 107, 114, 115, 128, 131, 136, 137, 138, 139, 140, 142, 144, 145, 149, 151, 154, 155, 156, 163, 165, 169, 170, 171, 180, 183, 184, 189, 190, 194, 195, 196, 197, 199, 201, 204, 205, 206, 215, 216, 217, 223, 225, 230, 237, 241, 242, 251, 254, 257, 262

Goethe, vii, 36

good and evil, 222, 243

Gorenfeld, 107, 108, 256

Gospel, 61

Gottlieb, xi, xii, xviii, 16, 17, 21, 253, 256, 267

Graham, 60, 81, 177, 250, 256

Gray, 230, 262

Greece, 11, 235

Greek, xvi, 6, 9, 10, 28, 31, 56, 136, 173, 193, 208

Gregory, 110, 256

guidance, 106, 161, 172, 173, 179, 202, 215
Guindi, 198, 199, 201, 255
Gülen, 15, 47, 191, 202, 203, 208, 216, 217, 222, 257, 269
Gülen Movement, 15

H

Hadith, vii, 9, 16, 169, 190
Hafiz, 12, 47
Haiti, 129
hajj, 65, 66
Hamilton, ix, xiii, xiv, xv, xvi, xx, xxi, xxii, xxiii, 3, 13, 21, 28, 30, 31, 33, 36, 48, 54, 55, 56, 59, 61, 63, 66, 69, 77, 79, 89, 94, 96, 98, 99, 100, 101, 102, 103, 104, 106, 108, 109, 111, 122, 129, 135, 144, 145, 146, 150, 151, 153, 154, 155, 156, 163, 169, 189, 192, 206, 207, 208, 211, 221, 226, 227, 238, 239, 246, 247, 248, 257
haqiqat, 24
haqq, 13, 33
Hasan al-Basri, 12
Hayek, 163
heart, vii, viii, ix, x, xi, xii, xiii, xiv, xv, xx, xxi, xxii, xxiii, 11, 14, 15, 17, 20, 21, 22, 24, 28, 33, 34, 35, 40, 41, 43, 44, 45, 46, 49, 53, 54, 57, 58, 61, 63, 66, 67, 71, 72, 75, 77, 83, 87, 88, 96, 103, 115, 120, 122, 126, 130, 131, 135, 136, 138, 139, 141, 142, 146, 147, 148, 149, 150, 152, 154, 155, 156, 157, 162, 163, 165, 169, 171, 172, 173, 176, 178, 179, 180, 182, 183, 184, 185, 189, 190, 191, 192, 194, 195, 196, 197, 199, 204, 205, 206, 211, 215, 216, 217, 218, 219, 220, 221, 222, 223, 224, 225, 227, 228, 230, 232, 235, 237, 238, 239, 242, 243, 245, 246, 247, 248

Hebrew, 10
Hegel, 33
Heidegger, 7, 75, 76, 128, 176, 257, 259
Hephaestus, 174
Heraclitus, 28, 35, 229
Hermetic, 7, 12, 37, 264
Hesychast, 62
Hicks, 236
Hillier, 210, 257
Hillman, 180, 181
Hobbes, 94
holism, xix, 53
Holland, 18
Holloway, 109, 258
Hollywood, 107, 108
Homer, 174
Hong Kong, 55
Houghton, 167, 258, 265
Hubbard, 107, 108
Hudavendigar, 4
Husamuddin, 6, 195
Husserl, 223

I

Ibn al-Arabi, viii, x, xi, 7, 9, 15, 16, 21, 23, 28, 30, 40, 41, 44, 115, 136, 139, 140, 144, 145, 146, 148, 149, 151, 152, 154, 156, 158, 165, 166, 168, 170, 180, 181, 182, 183, 184, 185, 192, 194, 200, 206, 253
Iceland, 235
imagination, 42, 65, 171, 179, 180, 181, 182, 183, 184, 199, 240
Inayat Khan, xi, xiii, 4, 12, 18, 22, 24, 26, 34, 38, 39, 40, 46, 88, 153, 164, 172, 176, 181, 195, 204, 209, 220, 223, 224, 225, 227, 229, 231, 242, 246, 247, 267
India, xi, 11, 15, 25, 65, 121, 123, 129, 181, 233
Indonesia, 22, 129, 238
infinity, 27, 140, 157
Innenwelt, 95

inner eye, 184
insan-i-kamil, 241
insight, viii, xi, xiii, 9, 11, 86, 131, 148, 152, 156, 159, 173, 177, 181, 196, 197, 230, 241
intelligence, 34, 86, 107, 141, 142, 149, 155, 181, 198, 203
interconnectedness, xvi, xix, 10, 19, 33, 39, 46, 127
intuition, xxi, 11, 36, 63, 144, 161, 163, 182
Iraq, 22, 127, 266
irfan, 9
ishq, xii, xxiii, 131, 138, 158, 189, 190, 191, 194, 204, 221
Islamophobia, 22

J

Jablonka, 80
Jackson, 129, 130
Jahn, 60
James, 9, 57, 171, 174, 180, 181, 235, 258
Japan, 120, 148
Jefferson, 97
Jesus, 25, 26, 31, 73, 107, 231
jihad, 23, 24
Joas, 175, 219, 258
Johnson, 234
Jung, xii, 63, 180, 181
junk food, 70

K

Ka'ba, 66
Kabbalists, 108
Kafka, 96, 97, 253, 258
Kaku, 40
kalam, 35, 242
Kapoor, 234
Karma, 46
kashf, 11
Kasser, 98
Kawthar, 182
Keen, 236, 258
Keith, 64, 100, 123, 124, 128, 258

Kellner, 55, 57, 259
Kharaqani, 172
Khayyam, 12
Khazari, xiii, 12, 17, 18, 151, 202, 255
Khidr, 240
Khoromi, 190, 259
Kinney, 13, 19, 259
Kirman, 236
Klein, 108
knowledge of mysteries, 9, 136
Koran, 56, 138, 259
Krishna, 23, 25, 26, 31, 81
Kumar, 65

L

Lama, 239
Lamb, 80, 128
Lamont, 235
Lao-Tzu, 7, 30, 157, 158
Latour, 155
Lauder, 78
Laughlin, xix, 36
Layla and Majnun, 197
Lefort, 224
Leibniz, 143, 144, 153
Lings, xii, 6, 8, 9, 12, 24, 26, 259
logos, xv, xvi, 35, 222, 223, 242
London, 78, 122, 249, 250, 251, 252, 253, 254, 255, 257, 258, 259, 260, 261, 262, 263, 264, 265, 266, 267, 268, 269
loneliness, 18, 74, 82, 105, 180
Lonsdale, 69, 70, 259
Lorenz, 110, 252
love, vii, ix, x, xi, xii, xxiii, 18, 19, 20, 26, 31, 40, 44, 57, 65, 85, 87, 94, 100, 102, 108, 109, 126, 127, 131, 138, 158, 168, 169, 174, 179, 185, 189, 190, 191, 192, 193, 194, 195, 196, 197, 200, 201, 202, 203, 204, 205, 206, 207, 208, 209, 210, 211, 214, 216, 218, 220, 221, 222, 223, 224, 226, 228, 230, 232, 237, 241,

242, 243, 245, 246, 247, 248, 249, 250, 257
Lovelock, 171, 259
Lutzenberger, 119
Lyotard, xxiii, 158, 223, 240, 241, 260

M

Mad Cow Disease, 113
Madonna, 108
Magonet, 22, 260
Maiden, 235, 236, 260
Maizebhandari, 173, 261
Malaysia, 22
mana, ix, 3, 28, 44, 66, 195
Mandela, 239
mantras, 26, 230
Margenau, 42, 260
marifa, x, xxiii, 9, 42, 58, 131, 135, 136, 137, 147, 156, 157, 158, 182, 184, 185, 196, 197, 221, 239
Markel, 97, 98
Marmot, 40
Martin, xii, 7, 8, 12, 40, 76, 106, 120
Marx, xix
Masson, 110, 260
master, xiii, 5, 6, 7, 148, 160, 164, 172, 173, 177, 237
materialism, vii, 14, 19, 33, 38, 62, 73, 81, 89, 94, 95, 98, 166, 198
Mathews, ix, xiii, xiv, xv, xvi, xvii, xviii, xx, xxii, xxiii, 3, 5, 13, 20, 21, 29, 30, 32, 33, 36, 38, 41, 42, 45, 54, 57, 59, 60, 61, 65, 69, 74, 95, 96, 102, 103, 108, 109, 111, 114, 117, 119, 130, 135, 137, 141, 143, 144, 145, 146, 147, 149, 150, 151, 152, 153, 154, 156, 157, 159, 161, 162, 163, 166, 168, 169, 178, 189, 191, 192, 193, 195, 196, 203, 204, 207, 210, 215, 216, 218, 219, 220, 222, 224, 225, 226, 227, 228, 231, 232, 233, 242, 245, 247, 260

Mathnawi, viii, x, 4, 6, 14, 18, 136, 191, 203, 204, 205, 220, 262
Maulana, 173
mawhiba, 196
McCord, 209, 210, 260
McDonough, 130
McFadyen, 127
McGauran, 112
McKnight, 60
McMansion, 58, 59, 60, 62, 64, 85
Mecca, 65
Meditation, 108, 230
Melbourne, xx, 55, 59, 251, 253, 254, 257, 259, 266
Merleau-Ponty, 222, 223, 224, 254, 261
metanarrative, xxiii, 158, 161
metaphysical empathy, xxi, 154
metaphysical psychology, xvi, xxi, xxiii
Mevlana, vii, viii, 4
Middle East, 14, 15, 22, 112
Mies, 213
Misri, 12
modernism, 14
Mofid, 125, 126, 261
Mongols, 159
Montaigne, 85, 86, 261
moral certainty, xxiii, 135, 155
Moses, 25, 240
Most Beautiful Names, 155
Muhammad, 4, 11, 23, 25, 26, 148, 172, 249
mujahada, 151, 165, 196, 205
Multiplicity, v, 3, 43
musabbib, 48
mutasawwif, 6
Muthanna, 202
Mutlu, 69, 261
mysterium coniunctionis, 184, 208
mystery, xv, 9, 10, 18, 27, 35, 36, 42, 74, 128, 130, 135, 139, 148, 153, 157, 158, 159, 169, 182, 185, 189, 207, 214, 215, 221

mysticism, x, xi, xviii, xx, xxii, 3, 9, 10, 11, 12, 13, 14, 21, 33, 36, 38, 85, 145, 156, 164, 181, 192, 216, 219, 229, 246, 253

N

Naess, xvi, xvii
nafs, xxii, 6, 19, 35, 93, 99, 119, 150, 168, 222
Naqshband, xii
narcissism, 100, 101
Nasr, xii, xxiii, 5, 14, 15, 36, 53, 54, 74, 83, 85, 89, 110, 135, 138, 140, 141, 142, 143, 145, 147, 149, 152, 153, 154, 155, 156, 157, 158, 165, 169, 170, 182, 183, 184, 200, 214, 216, 220, 221, 241, 261, 266
Naughtin, 105
Necessary Being, 7
Neef, 233
Newton, 42
New Zealand, 82, 103, 174, 251
Nicholls, 230, 262
Nicholson, vii, viii, x, xiii, 4, 6, 11, 12, 14, 96, 191, 195, 201, 204, 206, 222, 229, 231, 262, 264
Nietzsche, 83, 262
Niffarī, 5
Nigeria, 22
Nirvana, 31, 231
Nizami, 12
Northcott, ix, xv, 33, 62, 64, 94, 95, 103, 104, 115, 121, 125, 127, 128, 130, 166, 262
Norton, 163, 262
nothingness, 39, 169, 222
noumenon, xx, xxi, 28, 31, 94, 151, 155, 195, 208, 221, 226, 227
nous, 137, 181
Nursi, 198, 215, 232, 262

O

obesity, 66, 67, 96, 265

Oldmeadow, 145, 147, 149, 156, 262
Olfman, 61, 211, 262
Oneness, 8, 13, 28
Oneness of Being, 13, 28
Orwell, xiv, xv, 77, 83, 126, 175, 176, 179, 262

P

Pakistan, 15, 22, 129
panpsychism, xiii, xv, xviii, xxiii, 3, 13, 29, 30, 32, 33, 41, 130, 152, 156, 189, 219
Parmenides, 28, 265
partial intellect, 149, 150
patience, 179, 209, 239
Peirce, xii, xix, 34, 53, 174
Perfect Men, 195
Persia, vii, xi, 11, 12, 203
Persian, viii, x, xi, xiii, 12, 27, 114, 115, 258, 264
Pharos, 61
phenomenon, xi, xx, xxi, 8, 12, 39, 40, 54, 100, 102, 195, 197, 198
Philippines, 22
Phillips, 208, 263
Plato, xxii, 3, 11, 28, 29, 35, 44, 46, 47, 61, 85, 94, 137, 138, 139, 141, 150, 158, 160, 166, 172, 173, 174, 190, 193, 194, 195, 197, 203, 220, 229, 239, 253, 263
Plenitude, 7
Plotinus, xxii, 3, 28, 29, 37, 139, 147, 181, 230, 255, 261
Plumwood, xvii, 28, 29, 125, 137, 138, 189, 217, 218, 247, 263
plurality, 137, 139
Pocock, 104
Polanyi, xxiii, 32, 42, 135, 172, 263
Pollan, 68, 112, 263
poor man, 222
Pope John Paul II, 127
positivism, xvii, 34, 174
Postman, 161, 263

post-secular age, vii
poverty, xvii, 14, 106, 127, 128, 129, 194, 222, 231, 232, 233, 238
pragmatism, xii, 174, 175
presence, 4, 6, 9, 11, 17, 26, 42, 44, 60, 61, 85, 138, 152, 173, 178, 194, 216, 220, 231, 239
Prophet, vii, viii, 11, 23, 24, 26, 34, 36, 140, 148, 149, 154, 169, 172, 183, 195, 234, 241, 249
Pythagoras, 28

Q

qalb, xii, 155, 157, 169, 182
Qur'an, vii, x, 11, 12, 14, 16, 17, 23, 24, 35, 53, 138, 140, 149, 183, 184, 185, 204, 260

R

rationalism, xix, 38, 126, 141, 143, 156
Ravensthorpe, 117
Rawls, 109, 163
Razer, 55, 264
Real, vi, 17, 33, 34, 44, 114, 136, 140, 142, 143, 144, 145, 146, 148, 149, 151, 155, 157, 158, 166, 168, 170, 175, 176, 191, 194, 206, 219, 222, 226, 227, 228, 246, 261
Reality, xiv, xv, 32, 140, 141, 142, 151, 153, 170, 181, 183, 184, 190, 193, 226, 260, 262
Rees, 120, 264
Regan, 78, 264
religion, x, xi, xii, xiii, 8, 9, 10, 11, 12, 15, 17, 20, 21, 22, 23, 24, 25, 26, 35, 38, 40, 43, 55, 72, 74, 96, 107, 119, 145, 148, 152, 153, 174, 181, 193, 201, 220, 229
Rembrandt, viii
Revelation, 8, 12, 25, 32, 152
Rice, xi, xiii, 7, 12, 14, 20, 23, 68, 95, 151, 234, 264
Rida, 215

Rigby, 125, 213, 251, 264
Rinpoche, 119, 120, 264
Riyada, 215
Roberts, 108
Robinson, 9, 88, 89, 264
Roof, 108
Rorty, 147, 175, 264
Roshi, 229
Rumbaut, 82
Rumi, vii, viii, ix, x, xi, xii, xiii, xiv, xxi, xxii, xxiii, 3, 4, 5, 6, 7, 12, 14, 16, 21, 24, 25, 26, 27, 28, 29, 30, 35, 38, 40, 43, 44, 47, 48, 49, 53, 57, 58, 63, 66, 67, 70, 71, 75, 76, 77, 79, 81, 82, 83, 85, 88, 89, 95, 96, 100, 119, 122, 131, 135, 136, 137, 138, 139, 140, 144, 145, 147, 149, 150, 151, 152, 154, 155, 157, 158, 159, 164, 165, 169, 171, 172, 173, 180, 181, 182, 184, 185, 189, 191, 192, 193, 194, 195, 196, 197, 199, 201, 202, 203, 204, 205, 206, 207, 210, 212, 214, 215, 216, 217, 218, 219, 220, 221, 222, 223, 224, 226, 227, 229, 231, 236, 237, 241, 242, 245, 247, 248, 250, 251, 253, 255, 256, 258, 262, 264, 266
Rushdie, 241
Ruskin, 33, 60, 61, 64, 264

S

sabr, 229, 239
Sa'di, 12
Salleh, 88, 233, 265
Samuelson, 236
Sandel, 162, 265
Sanskrit, 45, 46, 61, 177, 190, 231
sapience, 139
Satisfaction, 215
sawm, 70
Scelfo, 106, 107, 108, 249
Schelling, 33
Schiller, 174

Schlegel, 33
Schleiermacher, 33
Schlosser, xv, 111, 265
Schrödinger, 40
Schuon, xii, 59, 74, 97, 98, 114, 115,
    117, 149, 155, 156, 164, 169, 170,
    178, 179, 180, 184, 195, 201, 203,
    204, 232, 233, 242, 246, 265
scientia sacra, xii, xxiii, 74, 135, 141, 145,
    146, 149, 152, 156, 183, 220
Scientology, 107, 108, 268
Sebeok, xix, 33
Second World War, 124
Şefik Can, 4, 127
self-consciousness, 6, 141
self-realization, xvii
semiotic knowledge, xxiii, 135
Sen, 238, 239, 265
Sennett, xii, xxiii, 115, 135, 173, 174,
    175, 177, 178, 220, 265
separation, 20, 44, 57, 63, 70, 71, 102,
    136, 141, 144, 149, 154, 183, 190,
    191, 192, 194, 195, 205
Seville, 202
Shabestari, 216
Shah, vii, xii, 6, 7, 13, 34, 189, 227, 265
Shams, vii, x, xi, 6, 28, 135, 149, 173,
    195, 253
shariah, 95, 232
shariah al-fitriyya, 95
Sharkawy, 15
shaykha, 202
Sheehan, 167, 258
sheikh, 5, 165
Shelley, 33
Shibli, 21
Shuhud, 190
Shukr, 215
Sichuan, 103
Siemens, 165, 166, 266
signs, xix, xxii, 17, 34, 36, 40, 44, 53, 95,
    96, 130, 141, 173, 243, 245

silence, xii, 43, 48, 89, 136, 203, 206,
    219, 222, 223, 224, 229, 230, 231
silsila, 172
simplicity, xi, xxiii, 60, 64, 72, 86, 118,
    130, 169, 206, 223, 232, 234, 242,
    245, 247
Singapore, 55
Singer, xv, 47, 111, 113, 266
Smith, 81, 94, 158, 260, 263
Solana, 82, 266
Solomon, 25
Solow, 236
Sophia, 6, 128, 152, 206, 262
soul, vii, xii, 9, 12, 18, 24, 25, 31, 34, 40,
    44, 57, 65, 73, 99, 122, 138, 160,
    174, 181, 190, 191, 199, 201, 205,
    208, 217, 225, 230, 237
South Korea, 238
Spinoza, xvii, 28, 30, 143, 144, 145
spirit, xi, xvi, 5, 8, 10, 11, 12, 22, 23, 28,
    33, 35, 37, 43, 44, 45, 47, 48, 59,
    61, 62, 63, 64, 70, 74, 79, 85, 112,
    115, 122, 126, 130, 138, 148, 151,
    161, 169, 174, 181, 190, 193, 215,
    217, 224, 227, 228, 237, 242
spirituality, xi, xviii, 6, 10, 12, 18, 23, 29,
    41, 42, 126, 152, 170, 224
spiritual struggle, 154
Stearns, 207, 266
Steelers, 107
stewardship, 15
Stiglitz, 126, 127, 234, 235, 236, 263, 266
Studdert-Kennedy, 80
subsistence, xxiii, 49, 60, 216, 217, 226,
    227, 232, 233
Substance, 76, 141, 257
Sudan, 22
Sufi, vii, ix, x, xi, xii, xiii, xiv, xviii, xxi,
    xxii, xxiii, 3, 4, 5, 6, 7, 9, 11, 12, 13,
    14, 15, 16, 17, 18, 19, 20, 21, 23,
    24, 25, 27, 28, 29, 30, 32, 34, 35,
    36, 37, 38, 41, 42, 45, 46, 47, 48,
    49, 53, 63, 66, 71, 72, 74, 75, 85,

99, 102, 109, 110, 112, 114, 115, 118, 135, 136, 137, 142, 143, 145, 150, 151, 152, 153, 156, 162, 164, 165, 168, 169, 171, 172, 174, 177, 180, 181, 189, 190, 191, 192, 194, 196, 197, 199, 200, 202, 203, 215, 216, 217, 218, 219, 220, 221, 222, 224, 225, 226, 227, 229, 230, 231, 232, 237, 240, 241, 242, 247, 248, 253, 254, 255, 259, 261, 265, 266, 267, 268

Sufism, vii, viii, ix, x, xi, xii, xiii, xviii, xxii, 3, 7, 8, 9, 10, 11, 12, 13, 14, 15, 16, 17, 18, 19, 20, 21, 22, 24, 25, 26, 27, 30, 31, 32, 33, 34, 35, 36, 37, 41, 46, 47, 63, 79, 87, 93, 99, 109, 112, 114, 122, 128, 130, 140, 141, 142, 144, 147, 158, 164, 165, 170, 172, 181, 183, 192, 194, 195, 201, 202, 209, 227, 231, 239, 243, 245, 246, 248, 250, 254, 255, 257, 259, 261, 267, 268

sujud, 151

Suluk, xx, 215, 217, 220

Supreme Knowledge, 152

sura, ix, 3, 44, 66

surrender, 36, 151, 164, 169, 174, 221, 232, 248

Suzuki, 173

Sydney, 55, 59, 60, 71, 72, 105, 256, 257, 258, 260, 267, 268

Symeon, 62

T

Tabanlı, 140, 148, 266

Tabriz, vii, 6, 262

Tacey, 10, 23, 74, 144, 170, 190, 267

Taoism, xxii, 3, 13, 30, 36, 142, 192, 224

Tatari, 46, 198, 199, 200, 267

Tawakkul, 215

tawba, 57, 136, 190, 245

tawhid, x, xxii, 3, 15, 28, 53, 71, 79, 93, 95, 99, 110, 136, 138, 146, 153, 157, 173, 182, 206, 245, 246

tawil, ix, 24, 33, 137, 182, 183, 218, 246, 247

Taylor, 72, 136, 137, 267

Thailand, 238

Thankfulness, 215

Theophrastus, xvi

theoria, 139

Thurow, 167

timelessness, 208

Toffler, 76, 267

topos, 139

tradition, vii, viii, xv, xvii, 7, 15, 17, 23, 24, 28, 33, 34, 61, 65, 82, 96, 140, 141, 142, 152, 153, 157, 164, 173, 190, 201, 203, 204, 223, 229

Trainer, 40

Transcendental Meditation, 108

trust, xiv, 19, 101, 108, 161, 168, 174, 179, 214, 232

truth, ix, x, 8, 11, 13, 21, 24, 25, 26, 32, 35, 36, 43, 45, 46, 74, 77, 78, 79, 81, 83, 87, 88, 95, 99, 100, 120, 136, 139, 149, 151, 152, 155, 158, 160, 171, 176, 183, 202, 204, 205, 220, 229, 242, 243, 246

Tuck, 82

Tucker, 17, 148, 266, 267

Turkey, iv, 4, 15

Twenge, 19, 267

Twinch, 16, 22, 23, 267

U

Uexküll, xix

Umwelt, 40, 95

UNESCO, viii, 4, 14, 18, 256

United Kingdom, 64

United States, viii, 58, 64, 93, 113, 116, 123, 209, 212

unity, vii, ix, x, xi, xviii, xx, xxii, 3, 8, 9, 12, 15, 16, 17, 19, 20, 22, 23, 25,

26, 27, 28, 30, 31, 32, 35, 46, 47, 48, 62, 63, 71, 79, 85, 93, 109, 120, 130, 136, 137, 138, 139, 140, 142, 143, 144, 149, 152, 153, 154, 157, 160, 161, 169, 180, 182, 189, 190, 194, 199, 200, 216, 217, 218, 242, 245, 246, 248
Unity of Existence, 13
Universal Intellect, 150
Unseen, 181, 182
unveiling, 11, 115, 137, 152, 157, 218
USA, 22, 55, 116, 251
Ustaoğlu, 118, 267
Uysal, 118, 267

V

Van Stolk, 172, 173, 267
Varghese, 42, 260
Vaughan-Lee, xii, 4, 5, 57, 72, 149, 154, 169, 190, 191, 194, 199, 200, 201, 202, 215, 216, 222, 230, 240, 241, 268
Vedanta, 31
Venus, 120
Veziroğlu, 118, 268
Victoria, 56, 67, 87, 105, 167, 257, 258
Vietnam, 121
Virilio, 176
virtue, xx, xxi, 31, 44, 93, 94, 155, 174, 182, 196, 215, 239
vision, xviii, 8, 12, 20, 21, 22, 23, 26, 29, 30, 35, 36, 38, 43, 47, 119, 120, 126, 131, 139, 141, 144, 149, 156, 158, 165, 184, 200, 202, 212, 217, 223, 230, 246, 248

W

Wachter, 81
wahdat al-wujud, 13, 16, 21, 136, 137
wahm, 33

Wainwright, 76, 268
Wara, 215
Warhol, 206
waridat, 196
Washington Times, 108
Watson, 86, 87, 268
Werbner, xii, xiii, 268
Wheeler, ix, xii, xiii, xv, xviii, xix, xx, xxii, xxiii, 3, 13, 32, 33, 34, 35, 36, 38, 40, 42, 47, 53, 75, 80, 81, 83, 95, 109, 117, 135, 146, 156, 162, 169, 172, 177, 189, 192, 233, 247, 268
Whirling Dervishes, 226
Williams, 19, 32, 34, 95, 148, 171, 247, 248, 264, 268
Wilson, 55, 76
wisdom, viii, ix, xxii, xxiii, 6, 12, 14, 36, 68, 108, 139, 141, 142, 152, 158, 164, 172, 174, 190, 194, 209
witnessing, 152, 184, 190, 235
Witteveen, 7, 12, 18, 38, 39, 40, 268
Womack, 210, 211, 268
Wordsworth, xx, 33, 65, 226
World Bank, 129
Worldwatch Institute, 129

Y

Yogi, 108

Z

zahir, 24, 44, 48, 183, 197, 199, 201
Zaidi, 16
Zakaria, 17
Zarathustra, 25
Zeitgeist, xiv
Zen, 71, 229
zikr, 230
Zimbabwe, 129, 252
Zoellick, 129
Zuhd, 215